BEVERLY

BEVERLY

AN AUTOBIOGRAPHY

BEVERLY SILLS

AND

LAWRENCE LINDERMAN

BANTAM BOOKS

TORONTO • NEW YORK • LONDON • SYDNEY • AUCKLAND

BEVERLY: AN AUTOBIOGRAPHY
A Bantam Book / May 1987

Library of Congress Cataloging-in-Publication Data

Sills, Beverly.
  Beverly: an autobiography.

  Includes index.
  1. Sills, Beverly.   2. Singers—United States—
Biography.   I. Linderman, Lawrence.   II. Title.
ML420.S562A3   1987   782.1'092'4   [B]   86-47567
ISBN 0-553-05173-3

Published simultaneously in the United States and Canada

PRINTED IN THE UNITED STATES OF AMERICA
BP   0 9 8 7 6 5 4 3 2 1

To Mom
who had a dream

To Pete
who fulfilled the dream

To Muffy
who is a dream

INTRODUCTION

On the night of October 27, 1980, after a career that had spanned more than thirty years and had taken me to the world's greatest opera houses, I sang for the last time at the New York City Opera. The next morning, I'd be taking over as the company's general director on a full-time basis. For more than a year, I'd been a part-time impresario, running the City Opera while fulfilling a final round of operatic and concert commitments that had been arranged years in advance. I thought I'd finished with all that, but a couple of months before, Albert Hudes, then the City Opera's director of special events, had asked me how I'd feel about a big farewell benefit. By then, I knew only too well that the City Opera was in dire need of funds, and there was no question that if we did such a benefit we could raise about a million dollars. I thought about it and said, "Okay, so long as it doesn't become a maudlin thing with film clips and how Beverly did this and how Beverly did that."

I told Albert I wanted to go out with confetti and balloons. I wanted to *celebrate* my years with the City Opera. I didn't want the evening to have a single sad note.

"It's almost twenty-five years to the day since my debut as Rosalinda," I said, "so why don't we do the second-act ball scene of *Die Fledermaus* the way it's done in Vienna on New Year's Eve."

The tradition there is that, in *Fledermaus,* Prince Orlofsky gives a ball during which everything stops as one star after another comes out and does a little turn. I have a recording of just such a performance, conducted by Herbert von Karajan, on which Giulietta Simionato and Ettore Bastianini, two great Italian opera stars, sing "Anything You Can Do, I Can Do Better" in the funniest broken English. That kind of thing still happens on New Year's Eve in Vienna. After a number of stars have come up and performed, Orlofsky says, "Enough, my friends, enough," and *Die Fledermaus* continues. Our idea was to dispense with the first act, and do the second act up until the ball scene, at which time various entertainers would take over the stage.

Trumpets rang out across Lincoln Center on the night the New York City Opera presented *Beverly!,* an abbreviated Act II of *Fledermaus*—and a nifty way to build up our bank account. The New York State Theater was packed with friends, colleagues, and opera lovers who paid as much as $1,000 a ticket to bid me goodbye. First a procession of my friends came onstage and performed. Dinah Shore sang "Blues in the Night." Mary Martin did "My Heart Belongs to Daddy." The late Ethel Merman belted out "There's No Business Like Show Business." Renata Scotto sang "Somewhere Over the Rainbow." Cynthia Gregory danced the *Fledermaus* ballet. Sherrill Milnes performed "Maria" from *West Side Story.* Leontyne Price sang "What I Did for Love." Placido Domingo sang "Granada." Flautist James Galway played "Danny Boy." Eileen Farrell sang "I've Got the World on a String." Donald Gramm got up and did a funny parody of "I Want What I Want When I Want It." It really was an unbelievable lineup of stars. The opera was going full blast—Alan Titus and I had just finished a duet—when Carol Burnett came bursting out on stage, loudly demanding, "What the hell happened to Gay Vienna?"

She and I then repeated the medley from our 1976 TV special: Carol sang arias, and I interrupted her with pop tunes. We wound up with me singing "The Man That Got Away" and Carol singing "Un bel di" from *Madama Butterfly.*

A lot of my nonsinging men friends wanted to participate, so when the orchestra, led by Julius Rudel, struck up a waltz, I danced with the likes of Burt Reynolds, Walter Cronkite, Mayor Ed Koch, and Zubin Mehta. My farewell turned out to be one of the happiest nights of my life.

I closed the evening the way I'd always closed my concerts: with a little Portuguese folk song my late vocal teacher, Estelle Liebling, had arranged for me when I was ten. I made a short speech paying tribute to Miss Liebling, and then began singing the song with lyrics I'd written for that night: "We have shared so much together/'Tis not the end but a new start/So, my dears, you know I love you/You'll be forever in my heart."

Charles Wadsworth, whom I'd worked with for many years, was accompanying me at the piano, and he started bawling. I walked behind Charlie, put my arms around him, and finished the song. There was a lot of screaming and applause, and a bouquet of red roses was brought up to me. I thought: *Terrific. We did that already. Let me get offstage.*

I walked off, and the crowd was still applauding. People in the wings said, "Get back out there and say goodbye." Fine. I walked back out and waved, and as I did, balloons and confetti came down and covered the entire stage. So I went out the way I wanted to, after all. No tears, just confetti and balloons—*thousands* of balloons—all over the place.

The evening ended on a very up beat, and we did indeed clear more than a million dollars for the City Opera.

The next morning I reported for work at nine o'clock. I arrived wearing a prima donna ensemble—at that point, I didn't have any other kind of clothing. Prima donnas do not wear inexpensive outfits, so I showed up in a sable-lined raincoat, a cashmere dress, Ferragamo shoes, with a ten-carat diamond ring on my finger and a carefully applied layer of makeup on my face. A prima donna face is a mask of confidence and self-assurance. Among the first things you learn as a prima donna are to smile, nicely, appear to be open and friendly, but not overly so, and look as though you're impervious to criticism, which you're most certainly not.

In 1978, when the New York City Opera first announced I was to be its next general director, I had been unprepared for the skepticism and hostility my appointment aroused throughout the opera world. There is, after all, no school for impresarios. Rudolf Bing of the Metropolitan Opera had been a floorwalker in a London department store. Kurt Adler of the San Francisco Opera had been a chorus master. Julius Rudel, my predecessor, was a conductor. Did being a diva *disqualify* me in some way? Even one of my severest critics once wrote that I'd had more impact on the public than any opera singer since Enrico Caruso. So why did so many people think I'd be the death of the City Opera?

Frankly, I didn't know. When I became the company's general director in July 1979, there were a *lot* of things I didn't know. For instance, I had no idea the New York City Opera was in debt up to its eyeballs. If I had known, there's no way I would have taken the job. I might have considered myself unsinkable, but the City Opera wasn't. In fact, the company was then on the edge of bankruptcy. God, was I naïve. I thought I could walk in and if I needed donors, they would automatically show up. I never for a moment imagined that when the opera was in season, I'd work fifteen hours a day, seven days a week. Prima donnas don't do that.

In my first book, *Bubbles,* which I wrote in 1976, I concluded by saying: "The fun is just beginning!"

Really? The first day I walked into my office—and worse, a few weeks later, when I finally got a look at the company's books—I knew I was in for a long, hard struggle. I wasn't a stranger to struggle. I was, however, a stranger to failure, and the possibility that I might fail in my new job was simply not acceptable. I was still the prima donna—and it wasn't until a bitterly cold day in a Godforsaken warehouse that I fully realized how much had changed.

As a retirement gift, the New York City Opera musicians had presented me with a silver rose, and the stagehands had given me a jumpsuit with a great big dragon embroidered on the back. I wore that jumpsuit beneath a down jacket the first time I visited the New Jersey warehouse where we stored our sets. Rik Kaye, the City Opera's technical director, had driven out there with me in order to solve a thorny problem. We had run out of warehouse space and had been storing some of our sets in trailer trucks, which were left in a parking lot. While this decreased our warehouse costs, it also resulted in our sets' being damaged by New York's icy temperatures. The trucks had also turned out to be easy prey for vandals—our entire set for *Le Coq d'Or* was destroyed in its trailer. At that point, Rik told me: "It's really necessary for us to go to the warehouse and decide which sets we want to keep and which we want to sell or throw out. Some of them will have to go, because we need to open up some space.

Otherwise, we'll just wind up renting more trucks and paying more parking fees."

It was freezing the day Rik and I visited our warehouse, a dank, dark place as big as an airplane hangar. Our sets were lined up in aisles wide enough to permit trucks to drive in, load up, and drive right out again. At that point we weren't computerized and didn't have our inventory listed on printouts. Rik took along a notebook to verify what was there.

When we walked in, two things happened: I was almost knocked over by the warehouse's overpoweringly foul odor, and then I stepped on something squishy. Rik told me that during the winter, rodents and birds would ferret their way into the warehouse seeking shelter from the cold, and would wind up starving to death. At home, if I see a cockroach, I scream and then yell, "Peter!" My husband calls the exterminator.

The first aisle started with the set for *Julius Caesar* and moved on to *Manon, The Tales of Hoffmann, I Puritani, Roberto Devereux, Maria Stuarda,* and *Anna Bolena.* Every one of these productions had been a major milestone in my career. As Rik and I walked along, I began remembering the place each of those operas had occupied in my life. Rik was taking notes; I was reliving moments that were irretrievably over. As we made our way down the darkened aisles, I stopped gaping at the sets themselves and instead began recalling specific performances of each opera. Suddenly I found myself searching for notes I'd left on various pieces of scenery or furniture. The set of *Julius Caesar* contained a little arcade to which I'd pinned a message reminding myself to sing the *"Piangero"* very slowly. On a chair used in *Anna Bolena,* I found a note asking the stagehands to make sure to angle the chair so that the audience could see my profile and I could see conductor Julius Rudel in the pit. When we passed the set of *Manon,* I remembered how tenor Michele Molese and I used to argue because he'd chew gum up to the moment we began a sensual scene in Act II. Molese would stick the gum behind his ear, and it was very difficult even to pretend to make love to a man with gum behind his ear. Mike eventually took to hiding his gum before that scene and I thought I knew where. I asked Rik: "Where's the door to the second act of *Manon*?"

When we found it, there were about two dozen pieces of gum stuck to the door.

The more we walked down those aisles, the more I was flooded with memories. I began weeping when we came to the sets used in *The Tales of Hoffmann*. The scenery for that opera had been tailor-made for Norman Treigle and me. *The Tales of Hoffmann* was the first opera in which Treigle and I began a collaboration that took both of us to a new level as performers.

As Rik and I continued to take inventory, my entire operatic life seemed to flash in front of my eyes. You could march me past a row of a thousand thrones, but I'd never forget the one that I occupied as Queen Elizabeth in *Roberto Devereux*. I was vividly remembering sights and sounds, all of them relating to my life as a performer, yet I was there to dispose of as many of those old productions as I could in order to make way for new ones.

I don't know that I've ever had a stranger experience. Rik knew I was reacting to our task with very strong emotions, but he didn't realize what I was going through, because he didn't know what these objects had meant to me.

Our visit to the warehouse took place more than two years after I retired as a singer. Until then, the fact of my retirement hadn't really hit me with finality, probably because a career doesn't truly end on the day one retires. For me, it ended the day I walked down that desolate warehouse lit here and there by naked light bulbs and littered with dead mice and birds. I realized then that a lot of things were dead and could never be revived, and I don't just mean the productions that Rik and I finally chose to throw out. I walked away feeling that a great big page in my life had been irrevocably turned.

For the first time in more than twenty-five years, I was sure no one would be shouting *"Brava, diva!"*

ONE

If anyone ever writes a definitive history of pre-World War II child stars, I'll be a footnote lost among chapters devoted to the likes of Shirley Temple, Deanna Durbin, Dickie Moore, Bobby Breen, and Freddie Bartholomew. In 1936, when I was seven years old, I became a "regular" on the *Major Bowes' Capitol Family* hour, which was then one of America's most popular radio programs. Each week I sang selections from French and Italian operas, which was considered freaky on the radio, even when adults did it.

I was not a hot show biz commodity, nor were my parents trying to make me one. In fact, my father wasn't particularly pleased that I was on the radio every week. My mother was just happy that her daughter shared her own lifelong love for opera, and was talented to boot.

Although opera was assumed to be the exclusive province of ladies in diamond headbands, it was the music we always listened to at home. We lived in Brooklyn, and Mama often went to Manhattan to buy opera records. She loved the prelude to the third act of *Lohengrin,* and really wore out her collection of recordings by Amelita Galli-Curci and Lily Pons. She played those records so often, even my two older brothers, Sidney and Stanley, could imitate Pons singing the Bell Song from *Lakmé*.

Our Victrola was kept in the kitchen, along with the crystal radio sets that my grandfather built for us. The kitchen itself kept changing. I was born at home—613 Midwood Street in Brooklyn—on May 26, 1929. My father, Morris Silverman, was an assistant manager for the Metropolitan Life Insurance Company, and since he worked on a commission basis, his income fluctuated wildly. Every once in a while he would land a very big client, like Mr. Schwartz of Chock full o' Nuts, who later changed his name to Mr. Black. Each time my father signed up an important new customer, we would move, though never more than a few blocks. Although the apartment where I was born was quite spacious, the first apartment I actually remember was a one-bedroom flat at 580 Empire Boulevard in Brooklyn. I shared the bedroom with my parents. My brothers—Sidney, six years older than I, and Stanley, four years older—slept in a Hide-A-Bed in the foyer.

The next apartment I remember, at 948 Lenox Road in Flatbush, was very large and lavish. We didn't stay there long, because I developed seriously inflamed sinuses. The houses there had been built on marsh flats, and it was just too damp for me. So we pulled up stakes and moved back to Empire Boulevard. Eventually we wound up in Sea Gate, a Brooklyn community on the ocean, past Coney Island.

My father was strong and formal, a handsome man slightly over six feet tall, who was thoroughly European in his attitude toward women. When I was born, he told my mother: "We already have two sons, Shirley. Belle is our dessert."

Belle Silverman came out of the womb with a bubble in her mouth, which prompted my mother's doctor to call me Bubbles. The rest of the family has always called me Bubbly, and it wasn't until I started school that I learned my name was Belle. I was shocked and not at all happy about that name. My friends called me Bubbles.

My father was a strict parent—there was absolutely no give-and take in our relationship. He laid down the law, and we obeyed. Papa never lectured us, nor did he ever lay a finger on any of us, but he knew how to make a point. He was a demanding man and expected no less of us than he expected of himself. I once scored a 98 on an arithmetic test, and I remember his saying: "I don't like ninety-eights. I only like one hundreds."

On the other hand, I could talk to him endlessly, and did. Until I was eleven years old, and he decided it was becoming unseemly, he would let me crawl into his lap, and at such times he was the most comforting papa in the world. On those occasions when it seemed there was no pleasing my father, my mother more than compensated for him: She felt that everything her children did was perfect. When I was in the third grade at P.S. 91, I won the spelling bee by correctly spelling *necessity*. My mother realized right then and there that she'd given birth to a genius.

I did nothing to dissuade her from that opinion. I'd been tested as having an IQ of 155, and if I didn't receive at least a 95 in every subject, it wasn't my report card. Grades weren't all that mattered, though. My mother put a premium on being cheerful—if nothing was wrong, there was no reason for any of her children to be whiners, and so we weren't.

My mother always thought of Sidney, Stanley, and me as the three musketeers, because we all looked out for one another. Actually, my brothers did most of the looking out—I was the baby of the family. Sidney, being the eldest, was the designated heir apparent. The family called him "Doc"—they picked out his profession before Sidney could walk—and he resembled my father and watched over me in much the same way Papa did. Stanley, on the other hand, was very frail as a boy and always had a kind of woebegone look. He was a beautiful kid with big brown eyes like saucers, but you'd have trouble seeing those eyes because his hair was always falling down over his face.

Sidney and I were chubby, and to this day we both blame Stanley for that. Stanley, you see, was very skinny, and my mother used to try to fatten him up with chocolate chip cookies and chocolate pudding with whipped cream on top. Sidney and I were quick to eat our desserts, but Stanley wasn't, so we used to eat his as well. Stan's frailness stemmed from the time he was hit by a car when we still lived on Midwood Street. Mama had really babied him after that accident, Sidney and I felt. Eventually, Stanley found his appetite, and now he puts away food like a human vacuum cleaner. He still has trouble keeping his weight up, but Sidney and I have absolutely no sympathy for him. Either of us can gain three pounds just by *looking* at an eclair.

My brothers and I were always very close. When I got scared at night, it was Stanley's bed I ran into, and it was Stanley who taught me how to play bridge. But whenever I had a serious problem to deal with, the older of my brothers was the one I'd turn to. Sidney did indeed grow up to become a doctor, and Stanley, after becoming head of Bobbs-Merrill, the book publishers, took over a lucrative sports publishing business. Both of them were highly individualistic, overbright children. I always sat between them at the dinner table, and I grew up playing the role of a wisecracking pacifier able to smooth over any arguments they'd start with each other. I also did what every little girl was expected to do: I sat up straight and never dirtied my dress. I was the best daughter in the world—ask my mother, she'll tell you. I still wear that title.

My mother was born Sonia Markovna Bonchikov in the Russian city of Odessa. Meyer Bonchikov, her father, was an electrical engineer and an inventor. He was also a socialist, and was suspected of plotting to overthrow the Czar. Grandpa somehow came to the attention of Eugene Debs, the famous socialist and labor organizer, and the two men corresponded. My mother was then too young to know the particulars, but two Americans came to Russia and took her father back with them to New York City, where he began working for the E. W. Bliss Engineering Company. Grandma Bonchikov had just become pregnant again when Grandpa left for the United States. He promised he'd send for the family before the baby was born, and he kept his word.

On July 18, 1917, the day before Alexander Kerensky came to power, my pregnant grandmother and her three daughters, none of whom spoke a word of English, boarded the Trans-Siberian Railroad bound for Vladivostok on the first leg of their trip to America. From there, they took a train to China and then sailed to Japan. In Yokohama they booked passage on the *Panama Maru,* a Japanese freighter that took them to Seattle, Washington. Then they traveled across the United States by train and were reunited with my grandfather in Brooklyn. Customs officials had already changed Grandpa's surname to Bahn. For no apparent reason they changed my mother's first name from Sonia to Sally.

My father's people had emigrated from Bucharest, Rumania, and were relatively wealthy. My father grew up in a big house in Brooklyn and enlisted in the army during World War I. He was gassed and wounded in the war, leaving him with shrapnel fragments in one leg. A few weeks before he was released from an army hospital, my mother, who was then sixteen, was wheeling one of her younger sisters down the street in Brooklyn when Mrs. Fanny Silverman saw her. My father's mother went up to her, pinched my mother on the cheek and said, "I have a son—he's wounded now, but when he gets better, I want you to meet him."

When her son Morris got back from the hospital, Mrs. Silverman began nagging him to meet this wonderful girl she'd found for him. My father told her: "Please, Mama, I just got back. When I find somebody, I'll come and tell *you*, okay?"

Fanny Silverman's house faced the street, and when my father was convalescing, he'd read while sitting at a front window. One day little Sally Bahn walked by, and my father called his mother over. "See that girl over there?" he said. "I'd like to meet *her*."

When his mother saw whom he was pointing to, she said, "That's the girl I told you about. See how easy it's going to be to meet the girl you're going to marry?"

It wasn't *that* easy. My father had a reputation for being a fast man with the ladies. He was good-looking and drove a yellow Stutz, and as my mom recalls, a lot of "American" girls were after him. My grandfather allowed Papa to go out with his Sonia, but only if her sister Anne, two years younger, came along. My Aunt Anne acted as their chaperone for a year and a half, at which point my parents signed papers to become engaged. They were married in 1923, when my father was twenty-six and my mother twenty. By that time, my father had begun calling my mother Shirley—don't ask me why; I really don't know.

My parents' wedding was a very elaborate affair—at one point, rose petals fluttered down from the ceiling, and at the conclusion of the ceremony, white doves were released. Grandpa Bahn spared no expense, especially since he knew that he was going to give my father the bill.

My parents' marriage always seemed ideal to me. My mother couldn't do enough for my father, and vice versa. They struck me as a very romantic couple. My father's job took him to different parts of Brooklyn every day, but he always managed to come home for a quick swim in the ocean, lunch, and much more, I suspect, than light conversation with my mother. He treated her like a queen. God forbid she should do heavy cleaning or have to write a check.

The nuclear family was still a generation away. My father had eight brothers and three sisters. My mother had one brother and four surviving sisters; Aunt Sylvia, the baby of the family, had died of congenital heart disease when she was twelve. I loved watching my mother and her four sisters together. Like Mama, they were all very attractive, and one of them, Aunt Adeline, whom we called Aunt Eddy, had been voted Miss Brooklyn. They always reminded me of the Gabors.

We got together with both sides of the family every Sunday, which was the best day of the week. Early on Sunday mornings, Grandpa Bahn would arrive at our house with hot bagels, tubs of cream cheese and butter, and plenty of sturgeon and black olives. He'd also bring every New York newspaper then published. He was determined to become Americanized, and by then all his daughters spoke flawless English. My brothers and I were each given our own newspaper. Sidney got the *Daily News,* Stanley got the *Herald Tribune,* and I got the *Daily Mirror.* We'd all eat breakfast, read the papers, and wait for Mama and Papa to wake up.

I was the apple of my grandfather's eye. He thought I was the prettiest little girl he'd ever seen, and he told me so every time he saw me. I think it was primarily because he was so dark. Grandpa had a shock of black hair and a black moustache. My father and my brothers were similarly dark, but I had my mother's coloring: very white skin and light-blond hair.

My father usually emerged from the bedroom at around ten o'clock, and, as was the rule, he made the coffee—Mother used a percolator, and he disapproved of percolators. He'd throw coffee into a pot of boiling water and then strain it. When he poured the coffee, he'd say, "That's how you grow hair on your chest." He said it often enough for me to worry about looking very peculiar when I grew up.

At noon, my mother, the original night person, would finally join us. During the week, she'd get up early to make us breakfast and sandwiches to take to school, and then she'd go back to bed. She's never changed her schedule, except that after her children left home, she would sleep late every day. Even now, when I want to speak to my mother, I don't call before one o'clock.

After coffee was served, Grandpa Bahn would go down to the basement and tinker in the workshop he'd set up with equipment borrowed from Bliss Engineering. Grandpa always made a racket in the basement, but one day he outdid himself: The gadget he was working on went through a concrete wall and punctured a water pipe. A couple of weeks later, Bliss Engineering bought his invention for a flat fee of $5,000, with the patent and rights owned by the company. Next time you walk by workmen tearing up a sidewalk with pneumatic drills, try to think kindly of my Grandpa Bahn. He later invented the automatic buttonholer, for which the Singer Sewing Machine Company also paid him $5,000.

We almost never went to Grandpa and Grandma Bahn's house, because by then she'd become very despondent and introverted. Grandma Bahn was a sensitive, stunningly beautiful woman who never really got over the death of her daughter Sylvia. She was a gentle creature, and I think she found life too tough for her and just decided to give up. I was very sad when she passed away. She and my grandfather were absolute opposites—he was such a dominant and domineering man. Without realizing it, I think my mother looked for a man who resembled her own father. My dad was also very dark and very domineering, and he spoke with a resounding period at the end of every sentence. I remember that when I was seven years old, my father summoned me into the living room, which in itself was an occasion, for we didn't use that room very often. He said, "I want you to listen to me. Your mother doesn't drink and your mother doesn't smoke, and you're not going to, either."

Frankly, at seven years old, it hadn't occurred to me to do either of those things. My father's little lecture put such fear into me that the first drink I ever had was with my husband—so you can see how Pete led me down the garden path from the very beginning.

On Sunday afternoons we'd go to Grandma Silverman's house on Eastern Parkway for dinner with at least three dozen relatives. Grandma Silverman was a wonderful, mysterious woman. If you opened her closet, you'd find twenty black dresses with high collars, and we never knew for whom she was in mourning. I remember many funny family discussions about whether one man had fathered all twelve of her children, and how come nobody could remember Grandpa Silverman.

Grandma Silverman served the family black Turkish coffee, and wine that she made in her basement. The kids were allowed to dip sugar cubes into the wine and we usually got a little bit loaded. My brother Sidney would demand, "Gimme booze, Gramma." There must have been fifteen first cousins running around the house, plus babies in their carriages. Dinner was served at around four o'clock, when several bridge tables would be piled high with food. Grandma Silverman made the best kreplach (think ravioli without the sauce), strudel, and challah (egg bread), but my personal favorite was her *tayglach,* little sticky balls of honey and nuts. After dinner we'd be home by seven o'clock so we could listen to the Fred Allen and Jack Benny shows on the radio. Sundays were terrific.

Saturdays were special too. On Saturdays my father took Sidney and Stanley to a baseball game or to the Turkish baths and then to a wonderful Rumanian restaurant named Mechel's that specialized in charcoal-broiled steaks. Mama and I, however, spent the day in "New York," which is how Brooklyn kids refer to Manhattan. I think my mother correctly sensed that if there was enough money to educate her children, my father would see to it that the boys would go to college, and if there was anything left over for me, fine; if not, that would also be fine—maybe I could win a scholarship. Marriage, after all, did not require a college education. My mother was one of the first women's libbers God put on this earth, and simply couldn't accept my father's philosophy. And so, when my father took off with his two sons, Mama took a long look at her chubby little blond daughter and decided I certainly *was* going to be educated.

My mother loved coloratura sopranos—she had a good voice and would sing along with Galli-Curci and Lily Pons in the kitchen—and soon enough, she began taking me to see Pons. On Saturdays. No Jewish child in the neighborhood could ice-skate; my mother had skated in Russia, and she took me ice-skating at Rockefeller Center. On Saturdays. Saturdays belonged to her and to her plans for making me an educated woman. She once told me: "Someday, you're going to sit at a dinner table with a Frenchman on one side and an Italian on the other, and you're going to be able to converse with them." That day came to pass.

When I was four years old, my mother saw a newspaper ad that read: WANTED: TALENTED CHILDREN TO GO ON BIG BROTHER BOB EMERY'S

RAINBOW HOUSE. TRAINING ATTACHED. Two kiddie shows then dominated Saturday-morning radio. *The Horn and Hardart Children's Hour*
was number one in the nation. *Rainbow House with Big Brother Bob
Emery* was the Avis of the genre.

My mother was pretty sure she had a talented child. I'd memorized the twenty-two arias that were on her Galli-Curci recordings,
and I could hit all the high notes. The year before, billed as Cutie Pie
Silverman (Cutie Pie was my father's pet name for me), I'd sung "The
Wedding of Jack and Jill" in Brooklyn's Miss Beautiful Baby of 1932
contest, and I'd won the talent award and the title as well. My mother
decided that since *Rainbow House* was broadcast on Saturdays, why
not give it a try.

So early one Saturday morning in 1933 (it's a thrill to see *that*
in print) Mama and I rode the subway into Manhattan and made our
way to 1440 Broadway, home of WOR radio and *Rainbow House*. Bob
Emery—I called him Uncle Bob—was a gray-haired, paunchy man
who wore granny glasses. He was kind and soft-spoken, and I instantly adored him.

Uncle Bob was a shrewd businessman. The hook in his ad was
that phrase *Training Attached*. In order to have a chance at getting on
his show, you had to spend 50 cents a week on lessons that began at
nine o'clock. From nine to nine-fifteen we learned how to tap-dance;
from nine-fifteen to nine-thirty we learned elocution; from nine-thirty
to nine-forty-five we sang. From nine-forty-five to ten, Uncle Bob
chose which twenty of his three dozen or so students would go on
the air with him. *Rainbow House* was broadcast from ten to eleven
A.M.

I was always picked to go on the show. Uncle Bob liked me
a lot, but not because of the way I sang "The Wedding of Jack and
Jill," Arditi's *"Il Bàcio,"* or any of my other biggies. He picked children
from each of his classes, and he initially selected me because of my
elocutionary skills. Or "thkillth," to be more accurate. I had lost my two
front teeth at a very early age, and I had the biggest lisp you ever heard.

But I wasn't self-conscious about it, and Uncle Bob never imi-
tated my lisp or made fun of me. Each week he and I would have
long discussions on the air. He'd say, "Well, Bubbles, how did you do
in your elocution lesson this morning?" And I'd say, "I'm trying not to
thpeak like I come from Brooklyn." And then I'd launch into my
elocution piece.

You can imagine why Bob wanted me on. He'd describe me to his audience (my mother had given me exactly sixty-five Shirley Temple curls), and then this four-year-old would talk her thilly head off. When my grown-up teeth finally came in, my ear had grown so attuned to substituting *th* for *s* that I had to go to a real elocution school to remedy the problem.

I never really got rid of it. To this day, if I'm fatigued or terribly upset, I'll sometimes start lisping, and it's happened at some spectacularly inappropriate moments. When I sang *Manon* with the New York City Opera, conductor Julius Rudel and I, who rarely differed over such things, had argued vehemently about the fast tempo he'd set for the opera's most dramatic and sensual scene: Manon Lescaut, nineteenth-century Paris's leading courtesan, has gone to the cathedral at Saint-Sulpice in hopes of winning her former lover, now a priest, away from the church by seducing him. At one of the performances I began singing the segment we'd argued about, which was a prayer, and damned if I didn't start lisping. Once I got into it, I couldn't get out of it—there was just no stopping me. Julius shot me an arch look from the podium, obviously thinking I was paying him back for the fast tempo. Then, seeing my genuine distress—you want to talk about sheer mortification?—he started to laugh. I looked over in the wings, and everybody backstage was laughing too. What's funny about "Than-Thulpithe"?

In any case, Uncle Bob soon expanded my role on his show. Each week he gave me a little ditty to prepare for the next broadcast. Most of the time I sang children's songs with memorable lyrics like:

> *Toodle-lumma-lumma, toodle-lumma-lumma,*
> *Toodle-eye-ay.*
> *Any um-ber-ellas, any um-ber-ellas,*
> *to fix today?*
> *Bring your parasol, it may be small,*
> *it may be big.*
> *He'll repair them all, with what he calls*
> *a thing-a-ma-jig.*

The most ambitious song Uncle Bob ever gave me to learn was "Alone," a beautiful ballad sung by Kitty Carlisle and Allan Jones in the Marx Brothers movie *A Night at the Opera.*

After he heard me on *Rainbow House,* Wally Wanger, a friend of the family and brother of movie producer Walter Wanger, arranged for me to sing at the opening of the Queen Mary restaurant in Manhattan. Wally decided to bill me as Beverly Sills, and my father was outraged when he heard about it. Wanger told Papa my name *had* to be changed. "You just can't have Belle Silverman on a theater marquee," he said.

"You certainly can't—and you aren't going to, either," Papa replied. My father finally went along with the idea, but by then it was clear that things were going further than he wanted them to go.

Mama, meanwhile, wasn't living her life through me, nor was she out shlepping me around to auditions. I think she just wanted me to become a worldly, educated woman.

By then I could speak French fluently. That came about because I'd been such a huge baby—I weighed ten and three-quarters pounds at birth—that after delivering me, my mother was quite exhausted and went away to a health farm for six weeks. While she was there, Papa hired a French girl named Janine to take care of me. Janine, whom we all called Jaye, was a red-headed seventeen-year-old who'd been brought to America by a relative of hers in Pennsylvania. By the time Mama came home, Jaye had fallen in love with my brothers and me, and my parents asked her to stay on. Jaye did house-cleaning and looked after the kids. She was what we'd call an *au pair* today. She could barely speak English, so she talked to us in French. The first songs I ever sang were little French tunes Jaye taught me, and I knew how to count to one hundred in French well before I could do so in English. When I got to kindergarten I could speak French, and so could my brothers. Jaye's six-week job lasted six years. At that point, she married a policeman whom she met while visiting her relatives in Pennsylvania.

I was on *Rainbow House with Big Brother Bob Emery* until I was seven. I wasn't there every single Saturday for four years, but I was a regular member of the show's family. In 1936, Mama screwed up her courage and took me to audition for *Major Bowes' Original Amateur Hour.* A weekly talent contest, *Major Bowes' Original Amateur Hour* had begun broadcasting the year before and had quickly become one of the ten most popular radio programs in the nation. Auditions for the show were held in the Capitol Theater Building, which the Major had built. Edward Bowes, then sixty-two, had made a fortune in real estate and collected honorary titles the way other men collect stamps. Bowes was an honorary major in the army reserves; it was one of more than a thousand honorary titles he held.

A lady by the name of Bessie Mack, the Major's top assistant, conducted my audition, and within five minutes of our meeting, she became my Aunt Bessie. After I sang for her, she went inside to talk to the Major. Major Bowes, an elegant, heavyset man, came out of his office and I sang the Bell Song from *Lakmé* for him. At the time, he was dating Mary Garden, one of the country's greatest sopranos, so he must have liked opera. He put me on the *Amateur Hour*.

Major Bowes had two weekly shows on CBS radio: the *Original Amateur Hour* and *Capitol Family*. Both were broadcast from the Capitol Theater Building. The *Original Amateur Hour* was like talent night at a vaudeville house—if the audience didn't like an act, a gong sounded and the contestant would slink off in shame. Whoever got the most applause won.

I appeared on the show as Beverly Sills, and I sang *"Caro nome"* from Verdi's *Rigoletto*. At the end of the aria, I hit and held a high E, which is roughly akin to a seven-year-old's running a four-minute mile. The audience's response was overwhelming. I won that week's *Amateur Hour,* and before the broadcast was over, Major Bowes brought me back out and announced he was going to have me as a regular guest on *Capitol Family*.

My debut on the *Capitol Family* hour coincided with the show's tenth anniversary, and photographs of the Major and me appeared in newspapers throughout the nation. Because of the publicity involved, Wally Wanger, who'd maintained his interest in my career, apparently thought I could become the next Shirley Temple. Not long after I began appearing on the *Capitol Family* hour, when I was still seven, he introduced me and my mother to a talent agent named Dorothy Cummings. Dorothy, in turn, introduced us to Jack Skirball, who would soon produce such Alfred Hitchcock classics as *Saboteur* and *Shadow of a Doubt.* Jack saw me as a walking incongruity, a little girl with a lisp and a Brooklyn accent who could belt out operatic arias.

Jack decided to use me in an episode of *Uncle Sol's Problem Court,* a series of film shorts he was then producing. Willie Howard, a burlesque comedian, played Uncle Sol, a judge who solved funny domestic problems in his courtroom. My little epic was called *Uncle*

Sol Solves It. I played a little girl with a great singing voice who was destined to become an opera star. My problem was that my parents wanted me to study singing in Europe, and I didn't want to go. That movie has been shown all over the Public Broadcasting System in the last couple of years. In the film, Willie Howard asks me: "Well, where would you like to study?" and I say, "Right here at home, Uncle Thol." And then I get up and take off my little sailor hat, and although the film isn't in color, you can see that my curls have turned from blond to auburn. I then launch into *"Il Bàcio,"* and when I finish, Uncle Sol faces the camera and says, "I find in favor of Bubbles—she studies right here at home." Uncle Sol was *so* wise.

Uncle Sol Solves It marked the beginning and end of my movie career. I enjoyed being in the film, but I had no interest in becoming a movie star. The only movies I liked were musicals starring Jeanette MacDonald and Nelson Eddy. I became a big Jeanette MacDonald fan, especially after seeing her sing an aria from *Faust* in *San Francisco.* (Clark Gable wasn't too shabby in that movie, either.) I was determined to become an opera star, no question about it. I would be a famous diva and sing at the Metropolitan Opera.

In the meantime, I was going great guns with Major Bowes. He worked with me the same way Uncle Bob had: We talked, and then I sang. For my first appearance, we rehearsed a little conversation and then repeated it on the show. The Major asked me: "Are you nervous?" I said I was, and the Major told the audience: "Well, I've given Beverly a little white elephant and she's clutching it in her hand for good luck."

Major Bowes' Capitol Family reached millions of homes, and by the following Sunday night's broadcast, listeners had sent me hundreds of little elephants. That was the start of a collection that at one time numbered thousands of glass, ivory, and jade elephants. Except for two of them, I've since donated my entire collection to various charity auctions. The only ones I've hung on to are the original ivory elephant Major Bowes gave me and one I received from my stepdaughter Lindley.

My parents did not raise a stupid daughter: The elephant episode prompted me to become a little con artist. During a broadcast on a snowy Sunday before Christmas, Major Bowes said, "Tell me, Beverly, what would you like for Christmas?"

"Oh, Major, I would just *love* to have a sled," I replied. The following week listeners sent me sixty-five sleds. Well, I soon got the hang of this. A few weeks later I mentioned how much I wanted a Mickey Mouse watch. I received dozens of them.

I was shameless. During one program, Major Bowes described the little ruffled dress my mother had made for me. I quickly cut in and said, "Yes, but my mommy won't make me a long dress, and I want one. Mama says little girls shouldn't wear long dresses, and I'm very upset."

I wasn't nearly as upset as my mother was when she heard that. She got more upset when scores of long dresses came pouring through the mails. One was a beautiful pale-blue taffeta dress with puffed sleeves, which I just loved—and that *really* made mother angry. She was so annoyed that she confiscated it and finally, finally sat down and made me a long dress.

Even though I embarrassed him a bit, my father tolerated my radio antics until a broadcast that took place while he was in the hospital for a hernia operation. I told the Major all about it, and how I hoped Papa would be all right so that he could go back to work soon, because we needed the money. Papa was listening and was not amused. We were not a charity case, and he did not want his Bubbly to extort money from people who listened to the *Capitol Family* hour. My days as a panhandler were over.

I earned $65 a week on the show, which was a very decent wage back then, even for adults. I wanted to replace the $5 spinet my mother had bought me with a grand piano, but my father insisted that I save my salary. The idea that I might need anything other than a funny little $5 piano never really crossed his mind. My father continued to have traditional goals for his daughter. Like many men of his generation, he thought that becoming a schoolteacher was about the only respectable profession for young women to contemplate. Investing time, energy and money in any other possible career for me simply would not have occurred to him. Papa didn't admire people in show business. He thought it was fine for his little girl to take piano lessons, and treated the subject very casually.

Mother knew I truly longed to get a quality piano to learn on, and so did Major Bowes. He decided to help me out. Major Bowes had enormous clout. When he heard that the Rinso laundry soap manufacturers were planning to make radio's first singing commercial, he told them to use me. Case closed: I was hired to do the singing, and the Major's announcer, Tony Marvin, who later moved to Arthur Godfrey's show, was hired to do the announcing and also the whistling on the commercial.

Recordings of that commercial are now in a couple of radio museums. It was an extraordinarily popular and successful commercial, and a lot of people can still recall the tune and the lyrics:

> *Rinso white, Rinso white, happy little washday song.*
> *Rinso white, Rinso white, birdies sing it all day long.*
> *Your fine-feathered friend has a message to send,*
> *So listen, you can't go wrong.*
> *Rinso white, Rinso bright, happy little washday song.*

There were no such things as residuals in those days, but sponsors weren't skinflints. I was paid $1,000 for the Rinso commercial. I got my Baldwin piano.

The Major found it amusing that he'd discovered this talented little child, and he was very interested in how I was making out. He began talking to my mother about getting me some formal vocal training. I remember his saying: "Why don't you give the child singing lessons? You ought to find a singing teacher for her."

I was on the *Capitol Family* hour until I was ten years old, at which point the Major became ill and ended the program. He continued on with the *Original Amateur Hour* almost until his death in 1946. CBS replaced *Capitol Family* with the *Cresta Blanca Carnival,* starring Morton Gould and his orchestra. I did a lot of singing on the show, along with a boy by the name of Merrill (né Morris) Miller—he later changed it to Robert Merrill. They tried to stick to the same format, but without the Major—who was as popular then as Arthur Godfrey would become—the show had a hole that just couldn't be filled.

When the *Cresta Blanca Carnival* went off the air after about a year, Aunt Bessie Mack sprang into action and lined up my first dramatic role. When I was eleven, I was written into *Our Gal Sunday,* a weekday radio soap opera. I was given the role of Elaine Raleigh, abused child opera singer. Each broadcast of *Our Gal Sunday* began with an announcer asking the question "Can this girl from a mining town in the West find happiness as the wife of a wealthy and titled Englishman, Lord Henry Brinthrop?" First time I heard that, I thought: *Why not? What's* her *problem?*

I played the daughter of the overseer of Lord Henry's estate. The overseer was a drunkard, and every time he got soused, he'd beat me. Every time he beat me, I'd run off into the hills and sing. When I was finished, I'd come back down and then the wicked overseer would beat me again.

I felt so grown up, reading scripts and acting on three or four episodes a week. Boy, was *that* fun. For those of you who may have missed it, Elaine Raleigh came to a good end. It happened like this: One day, our gal Sunday invites Marcella Hudnell, a famous opera star (played by Esther Ralston, a famous silent screen star), to spend the weekend at Lord Henry's estate. Madame Hudnell hears little Elaine sing between beatings, and realizes that the kid has a shot at becoming a great opera star. When the weekend's over—and without bothering to consult the drunken overseer—Marcella takes poor mistreated Elaine Raleigh back to New York with her. It took thirty-six weeks for her to accomplish that, and at $67.50 a week, I was glad she took her time.

My father then put his foot down, and he had a heavy foot. He'd had enough of my being on radio. He'd also had enough of his friends laughing about the way I'd accumulated sleds and Mickey Mouse watches. He and my mother were not laughing. My mother knew I dreamed of being an opera singer and that this childish period would pass and that I *would* become an opera star. My father wouldn't even acknowledge my dream—singing simply wasn't a respectable profession. I still find it remarkable that my mother, with her soft-spoken manner, could twist this powerhouse of a man around her little finger and persuade him to approve of my singing, language, and piano lessons. She'd find any way possible to manipulate Papa into thinking that her way was the right way. I remember her saying: "She's a chubby little girl—tap-dancing will be good exercise for her." To his very last day, I don't think Papa ever realized that everything that happened to his three kids happened precisely the way she'd planned it.

My radio career ended when I was twelve. I think my parents both decided that a little peace and quiet in our lives was very

important. My father wanted me to concentrate on my regular studies. Papa had always been a bear that way. He didn't believe in
children's books, which is why I didn't read *Winnie the Pooh* until I
was an adult. My father thought that if I could read, I should read
real books. And I did. I read *Gone With the Wind* when I was ten years
old. I'm sure I didn't know why, but I got very excited when Rhett
Butler put his hand on Scarlett O'Hara's bosom. (I didn't have one
yet.) I remember thinking: *Oh, my, this is the kind of book Sidney and
Stanley hide under their beds.*

I didn't miss being on radio, because I was at an awkward age. I
think *all* twelve-year-old girls feel awkward. For the past couple of
years I'd been the tallest kid in my classes at P.S. 91. I was always last
in line, which did nothing for my self-esteem. When adolescence set
in, I felt very unattractive.

Before the Bowes show ended, I'd begun to feel clumsy around
my mother. She was such a graceful, feminine woman—and when I
was ten I was horrified to discover that my feet were bigger than hers.
There was no question that I was going to surpass her in height, and I
began wishing I could stay Mama's size forever. To compensate for
feeling like a huge piece of lumber, I later began buying tiny accesso-
ries, and to this day that's still my tendency. I buy small purses and
tiny boxes, and I collect miniature, dainty things.

I developed breasts earlier than any of my classmates, and that
was a great source of anguish for me. I was already feeling tall and
gawky, and when it became obvious in gym class that I was the only
girl who needed a bra, I didn't just become miserable, I became
hysterical. I was so unhappy with the sheer size of me that my mother
bought me a garter belt, which was about seven inches wide, and I
wore it around my chest. It gave me the silhouette of a flapper, but at
least it made me feel less conspicuous. I started wearing that garter
belt when I was in the eighth grade at P.S. 91, and didn't take it off
until I started high school six months later.

I was also unhappy because of my wardrobe. My mother made
all my clothes, and they were beautifully cut, but they were unusual,
and so they, too, set me apart. The negative side of my mother's
nonconformity was that she never seemed to realize there were other
people around. When I went to school I just didn't look like the other
kids. I wore beautifully hand-tailored, hand-stitched clothes, some-

times with matching hats. There I'd be, sitting in class with a hat on, and naturally the teacher would ask me to remove it.

I didn't mind that, but I was always different. If it wasn't because of my clothes, it was because I was six inches taller than everybody else or because I was the only girl in class who never wore makeup. The Hedy Lamarr look was in, and my classmates were all experimenting with lipstick so dark red it was almost black. My father didn't permit me to use *any* cosmetics.

Show business was really the last thing on my mind at that point. It wouldn't have mattered if it had been the first thing on my mind, because I really had no place to go. Radio variety shows like *The Bell Telephone Hour* and *The Voice of Firestone* employed big stars—they weren't looking for twelve-year-olds. Shirley Temple had gotten her first screen kiss, and movie audiences were so unimpressed that Shirley quickly went into retirement. Almost overnight, it seemed, kiddie stars went out of vogue. The only thing I'd continue with would be my singing lessons.

That was my real legacy from Major Bowes—his suggestion to Mama that I take singing lessons. Within weeks after he'd mentioned it, Mother had searched for and found *the* singing teacher for me. Her name was Estelle Liebling, and she altered the course of my life.

TWO

Even though *Major Bowes' Capitol Family* was broadcast on Sundays, Mother and I still spent Saturdays in New York. A couple of months after I began working with Major Bowes—and after he'd told Mama to find me a singing teacher—we passed a newsstand just outside Carnegie Hall on West 57th Street. My mother bought a magazine called *Musical Courier,* which featured a cover photograph of Estelle Liebling with the caption TEACHER OF OPERATIC, STAGE, SCREEN, AND RADIO ARTISTS. Miss Liebling had been Amelita Galli-Curci's singing teacher, which really impressed my mother, for Galli-Curci was her favorite singer.

Mama felt that only the best would do for her Bubbly. She telephoned Miss Liebling for an appointment, and one Saturday morning, off we went to her studio at 145 West 55th Street.

When we got there, I held on to my mother's hand for dear life. Estelle Liebling, then fifty-four, was a chic, sophisticated, funny woman. When I first saw her I thought Miss Liebling was very tall, but she actually was a tiny woman who wore spike heels all the time. In spite of her funny, squeaky speaking voice, she was very imposing. She was also very rich; her husband was Archie Mosler, of the Mosler Safe Company. They lived in a penthouse high above the studio.

The first thing Miss Liebling said to my mother was: "Leave the little girl with Miss Minter, my secretary, and I'll hear you now." When Mama said the lessons were for her little girl, Miss Liebling was quite surprised. She looked at me and said, "I don't teach little girls. I don't even *know* any little girls."

My mother hung in there, though, and finally prevailed on Miss Liebling to listen to me. I rolled out the heavy artillery: whenever and wherever I sang it, *"Il Bàcio"* had never failed to knock 'em dead. As soon as I opened my mouth I knew I was making a good impression on Miss Liebling, because she smiled all the time I was singing. When I finished, she started laughing her head off. I mean, the woman was *cackling*. Nobody had ever laughed at me before, so I began to cry.

Miss Liebling hadn't meant to insult me. She quickly explained that she had taught *"Il Bàcio"* to Galli-Curci. I'd just done an imitation of my mother's Galli-Curci record, complete with every cadenza, or vocal embellishment, Miss Liebeling had written for the great lady—*bel canto* arias are embellished in much the same way jazz soloists improvise riffs. On top of that, my Italian was just plain ludicrous. I'd memorized the record, but at that point I didn't speak the language, so most of what I sang was gobbledygook. Miss Liebling apologized for laughing, but she'd never heard anything so funny.

Miss Liebling wasn't through with me yet. She asked me to sing another aria. By then, I was scared to death. She had a big Persian carpet in the studio, and in the middle of the carpet was the design of a large medallion. "You fidget too much," she said. "Stand in that medallion and stand still when you sing."

That was the first discipline I ever learned as a singer. I sang my second aria, and Miss Liebling agreed to see me every Saturday morning for fifteen minutes. It was the beginning of an association that lasted until her death thirty-four years later.

Miss Liebling became my mentor. She thought my voice was particularly well-suited to French repertoire, and appreciated the fact that I was already conversant in the language. But my French was like my English—I spoke both with urban accents. Divas can't sound as if they've grown up in a working-class Parisian neighborhood, which had been Jaye's background. Coloratura sopranos also need a flawless command of Italian. Two of Miss Liebling's neighbors were highly educated spinster sisters. For 50 cents each Saturday, they spent fifteen minutes polishing my French and forty-five minutes teaching me Italian.

Miss Liebling felt I'd benefit by taking piano lessons. Opera singers had to be musicians, she said. (Ezio Pinza was the only opera singer I ever heard about who supposedly couldn't read music. It was said that he had to memorize his roles one note at a time.) Paolo Gallico, a marvelous piano teacher, was a friend of hers, and despite the fact that he did not teach children, she arranged for him to become part of my Saturday-morning educational lineup. Mr. Gallico, the father of the great sportswriter and novelist Paul Gallico, was a tough man to please—to the point of sometimes rapping my knuckles with a ruler—which is probably why I got serious in a hurry about piano-playing. He wanted me to give up singing and instead pursue a career as a concert pianist. In the politest way possible, Mother and I told Mr. Gallico to forget it.

I addressed Miss Liebling as "Teacher." The only compliment she gave me was to concede that I had an extraordinary voice for my age. My lessons soon expanded from fifteen minutes to half an hour each week, and consisted mainly of scales and highly structured vocal exercises. Miss Liebling was the last surviving pupil of Mathilde Marchesi, one of the great vocal teachers of all time. Because I was so young, Miss Liebling put me through the entire Marchesi school of singing. At some point I intend to write a book on singing technique. I have the last copy of the original Marchesi book, and I want to make sure the Marchesi method doesn't simply disappear. I also want to leave behind notes on Miss Liebling's teaching techniques, plus my own observations on the subject.

I'd listened to Lily Pons on our kitchen Victrola ever since I could remember. A year after I began studying with Miss Liebling, when I was eight years old, Mama announced one day that our upcoming Saturday in New York would be spent seeing Pons in a matinee of *Lakmé*, by Léo Delibes. I'd never been to an opera, and I definitely wanted to see *Lakmé*—don't forget, my imitation of Pons singing the Bell Song from *Lakmé* had gotten me on *Major Bowes' Original Amateur Hour*.

Lakmé was put on at the old Metropolitan Opera House on 39th Street and Broadway. When we got inside, I couldn't believe my eyes. The theater was beautiful beyond anything I'd imagined.

After a little while, the house lights dimmed, the orchestra played its overture, the curtain rose, Miss Pons appeared on stage—and I was *shocked*. Pons was wearing a brief halter top. I loudly informed my mother and everyone else around us that Lily Pons's bellybutton was showing.

Mama gently told me to hush up, and for the rest of the afternoon I just sat there quietly and completely transfixed. Pons was beautiful, a Dresden doll come to life. Her voice was exquisite.

That was going to be me.

Several years later, when we heard Lily Pons sing at Carnegie Hall, we went backstage and stood in line to meet her. She gave me an autographed photo, which I still have. I was shattered, though, to find that I was already two inches taller than she was, and I probably outweighed her by a good twenty pounds. Pons was teeny to the point of being minute; I'm sure she was no more than five feet tall. Still, even that didn't really ruin the occasion for me. Lily Pons was like a fairy princess. She wore a beautiful gown, had a maid waiting on her, and I noticed all her stage makeup on her vanity table. I'd never been in a great performer's dressing room before, and it was everything I'd ever dreamed about.

In a curious way, being taller than Miss Pons made me think that perhaps my dream wasn't so impossible, after all. I felt that one day I'd be just like this woman. Purely and simply, Lily Pons became my idol. I really don't think I would have felt that way if I hadn't seen her in her dressing room. That was my first visit backstage at a major concert hall, and I knew I'd found my other home. Many, many years later, when I sang at Carnegie Hall for the first time, I was very upset to discover that its dressing rooms had been renovated. They were much smaller, less glamorous, and not nearly as beautiful as when Lily Pons had sung there.

After meeting her that day, I began collecting every Lily Pons record—and I mean *every* record. Whatever she sang, I wanted to sing. I kept asking Miss Liebling for Pons pieces, and for the most part she went along with me. She thought Pons's repertoire was perfectly suited to my voice.

I lived for my Saturday lessons, and neither rain nor sleet nor occasional bouts with the sniffles ever dampened my enthusiasm for them. My mother occasionally worried that I was *too* enamored of the whole thing. Sometimes she'd say, "Honey, there's such a nice movie playing down at the Savoy today—why don't you go see it with one of your friends?" No way.

Miss Liebling also thought I was focusing too narrowly on my music. She once asked me what I did on the hour-and-a-half subway ride home.

"I study my music," I told her.

Miss Liebling said, "You don't have to do that—you've just *had* a lesson. Read a book."

She enrolled me in Womrath's lending library and paid the $10 deposit that Womrath's required. Miss Liebling gave me a list of books to take out, and I read them all. Between her and my father, I got a very early grounding in such classic literature as *The Way of All Flesh, Pride and Prejudice,* and *Little Women.* Miss Liebling had great plans for me.

"You're going to be a cultured woman," she once told me. "Don't think you're like every other girl in school, because you're not. I don't want you to have a lot of friends and I don't want you to do things other girls your age are doing."

I'm afraid I couldn't accommodate her. After school, I'd change out of the special outfits Mama made for me, and I'd act like any other kid from Brooklyn. When I was nine, I had been the neighborhood potsy champ. (Potsy is the game many people know as hopscotch.) We all had our favorite little potsy pieces. Mine was a doll Mama made for me out of three large dried beans she pasted together and then painted to resemble a little girl. I also became the neighborhood Hi-Lo champion. Hi-Lo was the brand name for a little wooden racquet that came with a rubber ball attached to it by a long rubber band. The object was to keep smacking the ball, which would travel about five feet and come back, until you missed. I once got up to a thousand on Hi-Lo, and I defy even John McEnroe to match that figure.

When I was nine, I fell in love for the first time. His name was Bobby Beecher, and he was twelve. Every day, Charlotte Shapiro, my best friend, and I would play jacks on the pavement across the street from where Bobby lived. I was desperately in love with him, but Bobby never even knew I was alive.

My folks were very happy when my brothers and I started going away for the summer to Camps Lincoln and Laurel in New Jersey.

"Uncle" Al and "Aunt" Sady Tisch, who owned the camps, were friends of my parents, and their sons, Larry and Bobby, were childhood buddies. They grew up to form the Tisch financial empire, and Larry took over CBS not long ago. Whenever we see each other, which is often, it's still Bobby and Larry and Bubbles.

Aunt Sady gave my parents a break on the price, or else they'd never have been able to send the three of us away for the summer. The head of the camp was a show business lawyer named Jack Heller. "Uncle" Jack loved opera, and he put on several Gilbert and Sullivan operettas at camp. When I was ten years old I got my first leading role there. I played Yum-Yum in *The Mikado* (Mother made my costume), and Buddy Israel, who played Nanki-Poo, gave me my first stage kiss. Buddy later changed his name to Jules Irving, and for many years he ran the Vivian Beaumont Theater at Lincoln Center. Buddy died in 1979. His daughter, actress Amy Irving, is married to Steven Spielberg.

I arrived at camp with a tennis racquet, courtesy of my father. Papa admired Helen Wills Moody, and thought tennis was a very ladylike form of exercise. Arlene Harris was the only other girl at camp with a tennis racquet. Day after day, Arlene and I stayed out on the tennis court like two drippy kids, but by the end of the summer, I had become a crackerjack tennis player. I swam, I played softball and volleyball, and one summer I was voted Camp Laurel's outstanding athlete.

At home, I started going to Brooklyn Dodger games with my brothers. My favorite Dodger was Van Lingle Mungo, but my *very* favorite player was Lou Gehrig of the Yankees. My brothers and I collected the baseball cards that came in packages of gum, and I adored Lou Gehrig's dimples. For some reason I was sure that when I grew up, he was going to be mine. I didn't care at all about Mrs. Gehrig; I was in love with Lou. Gehrig died when I was twelve years old, and I reacted as if a member of the family had passed away. I was heartbroken and cried for days. My brother Stanley said, "What you're doing is idiotic."

I answered, "But he was *mine*." It was a terrible few weeks for me.

Right about then, I retired from radio and started studying twice a week with Miss Liebling. New York's subways were then quite safe to ride, and on Tuesdays and Saturdays, I often traveled in from Brooklyn by myself.

I became very serious about my opera-going. I looked at every opera with an eye toward whether or not I could see myself taking part in it. When I saw Pons in *Lucia,* that was going to be me. After my lessons, I'd buy a standing-room ticket to the Metropolitan Opera. During that period I saw such great performers as Risë Stevens, Lauritz Melchior, Richard Tucker, Jan Peerce, and Leonard Warren.

Sometimes Miss Liebling arranged for me to go to the Met. One night she gave me a pair of tickets and told me some singer was making her debut, but Miss Liebling wasn't interested in going. I gave one of the tickets to a friend who was always on the standing-room line with me. There we were, two teenagers in the fifth row of the orchestra, me in my brown-and-white saddle shoes, bobby sox, and Sloppy Joe sweater, watching what turned out to be an historic event: Ljuba Welitsch singing Richard Strauss's *Salome* for the first time at the Met. Welitsch seemed to shine with an inner light a hundred times brighter than anything a stage technician could produce. Fritz Reiner conducted, and I'd never seen technique like his. Reiner kept his hands in front of his nose and led the orchestra by making teeny, tiny triangles with his fingers. When the opera was over, the audience went slightly batty—that was the first time I had ever witnessed pandemonium in a theater. Ljuba and I later became close friends. We have often discussed that *Salome.* Some 25,000 people claim they were there. I *really* was.

We moved to Sea Gate just after I graduated from P.S. 91, which went up to the eighth grade. I was then accepted into the High School of Music and Art, then located on Convent Avenue at 135th Street in Manhattan. To get there from Sea Gate, I took a bus, a trolley, the BMT subway up to 42nd Street, and then transferred over to the IRT subway, where I took an express uptown to 125th Street and then transferred again to a local, which took me within a few blocks of the school. It took almost three hours to get to Music and Art, which meant that to be on time for my eight o'clock class, I had to leave home at five A.M. If I left school promptly at three o'clock, I didn't get home until six, which left no time for singing or piano practice or even homework.

After my first week at Music and Art, Papa and I had a long talk. He thought all that commuting was too much for me, and I agreed.

The problem was what to do about it. At the time, *the* school to go to in Brooklyn was Erasmus Hall. It was unlikely I'd be accepted there, however, because we lived way out of the district. My mother nevertheless phoned Mr. Lipschitz, the principal of P.S. 91. She told him about the problem I was having with Music and Art and that I wanted to attend Erasmus Hall. Mr. Lipschitz advised her to send me to Abraham Lincoln High School, which was in our district. Mama insisted that I wanted to go to Erasmus, and that my father had volunteered to drive me there every morning and pick me up every afternoon.

Mr. Lipschitz liked me—I'd been the valedictorian of my graduating class—so he wrote a letter to the principal of Erasmus Hall saying that I was an outstanding student, and that as long as my father provided transportation for me, the school should make an exception in my case. Erasmus Hall accepted me on that condition: Papa had to drive me to school in the morning and pick me up in the afternoon. There simply wasn't any way to get from Sea Gate to Erasmus Hall by public transportation.

I got to know my father very well during those years. Papa had to be in his office at seven-thirty each morning, and my first class didn't start until eight-forty. Every morning, he'd drive me to DuBrow's cafeteria, right next door to Erasmus. We'd get there before seven o'clock, and we'd arrive with copies of four morning newspapers— the *Times,* the *Daily Mirror,* the *Daily News,* and the *Herald Tribune.* He'd get a cup of coffee for himself, a half cup for me (I'd fill the rest up with cream), and we'd both feast on hot almond horns. To this day, whenever I see one of those pastries, a wave of nostalgia washes over me.

We'd then sit and read the papers, and Papa would ask me questions about some of the day's news stories. It was a wonderful way to learn what was going on in the world. I felt very close to my father. He'd leave me in DuBrow's at around seven-twenty, and I'd sit there reading the papers until it was time to go to school.

The news then was awful, of course. It was a somber time for the family and for our country. World War II had started. We learned what the Nazis were doing to Jews in Germany and how they were out to conquer Europe and the rest of the world. We knew how important it was for America to win the war.

A lot of neighborhood boys went off to fight in Europe and

never returned. My brothers had a friend named Stanley Greenberg, whose father owned the Baltic Linen Company—he always used to say his dad worked in a sheet house. Stanley was killed in the war. So were a lot of other boys we knew. Sea Gate is a residential community of single family houses, and when I'd walk down the street I'd see many windows displaying the Gold Star.

My brothers both enlisted in the army and were sent to Europe. Sidney became a medical corpsman in the infantry and won two Purple Hearts and a Bronze Star during the Battle of the Bulge. He was missing in action for weeks, and I remember how much my parents and I feared for his life. Stanley joined the army air corps when he was seventeen—he didn't want to be left behind—and came through without a scratch. I don't think I had a single male cousin of age who didn't fight during World War II. Miraculously, none of them was killed.

Our safe little haven was turned upside down during the war years. Our house was right on the ocean, and we'd see troopships leaving for Europe every day. Over the sound of the waves and the engines, we could hear a low roar—it was the sound of the thousands of men on board talking to one another. It's hard to describe the joy we all felt when the Nazis were finally defeated.

During the war, I continued my studies with Miss Liebling, who was helping me to become quite a little lady. Miss Liebling often invited me to the fancy dinner parties she had in her apartment. My parents would drive me into Manhattan, drop me off, and then go to a movie. I'd sit down to dinner in the company of perhaps two dozen famous people. Afterwards, I'd sing for them. Miss Liebling's guests included such patrons of the arts as Fan Fox and her husband, Les Samuels, and opera stars like Maria Jeritza, Lauritz Melchior, Jessica Dragonette, and Grace Moore. At one dinner I met Marcel Prawy, who was then head of the Vienna Volksoper. After he heard me sing, Prawy insisted that I come to Vienna and study with him. There wasn't a prayer of that's happening.

The food at those dinners was marvelous. I'd never seen a soufflé before, nor had I ever had to contend with three forks and three different wineglasses—I knew about Grandma's wine with seltzer, but that was it. Three-quarters of who I am came from my family; the other 25 percent came from Miss Liebling. She was funny, attractive, intelligent, and knew everyone in opera. She also could pick up the phone and reach anyone in America, and that alone fascinated me. Did *I* want to be like her? Of course I did.

Miss Liebling furthered my education in a very special way. She would show me fashion designs and make me aware of why leading sopranos like Lily Pons and Mary Garden had their gowns made by Worth, Mainbocher, and Balenciaga. There was a look to quality clothing, and my mother was able to copy some of those extraordinary designs for me.

Miss Liebling's guests thought my singing was pretty remarkable for my age, but my solos weren't the real highlight of those evenings for me. I just loved to watch Estelle Liebling entertain her guests. She had an endearing way of putting herself down at the start of every speech, and I've consciously copied her speaking style. Miss Liebling sometimes would begin by saying: "Now understand, I don't know anything about this topic, but that doesn't mean I can't talk about it for five hours." Many years later, when I began making speeches, I'd start out by saying: "My husband will tell you I can talk for two hours straight about nothing at all. My real problem is that I can't talk for five minutes about anything in particular."

Miss Liebling often introduced me to important women in the hope that their sophistication and manner of dress would rub off on me. Soprano Maria Jeritza was one of her favorite people, and mine as well, and Miss Liebling usually brought me along when she went to dinner at Miss Jeritza's beautiful home. Miss Jeritza always had a very handsome man seated on her right; on her left would be this teenage girl watching her and thinking she was the most beautiful creature the girl had ever seen. Maria Jeritza was one big sexy lady. She was also quite a character. The first time I went there, Miss Jeritza opened her beaded purse after the main course was served and took out a gold toothpick. She held a napkin very daintily in front of her mouth and proceeded to use the toothpick. She then turned to me and whispered, "In tventy secunts, diss hull table vill be talking Jeritza juices gold toothpick to clean teeth. Alvays remember: Iss important for opera zinger to be kerukter. Never let people tink you afferage."

Years later, Jeritza gave me the gold toothpick and the gold beaded purse I'd so admired.

In 1944, Miss Liebling decided it was time for someone other than her dinner guests to hear me sing. By then, I was ready to resume performing. I was no longer a chubby little girl. I'd become a striking young woman who was 5 feet 8½ inches tall, weighed 130 pounds, and had a figure that measured 38–24–36. I'd walk down the street and men would get whistly, and back then it was okay. I attracted a lot of attention when I entered a room, and I didn't mind that one bit.

Miss Liebling was a great friend of J.J. Shubert, and one day she called him and said, "J.J., I want you to listen to one of my students. She's only fifteen, but I think you ought to see her and hear her."

He said, "Okay, Stella, send her over."

Mother came with me when I went to see Mr. Shubert. He lived in a lovely apartment above Sardi's restaurant at 234 West 44th Street. Mr. Shubert was a charming elderly man, and he very quickly and easily made Mama and me feel at home.

After I sang for him, Mr. Shubert mentioned that he was producing a Broadway musical called *Love in the Snow* starring Anne Jeffreys, and he offered me a job as her understudy. I took it. Today, understudies are costumed, rehearsed, billed in the program, and literally prepared to go onstage on five minutes' notice. In those days, being an understudy was a far more casual affair. I received some musical coaching and I knew all the dialogue, but nobody had any idea how well I could perform the part. *Love in the Snow* ran for only a few weeks.

The real reason Mr. Shubert offered me that job was to get me on his payroll. J.J. Shubert had made a fortune on Broadway by producing *The Student Prince, Blossom Time, The Merry Widow,* and many other operettas, and he thought their appeal would last indefinitely. I didn't know it at the time, but he was then planning Broadway revivals of all the old Rudolf Friml and Sigmund Romberg operettas, and he had me in mind for several leading roles. Before *Love in the Snow* closed, J.J. offered me a contract to go out on a two-month Gilbert and Sullivan tour that would hit all the major Shubert theaters in the East and Midwest.

Mother and I were thrilled; Papa wasn't. Nice young women didn't go on the stage; they went to school, he said. If I went on the tour, I'd have to drop out of Erasmus Hall High School. My mother stood up to him. Working for a wonderful man like J.J. Shubert would be both an honor and an opportunity, she said. My education could be taken care of through correspondence courses at the Professional Children's School.

Mama defied my father and signed the contract for me. This was a woman who waited on her husband hand and foot, who used to say that my father never knew what color her kitchen was painted because he never went into it, and who always had a drink waiting for him when he came home. Looking at him from today's perspective, my father was truly a male chauvinist, but Papa never would do anything to make my mother unhappy. He accepted Mama's *fait accompli* with as much grace as he could muster.

Before the tour started, I had one commitment to fulfill. After *Major Bowes' Capitol Family* went off the air, Aunt Bessie Mack was hired as talent coordinator for Arthur Godfrey's *Talent Scouts* program. Aunt Bessie invited me to sing on the very first Godfrey broadcast, and that was fine with me. It was not so fine with J.J. Shubert. Because of the contract we had signed, I had to ask his permission to be on the show. Mr. Shubert refused to allow me to appear as Beverly Sills. He planned to present me as "the youngest prima donna in captivity" and was afraid he'd lose credit for discovering me if I went on the Godfrey show before doing his Gilbert and Sullivan tour.

I wound up going on the Godfrey show as "Vickie Lynn," which was the name on the label of the blouse I wore that day. Vic Damone was also on that first show with me. Arthur Godfrey introduced me to his audience by saying: "Vickie Lynn is a beautiful girl with mounds of auburn hair and two of everything she needs."

My father went into a rage when he heard that—there was no containing him. He couldn't believe CBS radio would allow Godfrey to get away with that remark. Papa was more convinced than ever that show business was no business for his little girl.

If I had any qualms about leaving Brooklyn for a couple of months, they probably centered around my first real boyfriend, Sandy Levine. Sandy and I had been going out for more than a year at that point. He was a good-looking blond boy and an excellent athlete. Sandy had given me the little gold baseball and the track letter that he received for being on varsity teams at Lincoln High. Sandy and I rarely went out alone. As was the style then, we traveled in groups that went bowling in Luna Park or to the movies or to the Sweet Shoppe, a local hangout, or to somebody's house where we played records and danced. When Sandy came to call for me, he would stand at the front door and whistle "Rinso White," which prompted my father to ask, "Is he a boy or a bird?"

In 1945, not long before I went out on the Shubert tour, Sandy gave me a beautiful Mexican silver bracelet with the inscription TO BUBBLES, THE STAR OF MY HEART. When I returned from the tour, I found out Sandy had started dating a blues singer. I was a little surprised that our breakup didn't bother me at all, but I guess I shouldn't have been. I came back to Brooklyn a much worldlier young woman than when I'd left it.

THREE

The Shubert tour marked the first time I'd ever been away from home, if you don't count camp—which I didn't. The company numbered about forty people, including a twenty-piece orchestra. The prospect of performing six nights a week was only one of the lures the trip held for me. I'd never slept on a train or been on a plane, and I was about to get my first look at life outside New York City. When we left Penn Station, I was one excited young lady.

I was also very naïve. I was such a baby, in fact, that Mama hired one of the ladies in the chorus to be my roommate and act as my chaperone. Her job was to see to it that I got to the train station on time and do my hair for the various Gilbert and Sullivan roles I was playing.

My roommate was a terrific girl with two weaknesses: gin and airline pilots. Like a lot of young women back then, she dyed her hair blue-black in the fashion started by Hedy Lamarr and Joan Bennett. I was then using a tar soap shampoo, which was as black as my roommate's dye. The big joke between us was that one day she'd get the bottles mixed up and dye my hair black, and that's exactly what happened. Unfortunately, she poured dye on my hair as liberally as if it were shampoo. When we realized what she'd done, we used the shampoo, but that only made things worse: The dye washed out in streaks. I looked like a skunk.

The cosmetics industry wasn't nearly as sophisticated as it's since become, which is one reason why women weren't changing their hair color at whim, the way we do today. There wasn't a product on the market that could undo the damage my roommate had wrought. The only thing she could think of was to run down to the corner grocery and buy a bottle of household ammonia. The ammonia bleached my hair chalk-white.

I decided it was time for a talk with Mama. I was in the habit of calling home collect every Wednesday. My father would always pick up the extension, but since he wasn't enthusiastic about this tour, he was not very talkative over the phone, although I'd hear him puffing on his cigar while Mama accepted the charges. This time it wasn't a Wednesday and I didn't call collect. I was crying when I telephoned. "Mama, Mama," I sobbed, "something terrible has happened to me."

My mother didn't answer.

"What's wrong?" my father asked.

"My hair was accidentally dyed black, and we used ammonia on it and now it's *white!*"

There was dead silence on the other end. "Hold on for a minute," Papa finally said. "I have to pick up your mother—she just fainted."

When Mama was able to speak to me, she told me to start from scratch again. My roommate and I got my hair back to its natural unnatural color—a strawberry-blond that showed up better onstage than my natural auburn, according to Mr. Shubert.

Our itinerary on that tour was exhausting. In two months, we played Providence, Boston, Hartford, Montreal, Toronto, Detroit, Cleveland, Madison and Milwaukee, Grand Rapids, Indianapolis, and Cincinnati. We performed three or four nights in each city or else we stayed for an entire week, which was considered a major engagement.

We performed seven different Gilbert and Sullivan operettas: *The Mikado, The Pirates of Penzance, HMS Pinafore, The Gondoliers, Patience, Iolanthe,* and *Trial by Jury.* Gilbert and Sullivan were gifted, funny writers, and I could always count on certain songs of theirs to bring down the house. "Sorry her lot" in *HMS Pinafore,* "Poor wandering one" in *The Pirates of Penzance,* and "The moon and I" in *The Mikado* were all show-stoppers.

I played the title role in *Patience,* and I absolutely loved the character, because Patience is a very funny, flaky girl. My favorite line in the operetta occurs when someone comes up to her and says, "Tell me, girl, do you ever yearn?" And Patience replies, "I yearn my living." I played her as a dumb Dora all the way through and really had fun with the role. Patience is usually portrayed as a dainty ditz, but I made her into a bit of a klutz, as well. My Patience grew clumsier and clumsier with each performance, and audiences seemed to like her all the more for it. *I* certainly did. I found that I had a gift for slapstick humor, and it was fun to exercise it onstage.

As my career progressed, I discovered that, in addition to wanting to sing the great tragic roles, I was equally attracted to playing comic characters, particularly if I could make klutzes out of them. In later years, after I'd played Rosalinda in Johann Strauss's *Die Fledermaus* many, many times, I eventually got bored with that particular glamour puss. I remembered how much fun I'd had with Patience, so I started playing Adele, Rosalinda's maid, who reminded me of Patience. I decided that Adele was the kind of maid who wouldn't just dust objects—she'd bust them. My Adele knocked over pictures with her feather duster, broke flower vases, and after puffing up pillows, somehow managed to throw them on the floor instead of back on the settee where they belonged. In her first scene, she sings an aria while cleaning up, and by the end of it, Adele, as I played her, has turned an extraordinarily beautiful Viennese sitting room into a disaster area. And she has no idea of the havoc she's wrought. Quite the opposite: Adele is very pleased by her efforts. She was an extension of Patience, and I treasured both those birdbrains.

Whenever I could add that quality to any of the comic roles I played, I would. I did it to Marie in Donizetti's *The Daughter of the Regiment,* and in his *Don Pasquale,* when Norina tried to disguise herself, I again went back to my characterization of Patience and made her a bit of a scatterbrained klutz. Why did I have the urge to do that to those ladies? I guess it's because, as an adolescent, I was such a big kid and felt so awkward that I often thought of myself as a klutz. When I got older and realized that tall, voluptuous women were rather desirable after all, I was so relieved that it gave me great pleasure to act clumsy deliberately.

Patience was the first show I nearly carried by myself, and the prospect of doing it frightened me at first. Mr. Shubert had placed a lot of responsibility on my shoulders, and I didn't want to let him down. But when opening night came and I walked out onstage for the first time, I was almost high with excitement, and I didn't blow a single line. I was probably too young even to *think* about doing that. Whatever the reason, that performance set a pattern for me: I never developed stage fright. The rationale I eventually dreamed up was that if somebody in the audience could sing my part better than I could, our roles would be reversed—I'd be sitting in the audience, and she'd be onstage.

Another reason I never suffered from stage fright, I suppose, is that I loved performing. To me, being onstage was never anything less than a joyful occasion. I'd been an innately shy child because of my height, but even in the Major Bowes days, all that self-consciousness went away when I got onstage. In a sense, I'd always used the stage as an escape from reality. I continued to do that, although the escape took a different form: I looked forward to becoming somebody else every night.

My size, which only a few years before had been a source of acute embarrassment, had now turned into an asset. My figure did a lot for my stage costumes.

My salary on the tour was $100 a week, which was good money in 1945, but it didn't seem to go very far. My father made me buy a $50 U.S. Savings Bond every week, so $37.50 was taken out for that, plus another $5 or so for taxes. (The IRS wasn't nearly as hungry in the 1940s as it is in the 1980s.) We had to pay for our hotel rooms and our food, so we all lived as inexpensively as possible. Hotel rooms were about $6 a night, and I always shared one with my chaperone, so that came to less than $25 a week. Food was very cheap. My roommate bought a little electric hot plate and a small pot, and several times a week we'd fill the pot with water and heat up cans of Dinty Moore beef stew. We ate straight out of the can, and supplemented our diet with fresh fruit and vegetables. And peanut brittle. Neither of us had ever cared for the stuff, but we spent a lot of our afternoons going to the movies, and I think that's how we got hooked on it. We became formidable peanut brittle mavens, and even today I think I can still remember the best places to buy peanut brittle in the cities we visited.

I was often homesick and lonely at night, but that was mostly because my roommate continued to make connections with airline pilots. She wasn't the only cast member who found romance on the tour. As we went around the country, a lot of the men and women in the cast began pairing off, and I suppose I found that slightly scandalous. I was a nice Jewish girl, and in those days nice Jewish girls lived at home with their parents and remained virgins until they got married. My idea of a big evening was an occasional dinner out with my roommate and Jimmy, who sang in the chorus, and Frank, my leading man. We'd order two steak dinners and split them four ways, and then abscond with all the rolls in the bread basket.

Jimmy knew how lonely I was as a result of my roommate's nightly excursions, so he took it upon himself to inform Mama of what was going on. My mother was very grateful and wound up hiring *him* as my chaperone.

It didn't take me long to discover that Jimmy and Frank were gay. It was the first time I'd ever come into contact with homosexuality, which was still very much in the closet then. Nobody talked about it at all.

Jimmy and Frank trusted me, and I liked them a lot. They and their friends were very cozy people, and made a point of including me in all their parties. In those days, there was an underground network of homosexuals, and they took care of their own. Very few of the gay men stayed in hotels; wherever we went, they had friends to stay with. Jimmy never failed to invite me to their friends' houses, and boy, did they have splendid furniture. My initial impression was that homosexuals had a natural gift for finding the best places to shop.

At that point, I really thought homosexuals were people who just felt differently about certain things—I had no idea what their sexual orientation was all about. Sometimes I was very confused. When Frank, Jimmy, and I went shopping or antiquing (we never bought anything; we just looked) they behaved in a way that was totally acceptable to everyone. But when they went to their friends' houses, they became different people. They changed the kind of clothing they wore, which isn't to say they dressed up as women, but their style and mode of behavior became effeminate. Even when we traveled on the train and they would come into my tiny compartment to play cards, their behavior would change a lot. I really didn't understand Frank's relationship with Jimmy. Frank was so obviously manly and handsome that, if he'd asked me, I'd have gone out with him. I couldn't comprehend their attitude toward women, either, and I began buying books on homosexuality to try to figure it all out. Such books weren't easy to find forty years ago, and when you did find one, you had to carry it around in a brown paper bag—God forbid someone should see you reading it. I bought several books written by psychiatrists, and I also bought *The Well of Loneliness,* an autobiographical novel written by a lesbian whose pseudonym was Radcliffe Hall.

I learned what there is to learn about the subject, or at least what there was to learn about it then. The plague of AIDS had not yet surfaced, of course, and at this moment I think we've seen only the tip of the iceberg. There *are* a great many homosexuals in the arts, and in 1986 alone, more than a dozen friends of mine died from the disease. At one point recently I had the ghoulish feeling I was becoming a full-time mistress of ceremonies at memorials held for AIDS victims. I think AIDS has been around a lot longer than most people suspect. Years before the disease was diagnosed, a number of gay men I knew seemed to be dying of rare forms of cancer.

It was a much simpler time when I met Jimmy and Frank. Both of them were steeped in certain areas of stagecraft, and they were always there to lend a helping hand. In one city, for instance, a reviewer commented that, as Patience, I looked like a very healthy milkmaid because of all the rouge I had on my cheeks. The next day Jimmy sat down with me and patiently and expertly taught me how to make up my face.

I heard from Jimmy again many, many years later—he was in San Luis Obispo prison for shooting his lover (not Frank). His friend had been killed with his own gun, and Jimmy claimed it had been an accident. He was up for parole, and he asked my husband and me to write to the parole board on his behalf. We corresponded fairly often with Jimmy then—Peter referred to him as "our *real* pen pal." He sent us commendatory letters about himself from a priest and several other people, so I wrote to the parole board about my earlier experiences with him. I said that I felt Jimmy was a gentle man, and that I believed his story. And I really *did* believe it. When Jimmy's parole came through, my husband and I sent him money for a little mobile home, and we agreed to back him in a pet shop. I was coming out to sing in California, and we helped him financially in setting up the business. Ten days before we got to California, Jimmy died of a heart attack.

The Shubert tour opened my eyes to a lot of things. The experience I got as a performer was invaluable, but more than anything else, it was a terrific adventure.

J.J. Shubert had closely monitored my progress, and when I returned, he signed me to do another tour that would begin in eight months.

My parents were delighted to have me home again. My father, still displeased at what was happening to my education, was determined to keep me there. While I was away on the tour, I had completed all the correspondence courses necessary for me to graduate from the Professional Children's School. My father thought the whole thing was a sham, but he and Mother accompanied me to the school's graduation ceremonies. For some reason, Frank Fay, a comedian who'd once been married to Barbara Stanwyck and who was known to be a heavy drinker, was in charge of presenting the school's graduates with their diplomas. Mr. Fay had had a couple of shots that day, and when I came up to get my diploma, he put his hand on my behind and said, "Boy, they weren't built like that when *I* got out of school."

That was quite enough to send my father into still another tirade about the evils of show business. Although my father approved of some of the accomplishments I had acquired as I trained to be an opera singer—I was multilingual by then and a skilled pianist—to him they were no more than that: accomplishments. He did not approve of the direction in which they were taking me; Papa realized I was acquiring a culture of my own that went far beyond the streets of Brooklyn. I'd won a mathematics scholarship to Fairleigh Dickinson College in New Jersey, and Papa tried his best to get me to accept it; in spite of his earlier doubts about the importance of a college education for me, he had become very proud of my academic record. But I wouldn't hear of it, and neither would Mama. I wasn't interested in math; I was going to be an opera singer.

The next eight months became a period of intense study for me. I resumed my lessons with Miss Liebling, who began working with me three days a week. I don't know if I shared my brother Stanley's gift of a near-photographic memory, but I began eating up operas almost as fast as it takes some people to dawdle over a leisurely dinner. I could learn an opera in hours. Before I was seventeen, I must have known fifty or sixty operas. What's more, I learned *all* the roles, not just mine. Later in my career, this knowledge proved very helpful.

There was no place in the city for me to perform, of course. The Metropolitan Opera was reserved for the world's most famous singers, so forget that. The year before, in 1944, with the support of Mayor Fiorello La Guardia, the New York City Opera had had its inaugural season, but nobody there was interested in having a sixteen-year-old girl join the company. It wasn't even a principally American company. Opera was thought to be such a foreign art form that American singers changed their names in hopes of passing for European. Anne McKnight, for example, changed her last name to Cavallieri, close to the Italian word for *knight*.

Mr. Shubert stayed in touch with me between tours. He'd often call my mother to find out when I was coming into Manhattan for a singing lesson, and he'd invite me to have lunch with him in his apartment. Occasionally, Mom would come along, and when she did, J.J., with a little twinkle in his eye, would say, "With a mother like that, you're going to grow up to be very pretty."

J.J. Shubert did not have the best reputation when it came to the ladies. In fact, he was a notorious womanizer. He loved beautiful women, and my mother was a very beautiful woman, and I was a pretty good-looking teenager. But I must say that with us, he couldn't have been kinder. If I mentioned that I loved to do wooden jigsaw puzzles, he'd buy me wooden jigsaw puzzles. I remember his saying one day: "You're a big girl now—you shouldn't be wearing flat shoes. Don't you have any high heels?"

I told him no, I didn't. The next time I saw him, Mr. Shubert presented me with a pair of black leather high heels with white bows from Bergdorf Goodman. He gave me a number of books on opera singers, and on one occasion—I don't remember if it was Christmas or my birthday—he bought me a pretty fur-trimmed suit. Mr. Shubert was a charming, generous man. And yet somewhere in his apartment—I can't recall whether it was embroidered on a sofa cushion or on a plaque that sat on his desk—there was a little saying: PROPINQUITY BREEDS FAMILIARITY. I ran home as fast as I could to look up *propinquity. Familiarity* I knew. That was my only clue to all the talk about him. As far as Mother and I were concerned, he was a dear.

Miss Liebling didn't want me to lose confidence in my ability to sing in front of an audience, so in between Shubert tours, she suggested I audition for chorus roles in Broadway musicals. If I was offered a job, I wasn't to take it; I was only there to audition. Her idea had a certain logic, so I went along with it. I began buying the trade paper *Show Business,* and any time I saw an ad for a chorus audition, I showed up.

Chorus auditions are the worst. They're known as "cattle calls," and people *are* treated like cattle; their anxiety is almost palpable. My audition number was Gershwin's "Summertime," and I always was allowed to sing it all the way through. Invariably, I was either offered a job or told: "That voice doesn't belong in a chorus." I always made a strong impression, one way or the other. After one audition, a director asked me if I could sing like Gertrude Niesen, a very popular performer best known for a Broadway show called *Follow the Girls.*

"No, I can't," I snapped. "Can Gertrude Niesen sing like me?" I was a fresh kid.

The second Shubert tour lasted from the end of September to shortly before Christmas. Mr. Shubert raised my salary to $150 a week and rented a beautiful silver fox cape for me to wear in my entrance as the Merry Widow. I also sang the lead in *Countess Maritza,* but I wasn't cast in *Rose Marie,* the only other operetta we presented on the tour. I did manage to take part in that production, however. Here's how a reporter for the *Detroit Times* informed readers of my appearance:

> Sunday's customers and cast saw a red-headed Indian. After the first shock wore off, many in the cast had a brief spell of hysterics. The Indian wasn't too calm. Seventeen-year-old Beverly Sills, who plays the leads in *The Merry Widow* and *Play, Gypsy, Play [Countess Maritza],* has seen *Rose Marie* about 30 times. She was standing in the wings when Beth Dean, who plays the Indian girl, collapsed from exhaustion. Beth's understudy had been called out of town, but there was Beverly, auburn curls and pigtails and wearing a borrowed costume. There was no time to rent a wig or fit an outfit. She went on without rehearsal.

The *Detroit Times* critic didn't comment further on my performance, which was just as well. I don't think I was too convincing as a tom-tom dancer, and I flubbed my only big line: Instead of asking the romantic lead to visit me in my cabin, I asked him to meet me in my castle. In addition, my hair had been curled for the evening performance of *The Merry Widow*. In order to hold the pigtails straight, they braided my hair with wires that were used to hold the caps on milk bottles. During the evening the pigtails kept curling up, which added enormously to the audience's amusement.

Except for my increased maturity as a performer, the second Shubert tour was very much like the first. When it ended and I got back to Brooklyn, my father sternly informed me that if I really wanted to be an opera singer, I had to stay home and study full-time. I didn't give Papa an argument, but I knew how I felt and what I wanted to do. I wasn't in love with operettas and life on the road, but Mr. Shubert paid good money, and I loved entertaining audiences. Had there been another Shubert tour, I assure you I would have been on it. But there were no further tours. In 1946, the popularity of operettas plummeted like a lead balloon, and our ticket sales reflected that fact. J.J. Shubert set aside his dream of reviving operettas on Broadway and never produced another one.

That was probably a serendipitous turn of events for me, for without a performing outlet, I studied more seriously than ever with Miss Liebling. I was already a very disciplined singer. Ever since I was a little girl, Miss Liebling had been giving me one act of an opera score to learn at a sitting and to memorize by the next time I saw her.

Miss Liebling was very strict and formal with me. When she was at the piano, she never let me read music over her shoulder, and she got *very* annoyed the few times I showed up unprepared. One of Miss Liebling's favorite admonitions to me was "Text! Text! Text!" which she said whenever she felt I was merely singing notes and not paying attention to the meaning of the lyrics. Miss Liebling wanted me to sing the way Olivier acts, to deliver what I was singing in such a way that my audience would respond emotionally.

Less than a month after we started working together again, Miss Liebling began sending me down to Philadelphia every Saturday to study for an hour with Giuseppe Bamboschek, the artistic director of the Philadelphia Opera Company. Bamboschek had a special gift for Italian repertoire, and she wanted him to give me a better understanding of the "Italian style." Bamboschek had been one of the Metropolitan Opera's leading conductors during the golden era of Rosa Ponselle and Enrico Caruso. I thought he was adorable, and so was his wife; after each lesson, she'd make Italian sausage sandwiches for our lunch.

Bamboschek was a fine teacher, but he was no more successful than Miss Liebling in getting me interested in singing Puccini operas. I've always loved *watching* them, and I think *Madama Butterfly* is a masterpiece, but never for one minute did I picture myself singing that role. I would have been the biggest Butterfly in opera history. Licia Albanese probably came closest to pulling off what I still think of as a nearly impossible role. She was properly tiny, and even though her voice was essentially too light for Cio-Cio-San, it had the quality if not the quantity demanded by Puccini's score. As for *La Bohème,* I may have seen it a thousand times, but I've never walked out of a theater thinking I'd like to sing Mimi, that opera's fragile leading lady. The role calls for a darker, creamier voice than mine, and I saw no sense in kidding myself about it. *La Bohème* takes place in Paris, and I've always considered Mimi a French character who somehow got stuck in an Italian opera. In the last act of *La Bohème,* Mimi, a ninety-pound seamstress, has to sing like a nine-hundred-pound truck driver. Miss Liebling and I didn't knock ourselves out over my reluctance to sing *La Bohème,* but on separate occasions early in my career she practically forced me to sing Mimi and Musetta. I hated every minute of those performances and never sang those parts again.

Maestro Bamboschek felt it would be helpful for me to observe other singers in performance, so he hired me to understudy Florence Quatararo in Massenet's *Thaïs.* It *was* helpful. *Thaïs* is a French opera, and Miss Quatararo, a beautiful and talented singer, acted her role subtly and realistically. That was a revelation to me, and on a certain functional basis, that's one of the major differences between Italian and French operas. The Italian *verismo* repertoire requires a different style of acting than the French repertoire—a broader acting approach to match the broader strokes of the Italian composers' music. It's similar to the difference between silent-film acting and the contemporary style. While in Philadelphia, I made up my mind to concentrate on French repertoire.

I worked as an understudy for only a couple of weeks before

Bamboschek gave me a big break: In February 1947, I made my operatic debut as Frasquita in the Philadelphia Opera's production of Bizet's *Carmen*. It was a small role, but having it meant I was no longer just a student. I was now an opera singer. And since I was only seventeen years old, I knew great things were about to open up for me.

It's funny how dumb you can be at seventeen, isn't it? *Nothing* opened up for me, which shouldn't have come as such a surprise. Seventeen-year-old divas are rare. The Philadelphia Opera season ended in March, and after that I didn't work again until the summer, when I went out on my first concert tour. The tour lasted two weeks and was organized by a clever promoter named Lucius Pryor. Mr. Pryor hired five young American musicians—me, a male singer, a pianist, a violinist, and a flautist—and sent us to Council Bluffs, Iowa. We all prepared solo programs, and when we got to Council Bluffs, each of us was given an itinerary and an accompanist. Our salary was $150 a week, and out of that we paid the accompanist $40. If he had a car, we paid for gas; if he didn't, we took buses.

From Council Bluffs, the five of us fanned out around the Midwest and didn't see each other again until the tour ended. My first concert took place in a farming town about forty miles outside Kearney, Nebraska. I don't remember the name of the town, but I do recall that when the piano player and I got off the bus, the place was permeated with a really awful chemical odor. We were in cattle country and had arrived at the height of an epidemic. Local livestock were dying because of a foul-smelling fungus attacking the grain. The stench from the fungus, called stinking smut, was incredible.

Mr. Pryor had publicized all our concerts in the local media. Breathing through my mouth only, I went and picked up a copy of the town's weekly newspaper. They certainly spelled my name right. The front page of the paper carried a picture of a dead cow with the caption BEVERLY SILLS TO SING AT HIGH SCHOOL. Beneath that, a photo of me was captioned STINKING SMUT HITS NEBRASKA. It was a very auspicious way to begin my career as a concert artist. Actually, the concerts went well, but when the tour ended—we all met again in Council Bluffs—I was happy to get back home.

I spent the rest of the year immersed in my lessons with Miss Liebling and learned a number of French operas, including Massenet's *Manon* and *Thaïs*, Charpentier's *Louise,* and *The Tales of Hoffmann* by

Offenbach. I also learned that I hated being out of work and out of money. I wasn't the only one of her students in that bind, so early in 1948, Miss Liebling teamed me up with four other female students and a baritone and called us the Estelle Liebling Singers. We sang at colleges throughout New England, and each us made about $75 a performance. The work was fun, but it was also sporadic and ultimately depressing: What the hell did it have to do with being an opera singer?

And then my father suddenly became ill, and my priorities turned around completely. One night Papa began coughing up blood, and the family thought he had tuberculosis; Uncle Sydney, one of his brothers, had had TB. But that wasn't the case. My father had been gassed during World War I, and he had smoked three packs of cigarettes a day all his adult life. When he went in for a biopsy, our family doctor informed my parents that Papa had lung cancer. Midway through 1948 we moved into a three-bedroom apartment in Stuyvesant Town in Manhattan so that my father could be near Bellevue Hospital, where he began receiving cobalt treatments.

That winter, my parents went to Florida for four weeks, and Papa came back looking dreadfully thin. But then he began eating fattening foods, including lots of ice cream, and he seemed to be regaining his health. It was a false spring; his cancer was merely in temporary remission. When summer came, my father went to the hospital for a series of operations.

My parents never told me about Papa's lung cancer or the desperate nature of the operations he was about to undergo, which were a last-ditch effort to contain the spread of his cancer.

Just before the operations were to take place, I was offered $300 plus my passage to sing four concerts on a thirty-eight-day Moore-McCormack Line cruise to Buenos Aires, Argentina. My mother and father both told me to take the job. Papa was still going to be in pain when I got back, they told me, but eventually he'd recover. They said the doctors were fairly convinced he had tuberculosis, but that still wasn't a certainty. So off I went to Buenos Aires, and I had a wonderful time.

My father died five days before I returned to New York. He was only fifty-three years old. My parents and my father's doctor had all decided it was wiser for me to go to South America than to stay home and see Papa waste away. For a long time, I felt an enormous sense of guilt about having left my father's side when he was so sick.

I frequently tell myself that I'm very much like my father, and that if I were gravely ill, I'd also probably send away a child of mine. I know that years later, when I struggled with cancer, my tendency was to make light of it and to relieve my family by acting as if I were on some kind of a high. I actually preferred to be alone when I was in the hospital, and I've tried to console myself with the idea that perhaps my father was like that too. Except for my mother, he really didn't want anyone around him.

Shortly before I went to work on that cruise to Buenos Aires, I remember, I wore a black strapless dress when I went to visit Papa in the hospital. He looked at me and said, "You look wonderful. Don't let yourself get fat."

I laughed and said, "Why do you think I'll let myself get fat?"

"Because you like ice cream too much," he said.

That was the last conversation I remember having with my father.

The truth of the matter is that I always *have* liked ice cream a lot. And crazy as it sounds, I never take a bite of ice cream without thinking of him. Never.

Sometimes when I think about my father, I remember a small thing he did for me that eventually showed me a way to go through life without being weighed down by obligations that are more imagined than real.

When we lived in Sea Gate and I had to take a bus, a trolley, and three subway trains to get to Times Square, my father once handed me $20. "I want you to put this in your purse," he said. "You must never feel that there is no way out of a situation that makes you unhappy. If you're ever with a young man you don't like, or if anyone ever gets fresh with you, or if you're just having a lousy time, you'll always have money to come home by yourself in a taxi. That's what this twenty dollars is going to give you. It's your independence, your insurance, that you don't have to have a terrible time."

Over the years, that $20 became a kind of philosophical symbol signifying that there was always a way out of having a miserable time. Whenever I found myself in an unhappy situation, I always tried not to prolong it, but rather to get out as quickly as I could. That $20 took on a lot of other forms later on in my life. For a long time after I became successful, I accepted almost every operatic appearance I was offered, even when I really didn't want the job. There came a time when I finally realized it wasn't necessary for me to sing forever or to keep proving myself as an artist. At that point, my father's $20 took the form of a simple sentence: "I don't want to do that anymore, because it doesn't make me happy."

I still miss my father.

FOUR

We were devastated by Papa's death. Mother and I were utterly alone. Both my brothers were then attending college upstate. Sidney was in his last year of medical school at the University of Rochester, and Stanley, after graduating from City College of New York, was studying how to teach handicapped children at Geneseo teachers college.

I missed my father's love and care, but most of all I missed his strength. I didn't think that life had pulled the rug out from under me; the floor itself was gone, and beneath it—there was *nothing*. I fully expected my mother to be in even worse shape. My father used to tell her: "Shirley, you can look at garbage and see roses." That was no longer true. Mama was terribly frightened, and who could blame her? My father had always taken care of *everything*. He even used to wash my mother's hair.

As overprotected as she'd been until then, my mother began exhibiting a streak of courage and independence that I doubt even she suspected was there. Stuyvesant Town was and still is a wonderful private community of high-rise apartment buildings built in 1947 by the Metropolitan Life Insurance Company. It's almost a city within a city. Stuyvesant Town, which includes Peter Cooper Village, runs from 14th Street to 23rd Street along First Avenue and down to the East River. If he hadn't worked for Metropolitan Life, Papa wouldn't have been able to get us an apartment there, because even then Stuyvesant Town had something like a seven-year waiting list. More than 35,000 people live in the community, and another couple of hundred thousand would like to. It's the East Side's only affordable middle-income housing complex.

We'd been there just nine months when my father died, and we were practically broke. Papa's bank accounts were blocked until his will was probated, and we were told that would take at least six weeks. In the meantime, we couldn't afford, nor did we need, a 5½-room apartment.

A week after my father died—and the day after my mother finished sitting *shivah* for him—we went to see Mrs. Jones, who was Stuyvesant Town's head rental agent. Mother told Mrs. Jones about Papa's death, and pleaded with her to find us the cheapest apartment available. There *were* no apartments available, but Mrs. Jones told her: "Don't worry about a thing. Get rid of all the furniture you don't need, and in ten days I'll get you an apartment for seventy-eight dollars a month."

Mrs. Jones made good on her word. The following week, Mama sold all our extra furniture in twenty-four hours, and she and I moved into a one-bedroom apartment.

That was the only sunny moment in our lives for many, many weeks. My mother and I were desolate. I structured my time with my singing lessons—Miss Liebling had me come over five and sometimes six days a week, and as had been true since we first met, she charged me only a pittance compared to her usual fee.

For more than a month my mother and I did little but sit and mourn. Mama cried often, and not just because Papa was gone. Our rabbi, so friendly to the family when my father was making annual contributions to the synagogue, couldn't spare any time for her. The couples my parents had been so close to simply disappeared, and Mother knew why: She was an attractive forty-five-year-old widow. The wives of Papa's friends and business associates viewed her in a new, unflattering light—as a possible rival. Some rival. My mother never entered into another romantic relationship. A couple of years later, Sidney, Stanley, and I began pestering her to start seeing men, but she always put a quick end to those conversations by saying,

"When you've had perfection, why settle for second best?" These days, when I ask her about going out on dates, she laughs and says, "Who wants to go to bed with an old man?" Mama's genuinely content never to have married again, but it took her a long time to regain her equilibrium.

My mother had a lot to contend with after Papa died. The last days of my father's illness and his funeral had severely depleted the family's savings. His will was in probate for nearly a year, during which time money became very scarce for Mother and me. Uncle Louie, my father's older brother, had made a fortune selling blankets to the army during World War II. Because of our tight financial situation, Mother went to Uncle Louie and asked him to lend us a thousand dollars. My uncle said, "Okay, I'll lend you the thousand, but you'll have to give me your engagement ring as collateral."

I never forgave him for that. I never spoke to him again or even saw him again, except at my Uncle Sydney's funeral some years later, and I didn't speak to him there, either. I remember my brother Stanley telling him: "I don't wish you any harm, Uncle Louie, but I hope that for the rest of your life you have nothing *but* money."

That's exactly what came to pass: Uncle Louie died with nothing but money. I gave my inheritance from him to my mother, who should have received it in the first place. I did not attend his funeral. I don't think Uncle Louie had a positive effect on a single human being. Wherever he is, I hope he's happier than he was on earth. By now, I'm sure he's learned you can't take it with you.

After Mother sat by herself for six weeks, her old friend Faye Colbert, Sady Tisch's sister, finally said, "Shirley, are you going to sit like this all your life?" Faye asked my mother to talk to a friend of hers who was a Christian Science practitioner—a clergywoman. Faye's big convincing line was that if she liked what the woman had to say, Mother wouldn't have to change religions. She could practice Christian Science and still remain Jewish.

That's just what she did. The practitioner's name was Mrs. Ross, and her main message to Mother was that God is always there helping you; you never know what doors God will open for you or what he has in store for you.

After her first visit, Mrs. Ross took my mother by the hand and brought her down to the Traphagen School of Fashion and Design.

Mama already was an excellent designer and dressmaker with a strong knowledge of fabrics. After a year of study there, she was designing hats for Lilly Daché and selling her designs to some very well-known couturiers who had no qualms at all about putting their own names on her drawings. She became a functioning, independent woman and regained her cheery optimism.

By then, I'd also come out of my tailspin. My father left us a small annuity and enough money so we no longer had financial worries, although we couldn't live on the same scale as before. I hated not having a job, but that problem was remedied a couple of months after Papa's death. One day I was walking along Park Avenue and I stopped to look in the window of a flower shop. I was humming to myself, and as I looked around at the flowers, I noticed the reflection of an elderly gentleman who was standing next to me. The man struck up a conversation and asked me if I was a singer. I told him yes, I was, and he said, "May I walk along with you?"

He seemed harmless enough and looked very distinguished in a homburg and pince-nez, so I said fine. He wanted to know where I'd studied and with whom, and we walked and talked for a good ten or twelve blocks. The man gave me his card and said he owned an after-hours club on the East Side. I didn't even know what an after-hours club was. He explained that private, after-hours clubs stayed open until three A.M.; public bars had to stop serving at one A.M. He said that his establishment, the Hour Glass Club, was an exclusive men's club and that coincidentally, it was then in need of a singer. Was I interested? He said that of course I'd be singing popular music, and I'd have to accompany myself on the piano. Could I do that?

I said yes, and he offered me a job on the spot. My salary would be $125 a week, and he'd pay for two dresses I could wear while performing, which he later did. I'd be singing six nights a week, and he'd send a car to pick me up and take me home.

Although the gentleman will remain nameless, he was from a family that was extremely prominent in social circles. His club was located in a brownstone in the East Fifties, above the Hour Glass Restaurant, which was open to the public.

Mama and I were still living in Stuyvesant Town, and the first night I went downstairs to be driven to work, the owner's chauffeur was waiting for me in a green Rolls-Royce. The impact on our

Stuyvesant Town neighbors of having a Rolls-Royce pick me up was enormous.

The Hour Glass was probably the last men's club of its kind in New York. Everything about it was expensive. There were Aubusson carpets on the floors and Dufy paintings on the walls which came from the owner's private collection. The club employed great chefs, and their excellent food was served on extraordinary china. Each member maintained his own stock of liquor and wines. Some of the nation's biggest industrialists, social lions, and politicians frequented the Hour Glass.

I accompanied myself on a fifty-six-key piano on wheels. I would sing at one table for about ten minutes and then Charley, the maitre d', would move the piano to another table. Charley was a very kind man with a daughter my own age. We talked before I went out on the floor, and I told him all about myself.

During my first night there, I noticed little envelopes on each table. The very first man I sang for owned one of the largest silver companies in the United States. After I finished my ten minutes at his table, he put a hundred-dollar bill in one of the envelopes and handed it to me. I handed it right back and said, "I'm sorry, I don't sing for tips."

The maitre d's mouth dropped open. I very hurriedly said, "Move me to the next table, please, Charley."

As he did so, Charley said, "What the hell do you think you're doing?"

"What do you mean?" I asked.

"Don't refuse tips. That's how you make money around here," he said.

"That's ridiculous."

"*You're* being ridiculous," Charley said. "You're not doing this for fun. You told me you want to make money to pay for your lessons? Take the money in the envelopes and save it."

I soon got over my hesitation, let me tell you. For some of those men it was no big deal to tip me $100 or sometimes $500 in return for singing their favorite songs. I always managed a proper thank-you smile, but it continued to bother me a great deal to be tipped for my singing. When I told Mama about it, she was as disturbed as I was, and we both made a vow that I'd work there for exactly one year and save up as much money as I could.

I sang popular tunes of the day. Rodgers and Hammerstein's *South Pacific* was then running on Broadway, and members often requested songs from that show. Sometimes somebody would ask for an operatic selection. A number of Irish politicians frequented the Hour Glass, and I sang an awful lot of *Danny Boy*. One night a man whose name would surprise you asked me to sing *Danny Boy* over and over again. When I finished, he handed me an envelope containing $1,000, the biggest tip I ever received.

There were always plenty of women around. A number of New York's highest-priced call girls congregated at the Hour Glass. Arrangements between them and the members were handled with the utmost decorum. My friend Charley, the maitre d', acted as a discreet courier, shall we say, between the ladies and the men. The one rule everyone followed was that no action was allowed on the premises.

I didn't tell Mama about the women.

The call girls all seemed to own mink coats and important jewelry. They varied in age, and were either extraordinarily beautiful or had gorgeous figures, or both. I got to know several of them pretty well. One was the daughter of an American ambassador. Another was very anxious to have me understand she only did it because she liked it, not because she needed the money. Perhaps the most popular prostitute in the place was slightly crippled in one leg and walked with a noticeable limp. She once told me she thought men were attracted to her because they found her vulnerable. She was a very cultured lady who had her own box at the Metropolitan Opera.

Many years later, at the Metropolitan Opera, I noticed a beautifully gowned and bejeweled elderly woman wearing a long white mink coat. Her face was familiar, as was the peculiar way she walked, and I racked my brain for days trying to remember where I had known her. She was, of course, the congenial lady of the evening I'd met twenty-five years or so earlier at the Hour Glass Club. She died about ten years ago—I recall reading her obituary in *The New York Times*. Apparently, she was a member of a rather interesting family and had led a hectic life. The *Times* did not mention her activities at the Hour Glass.

With so many openly available women on the premises, members didn't bother me, except once. One night a member offered me $125 and put his hotel key in the envelope. I smiled prettily, stayed away from the man, and pretended that I didn't know what was going on. Charley chewed him out, and he never did it again.

I wasn't the only entertainer in the place. Three Mexican guitarists and a singer came in on weekends, when the club was nearly deserted—the men were home with their families.

The Hour Glass was always packed during the week. Members themselves often helped out with the entertainment. Three elderly gentlemen used to specialize in singing ribald, corny parodies of popular songs. Irving Berlin's *Annie Get Your Gun* was then running on Broadway, and they loved performing their own version of "The Girl That I Marry":

> *The girl that I married turned out to be,*
> *A walking and talking expense to me.*
> *The girl I keep alive,*
> *Wears a mink and just stinks*
> *of Chanel Number 5.*
> *A guy named Antoine has to do her hair,*
> *And Bergdorf-Goodman, they get their share.*
> *We've a nice house,*
> *Just one small room,*
> *But when I'm out of town*
> *It's a ball room.*
> *The girl that I married needs Tom, Dick, and Harry*
> *And me.*

The only lousy part of the job was my hours—I worked from ten at night until three in the morning, twenty minutes on and twenty minutes off. During my breaks, I'd go into a little room and study the music I'd worked on that morning with Miss Liebling. One night while I was on my break, I heard some really terrific piano playing. I came back out on the floor and saw a beautiful young man with black hair sitting at the piano. When I walked over and told him how much I liked his playing, he said he was hoping for a career in show business. He certainly achieved his goal. That was the first time I met Liberace.

After I was driven home each night, I'd usually be asleep by four A.M. and up by nine in order to make my ten o'clock lessons with Miss Liebling. For many weeks she thought something was seriously wrong with me, because I usually showed up in a bit of a daze. When I finally told Miss Liebling about my work at the Hour Glass, she strongly disapproved, but felt compelled to move my lessons to the afternoon.

Ever since I was a little girl, I'd been friendly with another of Miss Liebling's students, Jean Tennyson. Jean's husband, Camille Dreyfus, was chairman of the Celanese Corporation of America, and they were both staunch supporters of opera and opera singers. When Jean learned that retired soprano Mary Garden was down on her luck, she hired Mary to teach French repertoire to six scholarship students. Jean always took an active interest in my career and gave me one of the six scholarships. She paid Mary Garden $1,500 per student.

I never met the other five, because our lessons with Miss Garden were all private sessions. Mary Garden was no longer a young woman when we met. Her hair had turned white, but she still had a very trim body and extraordinarily beautiful legs. I got to see a lot of her legs, because Miss Garden was tiny and insisted on standing on a chair while teaching me. When I asked her why, she said, "Audiences have *always* looked up to me—that's why."

We spoke only French together, and in our six weeks of study she taught me *Manon* and *Thaïs*. Although I'd already started concentrating on French operas because of my love of Lily Pons, Mary Garden *really* got me hooked. That was in spite of her teaching methods. Charming, she wasn't. Mary Garden often struck me as the meanest woman I'd ever met. She was generous when it came to showing me how *she* performed Manon, and absolutely awful about allowing me room for a single creative thought. She received awe and admiration from me; in return, she made me feel like an awkward giant.

I used to think of Mary as Mighty Mouse. When we worked on *Manon,* every gesture she taught me was perfect for her and totally unsuitable for me. In that opera's famous seduction scene, for example, Mary wanted me to practically climb all over Des Grieux. She had this idea that I could pass in front of him with my arms raised over my head, reaching behind his neck. "Mary, I can't do it like that," I told her. "My bosoms will get in the way."

"Don't worry. The costume will flatten them out," she said.

"No, it won't. The costume will push 'em up and they'll look awful. Please—let me pass in front of him, facing him."

"Wrong, wrong, wrong," she said. "You can't have your back to the audience at that moment."

We worked on the seduction scene by switching parts back and forth. Mary played Manon to my Des Grieux and then she played Des Grieux to my Manon. Can you imagine a five-foot-eight American playing a sixteen-year-old French girl trying to seduce a young, handsome *chevalier* played by a five-foot-one middle-aged woman? It was a lot more easily said than done.

Mary was as acutely aware of my size as I was. For whatever reason, she had a real thing about my feet. She used to tell me to stop taking vitamins, so my feet would get no bigger. I told her she had nothing to worry about on that score—my feet had done all the growing they would. Mary wasn't mollified by that.

"Ladies simply do not wear size nine shoes," she said.

That remark brought out the Brooklyn in me.

"I wear size seven gloves," I replied. "Maybe I'll try walking on my hands."

When we weren't actually working, Mary seemed to undergo a personality transplant—she became patient and friendly then. She would sit and tell me fascinating stories about composers like Massenet and Debussy. She gave me several fans she'd used on stage, and when we finished *Thaïs*, Mary gave me the tiara she'd worn during the years when she alone owned that opera. She also gave me a stage photograph of herself wearing the tiara. "From now on," she said, "nobody but you can wear this crown." Coming from her, that was the most thrilling compliment I'd ever received.

Mary urged me to further my study of French repertoire under the guidance of Max de Rieux, artistic director of the Paris Opéra. That sounded more like a fantasy than a possibility, but Mary said I could get to De Rieux through Georges Sébastian, a conductor for the Paris Opéra and a great friend of Jean Tennyson. Jean wrote to Sébastian on my behalf, and he called De Rieux, who accepted me into a small class he'd be teaching in July and August.

Miss Liebling also thought it would be a very good idea for me to study with De Rieux, and she, as well, was instrumental in getting me into the class.

I was ecstatic about studying in Paris, and by then, Mama and I could afford to go. She cashed in some bonds Papa had left, and I had my squirreled savings from working at the Hour Glass Club. When the members found out I was leaving, they gave me a big party on the night of my twenty-first birthday. I received some wonderful gifts—a complete set of luggage made by T. Anthony of Madison Avenue, a silk robe, and a beautiful pearl ring. The women also chipped in and bought me a whole bag of travel goodies. Everybody sang to me, and a big bon-voyage cake was brought in. The owner of the Hour Glass gave me a gold ring with a crest he'd created for me and the inscription I'LL FOLLOW MY STAR. He thought I was going to have a great opera career, and I was glad he lived long enough to see some of my performances when I did make it. He was a very special man.

Miss Liebling knew her way around, and she advised us to sail to France on the *De Grasse*. The *De Grasse* was a one-class ship, which meant there was no first-class section, which we couldn't afford anyway, and no tiny tourist-class cubicles, which were where we would have wound up on any other ship.

Mother and I left New York at the end of June, and we had a very good voyage. Gypsy Rose Lee was also on the *De Grasse*. We became friends and put on a couple of shipboard benefits for the Seaman's Pension Fund. When Miss Lee performed, she would let anyone stick a $100 bill down her bosom. When some of the men wanted me to join in the game, Gypsy Rose told them: "No siree! She'll give you high C's for your C-notes, and that's all."

When we got to Paris, Mama and I checked into the Hôtel des Ambassadeurs, a fine hotel on the Boulevard Haussmann that Miss Liebling had found for us. Mother and I loved Paris. It's a city that's made for walking, and we did more than our share of it. I don't think Frenchmen were accustomed to seeing tall women—they stared at me as if I were a basketball player or maybe Sheena, Queen of the Jungle. A few years later I was at a party in Rome that was also attended by Ingrid Bergman, and whenever we looked around, our eyes met. We both suddenly realized it was because we were the tallest people in the room. We wound up in the ladies room together and of course she didn't know who I was, but she was very friendly and funny. "You realize," she said, "that we're probably the two tallest women in Italy." I was very taken with her, because Miss Bergman proceeded to scrub her face with soap and water—she wore no makeup at all. I don't think I've ever met anyone as beautiful in my life.

Mother and I toured Paris block by block, and naturally she found numerous little shops and bought miles of fabric. We went to the Louvre and the Eiffel Tower and did all the usual things tourists do. Miss Liebling had given me a list of people to get in touch with. One of them was Dick Smart, the owner of the Parker Ranch in Hawaii, which was one of the biggest ranches in the world. Dick was also a student of Miss Liebling's, and at the time he was singing at the Club Lido. Our visit there presented me with my first sight of bare bosoms jiggling around. Mama and I also went to the Folies Bergère, where we sat in big brown velvet armchairs and ordered Vichy water. We thought that was *very* sophisticated.

We wanted to go to the Paris Opéra, of course, but it was closed for the summer. That's where Max de Rieux conducted our classes. De Rieux brought his eight summer students on stage and gave us a grand tour of the Opera House, which was really rather awesome.

I went to class from ten A.M. to one P.M., five days a week. I was the only American in the class. The other students included a few Germans and a Swedish girl who spoke perfect English. De Rieux spoke no English at all; he conducted our classes in French.

At first we all found it more difficult to stand up and sing in front of the class than in front of large crowds. That probably had to do with feeling we were performing for highly critical peers. De Rieux rid us of that self-consciousness very quickly.

He taught us *Louise* and *Manon,* and after eight weeks of study, my pronunciation of French was good enough that I would never be embarrassed by it onstage.

When Mother and I got back to New York, I strongly believed I could support myself as an opera singer. But I was no longer a kid, and my dream of becoming an opera star had vanished. I knew how difficult and competitive the opera world was, and also that in my own country, the American artist was low man, or woman, on the totem pole. When I got back to the United States, nothing was going to change, because nothing had really happened. I'd picked up more training, and that was all.

As soon as I returned, Miss Liebling began teaching me my first German role: Sophie in Richard Strauss's *Der Rosenkavalier*. I'd been an opera student for fourteen years at that point, and I was itching to perform. I let her know about it, and a couple of weeks later she invited Désiré Defrère, a stage director for the Metropolitan Opera, over to her studio to hear me sing. Defrère was then getting ready to head up an opera touring company owned by Charles Wagner, and he liked the way I sang. Defrère had me audition for Mr. Wagner, and just like that, he signed me to a nine-week tour in which I'd play Violetta, the lead role in Verdi's *La Traviata*. I was in heaven. *La Traviata* was the operatic antecedent of *Camille,* the 1936 movie classic that starred Greta Garbo as the fatally consumptive heroine whose death leaves Robert Taylor sadder but wiser. I'd seen the movie when I was a kid, and I'd always loved *La Traviata* because of it.

During rehearsals, Defrère taught me several things I used until the end of my career. One of the first: When you want to get the audience's attention onstage, stand absolutely still. He taught me the finer points of how to apply makeup, how to curl my hair, how to walk on a stage, and how to assume the character I was playing—he wanted me to establish in my own mind what Violetta looked like and how old she was. *La Traviata* was actually based on a semiautobiographical novel and play by Alexandre Dumas *fils,* both titled *La Dame aux Camélias,* and I had read them both. Defrère told me always to read up on any character I played that was based on a literary or historical figure.

When he wasn't instructing me, he was flattering me. Defrère constantly told me that I was going to be famous and that I'd become the finest Violetta of my generation. That may or may not have been true, but I sang Violetta more than three hundred times during my career, and I certainly was very successful in the role.

Defrère was a jolly Belgian who spoke French all the time and told the world's filthiest jokes. He was hilariously funny, and he had an insatiable lust for women. My mother came along a couple of times when I went to dinner with Defrère and several other people from the company, and Defrère made a very serious play for her. Mama told him she didn't want to get involved with another man until I was married, which was a lie—she really didn't know how else to put him off without hurting his feelings.

The Wagner tour left New York in late September of 1951, and for the next nine weeks we played one-nighters. We probably broke every union rule then in existence, for we played sixty-three straight nights without a single day off. We were a bus-and-truck company:

The singers, orchestra members, and props were in the bus; the costumes, scenery, and instruments were in the truck. We literally lived out of a suitcase; because of the limited space on the bus, we were allowed only one suitcase each. Some days we'd travel 350 miles between cities, get off the bus, grab something to eat, change at once into our costumes, and go onstage. Some of the places we performed in didn't have dressing rooms, so we'd get into our costumes on the bus, ladies first. In *La Traviata,* the men all wore cutaway coats, so it never took them long to catch up.

I'm sure I learned more about opera during that tour than in any other nine weeks of my life. For one thing, I learned that I could sing *Traviata* even if I had a bad cold or was hoarse or had a sore throat—I *had* to go on, because the girl who was supposed to alternate with me *really* got sick. I wound up singing fifty-four of the sixty-three *Traviatas* we performed.

I also learned how much I enjoyed acting. Defrère gave me a great deal of latitude, and I did plenty of experimenting. I tried never to play Violetta the same way twice. It's a fascinating role, and I never stopped finding new aspects of her personality, subtle as the nuances may have been. I don't think I ever really finished Violetta.

Defrère taught me that there are two schools of opera singing. One is concerned exclusively with making beautiful sounds, and there's nothing wrong with that. We're talking about a God-given talent few people possess. The other school features equally talented singers who, in certain instances, will sacrifice a beautiful sound in order to make a dramatic point in an opera. Maria Callas was such a singer.

Maria Callas had a flawed voice. Her high register was very strident, and in her later years she developed a wobble—a very wide vibrato—but those things never bothered me. I became a Callas fan simply because of her sense of drama.

Everyone credits Callas with the rebirth of the *bel canto* repertoire—the "beautiful singing" found in the works of Bellini, Rossini, and Donizetti. Not to take anything away from Callas, but Lily Pons was singing *bel canto* repertoire long before Callas ever stepped foot on a stage. In the late 1930s and 1940s, Pons frequently sang *La Sonnambula, Lucia di Lammermoor, The Daughter of the Regiment,* and *Linda di Chamounix.* She was the twentieth century's real pioneer of *bel canto* opera, and I loved hearing Pons's virtuoso offerings of high notes, trills, and runs. I also loved the way she looked, which I knew I could never duplicate. But I never wanted to act like Pons, because she did little, if any, acting.

Callas's contribution was to redefine *bel canto* opera, which had always been regarded as a showcase for birdlike singers who could hit all the fine little high notes. Callas showed the world that in addition to being vocal *tours de force,* such *bel canto* works as Donizetti's *Anna Bolena* and *Lucia* were tremendous dramatic vehicles, true masterpieces of character development. Pons was always perfectly coiffed, always beautiful, and she sang spectacularly, but Callas dug deeply into the tragedy of these operas and gave their texts new meaning that audiences had never thought about before.

I dreamed of being as great a star as Pons, but that's all it was—a dream. Defrère may have been filling my head with intimations of stardom, but at that point I felt very fortunate just to be singing in the succession of high-school gyms, auditoriums, and meeting halls visited by the Wagner company.

If the work was exhausting, at least it paid well—I got $75 a performance, which is more than comparable tours pay these days. That was a lot of money in 1951, but you wouldn't have known it from the way we lived. John Alexander, who was later to become a renowned Metropolitan Opera tenor, played Alfredo, Violetta's lover. John was saving his money because right after the tour he was going to marry his fiancée, Suzie. With no prospect of employment beyond the tour, I also tried to sock away every cent I could. A couple of times a week, John and I would go into restaurants together and split a steak dinner. Being a savvy traveler by then, and remembering what I'd learned on the Shubert tours, I wouldn't leave a restaurant without stuffing my purse full of rolls. I had a fancy little electric burner, and in the mornings I'd make coffee on it and eat those rolls for breakfast.

On the Wagner tour we were housed in really tacky hotels. Tour members did serious cooking in their rooms—at night, the hallways of those crummy joints would absolutely reek of garlic. After most performances we'd all get together to eat pasta, drink red wine, and play poker. John, a lifelong friend and the tenor with whom I sang most often, taught me how to play poker on the bus, and in head-to-head competition, my lessons cost him $132. Our pasta-and-poker parties often lasted until three in the morning, which didn't leave us much time for sleeping: We'd be on the bus again at eight A.M. By eight-thirty, however, most of us were already in a deep, daylong doze. One way or the other, we got our rest.

Unlike the Shubert tour, on the Wagner tour not a single love affair got started. We all stayed in single rooms, and I suppose because we spent so much time together during the day, we longed for privacy at night. At the same time, we were like a very close-knit family, and at the slightest excuse, out would come the pasta and poker chips.

One drawback of the tour was that I didn't get a chance to get acquainted with the dozens of cities we visited. Grizzled vet that he was, Defrère usually knew the best cheap restaurants in every town, and occasionally he'd show me where to buy used books; when I wasn't sleeping on the bus, I was reading. Defrère was an antiques collector, and he took me along on his shopping expeditions, but that was it for sightseeing. What I got to know best on that tour was the inside of the bus.

When the tour was finally finished, I was exhausted. It was at least a week before I was ready to go to work again, but it took several months to find my next job. I don't recall how I got the engagement, but early in 1952, I sang a few concerts with the St. Louis Symphony. They were doing the Bach *Magnificat,* and whoever they'd lined up must have canceled out, because they were in desperate need of a soprano. Other than that, the first half of 1952 was a very lean period for me.

I continued my lessons with Miss Liebling, of course, and just before summer, I signed on with my first agent, Charles Rapp. The big booking he got me was a series of Wednesday-night appearances at the Concord Hotel in New York's Catskill Mountains. Hotels in the Borsht Belt then featured the biggest names in show business, but I was not what you'd call a headliner. Wednesday was concert night at the Concord, and Mr. Rapp arranged a series of eight appearances for me there. I sang four or five songs each Wednesday night, for which I was paid $100 minus Charlie's ten percent commission. He always signed his checks "C. Rapp," which was *exactly* how I felt about singing at the hotel. I've often made fun of those Wednesday-night performances, but in retrospect, the $720 I earned at the Concord was important money.

Miss Liebling continued to look out for me. That summer, she arranged for John Alexander and me to sing concert versions of *Traviata* at a number of music camps, which were very much in vogue then. During the summer, well-to-do ladies and gentlemen who were amateur musicians would take off to rustic retreats throughout New England, primarily in Vermont, and musicians would be brought in to perform concerts. Johnny and I did a lot of those and really enjoyed them. We were paid either $50 or $75 a concert, depending on the size and generosity of the particular music camp that Miss Liebling had muscled us into.

In September, I went out on another Charles Wagner tour, which again lasted nine weeks. This time I played Micaela in *Carmen.* Georges Bizet wrote the part of Carmen for a mezzo-soprano, a lower voice than mine, so I couldn't feel slighted about not getting the title role. Still, I was no longer a leading lady, and that was a bit of a comedown. My one consolation was that I earned more money than anyone else, because I was singing every night and getting $100 a performance. I did sixty-three consecutive Micaelas, and that's called going bonkers. It was a numbing, unrewarding experience—I didn't learn a thing on that tour. For several years afterward, it was very hard for me to listen to *Carmen,* let alone sing it. Micaela, Don José's country sweetheart, appears in the first and third acts of *Carmen,* and after that, she's not heard from again. There were long stretches of time to kill, and I occupied them by reading English novels, starting with those of Sir Walter Scott. I was really bored to death on that trip.

I was also very lonely. Johnny Alexander wasn't along because the role of José was too heavy for him to sing, and although I got very friendly with Lydia Ibarrondo, the girl who sang Carmen, we didn't spend much time together. Lydia was a real spitfire whose boyfriend had a matching temperament. At the start of the tour he drove alongside the bus every day, but after a couple of weeks she decided to travel with him, so I lost my road companion. I bought a $15 guitar and a how-to book, and began killing time on the bus by working very hard at learning to play the instrument. Eventually I took classical guitar lessons. I also learned to play chess on that tour.

Sitting in the wings every night, I wound up memorizing every part in *Carmen.* A few years later, when I became lunatic enough to sing the role of Carmen, I didn't have to learn it—I already knew it.

Désiré Defrère was again in charge of the tour, but he was ill most of the time. Defrère taught me how to play chess, but we didn't spend nearly as much time kidding around together as we'd done the previous year. Micaela was not a very intricate or difficult role, so there was little for us to talk about. Looking back on it now, the second Wagner tour was my first operatic experience with TTMAR—"take the money and run." It didn't feel good at all.

I got back to New York in November 1952, and I was now very, very antsy. The Wagner company had decided to tour with *Madama Butterfly* in 1953, and I've already told you that I felt mine was not a Puccini voice, so my only real source of income was out the window. But even if Charles Wagner had offered me the lead in an opera I liked, I might well have turned him down. Aside from the money, there didn't seem to be any point in doing more tours. I hadn't been studying most of my life for the privilege of singing in high-school auditoriums two months a year. I was looking for something more substantial, and if it didn't start happening soon, maybe I'd just pack the whole thing in.

FIVE

Miss Liebling felt that my apprenticeship was over. At the start of 1953 she called Jean Tennyson, who'd paid for my lessons with Mary Garden and who'd helped arrange my Paris studies with Max de Rieux. Jean was an important contributor to the San Francisco Opera, which was then considered second only to the Met as America's finest opera company. Miss Liebling had heard that Gaetano Merola, head of the San Francisco Opera, was coming to New York in early February to audition singers for a scholarship program he was about to start. She thought I was ready for the big time, and asked Jean to see if Merola would let me audition for him—not for a scholarship, but for a job with his opera company. Jean called him, and on a very cold winter day, I went to sing for him at a place in Manhattan called Judson Hall.

Merola was an amiable, seventy-two-year-old gentleman. In 1899, the Metropolitan Opera had brought him over from Naples to serve as its assistant director. After leaving the Met, Merola spent nearly twenty years with several other opera organizations. He eventually founded the San Francisco Opera in 1923 and had been its artistic director ever since.

Merola was gentle but decisive. He liked my voice and was

impressed by my performing experience. Right then and there, he hired me for the full run of the San Francisco Opera's 1953 fall season. I'd make my debut as Helen of Troy in Boito's *Mefistofele,* and I'd also sing the far juicier role of Donna Elvira in Mozart's *Don Giovanni.* Merola offered me a salary of $175 a week and asked me to come out to San Francisco at the end of August. He wanted me to be his house guest for two weeks, which would give him enough time to coach me in my roles.

I said yes to everything.

I walked out of Judson Hall a different woman. If Merola hadn't hired me, it wouldn't have been a tragedy, but the fact that he did removed any lingering doubts I had about wasting my life chasing an unattainable goal. I *was* going to be an opera star.

For several days my brain was on automatic pilot. I just couldn't conceive of life's being sweeter.

San Francisco was almost seven months away, though. I had to do *something* before heading west, so I started phoning around for work. One of the first people I called was Giuseppe Bamboschek, the kindly maestro from Philadelphia. His casts were already set, but Bamboschek had been in touch with Rosa Ponselle, who had been appointed artistic director of the Baltimore Civic Opera Company in 1952. Miss Ponselle was planning to present *Manon,* and if I was interested, he'd arrange an audition for me.

I was and he did.

A few days later, on a cold, gray morning, I caught a train down to Baltimore. From the railroad station, I took a bus to Rosa's estate, which was several miles northwest of Baltimore. When the bus driver let me off, I saw an immense house, an outdoor pool, and acres of manicured lawns. This was the famed Villa Pace.

A uniformed maid greeted me at the door. She didn't take my coat. Beneath my arm, I carried a large G. Schirmer envelope, the shopping bag of a 1950s music student, with my music in it. The maid told me that Madame Ponselle was upstairs and expecting me, so we climbed a beautiful staircase and I was ushered into Rosa's bedroom.

It was one P.M. and Rosa was just finishing breakfast in bed. That was some bed: A silver headboard framed Rosa's great wide face, huge brown eyes, flat broad nose, and generous mouth with its slash of bright-red lipstick. Rosa's face was etched with lines of anguish, and her eyes were as sad as a cocker spaniel's. Cocker spaniels were not her thing, however. Poodles were. Her bed was covered with poodles, and there were probably a dozen more that couldn't get on the bed, running around the room. The dogs on the bed were yapping and scattering leftovers from Miss Ponselle's breakfast tray all over the place.

Rosa seemed oblivious to them and to me. She had a piece of pink netting tied around her hair in a big bow that made her look as if she had pussycat ears. Rosa was wearing a pink satin bedjacket and a pink nightie.

Her bedroom was freezing. I'd heard that Rosa liked backstage areas to be ice-cold wherever she sang—so cold that Ezio Pinza had once refused to walk into the opera house until some heat was put back on.

Rosa called out for her maid and then got out of bed—several poodles had to move to allow her to put her feet down. Miss Ponselle then removed her bed jacket and nightgown and stood naked, waiting for her maid to come and dress her. More to herself than to me, Rosa said, "I'm overweight."

All I could think was: *Rosa Ponselle is standing stark naked in front of me!*

Her maid then hurried in and began dressing Rosa. There was no need for me to say anything, because Rosa never stopped talking to the maid. She gave the woman a long list of orders pertaining to the dogs' meals, luncheon for her and me, several things she wanted done around the house—on and on. After ten minutes, Rosa, the dogs, the maid, and I (in that order) finally left the bedroom, descended the staircase, and went into the music room.

Miss Ponselle finally addressed me. "Take your coat off," she said. "You can't sing with your coat on, honey."

We sat down on a sofa. "Let's talk about *Manon*," she said. "Let's hear you sing it."

I sang the Saint-Sulpice scene that Mary Garden and I had labored over. I sang, we talked, and then we *both* sang. Even at that point—she was then fifty-six—Rosa Ponselle still had a great voice. Her face was exceptionally broad between the cheekbones—singers call that area the "mask." The width of Rosa's face enabled her to sing "in the mask" even above the staff—her high notes were all up front. When I reported this later to Miss Liebling, she said that was the reason Rosa had trouble early on with her high B's and high C's. "She never had enough head tone in her high notes," Miss Liebling said. "Too much open-throated singing is dangerous."

In spite of that, Rosa still had a large, thrilling, creamy Italian voice. An authentic Italianate soprano voice is hard to describe, but I know it when I hear it. I have only heard a few sopranos in my life who really had it: Ponselle, Renata Tebaldi, and Leontyne Price. The sound is emotional with a vibrato that ripples and throbs. Listen to Tebaldi's early recording of *Madama Butterfly* and you'll feel it as well as hear it.

Rosa and I had a terrific time, and after a couple of hours, she said, "*Manon* is yours. We will work on it together."

I was thrilled, but in the back of my mind I had one small worry: After I'd been coached in the role by Mary Garden and Rosa Ponselle, would a Manon of my own ever emerge?

At about four in the afternoon, we ate lunch on trays that were brought into the music room. Rosa and I had been talking about dieting; lunch was a plate of pasta and garlic bread.

After lunch, we went back to work. Rosa was tireless; I wasn't. She had still been in bed at one, but I'd been up since five and the music room was every bit as cold as Rosa's bedroom. As it grew dark outside, I began getting nervous about making my train back to New York. When I mentioned it to her, you can't imagine her look of shock. Rosa told me to forget about going home: I was to be her guest overnight.

I stayed at the Villa Pace for five days. We worked hard, and when we needed a break, we'd take a walk on her property. Rosa lent me one of her mink coats for those walks—she had at least a dozen in her fur closet. During our walks, I learned that Rosa's husband, Carle A. Jackson, the son of a former Baltimore mayor, had recently divorced her in order to marry another woman. She was lonely and depressed, and I think that's why the Baltimore Civic Opera became such a passion of hers.

It's odd to think that when we met, I wasn't quite twenty-four years old and she was fifty-six. I'm fifty-seven as I write this, and realize now, as I didn't then, that Rosa wasn't an old woman. She was old for a singer, perhaps, but judged by today's lifespans, she was relatively youthful.

Rosa had never sung Manon, but she had very definite ideas about how the character should be played and what vocal approach I should take. Mary Garden had concentrated primarily on acting and had only hinted at how I should sing certain musical phrases. Rosa dissected the role a note at a time. I insisted she was singing and acting Puccini's Manon Lescaut, not Massenet's Manon. I thought her interpretation was too broad and too heavy.

I didn't see Manon in that light at all. When she first comes onstage, I wanted the audience to see a fifteen-year-old farm girl, not a slut. Manon is being sent to a convent because her mother probably found her in the hay with a hired hand once too often, but that doesn't mean she's the village whore, which is how some sopranos have played her. I didn't, because to me, Manon isn't immoral—she doesn't even know what she's done wrong. When she meets the Chevalier des Grieux, who falls for her in two seconds flat, Manon tells him: "My parents think I'm having too much fun, so they're sending me to the convent."

I pictured Manon as a farm girl who's never been to a big city and who looks it when the audience first sees her. I wanted her to be flirtatious in a childlike way, and not at all graceful in the first act. At the start of Act II she has begun living in Paris, and I wanted her to be a little more polished then. By the end of that act, the audience would see her transformation into a courtesan.

We fought like cats and dogs about that character for five days, but Rosa didn't pull rank on me. She treated me as a colleague. When I took the train back to New York, I can't tell you the sense of loyalty I felt toward that woman.

I returned to the Villa Pace a few days later for the start of rehearsals. We'd be presenting two performances of the opera, and we had quite a long rehearsal period—nearly two months. Rehearsals were held every night in Rosa's music room from seven o'clock until close to midnight. She drilled us like a marine sergeant. Rosa finally allowed me to play the first act the way I wanted to, which was gracious of her. Except for two incidents, we got along perfectly.

Our first run-in took place during a big dinner she put on at the Villa Pace. Rosa had invited Baltimore's leading citizens and most ardent opera lovers to meet the cast of *Manon*. At the dinner table, she introduced me to the gathering as her newest protégée, which was a huge compliment. I stood up and thanked her and told everyone what a wonderful time I'd been having, working with Miss Ponselle— but I had to point out that I'd been studying with Estelle Liebling since I was seven years old, and that Miss Liebling had taught me everything I knew.

When I sat down, I could tell Rosa was furious. But I thought she'd been unfair to Miss Liebling, and I had to say so.

Our other disagreement occurred a couple of weeks before opening night. I don't remember who got me the job, but I was invited to sing with the Erie Symphony Orchestra in Pennsylvania. The conductor was a man named Fritz Mahler, who said he was a nephew of Gustav Mahler, the great Austrian composer and conductor. Believe me, I didn't bother checking the man's pedigree. The important thing was that I could earn $350 in one night, so I asked Rosa to release me from rehearsals for three days. At this point I had Manon down cold, and we were just marking time until opening night.

Rosa said, "If you leave to do this, I'm not going to let you do the first performance of *Manon*. I'm going to give it to a girl named Phyllis Frankel."

Phyllis Frankel was a soprano from Baltimore who'd already played several leading roles with the company, including Violetta in *La Traviata*. I didn't believe Rosa would do that to me, but I didn't argue with her. I needed the money, so I went to Erie, rehearsed for one night, sang the next night, and then came back.

Rosa was a woman of her word. Phyllis Frankel sang the first *Manon,* and on April 18, 1953, I sang the second performance. The audience and local critics were very responsive, but my performance didn't measure up to my own expectations. I thought I was fine vocally, but my characterization wasn't nearly as good as I'd wanted it to be. A lot of that stemmed from my strained relationship with Rosa. Despite what she'd said, I knew Rosa had taken the opening night away from me because I hadn't let her claim me as her protégée. During my performance, every time I deviated from her concept of Manon to mine, I knew she was aware of it and disapproved. I wound up feeling very self-conscious onstage, and what resulted was not a totally committed performance.

In later years I came to understand Rosa very well. She had retired from singing early (even earlier than I did), when she was one of the world's leading sopranos, as was later true of me, and she had returned to run an opera company, as I did. Rosa had retired in 1937, a year after her marriage, at the height of her vocal powers. Her return to the opera scene as an artistic director sixteen years later was an experience I'd eventually come to appreciate only too well. If you work at it just a little bit, opera offers a terrific escape from problems that might otherwise overwhelm you. Rosa and I worked at it a *lot*.

Rumor had it that Rosa's retirement had been caused by Olin Downes's devastating review in *The New York Times* of her *Carmen*. When I asked her about that, she denied it. One night after she'd had a couple of brandies, however, she took me down to the basement of her home, where she'd stored cartons and cartons of that *Times* review. To me, it seemed as if Rosa had tried to buy up all the issues the *Times* had printed that day so that nobody could read the scathing review. I urged her to destroy them.

"What could a newspaper critic do to the great Rosa Ponselle?" I asked her.

Plenty, apparently. If that review hadn't caused Rosa to retire, it had certainly wounded her deeply.

On August 31, I flew out to San Francisco, where Gaetano Merola had arranged to have a driver meet me and take me to his home. Anyone familiar with my career knows what happened that day: I waited and waited, but the car and driver never appeared. I telephoned Mr. Merola several times, but his line was busy, so I copied down his address and went to see him. I had only $20 with me, which is why I didn't take a cab. Instead, I picked up my two suitcases and boarded a succession of buses and cable cars. It took me four hours to get to Mr. Merola's house.

When I arrived there, the door was open and I walked in. All around me were people who looked terribly unhappy. I wandered into the parlor, and there was Mr. Merola—laid out in a coffin. The night before, he had died while conducting a performance of *Madama Butterfly* at Stern Grove. His house was filled with a crowd of grieving people.

I was shocked, confused, and totally alone. No one knew who I was, and I couldn't find Mrs. Merola—I really didn't know *what* to do. The only thing I could think of was to get back on the buses and go to the opera house. A couple of people there confirmed that I was expected, but not for two weeks. And they could do nothing for me in the way of lodgings. A switchboard operator finally referred me to a horrible little joint on Market Street. It was a flophouse. Winos, prostitutes, and one newly arrived opera singer lived there. Rehearsals were due to start the following week, and when they did, I'd be able to draw against my salary. For whatever reason—I probably didn't want to worry her—I was reluctant to call my mother for money. I wound up spending the loneliest week of my life at that hotel. It was the hungriest week of my life, as well. My biggest meals consisted of coffee and white-bread-and-ketchup sandwiches, which were free at the corner diner. God, I was miserable. When that week finally ran its course and rehearsals started, I was out of that fleabag in a flash.

Kurt Herbert Adler had been the San Francisco Opera's chorus master, and in the wake of Merola's death, he was appointed interim artistic director. Adler was quite nervous in his new job. He did a lot of yelling and screaming, and the more he raved and ranted, the more uptight everybody got. Our rehearsals became very tense little affairs, but I was singing with great stars, and they didn't let it bother them.

I learned a lot that fall. I attended every performance of every opera; I practically lived at the opera house, morning, noon, and night. I was an unknown young kid, but here I was onstage with internationally famous singers—Licia Albanese, Jan Peerce, Giuseppe di Stefano, and Nicola Rossi-Lemeni, who was then Italy's foremost bass. When I wasn't performing, I was watching singers like Cesare Valletti and Giulietta Simionato, both of whom were very kind to me.

I was terribly lonely before my mother joined me in San Francisco. Italo Tajo, who played Leporello in *Don Giovanni* and was one of the most famous Leporellos of his time, took it upon himself to cheer me up. Italo knew all the wine people in the Napa Valley, and on Sundays he used to drive me up to spend the day with the Mondavi and Martini families. Have you ever seen photographs of big Italian families posed in front of long tables piled high with food and wine? That's what those days were like in my memory.

Italo taught me a lot about adding subtle touches to flesh out a character. He was a mischievous man and took great pleasure in doing stage business with his feet. In *La Bohème,* for instance, he'd slip off one shoe, and then spend ages rubbing his foot.

Helen of Troy in Boito's *Mefistofele* is a nice debuting role. All you need is a good body, a firm bosom, a couple of high C's, and you've got it made. I stood there in my little Greek toga, sang prettily, and received good notices. I got much more attention from critics for my performances as Donna Elvira in Mozart's *Don Giovanni*, a show-case role for a soprano. I also understudied Dorothy Kirsten in *Traviata* and sang a dress rehearsal for her when Dorothy left town for a few days to visit her husband, who'd become gravely ill. Altogether, I learned about a dozen roles while I was in San Francisco.

I was there for more than three months, and I'm afraid I didn't leave town on the best of terms with Kurt Adler. I've made light of this story for more than thirty years, but when it happened, believe me, it was no laughing matter. One night, a singer in Wagner's *Die Walküre* canceled at the last minute, and Mr. Adler asked me to step in for her. That was fine with me—I'd always wondered what it would feel like to dress up in a vintage Wagnerian costume. I played one of eight lady Valkyries, and we all wore long robes, shields, breastplates, and horned helmets. In the rush to get me ready, no one, including me, thought about making sure my helmet fit. It didn't. When we all came clanking out onstage before our final exit, my helmet fell off and rolled toward the front of the stage. I wasn't quite the seasoned pro I fancied myself: Instead of ignoring the incident, I scurried out and put the helmet back on my head. The audience laughed and then applauded.

When I got off the stage, Adler came up to me and said, "Sills, are you drunk?"

You could take the girl out of Brooklyn, but, at least at that point, you couldn't take Brooklyn out of the girl. I told Adler to drop dead.

As a result of that remark, I didn't sing with the San Francisco Opera again for eighteen years. Kurt and I reconciled at a San Francisco concert of mine that he attended seventeen years later. When I came out to sing my first encore, a man in the audience shouted over to Adler: "When are we going to get her in the opera, Kurt?"

From where he was sitting, Kurt yelled back: "Next season!"

The man in the audience called out, "We want *Manon*!"

Kurt then looked toward the stage and shouted, "Will you come and do *Manon*?"

"Yes," I said, and the audience gave both of us a standing ovation.

It was more than time for us to let bygones be bygones. In 1953, we'd both been in our first seasons, and we'd simply blown up at each other. When I returned to the San Francisco Opera in 1971, the first thing I saw in my dressing room was that very same helmet, filled with orchids, a bottle of wine, and a card from Kurt that said, "Welcome Home." Inside the helmet, on a strap, was a faded name: SILLS. I now use the helmet as a planter.

I got back from California at the start of December 1953, and I hadn't been home for more than a week when my great booster Giuseppe Bamboschek of the Philadelphia Opera Company introduced me to Carlo Vinti, one of the first men on Madison Avenue to realize television's enormous potential for quality programming. Vinti came up with the idea of doing a weekly half-hour show of opera highlights, and Progresso foods agreed to sponsor the program. The first broadcast of *Opera Cameos* went on the air before Christmas.

The format of the show was very simple: We presented condensed versions of various operas. Giovanni Martinelli, a great tenor who looked like a lion, narrated the program and tied up the story between arias. The wonderful thing about Martinelli was that everyone thought he was doing the narration in Italian—you could barely understand a word of his English.

I sang *Thaïs, Tosca, Traviata,* and a lot of other things on the show. *Opera Cameos* was broadcast on the Dumont Television Network, and it attracted a lot of attention. Before long, Vinti had no problem persuading a number of singers from the Metropolitan Opera to appear on the program.

He then came up with a second sponsor: Gallo wines. In addition to singing, I did commercials—we all did. I'd bring out a tray full of Progresso foods and push that, and then I'd do a pitch for Gallo's Tawny Port, which I always called Torny Pawt. I got very little money, but the exposure was great, the experience was fun, and each week I'd wind up with a closetful of Gallo wine and cases of Progresso soup.

I liked working on television, but it posed problems far different from those of singing in an opera house. I was very aware that the camera was right on top of my face, so I tried to look as pretty as I could while singing, which isn't easy. You feel as though you're under a magnifying glass, and there are certain things you have to watch out for on TV. Many singers shake their heads too much, or their tongues may move a lot. That might not mean much in an opera house, but if you do that on television, you can wind up looking like a hippopotamus. Nowadays, television directors know when to avoid certain angles and close-ups.

No matter what the camera angle, TV always detects the presence of sweat. I've seen a televised production of *La Bohème* in which Mimi appears properly delicate and perfect—until she starts singing and beads of perspiration can be seen on her forehead and upper lip. Makeup is also a problem. In studio-mounted operas, singers' makeup and wigs appear unnatural. In those *Live from Lincoln Center* telecasts of operas performed at the Met or the New York City Opera, every singer's makeup has to be strong enough to "read" to the last seat in the balcony. In close-ups, the makeup often looks overdone to the point of oddity. But then again, Butterfly is fifteen, Manon is sixteen, and Salome is hardly older than Lolita; I haven't seen any prima donnas who qualify. Luckily, opera rises above such matters. *Everything in opera is larger than life.*

When I began appearing on television, Miss Liebling decided it was high time I got myself a legitimate opera agent. Gerard and Marianne Semon were two of the best in the business, and they took me on at her request. The Semons were very kind to young singers. They frequently asked Mama and me to dinner at their home.

Marianne and Gerard were very close to Dr. Joseph Rosenstock, who was then the head of the New York City Opera. Like Miss Liebling, they felt I was now ready for the City Opera. To be honest about it, I thought I'd be a shoo-in. I had just done a leading role in *Don Giovanni* and I'd come back from San Francisco with a fistful of good reviews. Just before Christmas of 1953, the Semons arranged an audition for me with Dr. Rosenstock.

Marianne and Gerard accompanied me to the City Opera's theater at City Center to witness the big event. I wasn't nervous about my audition. I walked briskly out onstage and sang Violetta's first-act aria from *Traviata*. Dr. Rosenstock seemed singularly unimpressed. He said, "Thank you," and that was it.

Marianne and Gerard thought I'd sung very well, but I knew I hadn't. I was just off—who knows why? I hadn't sung the way I knew

I could, so I wasn't terribly disappointed. I was just anxious to get a second try.

A couple of months later, Dr. Rosenstock invited me to audition again, and this time I was ready with my coloratura warhorses: *"Caro nome"* from *Rigoletto* and the Bell Song from *Lakmé*. I wasn't off *this* time. In fact, I expected Dr. Rosenstock to do handstands.

He didn't.

Several weeks later, he called Marianne to set up still another audition for me. Same result: no sale. I did five auditions for Dr. Rosenstock that year, and after each one, all he'd tell the Semons was: "Fine. I'll let you know."

Just as I started to get terribly depressed, I got a call from Georg Solti, who was then music director of the Frankfurt Opera. Solti had been a guest conductor with the San Francisco Opera the year before, and he was on the podium when I ran after my helmet in *Die Walküre,* and when I sang the fifth slave girl in Richard Strauss's *Elektra.* I must have been either a very good fifth slave girl or an extremely poor one, because Solti rehearsed me a lot. He was and still is a very handsome man, and rumor has it that before Solti married, he was a great lover. Supposedly, the maestro's many former girlfriends at one point formed a White Mink Coat Club—Solti supposedly was very generous to the ladies he liked.

Solti was enamored of the way I sang my role as a slave girl. He asked me to learn Marguerite, Micaela, and Violetta in German; in the early 1950s, every opera presented in Germany was sung in German. Solti told me he wanted me to sing in Frankfurt, and that he'd send me an airplane ticket.

He did. Solti sent me a one-way ticket and told me I'd be staying at the Frankfurterhof Hotel. I thought it would be an inexpensive little *pension,* but I was wrong. I arrived in Frankfurt in the midst of a snowstorm and checked into a beautiful suite. I was very impressed and immediately went to the opera house and asked for Maestro Solti.

Georg was glad to see me—a little *too* glad. He said he wanted to hear my arias in German, and when I stood next to him at the piano, he made a pass at me. In putting him off, I accidentally slammed the piano lid on his fingers. I ran out of the opera house and kept going. When I got back to the Frankfurterhof, I realized I didn't have enough money to fly home. I did, however, have a letter of introduction from the Semons to Rudolf Hartmann, the head of the Munich Opera.

In a panic, I boarded the next train to Munich, thinking I'd audition for Hartmann and maybe earn enough money to get back to New York. Unfortunately, I developed a fever and laryngitis on the train. That didn't stop me from going to see Hartmann. When I told him what had happened to me in Frankfurt, Hartmann was so sympathetic that he bought my ticket home and personally drove me to the airport. I cried a lot on the flight home. Later I paid him back for the ticket.

Aside from my appearances on *Opera Cameos,* the only bright spots of 1954 for me were an *Aida* I sang during the summer at Brigham Young University's football stadium in Salt Lake City—which Miss Liebling had a hand in arranging—and summer-stock work in Cleveland, which I arranged.

In the 1950s, proprietors of summer music theaters throughout the country came into New York and held mass auditions for singers. Several of my friends and I showed up to audition for John Price, who was in charge of Cleveland's Musicarnival, at that time the largest tent theater in the country. Musicarnival seated about 1,500 people, and was a first-class operation all the way. I got lucky with Mr. Price: He hired me to sing the leads in Franz Lehár's *The Merry Widow* and in *Rosalinda,* the Broadway version of *Die Fledermaus.*

Several of my unemployed pals also landed jobs with Musicarnival. I don't remember what we were paid—it wasn't much—but it didn't matter. Musicarnival's management made things very pleasant and homey for us. They put us up in various people's houses, and in addition to our salaries, we also received a per diem allowance for food.

We were very well looked after. Thirty years ago, the people who ran summer tent shows felt a great responsibility toward their performers. In addition to housing us, they made sure we got safely to and from the theater, and they were genuinely interested in our welfare. They wanted us to enjoy ourselves while we were there.

Not long after I started singing at Musicarnival, the cast was invited to a pool party held at the estate of a wealthy, pleasant man named Bob Bishop. Bob was one of Musicarnival's backers, and we started going out together. We saw each other on and off for about a year—my first real beau.

That's the way it was back in those days. I'd dated a lot of different men, but I'd never had a great romance. My mother wasn't disturbed by that; my brothers were. Sidney and Stanley were convinced that their twenty-five-year-old baby sister was going to be an old maid, so they began fixing me up with all their friends. Sidney really got to be a pest about it. One year he mounted a serious campaign to set me up with a doctor he was thinking of going into business with. He even conned my mother into pushing me to go out with the man. I refused even to meet him.

When I got back from Cleveland, it was time for me to resume further humiliation at the hands of Dr. Rosenstock. After my final two turndowns in 1954, I went through two more pointless waltzes with Rosenstock in early 1955. I was getting damned upset. If he didn't want to give me a job, why did he keep asking to hear me?

Yet, in the spring of 1955, Dr. Rosenstock again called Marianne to arrange an audition for me. She knew how I was feeling, so Marianne said, "I'm sorry, but before I let Beverly sing for you again, you'll have to explain why you haven't hired her."

Rosenstock told her he thought I had a phenomenal voice but no personality. No personality? Fine. Throughout all those auditions, I'd wanted Dr. Rosenstock to know I was a serious singer, so I'd always dressed in very subdued clothing. Well, forget *that*. I'd worn jumpers and high-necked blouses to the previous auditions. The eighth time out, I showed up in a jumper—but without a blouse underneath. I bought myself a pair of black mesh stockings and the highest heels I could find. I'd always tied my hair back in a bun; this time I let it hang all the way down my back.

When I came out onstage that day, Dr. Rosenstock addressed me directly for the very first time. He walked down the aisle and said, "Vell, vell, vot have ve got here?"

I told him I'd already sung my entire repertoire for him, so I was going to sing an aria that *wasn't* in my repertoire. He burst out laughing. "So vot are ve going to sing?" he asked.

"Ve are going to sing an aria from *Andrea Chenier* called 'La mamma morta,' " I said.

You have to understand that "La mamma morta" is an aria sung only by ladies with huge, heavy, dramatic soprano voices. At twenty-five, I had a light, high, lyric coloratura soprano voice. It was definitely the wrong thing for me to sing, but I was *very* angry, and I wanted him to know it. Believe me, he knew it.

Surprise, surprise: I sang the aria for him and Dr. Rosenstock said, "Uhkay, up to the office, Seals."

I signed a New York City Opera contract to do one performance of Rosalinda in *Die Fledermaus* and to understudy Phyllis Curtin and Jean Fenn in two other operas that fall. It had been a long haul, and I was not so much elated as relieved.

S I X

The New York City Opera owes its existence to a garish, cavernous, mosquelike structure built by the Shriners in 1924 and abandoned by the Ancient Order in 1939. By 1942, owing to nonpayment of back taxes, legal title to the Mecca Temple on West 55th Street had passed to the City of New York. It was then that Mayor Fiorello La Guardia, fueled by the spirit of Franklin Delano Roosevelt's New Deal, put City Council President Newbold Morris in charge of finding a use for the building. That was no easy task. The Mecca Temple seated 2,692 people, was costly to operate, and was terribly run-down.

Morris, a patrician public servant, consulted with Morton Baum, a financier and music lover, and together they came up with the idea of using the Mecca Temple as a site to present opera, ballet, drama, musical theater, and concerts at prices the average New Yorker could afford. Mayor La Guardia agreed to lease the Mecca Temple to the new City Center of Music and Drama for $1 a year—though the city subsequently reneged on that promise.

Baum was the guiding force in establishing a resident opera company at City Center. In 1943, Laszlo Halasz was appointed the City Opera's first general director, and in February 1944, the company's opening season presented Flotow's *Martha,* Puccini's *Tosca,* and *Carmen.* Ticket prices were scaled from 75 cents to $2.

Dr. Rosenstock replaced Halasz as general director in 1951, and he continued to fulfill NYCO's aim of being "an opera company for the people." When I joined the City Opera in 1955, the most expensive seats in the house cost $2.95. George Balanchine and his New York City Ballet were also performing at City Center, which really put it on New York's cultural map.

The City Opera's fall season was then one month long; its spring season lasted all of three weeks. We were hardly in the same league with the Met or the San Francisco Opera, both of which employed great stars and offered their resident singers up to six months of employment. Few regional opera companies were alive back then, which meant that if you didn't sing for one of the top two, you had to scramble to find work.

Rehearsals began for *Die Fledermaus* with the City Opera. I worked hard, and so did my mother. Mama made all my *Fledermaus* costumes, including a lovely white gown and a tiara. For my big entrance number, she went to the Ritz Thrift Shop and bought me a white fox stole for $5. The opera company was very grateful. Their set of Rosalinda costumes had been built for Phyllis Curtin, who was shorter and much skinnier than I was. Altering them to fit me might have been one of life's little nightmares.

Mother and I were strapped for money, but I was being paid $75 for my performance in *Die Fledermaus,* so when the opera opened, I decided to splurge. I bought my mother a corsage and a seat in the orchestra section, and gave her cab fare to City Center. On October 29, 1955, my opening night in *Die Fledermaus,* I decided to save a little money, so I walked from our apartment to City Center, more than two miles away. *That* was the last time!

Rosalinda was a good role for me, because *Fledermaus,* Johann Strauss's most popular operetta, contains a lot of humor. I was funny onstage and sang well that night, and my debut was a success. The next morning, Harold C. Schonberg, who was then just breaking in as opera critic for *The New York Times,* wrote that the City Opera had added "an accomplished singing actress to its roster," and that *Fledermaus* was "easily the best musical that you can see in this city on or off Broadway."

Despite getting a seal of approval from *The New York Times,* I didn't feel my life was going to change. There simply wasn't anything else on the horizon for me, and that was especially true in regard to the City Opera. Nobody in the company had a long-term contract—Dr. Rosenstock didn't operate that way. Instead of finding operas to suit his singers, he'd pick the repertoire first, and then the singers would hold their breath, hoping he'd pick them to perform a role or two.

Rosenstock never called me anything other than "Seals." I know that he liked me as a musician, but other than that we had no relationship. He did like the fact that I was always ready to go on. Several hours before a performance of *Carmen,* Madelaine Chambers, who played Micaela, called in sick. Dr. Rosenstock told one of his assistants to "Get the redheaded girl—*she* knows Micaela." Having done it sixty-three nights in a row on that Wagner tour, I certainly *did* know it. The only problem was outfitting me—Madelaine was tiny compared to me. The problem was solved by dressing me in Dolores Mari's costume as Nedda in Leoncavallo's *I Pagliacci,* which the City Opera also was presenting that fall.

One of the highlights of that first season was a new production of Tchaikovsky's *The Golden Slippers,* starring Jean Fenn, a tall, beautiful blonde. Jean was the protégée of Edwin Lester, head of the Los Angeles Civic Light Opera. At the time, the L.A. Civic Opera was a highly prestigious company—*The Great Waltz* and all kinds of wonderful new shows had originated there.

I understudied Jean as Oxana in *The Golden Slippers,* and during rehearsals it seemed pretty evident that our production wasn't going to fare too well. The opera itself isn't very interesting, and neither was our production. I remember one very bizarre moment in which witches with broomsticks flew across the stage on a wire. *The Golden Slippers* seemed corny and contrived, and I began calling it *The Golden Shlepper.*

God knows what Jean Fenn called it. Jean was a very fine singer, but the opera turned out to be a dud and wasn't given good reviews. After Jean's second appearance as Oxana, Edwin Lester suddenly decided that Miss Fenn should forget about the third and final performance. We were all caught off guard by the news, and I had no more than an hour of rehearsal to get ready for the role. At least Jean was my size, so all her costumes fit me. Throughout the opera, Oxana is out there singing, "Bring me back the golden slippers if you want to marry me." In the last act, tenor Dick Cassilly finally brought the slippers onstage, at which point he and Oxana danced together and presumably lived happily ever after.

The Golden Slippers turned out to be a case of Die Walküre and der helmut revisited. In my haste to get ready, I forgot to try on the golden slippers. Jean's shoes were at least a size and a half too big for me, and as soon as Dick and I started dancing, they fell off my feet. I didn't repeat the mistake I'd made in San Francisco—instead of trying to retrieve them, I danced barefoot. Dick and I both broke up during the dance, and when the curtain came down, those two golden slippers were sitting right in the middle of the stage.

Dr. Rosenstock was not amused. He stopped speaking to me for the rest of the season, but I think his respect for me increased enormously that night. I know it did, because he engaged me for the upcoming spring season.

When we finished our five weeks at City Center, the company went on a month-long tour that began in Philadelphia and ended in Cleveland.

That's where I met Peter Greenough.

Julius Rudel, the City Opera's assistant conductor, was a buddy. Julius had been with the City Opera since its founding in 1943–44, when he'd been hired as a musical assistant at a salary of $50 a week. He'd accompanied me on the piano during some of those awful auditions with Rosenstock and had conducted me in Carmen that fall. Rudel led the orchestra during every performance on the tour, and he was a joy to work with. Julius had an uncanny ability to sense how long I wanted to hold a note, when I wanted to pause, when I wanted to speed up or slow down the tempo—he really was extraordinary.

During the tour, Julius was acting general director, a job that made him very nervous. In Cleveland, he was not a happy man. There was nothing wrong with our work, but we weren't doing well at the box office. When the Cleveland Press Club decided to throw a party for us on a Friday night, Julius asked me to attend. I told him to forget it. I planned to have dinner, see a movie called The Man Who Loved Redheads, and go back to the hotel to wash my hair.

Julius is Austrian, and in his most formal English he said, "I'm sorry, Beverly, but we are not selling tickets in Cleveland, Ohio, so you will come to the Press Club." That did not sound like a request.

I figured that as long as I had to be there, I might as well get all dolled up, so I wore a very low-cut dress to the party. I remember walking up a flight of stairs and being greeted at the landing by a tall, handsome man with hair so blond it was white. His name was Peter Greenough. Peter was president of the Press Club and associate editor of the *Cleveland Plain Dealer.* He and I sat at the same table, and although we didn't have a chance to talk to each other very much, I knew that he was interested in me. And that I was interested in him.

Peter asked me to have dinner with him on Sunday night, but I said I couldn't: I was supposed to go beagling with Bob Bishop and then catch a six o'clock flight back to New York. Beagling is sort of like a foxhunt without the fox. Something that smells like a fox is dragged through fields by a rider, and a bunch of beagles chase after it, and then a bunch of "beaglers" on horseback chase after the beagles. We're talking serious WASP recreation here.

I told Peter to come to the Saturday night performance of *Die Fledermaus* and to a party Connie and John Price were giving for me afterward. Peter declined; he had a date for Saturday night. Well, that was that, I thought. Just before I left the Press Club party Peter passed me a note, written on the inside of a matchbook, that said "Please don't go back — 912 — you'll need some good food after beagling." He wrote down his telephone number and signed it *Pete Greenough.* (My hotel room number was 912. At least he didn't call me Seals.)

I've never forgotten the first time I saw Peter. I know every inch of him now, but when I laid eyes on him that night I thought he stood six foot eleven—he just blotted out everything else in the room. Peter, then thirty-nine, was a husky six foot one, but he seemed so strong and powerful that I thought he was a giant. After Sandy Levine, I'd never dated men who were my size or shorter. I may have liked my purses small but I liked my men big, and boy, did Peter fill *that* bill.

I believe the word is *smitten.*

Peter's reaction to me was no less intense. Peter says it was what the French call a *coup de foudrè*—a thunderbolt. We looked at each other and we fell in love. Just like that.

Peter didn't come see me in *Die Fledermaus,* but he dropped his date off early and made it to the party. We talked and talked and talked. Peter told me he was going through a difficult divorce and that he'd won temporary custody of his three daughters—and it all went in one ear and out the other. We were *very* attracted to each other. I again wore a low-cut dress, and as I've often reminded Peter, I don't think he saw my face for the first three days we knew each other.

He invited me to dinner the following night, and I again refused—I had to catch that plane, after all. The next day, while I was out beagling, I changed my mind. I found Peter's matchbook—I didn't have to search very hard for it—called him, and he said he'd pick me up at the hotel. I then called my mother and told her I wouldn't be catching the plane home that night. "Why not?" she asked. I gave her a lame excuse about being tired from all that beagling. Mama didn't believe me for a second, but she was kind enough not to push. If I wanted to come back on Monday, that was fine with her.

It was *very* fine with me. A couple of hours later, Peter showed up at the hotel with two of his three daughters: Lindley, nine, and Nancy, who was six. I looked at them and said, "Who are they?" Peter had of course told me about them the night before, but obviously nothing he'd said had registered.

Nancy, the little one, looked at me and asked, "Are you going to be my new mommy?"

I said, "I don't think so, dear." I asked Peter where their mother was.

"I have no idea," he replied. She had flown off to Europe with another man.

He then drove the three of us back to his house, which was only about fifteen minutes from downtown Cleveland. Still, it was a pitch-dark night, and I didn't have a clue as to where we were going. I kept thinking: *Here I am with a man who's got three kids. His wife's disappeared. What in hell am I doing?*

Peter had just moved into an enormous chateau-style house situated on three acres of land that fronted Lake Erie. Cities along the Great Lakes probably have the ritziest suburbs in America. If you've ever driven past Chicago to Lake Forest, Illinois, or past Detroit to Grosse Pointe, Michigan, you'll know exactly what Bratenahl, Ohio, was like: drafty mansions and lots of old money. They just don't build houses like that anymore. I still can't figure out why they built 'em like that in the first place. Peter's was among the last of these great white elephants, except that his was painted pink and had green shutters; his estranged wife had picked out the colors. The house was

Three-year-old Cutie Pie Silverman, creator of the topless swimsuit and future sex goddess.

My debut on *Major Bowes' Capitol Family* hour coincided with the radio show's 10th anniversary. Like Shirley Temple's, my own days of being "cute" were just about over.

In 1953, when I began singing on *Opera Cameos,* I also did commercials on the show. Here I am carrying my perks and my product—a tray of Progresso foods.

Every teenager in Brooklyn knew that the height of sophistication was the Cary Grant Raised Eyebrow Look.

PHOTO BY BRUNO OF HOLLYWOOD, NYC

The only two men who were ever able to boss me around: my late father, Morris Silverman (left), and my husband, Peter Bulkeley Greenough.

Peter and I on our wedding day, November 17, 1956. And (right) my mother, Shirley Silverman—the beautiful dreamer who helped make all my dreams come true.

My perfect daughter, Muffy—
the gentlest, kindest young
woman I have ever known—
and her proud mama, photographed in the early seventies
(right) and when Muffy was 27.

My son, Bucky, at Martha's Vineyard. He's now in his mid-twenties.

Peter, Muffy, and I relaxing around our pool at Martha's Vineyard. That's Paul Newman on my T-shirt. Every woman should have Paul Newman on her bosom.   ALFRED EISENSTAEDT,
LIFE MAGAZINE © TIME INC.

Mama's dynasty—at the wedding of one of her grandchildren: my brothers Sidney (left) and Stanley.

Estelle Liebling, the great lady who was my singing teacher for 34 years.
LEONARD McCOMBE, LIFE MAGAZINE © TIME INC.

In the summer of 1960, my stepdaughters Nancy and Lindley and I rode in a parade promoting "The Central City Stars"—a bit of an exaggeration—in Central City, Colorado.

Me in my all-purpose costume—low-cut, I was Carmen; without decolletage, I was Micaela in *Carmen* or Nedda in *Pagliacci*. PHOTO BY BRUNO OF HOLLYWOOD, NYC

March of Dimes poster child Carmen Donesa—like the other girls and boys who've fulfilled that role—was the bravest of the brave.
MARCH OF DIMES BIRTH DEFECTS FOUNDATION

Zubin Mehta and I hosted Young People's Concerts at Lincoln Center and encouraged children to adopt a "try it, you'll like it" attitude toward classical music. PHOTO COURTESY OF NEW YORK PHILHARMONIC

Getting ready for *Sills and Burnett at the Met*: Carol and I rehearse the *Aida* duet. It was cut from the show—she said I had all the high notes.

The chairman and president of the Beverly Sills/Arlene Francis We-Only-Want-to-Be-Loved Club. © HELEN MARCUS 1980

Carol and Bubbles discuss the arms race and the Middle East.

Bette Davis, Mae West, and Bubbles at director Billy Wilder's home.
We were discussing a revival of *Little Women*.   PHOTO BY RODDY McDOWALL

My Sarah—Caldwell, of course. Sarah's the most innovative female director
in opera history, and she's also a brilliant conductor.   UPI/BETTMAN NEWSPHOTOS

I was Prince Charles's dinner partner at the White House, and Princess Di and I have met several times.   THE WHITE HOUSE

Peter and I with my royal family: Queen Barbara and King Merv Adelson.

Johnny Carson will never be mistaken for Nelson Eddy, but he gave it his best shot when we sang "Indian Love Call" on *The Tonight Show*.

When I stepped in for Johnny as a guest host, it turned into a meeting of the Best Friends Club—Eydie Gormé, Carol Burnett, Dinah Shore, and me, joined by Rock Hudson.

Any number of sopranos spend their whole lives hoping for the day they, too, can sing with Miss Piggy's pals. © HENSON ASSOCIATES, INC. 1980. ALL RIGHTS RESERVED REPRINTED BY PERMISSION.

What terrific First Ladies we've had. Our Presidents have been lucky men.

To Beverly Sills—
my great friend
Jimmy Carter

What Becomes a Legend Most? How should I know? But when Madison Avenue
beckoned, I was happy to pose in a Blackglama mink.   BILL KING. FUR BY MAXIMILLIAN FURS

This is my favorite photo of Sills as
starlet, all gussied up in a borrowed
fur and jewels that were auctioned off
at a benefit gala.

definitely not my style. It had maybe twenty-five rooms and lots of uniformed ladies running around to keep it clean and to serve dinner. Peter told me he was an excellent cook and then sent out for Chinese food. He *is* an excellent cook, by the way. After the four of us had finished dinner, the maids took his daughters off to bed.

Peter and I repaired to the living room, which was about thirty-five feet long, thirty-two feet wide, and contained absolutely no furniture. The land Peter's previous house had been built on had been sold to the U.S. government for a Nike missile site, and the house had been torn down. Peter and his ex-wife had decided to start from scratch in furnishing the new house. The living room did have a phonograph and a large marble fireplace, however. Peter put on a Sinatra record and began to build a fire. Everything was very romantic—for at least two minutes. Peter had never used the fireplace before; as soon as the flames got going, the room filled up with smoke—we had to run outside in order to breathe. Peter said the chimney was defective, but he just might not have opened the flue.

When the smoke finally cleared, we came back in, opened the windows, and then sat down in the kitchen. Peter proceeded to tell me a great deal about himself. He had grown up near Boston. His family had literally come over on the *Mayflower*—he was a direct descendant of John Alden. His father, Henry V. Greenough, had wanted Pete to attend Harvard and then become involved in his business, Ludlow Manufacturing, which had been the world's largest producer of jute. The company was more than ninety years old and had never failed to pay its stockholders a dividend.

Peter loved his father dearly—they hunted and fished together—but he wanted to be a journalist, not a businessman. For more than a century, an unbroken line of Greenough men had gone to Harvard, and that was another family tradition he did not intend to continue. After Peter won a four-year academic scholarship to Princeton, he and his father struck a deal: If Pete would go to Harvard, it would be okay with Harry if his son became a journalist. They shook hands on it. Peter graduated from Harvard in 1939 and got a master's degree from the Columbia School of Journalism in 1940.

During World War II, he flew transports over Europe and later was sent to Air Combat Intelligence School in Orlando, Florida. Peter investigated and analyzed the biggest air screw-up of the war. During the invasion of Sicily, the American, British, and Greek navies shot down forty-seven American planes in one night, killing more than eight hundred paratroopers in the process. Peter found out why: At low altitudes, the C-47 looked exactly like the German Heinkel 111, their torpedo bomber. Ten minutes before the C-47s passed over-head, the navy fleet had been torpedo-bombed by a squadron of 111s. Somebody failed to tell the navy the C-47s were coming. Peter helped track down the officer responsible for that; within a month, a certain lieutenant general whose name will go unmentioned here was stripped of his rank and booted out of the service. That analysis put Pete into the Pentagon in air intelligence work.

After the war, Peter went to work as a general assignment reporter for the *Cleveland Plain Dealer*. Peter's mother came from Cleveland—her father, Liberty Emery Holden, had bought the *Plain Dealer* in the late 1880s. Peter told me that night about some colorful murder cases he'd covered, including the Dr. Sam Sheppard trial. Peter was no dilettante. His promotion to associate editor reflected that.

I told Peter all about my life, and before we knew it, we'd talked the night away. He drove me back to my hotel just before dawn, and later that day he returned to take me to the airport. We made plans for him to visit me in New York.

When I got home, I told my mother: "I think I've met a man I could marry."

She was ecstatic.

Then I told her that Peter was still married, had three children, was twelve years older than I, and wasn't Jewish.

My mother started crying. "Why does everything have to happen to my baby?" she sobbed.

I had figured she wouldn't be overjoyed.

Peter flew to New York a couple of weeks later, and he charmed my mother from the moment they met. He brought her flowers, he complimented her on everything, and I mean *everything,* and was such a perfect gentleman that Mama quickly dropped her objections to the idea of my marrying a gentile. Peter declared himself very, very early on that subject. He wanted to marry me as soon as his divorce became final. The man had swept me off my feet, and I was looking forward to our wedding as much as he was.

In the meantime, my mother didn't want me to be seen around

New York with a married man. Peter said he was in absolute agreement with her on that—I couldn't believe my ears. And so the three
of us went to dinner together, went to the theater together—actually,
we shared some great times.

One reason both my mother and I got along so well with Peter
was that in many respects, he resembled my father. Peter has a
tendency to be very bossy, and he's completely self-assured. Those
traits appealed to me, because as a child I'd gotten so used to them in
my father. Peter, however, was a complete WASP. One look at him
and you knew that this was a man who'd never wanted for anything.
Peter was born and raised in Brookline, Massachusetts, which is very
far away from Brooklyn, New York. He was a true Boston Brahmin.
Like his father, Peter believed there were only three times your name
should be mentioned in a newspaper: when you're born, when you're
married, and when you die. He learned very quickly that there are a
few more times in between.

I didn't really care what he thought. I'd never been in love
before, and was I enjoying it!

On January 1, 1956, Giuseppe Bamboschek once again came
through for me. Vivian Della Chiesa, a well-known opera singer and
radio personality, was slated to star in a production of Montemezzi's
The Love of Three Kings that Giuseppe was about to present in
Philadelphia. Vivian had taken ill, and he wanted to know if I'd sing
the role of Fiora in her place.

"Sure, why not?" I told him. "When's opening night?"

"January ninth," Giuseppe said. "You think you can learn it by
then?"

"I probably can," I said.

When we hung up, I realized I might have bitten off more than I
could chew. *The Love of Three Kings* is a very difficult opera, because
it doesn't contain arias and duets in the traditional sense. It's more
like one continuous tone poem. *The Love of Three Kings* is one of the
few operas that never gives audiences a chance to break the action
with applause.

Peter was in New York at the time, so he ran around and
managed to find a very old recording of the opera, and I went and got
a copy of the score. The only way to learn a part so quickly is to keep
singing it over and over and over again. I must have crammed about

four weeks of singing into four days, and my mother worked just as hard. She made my costumes, including a beautiful low-cut gown of clingy blue silk. It was a very sexy get-up for a very sexy character. At one point, Fiora stands on a parapet and waves goodbye to her husband—and her lover is standing right behind her.

I learned the part in four days and then went down to Philadelphia. Over the next four days Giuseppe coached me, and by opening night I was ready.

Bamboschek had given me a great opportunity; I was singing with a cast of international stars. Avito, Fiora's lover, was played by tenor Ramon Vinay, who was *the* great Otello and matinee idol of his time. Without question he was the sexiest man I ever sang with. He didn't just act love scenes—I mean, things started *happening* out there. In Act I, when he began pulling my dress off my shoulder, I was panic-stricken. I really didn't know how far he planned to take things.

Manfredo, Fiora's husband, was played by Frank Guarrera, a baritone who sang with the Metropolitan Opera. Fernando Corena, the Met's number one basso buffo, sang the role of King Archibaldo, Fiora's father-in-law. Corena was a small man, and every night he had to pick me up and carry me across the stage of the Philadelphia Academy of Music. I really was skinny at the time—I have the photos to prove it—but I was still a big woman, and it was no picnic for Fernando to do all that shlepping. For years afterward, whenever we saw each other—and no matter how fancy the reception might be— Fernando would grab his side as if he'd just developed a hernia and then mutter, "Sills, it *hurts*."

The Love of Three Kings was a terrific experience on every conceivable level. I had a lot of fun doing the opera, and we all got rave reviews. Bamboschek, a truly accomplished conductor, was as friendly on the podium as he was in private. The maestro didn't rattle easily, and he had an antic sense of humor. When a reporter asked why he'd gambled on me to learn the role of Fiora in less than ten days, Giuseppe said, "I didn't know anyone else stupid enough to try it or smart enough to learn it."

Before the opera, I was a nobody. After it, I was a nobody with an asterisk. I now had a reputation among conductors throughout the country for being a phenomenal musician who could learn anything at all, and for being absolutely unflappable. So why weren't they breaking down my door?

In the spring of 1956, I again sang Rosalinda in the City Opera's production of *Die Fledermaus*. I also sang Madame Goldentrill in a new production of Mozart's *The Impresario*. That was a major coup. *The Impresario* is a comic *All About Eve* with high notes. There are two sopranos in the opera, and Madame Goldentrill, the established prima donna, has better music to sing than Miss Silverpeal, the soprano who pulls every trick in the book in an effort to unseat her. The role of Madame Goldentrill is loaded with high F's, and really allows coloratura sopranos to strut their stuff. Every soprano in the company wanted the part, and several of them campaigned hard for it. In the fall, I'd been one of twenty-two sopranos with the company, and since I'd just joined up, I knew it would be out of place for me to be the least bit aggressive about going after the role. So I took a wait-and-see attitude, and I was surprised when Dr. Rosenstock handed me what I considered a very juicy plum.

Even at that point in my career I was very outspoken. If I didn't like the way things were going, I'd say something. In *The Impresario,* which we performed in English, there's a scene in which Madame Goldentrill and Miss Silverpeal battle it out to see who can sing higher. Jacquelynne Moody played Miss Silverpeal, and after she finished her aria, I'd give Dr. Rosenstock the signal to begin mine—I'd pull a purple handkerchief from my bosom. During one of our stage rehearsals, I felt he was setting too slow a pace. I walked over to the footlights, pulled out my handkerchief and began waving it at him and beating time. Dr. Rosenstock said, "Is dot a piece uff stage business or a piece uff criticism by Miss Seals?"

I said, "Well, Dr. Rosenstock, let's say it's a piece of criticism by Miss Sills turned into a piece of stage business."

Rosenstock didn't like that one bit.

The Impresario is a one-act opera, which means you need something else on the program. Dr. Rosenstock decided to pair it up with the world premiere of *School for Wives*, a one-acter written by Rolf Liebermann. *School for Wives* was just plain awful. Liebermann hung around during rehearsals, and on more than one occasion he heard me say subtle things like "Boy, you really have to have *chutzpah* to put this on a program with *The Impresario*," and "Thank God I'm doing the *Mozart*." I was most unkind, and Liebermann never forgave me for it. He later ran the Hamburg and Paris operas, and I was never invited to sing at either place. In the mid-1970s, when I was the most famous Manon in the world—there was just no question that I owned the role—Liebermann staged a new production of *Manon* at the Paris Opéra and called in Jeannette Pilou to sing it. I know he did that to punish me for shooting my mouth off about *School for Wives*. When his production of *Manon* fell flat on its face, I was not exactly reduced to tears.

School for Wives laid a very large egg, and critics weren't knocked out by *The Impresario*, either. Audiences almost boycotted the double bill: We played our two performances to houses that were two-thirds empty. The company's nine other productions didn't do much better at the box office—attendance that season averaged just a shade over 50 percent of our seating capacity. I didn't know it then, but the City Opera had been losing business for several seasons. The previous fall, when I had joined the City Opera, Rosenstock had sat down with Morton Baum, the company's founder, to discuss the situation. They both decided that the wisest move for Dr. Rosenstock was to resign. In November 1955, Erich Leinsdorf was secretly hired to succeed Dr. Rosenstock. On April 11, 1956, after eight years with NYCO and after conducting *The Impresario*, Dr. Rosenstock formally resigned as general director of the New York City Opera. If nothing else, Leinsdorf certainly inherited a strong complement of singers.

SEVEN

I know this may sound strange, but one of the things I've always loved about Peter is that he really never gave much of a damn about my singing. Yes, he's very proud of me, and he loves my voice, and he's always respected my art and my enthusiasm for it. But with Peter, I never had to worry that he was attracted to me because he liked the idea of going out with an opera singer. Peter comes from a very musical family—his late brother, Vose, was one of the nation's finest accoustical engineers—and he loves symphonic music, but he's never been as great an opera fan.

From the moment we met, I knew Peter loved me for *me*. I didn't have to think about why I loved *him*. Peter was a bright, articulate, great-looking man who was very romantic and caring and funny and sophisticated and strong and—well, I guess you get my drift. He's also very opinionated and stubborn, but I can live with that, and have for thirty years. Peter will tell you he's put up with a similar burden, but that's nonsense. Compared to him, I'm a pushover.

After the City Opera's 1956 spring season ended, Peter and I wanted to make our marriage plans definite. We decided to get married right after his divorce became final, which we hoped would happen before the end of the year. My mother strongly objected. She insisted we wait six weeks after Peter's divorce, and since I'd already waited twenty-six years, that didn't seem like a great sacrifice.

Peter's divorce was painful and messy. That had also been true of his marriage. Peter had been married to Clara Jane Diana Thomas, a woman who ranked very high in Cleveland social circles. Her mother's family had founded Wells Fargo and American Express. Her father was in shipping—there was a lot of money there. Unhappily, Peter's wife became very ill. She was a manic-depressive alcoholic and was institutionalized several times. After their third daughter was born retarded, her illnesses got worse. Several months before I met Peter, his wife cleaned out their bank accounts and ran off with another man. Peter had had enough. He instituted divorce proceedings and incurred the wrath of Cleveland's country club set by suing for custody of the children. That was almost unprecedented thirty years ago, but Peter had won temporary custody of the girls.

It was not a wonderful situation to walk into.

I suppose it was understandable that both our families—mine more than his—strongly opposed our marriage. My mother and brothers had had a chance to get to know Peter, so they were no problem. My mother's sisters didn't approve, but at least they were cautious about what they said. My father's side of the family felt no such constraints. They'd say to me: "If your father knew you were marrying a gentile, he'd turn over in his grave."

I was very offended by that. And I think they were wrong. My father would have had a lot of knockdown drag-out arguments with Pete, but he would have liked him. Papa would not have tried to prevent me from marrying Peter. We would not have had a rift in our relationship because of my marriage. That much I know about my father.

Peter wanted me to get to know *his* father, and in July he invited me to spend a weekend at his family's summer home on Martha's Vineyard in Massachusetts. His father told Peter not to bring me along. Harry Greenough refused to meet me until Peter's divorce was final. Even then, he chose to remain aloof. I didn't meet my father-in-law until the day of the wedding.

At the wedding reception I asked him what his reaction had been when Peter told him he was going to marry a Jewish opera singer. "Well," he replied, "we were out fishing on my boat. It was terribly foggy, and we were lost. But the fishing was sensational. I had two choices. I could have thrown myself overboard, or gone on fishing. Being the intelligent man that I am, I decided to go right on fishing. I asked Peter to tell me about you. He *could* have described you as a very beautiful woman. Instead he said you were damned funny." At that point Harry Greenough turned to me and said, "Call me Dad."

I already had one staunch ally in the Greenough family before I met Peter's father. When Peter announced his intention to marry me as soon as his divorce went through, his Aunt Constance invited me to lunch at the Colony Club. Everyone called her Aunt Cocky, and she was an incredible old lady. Her husband, Sam Fuller, had been one of the original partners in Merrill Lynch. During the winter, Aunt Cocky lived in a large house in West Chop, on Martha's Vineyard. Every June she'd stroll across the street and move into her summer house. She was a remarkable woman. Aunt Cocky swam every day, played tennis until she was ninety-one, gave up golf at ninety-two, and played bridge till the day she died at ninety-eight.

When we met at the Colony Club, she was already seated at our table, smoking a cigarette in a long holder—I never saw her without a cigarette. She was a well-dressed, attractive woman. But when she greeted me I became slightly unsettled—Aunt Cocky's voice was so deep it sounded like a foghorn.

After we said hello, she stared at me for perhaps half a minute and then said, "Well, you certainly are pretty."

"Thank you," I said.

"How old are you?"

I told her I was twenty-seven. "Peter's much too old for you," she said.

"He's only twelve years older than I am," I said.

"Is that all?" she asked. I nodded. Aunt Cocky—she insisted I call her that—then asked, "What about those two little prima donnas of his?"

That was how she referred to Lindley and Nancy; Peter's third daughter, Diana, was living at a special school for handicapped children near Philadelphia. I didn't meet Diana until after Peter and I came back from our honeymoon.

I told Aunt Cocky that I didn't know Nancy and Lindley very well, but yes, I was sure there'd be some problems. At the time, I didn't know whether Peter would win permanent custody of the girls.

I felt that if he did, I'd either have a major problem with his daughters, or else a series of minor problems such as all stepmothers have to tiptoe their way through. As it turned out, I got both.

Toward the end of our lunch, she said, "You know, I can't imagine why you want to marry him—Greenough men are *very* difficult to live with."

"I can handle Peter Greenough any time, any day," I told her.

She looked at me and smiled. "What would you like for a wedding present?" she asked. Aunt Cocky and I grew very close, and she became a kind of emotional anchor for me. Whenever there was a family problem, she was there to help.

A month later I returned to Cleveland to sing at Musicarnival again. My brother Stanley had gotten a job in Cleveland, and I moved in with him and his wife, Shirley, who was then pregnant with their son Mike.

Bob Bishop was the only one of our friends who knew how serious Peter and I were about each other. Peter, meanwhile, was going through difficult times. Several of his cronies had suddenly started snubbing him. I remember Peter's saying to me one day: "They're treating me like a pariah."

That's exactly what he had become. Peter was ostracized by Cleveland's rinky-dink version of high society because he had the nerve to fight for custody of his children. That just wasn't *done*. In the 1950s, a husband couldn't get custody of his children unless he proved their mother guilty of either moral turpitude or gross neglect of duty. Peter chose gross neglect of duty and eventually won, but it was a costly victory. Cleveland's press covered his divorce as if it were a particularly grisly murder. The *Plain Dealer* was owned by the family, including Pete, so its treatment was conservative. The rest of the city's media focused their sights on a business competitor and really let Peter have it. He tried hard, but Peter wasn't able to shield the kids from hearing or reading about their mother's problems.

I spent that August getting to know Lindley and Nancy, meeting the Cleveland chapter of Peter's family, and being introduced to his buddies. I ran into a solid wall of anti-Semitism. One of Peter's friends said, "If Peter's mother was alive, she'd die all over again if she knew he was marrying a Jew."

That man has since committed suicide, and yes, I *do* hold

grudges. I can't tell you how much I resented all the anti-Semitism I encountered in Cleveland. I'd never experienced it before, probably because I'd always stayed in my own little circle and, until Bob Bishop, I'd always dated Jewish boys. Most of my dates with Bob had been spent with friends from Musicarnival. Peter was the first and only man I ever fell in love with, and I was meeting a lot of people who, like him, were rich gentiles. I was shocked by their religious bigotry. I don't even know if it had to do with the religion per se. It *did* have to do with the fact that I was a Jew. If Peter was hurt by the way his peers were reacting to his pending divorce, well, that was just a preview of how they treated him after word got out that he was going to marry a Jewish opera singer.

I just don't *understand* anti-Semitism. A crowd of us from the City Opera would often get together and go see an opera at the Met, and I realized I was often the only Jew in the group, but it never mattered to me or to my colleagues.

In Cleveland, it mattered. A lot.

The only people who welcomed me with open arms were Senator Roy Bulkeley, Peter's cousin, and Roy's wife, Helen. Helen felt that Nancy and Lindley needed a lot of help—she knew how sick their mother was. She thought I'd have a healthy influence on their lives and wanted the three of us to get to know each other as quickly as possible. To expedite that, Helen began bringing Lindley and Nancy to lunch at her house, where I'd be waiting for them. I couldn't see the girls in Peter's house, because my mother asked me not to set foot in Peter's house until his divorce was final. I *told* you I was the best daughter in the world.

I have to admit that I was very naïve. I was in love with this big, handsome man and I was going to get married. So maybe there were a couple of children I'd have to raise—I was sure everything would work out fine. I generally enter into projects with a great deal of optimism, and I'm shocked if they turn out differently from the way I've envisioned them. Lindley and Nancy were intelligent, pretty girls. I'd love them and they'd love me back, and we'd work it all out within a few weeks, and wouldn't their daddy be proud of us? No problem. Love conquers all.

Peter and I were completely infatuated with each other, and that was the only thing that counted. And, having sung too many Micaelas and never the title role, I was having a ball singing *Carmen* at

Musicarnival. Carmen is almost always sung by a mezzo-soprano. However, I didn't think twice about doing it. It was one of the few times in my life I haven't taken my work all that seriously. I just wanted to have fun with the role.

Norman Treigle, one of the skinniest singers I ever knew—Norman was 5 feet 11 and weighed 140 pounds soaking wet—had joined the City Opera two years before I did, and we'd become good friends. This absolute rail of a man had one of the finest bass voices of his generation, and I was eager to work with him. Norman played the toreador, and he was sensational. Lloyd Thomas Leech, the tenor who'd played my husband in *Fledermaus,* was Don José, the soldier Carmen seduces and spurns, and who kills Carmen in the final moments of the opera. Lloyd and I had been a good comic team in *Fledermaus,* and even though we weren't supposed to, we had spent a lot of time breaking each other up onstage. Norman and I wound up doing the same thing. That August, I think I set a world record for consecutive performances of *Carmen*—I sang eighteen in a row. Despite the fun I had, I knew Carmen really *should* be sung by a mezzo-soprano, because the role calls for a dark, sexy sound. Mezzo-sopranos have a fuller, more sensual sound in the lower register. The soprano's strength is in the beauty of her high notes. After my engagement at the Musicarnival, I never sang Carmen again.

Norman and Peter hit it off as soon as they met. Since my mother had asked me not to be seen alone with Peter, Norman acted as our chaperone. The three of us went out together several times a week, and later, Peter and I grew very chummy with Norman and his wife, Linda. Norman and I became like brother and sister. In the years to come, we performed so often and so well together that people began referring to us as the Lunt and Fontanne of the City Opera.

Peter's divorce became final at the end of September. In line with my mother's wish, we arranged to be married six weeks later. By then, the City Opera's fall season would be over, but the year before, the Semons had committed me to a long tour following NYCO's season, so our honeymoon was going to be a catch-as-catch-can affair.

Erich Leinsdorf, the City Opera's new general director, was unquestionably one of the world's greatest conductors. He had begun conducting performances at the Metropolitan Opera when he was not yet twenty-six, and he'd been head of the Rochester Philharmonic for nine years when he was hired away to take over for Dr. Rosenstock. I'd met Leinsdorf. He'd seen my work and liked it—he was one of the first conductors to catch on to me.

In his first season as general director of the City Opera, Erich cast me as Rosalinda in *Die Fledermaus* and as Philine in Ambroise Thomas's *Mignon*. Rosalinda was already a comfortable role for me—I'd sung it on tour and I'd be singing it for the third time in my three seasons with the City Opera.

I was much more excited about Philine, because one of the arias she sings, *"Je suis Titania,"* is one of the most famous and often performed coloratura soprano showpieces. Although Madame Goldentrill had been a showy role also, *The Impresario* is almost an obscure work. *"Je suis Titania"* is a kind of litmus test for coloratura sopranos. Critics and opera buffs look forward to what you can do with the aria, and if you sing it well, they get all fired up.

I didn't have a chance to work with Leinsdorf. He graciously brought Dr. Rosenstock back to conduct *Die Fledermaus,* and engaged France's Jean Morel to conduct *Mignon*. I adored working with Morel, and the feeling was mutual. We used to speak French together, and our rehearsals were always great fun. Morel had a tremendous sense of humor and was more Gallic than Jacques Tati. When he spoke English, he sounded like Peter Sellers doing Inspector Clouseau, and that would really crack us up. *Mignon* had quite a cast. Frances Bible played Mignon; Donald Gramm, a brilliant bass/baritone, played Laërte; and Emile Markow, a bass, played Lothario.

Mignon got excellent reviews, and Philine's aria lived up to its reputation as a showstopper: On opening night, I got the first standing ovation of my operatic career.

We did a lot of interesting operas that fall, but the season turned out to be a financial disaster. Leinsdorf had the makings of a great opera impresario; he had a lot of terrific ideas, but he couldn't carry them out properly on the City Opera's tiny budget. For instance, he brought in a number of talented directors and designers, but their fees far exceeded the City Opera's normal payments for those functions, and they were also not used to working under strict budgetary restraints. Leinsdorf's most controversial innovation was a revolving stage, which cost a bundle to build and install. Unfortunately, the damned thing just didn't work the way it was supposed to—it was very slow and noisy. He'd had several financial run-ins with the company's board of directors before the season started, and when it ended, Erich resigned. The City Opera lost more than $150,000 that season, which was more than 300 percent greater than any operating loss in its history. The company was in serious trouble.

Our season ended on November 3, and Peter and I set our wedding date for exactly two weeks later. The City Opera was going to play a week in Detroit, and I was supposed to sing Rosalinda in *Die Fledermaus*. Since I had to be in the Midwest, I flew to Cleveland first, where I stayed with Stanley and his wife and visited Peter. Maybe I shouldn't have traveled, because right after I got to Cleveland, I came down with a fearsome case of laryngitis. I'd sung before with laryngitis, but this time I couldn't talk, let alone sing. My mother had made my costumes, and I gave them to my understudy, Beverly Bower, and volunteered to go to Detroit and help coach her in the role.

Peter drove me there. When we got to the Shrine Auditorium, we were met by Julius Rudel and John S. White, who was then the company's administrative director. Peter had never met them, and I'm sorry to report that both men were rather rude to us. They acted as if I'd intentionally gotten sick. Peter took their attitude personally, but I tried to convince him that's the way all opera officials behave when you have to cancel and they have a crisis on their hands. After a few days in Detroit, I flew back to New York for our wedding.

On November 17, 1956, Peter and I were married by State Supreme Court Justice James McNally in Miss Liebling's studio. My mother made my wedding gown, as well as my trousseau, and I wore a veil given to me for the occasion by Jean Tennyson, my longtime patron. It was a very small wedding. The only people we invited were my mother; my two brothers and their very pregnant wives; Sue Yager, my best friend; Désiré Defrère, who still regarded Mama with lust in his heart; my Uncle Sydney, my father's youngest brother; and Peter's father, stepmother, brother Vose, and sister Barbara.

Miss Liebling played the Bridal March, and Peter and I were married standing in the same Oriental carpet medallion Miss Liebling had ordered me to stand on when I was seven years old.

The wedding took place at noon, and at five o'clock we boarded a plane to Florida. Peter and I spent our first night as husband and wife at the Miami Springs Villa, near Miami's airport. I was a twenty-seven-year-old woman and I was far from wide-eyed and innocent, but I'd lived my life in accordance with my parents' wishes. I'd been raised at a time when a Jewish girl was supposed to live at home and remain chaste until she got married, at which point her mother would weep at the thought of some man defiling her gorgeous Jewish virgin. I can't prove it, but I'll bet you anything my mother cried her eyes out that night. *I* certainly didn't.

The next morning we flew down to Nassau to begin a three-week honeymoon. An Associated Press photographer shot a picture of us upon arrival in Nassau. The photograph was printed in some papers with the following caption:

> Peter Greenough, editor of the *Cleveland Plain Dealer,* and his wife, Jackie Searles.

Jackie Searles was a boy comedian!

Peter may have been hurting a bit financially after his divorce, but he was intent on giving me my first real taste of what I've always called the Beverly Greenough treatment. When we landed at the airport in Nassau, Peter rented a fast little British sports car and drove us to a lovely villa at the Balmoral Club. Peter then let me in on his big surprise: He'd chartered Errol Flynn's yacht for us. We went down to the dock for a quick little spin, and Peter still has a photograph of me throwing up all over Errol Flynn's yacht. I also got seasick the couple of other times I went on board, so in that department, at least, the new bride was a complete washout.

Later that morning, Peter and I went swimming. Before we left the beach my new husband informed me that he'd lost his wedding ring in the water. That really annoyed me because, in my very proud manner, I'd insisted on paying for Peter's ring, which was platinum to match the one he'd given me. Peter thought I was dumb for doing that—I didn't have any money and had had to charge the ring at a Cleveland jewelry shop. When he lost the ring the first morning of our marriage, I made him pay for the one I'd bought him as well as its replacement. He considered that fair. Several years later, when our daughter was still a little girl, the three of us went swimming in the ocean off Deal, New Jersey. Peter lost his second wedding ring somewhere on the beach. The next day, my daughter went back down to the beach and found the ring. To this day, Muffy claims she's responsible for keeping our marriage together. I'm sure Dr.

Freud would have had a lot to say about Peter and his wedding bands.

Peter and I became friendly with the publisher of a New Haven newspaper who was also on a honeymoon with his second wife. The publisher had the uncomfortable habit of referring to his new bride by his first wife's name, which is not the way to score brownie points with a bride. She was very upset about it. In an effort to console the woman, Peter told her, in front of me, "Listen, the only reason I was able to go on this honeymoon is because my newspaper is on strike."

That didn't sit well with me at all. What you had were two rather forlorn new brides consoling each other while their husbands went off fishing in Errol Flynn's yacht.

Before our marriage, I'd told Peter that gardenias were my favorite flower. He thought I'd said camellias, which is why my bridal bouquet was made up of camellias. I mentioned gardenias to him again in Nassau, which was definitely a mistake. Peter disappeared for a couple of hours one day and returned with a gallon of a gardenia-scented perfume called Byzance. That was my first experience with Peter's typical behavior: Send him out for a package of cream cheese and he buys you Zabar's entire delicatessen.

My husband never buys one of anything. His attitude is contagious, too. Some years back, the Smucker's jelly people came out with a chocolate syrup called Magic Shell that hardens when poured over ice cream. When Smucker's discontinued distribution of the product on the East Coast, I panicked. I sat right down and wrote a letter to Mr. Smucker himself, who turned out to be an opera fan. He sent me a case of Magic Shell, along with an adorable note telling me the name of the lady to write to for more. There are eighteen jars to a case. I ordered six cases.

My husband is a very normal man, but his shopping habits are eccentric. Because we travel a lot, Peter's clothes take a real beating. Twice a year, he goes to Brooks Brothers and gets himself fully outfitted. The first time he orders all his summer suits, and the second time he orders all his winter suits. The thing is, he buys the same suits every year. Every once in a while he'll say, "You haven't told me whether you like my new suit."

My reply is always the same: "How can I tell it's new? It looks exactly like last year's suit." Which it is.

I think I married the world's most compulsive buyer. I soon

found out Peter buys things in quantity only because he detests shopping. He's not big on browsing, either. My husband once ordered me a sable coat from Galanos over the phone. He very emphatically said that not just *any* sable coat would do. Peter told them to make me a *great* coat. Galanos took my husband at his word: They made me a great coat. Just like the coats worn by Russian soldiers. It has big lapels and huge pockets, and whether or not that style was Peter's intention, I wound up with the most sensational sable coat I've ever seen. It never even *dawned* on Peter that I might not like it.

After our honeymoon, Peter and I flew back to Cleveland. I was there just long enough to change clothes. A year before, my agents, the Semons, had booked several concert dates for me in December. The first took place in Palestine, Texas, and the next night I sang in Baytown, Texas. When I got there, I realized I'd lost a beautiful diamond pin Peter had given me not long after he'd presented me with my engagement ring. I want you to know that some wonderful people in Palestine called me in Baytown to report that they'd found the pin and that they'd insured it and mailed it back to my new address in Cleveland.

Before Christmas, I did a concert with the Miami Symphony and was about to return home when I got a call from Earl Wrightson's manager. Earl Wrightson and his singing partner, Lois Hunt, were classical music's answer to Steve and Eydie, and wherever they played, their concerts always sold out. Their manager told me Lois was ill and asked if I'd fill in for her at a concert they were supposed to give in Florida a couple of days later. Since I was in the neighborhood, I said yes, and Peter flew down to join me—I remember that we stayed at a very elaborate resort. I'd met Wrightson before. He was a bearded, distinguished-looking baritone.

Alfredo Antonini conducted our concert, and Earl was all business onstage that night. The concert went very well, and afterward we were invited backstage to a reception given in our honor. Earl and I stood on a receiving line, which Peter wouldn't join. He felt he'd be out of place there, so he stood about ten feet away. The city's leading patrons of the arts—almost all of them women—began parading up to greet us. The woman in charge of the event brought forward the first person in line and said, "Mr. Wrightson, this is Mrs. Jones."

Mrs. Jones shook Earl's hand and said, "Mr. Wrightson, I *so* enjoyed your performance."

Earl smiled sweetly and replied, "F—k you very much."

I told myself: *I am not* hearing *this.*

Earl then turned to me and said, "Mrs. Jones, this is Miss Sills." Mrs. Jones shook my hand and told me how much she had enjoyed my performance.

When Wrightson repeated his little greeting to the second lady on line, I waved like crazy for Peter to come over. He did, and this time both of us heard Wrightson say the same thing to the next six women. Not one of them blinked an eye, or seemed to understand why Peter and I were laughing so hard.

We got back to Cleveland in mid-December. The kids gave us a warm welcome and had a great time at a big party we threw for our friends. One of the tenors with the City Opera distinguished himself that night by falling up the stairs and knocking down every painting on the stairway wall. I'd never seen anyone fall *up* a flight of stairs before, but he always was a very athletic performer.

Eileen Farrell was then in town getting ready to sing with the Cleveland Orchestra, and she was a frequent visitor. She had a very low opinion of conductor George Szell—she felt he was allowing the orchestra to drown her out. Eileen would stomp into our house after rehearsals and say, "Where the hell is the gin?" Eileen didn't really use the word *hell;* when she gets her dander up, her vocabulary starts where Earl Wrightson's left off.

My stepkids loved her, because Eileen would curse Szell in the most imaginative descriptive terms they'd ever heard. She was doing the Verdi *Requiem,* and she'd say things like "If that louse thinks he's going to have his orchestra play louder than my high C, he's got another think coming."

Okay, so she didn't say louse, either, but I think I've already used up my quota of swear words.

Eileen told the girls lots of wonderful stories. Lindley and Nancy especially liked the one about Eileen taking her little girl, Kathleen, to church one day. Kathleen told her that every time the priest walked by, she smelled whiskey. Eileen leaned over and whispered, "What?"

Her daughter said, "Whiskey."

Eileen again whispered, "What?"

And her little girl yelled at the top of her lungs: "WHISKEY! ARE YOU DEAF?"

Lindley and Nancy thought that was the best story they'd ever heard. They *really* loved it when Eileen used dirty words, because they knew I couldn't do anything about it.

At Christmas time, Peter's father and my mother came out to visit us. My mother loved Peter, but she was still apprehensive about our marriage—not because Peter wasn't Jewish, but because he had a sick ex-wife and three children. Mama told me: "If his wife was a normal woman, you could sit down and make proper arrangements about visits and how the children will be raised. But you have nobody to deal with here. You have a mentally unbalanced woman who's an alcoholic, and that's that."

In that respect, she was absolutely right. It took my mother a long time to overcome her feeling that Peter had laid too many problems on me from the very start of our marriage.

My father-in-law liked my mother because of her insistence that we maintain proper decorum and wait six weeks after Peter's divorce before getting married. Dad was a tough old bird. He was stocky, had a big bushy moustache, and very dark hair that turned pepper-and-salt when he was in his 80s. He had the look of old money, and he also had the traits one associates with that phrase. He was totally self-assured, conservative, and sophisticated.

My father-in-law and I respected and loved each other from the moment we met. I was extremely outspoken and so was he—Dad laid his cards right on the table. He often told me about the difficulties I'd face as Peter's wife, and then he'd say, "Well, now you know what the problem is, and now I'm going to help solve it."

He did, too. When I moved into the house it was still almost completely unfurnished. Peter told me to move very slowly in furnishing the place, because it would take him a while to straighten out his cash-flow problems.

The first day my father-in-law visited us, at Christmas, he and I went into the living room. I brought in a couple of dining room chairs, and after we were both seated, my father-in-law said, "Do you like living in a pink house?" I told him no, but I felt it was important to get some of the rooms furnished before worrying what the outside of the house looked like. We had twenty-five empty rooms and three maids to look after them. It was a crazy situation.

"We have to talk about this a bit," Dad said. "I can't have my grandchildren brought up in this atmosphere. It's very unpleasant. How much does it cost to paint a house white?"

I told him I had no idea.

"What about furniture in the living room and dining room?" he asked.

"Well, we do have something coming for the dining room, but I don't have anything in the living room. The piano in the music room is mine—that's my dowry."

Dad laughed and said, "Have I given you a wedding present yet?"

He knew the answer to that one.

"Okay, here's your present," he said. "First, I want you to paint the outside of the house and then get this place furnished fast—I can't have the girls walking around a house like this. And I owe you something for raising them, so go ahead and get what you need."

"Up to what point?" I asked.

"Keep me informed, and I'll tell you when it's time to stop," he said.

I didn't take full advantage of my father-in-law's generosity. Peter and I needed to have our bedroom done, but after that, I furnished only the rooms I considered important from the girls' point of view. I did our living room, dining room, the girls' little playroom, and then I made a tiny library and television room for them so they'd have a cozy place to settle when they came home from school. I talked to my father-in-law every Sunday about what I'd bought and how much I'd spent, and sometimes he was interested and sometimes he was too bored to listen. Dad paid the bills to get our house painted white and to furnish five or six rooms. At that point, I sat down with him and said, "Thank you, Dad. I think from here on in, we'll make it on our own."

We had only about twenty rooms to go. That house was just too damn big.

EIGHT

Concert dates are usually booked at least a year in advance, and for the first time in my life, I had more work than I wanted. Instead of settling in with my new husband and family, I spent January, February, and early March of 1957 on the road. I left Cleveland just after New Year's Day for concert performances in Jamestown, New York, and Athol, Massachusetts. Peter was well acquainted with Athol and the one joke about the town; he couldn't resist warning me to watch my pronunciation.

I spent the weekend before that concert at my father-in-law's farm, a six-hundred-acre spread in Concord, Massachusetts, that had been in the family for many years. Dad and I continued to hit it off as if we were blood relatives, but I didn't get anywhere with Peter's stepmother. Aunt Cocky had predicted I wouldn't.

When we first met at the Colony Club, she had said, "You'll have to win over your father-in-law, and I think you will. Forget about your stepmother-in-law—that's not going to work. If it's any consolation, I know that if Peter's mother were alive, she'd adore you."

Dad's wife was a very difficult but gutsy lady from Philadelphia. As soon as I arrived, she made it perfectly clear that I wasn't too welcome in her home. My father-in-law spotted that immediately—it would've been hard to miss. Whenever I entered a room, she left it. It wasn't until after Peter and I had children that my stepmother-in-law became verbally offensive. She and Dad had vacationed in Hawaii every year, and I remember her telling me: "We used to go to Ocho Rios in Jamaica, but we had to stop because the Jews turned it into another Miami Beach." I was about to let her have it when my father-in-law looked at me and shook his head. I knew he wanted me to cool it. For once, I held my tongue.

When the weekend was over, my father-in-law's chauffeur drove me to Athol in the longest limousine I've ever seen. It was twenty degrees below zero, and without the mink lap robe Dad wrapped me up in, I would have frozen my fanny off. Some thirty-five people came to hear me that day. I invited them all to sit down front and gave them my very best. Armen Boyajian, my accompanist, had to soak his fingers in warm water off and on during the concert. Armen later became a singing teacher, and his pupils, including Samuel Ramey and Paul Plishka, sound like a Who's Who in Opera.

My next order of business was to get ready for an eight-week tour of "A Night in Vienna," a concert program that featured the works of Johann Strauss. The tour was set to start in mid-January, so after the Athol concert, I went back to New York to begin rehearsals. I don't think I was in town for more than a day when I got an urgent call from Norman Treigle. Norman told me that the City Opera's board of directors had voted to close down the company. He asked if I'd join him and a couple of other colleagues in a final plea to save the City Opera. Of course I would.

In the days that followed, meetings were held, committees formed, memos written—a lot of frantic activity ensued. Accounts of the crisis differ, but I vividly remember that the company had actually closed down—the 1957 spring season had definitely been canceled—and that a group of us (soprano Phyllis Curtin, baritone Cornell MacNeil, Norman Treigle, and I) went over to the Yale Club and had a long meeting with Newbold Morris and Morton Baum, the company's original founders. We did a lot of talking, but the essence of our message was quite simple: The four of us and everybody else in the company were prepared to work as hard and as long as it might take to make the City Opera solvent again. We didn't need a well-known outsider to come in and function as our key figure. We suggested that

Julius Rudel be appointed general director, and that we open the company again.

Morris and Baum both thought we had a very bright idea. Julius was one of "us," and he seemed like a very democratic choice. Instead of going to an extremely famous conductor and asking him to get us out of our own mess, we'd be working with someone already in the organization, someone who fervently believed the company was worth saving.

Morris and Baum, as it turned out, had really been looking for a way to save the City Opera—it was, after all, their baby. They promised to ask the board of directors to go along with our suggestions and assured us that we had nothing to worry about. Morris and Baum made good on their promises. A week after we met at the Yale Club, the New York City Opera was back in business and Julius Rudel was our new general director.

By then, I was singing Strauss waltzes in cities up and down the East Coast. Whenever he could get away, Peter flew to wherever I was singing and we'd spend the weekend together. I didn't enjoy that tour at all. I felt lonely and guilty about not being with my husband, and even guiltier knowing I had two stepchildren who needed me at home.

When I got back to Cleveland, I made up my mind to be the best wife and stepmother anyone had ever seen. Peter and I didn't have any problems; the girls and I did. They'd been badly scarred by their parents' divorce. At Christmas, in 1955, Peter had taken the girls to his sister's home at Martha's Vineyard. While Peter was away, the girls' mother arrived at Martha's Vineyard and kidnapped the children. She took them to New York and enrolled them in Miss Hewitt's private school. Even though the Ohio court had awarded temporary custody to Peter, that decision did not have to be honored by the New York court, and so temporary custody was awarded to the girls' mother while the case was being studied. Eventually the Ohio court gave permanent custody to Peter and visitation rights to his former wife. Peter immediately returned the girls to Cleveland. By the time I met the children, I think Lindley and Nancy felt like Ping-Pong balls.

Getting them to accept me was not going to be easy—and boy, did *that* turn out to be an understatement. Even though she knew her parents had broken up before I came on the scene, Lindley was sure they would have reconciled if not for me. If they hadn't, then at least she could have continued playing the role of little mommy. Before Peter and I were married, Lindley would sit at the head of the table and tinkle a little bell to signal the maid when to serve dinner and when to clear the dishes. It was tough for her to give up that role when I arrived, and it was even tougher for me to overcome her initial hostility. Lindley was nine going on thirty; she was *not* going to be jollied into loving me. Nancy was bright and funny, but she, too, was quite angry. I had a much easier relationship with Diana, the retarded child, simply because she didn't start out resenting me. Diana was very happy to have someone visit her, write letters to her, and bring her presents. And I loved doing those things for her.

Lindley, Nancy, and I did not have a wonderful period of adjustment. If anything, it was a tug of war. There were many moments when I knew it was time to pull in the reins, but that was easier said than done; I was reluctant to scold the girls, and when I did, Peter at first didn't back me up, which only made matters worse. Peter felt guilty about having caused them a lot of pain, and he didn't want to add to their problems.

After several weeks—and every stepmother in America will iden-tify with this—it was obvious that the kids were using their situation to escape discipline. That had to change, and I was the only one who could change it. When I moved into the house, the two girls had three maids literally picking up after them. Lindley and Nancy had no sense of the need to be self-reliant in practical matters. When they took off their clothes, they left them on the floor. Most children do that, and most mothers do what I did: I'd buy them pretty dresses and pretty hangers, and go through a whole routine showing them how to use the hangers. Every morning after they left for school, I found those pretty dresses on the floor, along with both girls' paja-mas, socks, blouses, and blue jeans. I could not get them to put anything away. That finally ended on the day they came home and found all the clothing they'd left on the floor—every little sock and every pair of pajamas—tied up in an enormous knot.

The kids and I really struggled at first; then they calmed down and we observed an uneasy truce. When you're a stepmother, it's difficult to find a middle ground that's comfortable for you as well as for the children you're raising. I tried hard, and the girls tried hard, but I think we were all victims of a lousy situation.

I felt very strongly about not cutting the girls off from their mother. As soon as I moved in, I called Peter's ex-wife to make arrangements for her to see them. I planned on going to New York once a week for singing lessons, and I offered to take the children with me. I could drop the girls off at her place for the day, and then pick them up in time to make an early-evening flight back to Cleveland.

Peter's ex-wife was noncommittal about the idea. She asked me to sit down with her and her mother and discuss it further, so I insisted we make an appointment to meet at the Plaza in New York. Neither woman showed up.

I knew how much the girls wanted to see their mother, but I just couldn't pin her down. Once she went to Bermuda and sent a telegram instructing us to have the children ready to receive a telephone call from her at seven o'clock that evening. Peter and I dutifully sat the girls down next to the phone at seven o'clock, and they waited there until ten-thirty, when they both fell asleep on the sofa. The girls were so forlorn the next day that I decided it was time for SuperStepmother to spring into action. I made an appointment to visit Peter's ex-wife in New York, and the following week I went to see her.

Our meeting was strange and depressing. Clara Jane Diana Thomas Greenough was living in an East Side apartment with her mother. When we met, Jane had just undergone a series of shock treatments to bring her out of a deep depression. I don't intend this to be cruel, but she acted like a vegetable, which is how many people behave when they first come out of shock therapy. Jane was an attractive woman and she was perfectly groomed; her hair, makeup, and fingernails had all been attended to in preparation for our meeting. But she hardly spoke. It was almost as if she weren't there.

Her mother did most of the talking that day. The kids' grandmother was an artist, and all she could talk about was how much she wanted to paint my portrait because she liked my red hair. I got the feeling that Jane's mother had always treated her daughter like an ugly duckling, but believe me, the ugly duckling was far better-looking than the old mouse.

The girls and their mother never got together again.

My own family, meanwhile, had written me off. Except for Uncle Sydney, all my father's brothers and sisters felt I'd dishonored Papa by marrying outside our religion. I was also persona non grata on my mother's side of the family. Mama's four sisters thought I'd had a huge wedding reception and hadn't invited them because I was too busy showing off for Peter's fancy friends and relatives. When my mother told me that, I sat down and called all my aunts. No matter how hard I tried to convince them of the truth, they didn't believe me. My aunts didn't speak to me for five years.

We probably never would have talked again if it were not for the party my brother Stanley gave for my mother on her sixtieth birthday. When Mama got wind of it, she called all her sisters and said, "You're invited, and you'd better come. Beverly and Peter will be here, and you either accept them or we're finished. I'll never talk to you again."

All my aunts showed up. Peter was at his genial, courtly best. In fact, he had them eating out of his hand until he stood up with a drink and said, "I want to make a toast to MGM."

My aunts looked at me as if I'd married a man who'd lost his marbles. I had no idea what he was up to.

Peter had a funny little smile on his face. "To MGM—*mein Gantze mishpocheh.*"

In Yiddish, that means "my whole family." My aunts laughed and thought it was very cute of this handsome *shaygetz* to try speaking Yiddish.

But five years had passed before that night. After my marriage, my Uncle Sydney, my father's youngest brother, was the only person on either side of the family who'd talk to me. I'd invited him to the wedding because I felt that somehow Papa should be represented there. A successful lawyer who lived in Greenwich Village, Uncle Sydney had been a very special person in my life. When Papa died in 1949, I began having dinner with Uncle Sydney two or three times a week at Nino and Nella's, a little Italian restaurant in the Village. He used to take me around to art shows and all kinds of cultural events, and he was always buying me little trinkets and introducing me to artists and the rest of his cuckoo friends.

When Peter and I were married, Uncle Sydney started crying so hard during the ceremony that he had to leave the room. By then, he'd become terribly unhappy, and we all knew why. Uncle Sydney had been engaged to an adorable, gamine actress named Sidney Fox. She had dreamed of becoming a movie star, and when she got a chance to go to Hollywood, she broke off their engagement. Sidney Fox was in a couple of movies, but her career didn't take off, and for whatever reason, she committed suicide. I don't think my Uncle Sydney ever got over her.

When I visited him after my honeymoon, things weren't the same between us. Uncle Sydney had been a kind of mentor to me, but he realized I was now a married woman whose husband was a worldly man. He also saw that Peter had great wealth, was supremely confident, and was at least as well educated as he was. Uncle Sydney still loved me as much as ever, but I knew he felt that my marriage had altered our relationship. It had, but I still loved *him* as much as ever.

Just before Peter and I went back to Cleveland for the first time as man and wife, the last thing Uncle Sydney said to me was: "Well, your life is beginning and mine is over."

I saw him several times after that, but our old intimacy never returned. The following year, Uncle Sydney killed himself by jumping out the window of his law office. I was not allowed to see the note he left behind. I strongly suspect his depression over my marriage may have contributed to his decision to commit suicide.

Having spent the first few months of my marriage away from Peter and the girls, it seemed like a damned good idea to stick close to home for a while. I'd been feeling very guilty about not spending enough time with my family, so I decided to cut down on my appearances. That's not to say I was in great demand, because I wasn't. But for the first time in my life, I turned down a few jobs.

I also changed agents. I still had nothing but trust and affection for Gerard and Marianne Semon, but they'd been absorbed by the National Concerts and Artists Corporation, which was the William Morris Agency of the opera world. Luben Vichey, the head of NCAC, was a former basso who'd sung at the Met several times. He'd married an heiress from Denver who bought him NCAC, and overnight, Vichey became one of the biggest opera agents in America.

A few months before Peter and I got married, I told Vichey about our plans. He did not approve, mostly because a married singer might not devote all her energy to her career. Right about then, I sang the role of Sophie in a concert performance of *Der Rosenkavalier*. Because Leonard Bernstein was the conductor that night, the concert drew a lot of media attention and I got a lavish little write-up and my photo in *Time* magazine. After that concert Vichey walked around telling people: "For her, no marriage—only career."

Peter took offense at that. Luben should have been smarter, but I wasn't terribly surprised by what he said. He was an agent. Agents tend to steer clients away from situations that might result in lower commissions. A married woman is likely to have children, which can temporarily, and sometimes permanently, put an end to her operatic career. Vichey was merely protecting a potentially profitable meal ticket.

But then he went too far. Peter and I invited Vichey to our engagement party in New York, and he spent part of the evening advising my mother that I should stay engaged to Peter for a couple of months and then get engaged to somebody else for a few months, and really just have fun, but avoid marriage at all costs. When Peter heard about that from my mother, well, that was the death knell for NCAC. We didn't have time to take care of it then, but Peter decided to buy me out of my contract with NCAC. He did that when I got back from the Strauss tour.

The only other major agency that handled opera singers was Columbia Artists Management. Miss Liebling arranged an appointment for me with the president of Columbia Artists, and Kurt Weinhold kept me waiting for two hours before seeing me. The man wasn't interested, thank you. He told me he had plenty of sopranos in his stable; I told him I wasn't a horse, and that was that.

Years later, at the 125th anniversary concert of the New York Philharmonic in Avery Fisher Hall, Mr. Weinhold came over to me and said, "Wouldn't you like me and Columbia Artists to manage you? We could do *so* much for you."

I said, "I would never work for anyone who keeps people waiting for two hours and who considers singers to be part of a stable."

Soon after I decided to change agents I went down to Baltimore to sing *Don Giovanni* with my skinny pal, Norman Treigle. His manager, Ludwig Lustig, was a polite, middle-aged gent with an enormous nose—he looked just like William Steinberg, the conductor of the Pittsburgh Symphony. Whenever and wherever Norman sang, Lustig always showed up, and that impressed me a lot. Lustig knew I'd left NCAC, and after he heard me sing with Norman, he invited me to sign with him. His client list didn't include a single star, but Norman told me Lustig worked very hard for his people, so I decided to become his client. And Norman proved to be right: Lustig *did* work hard for his singers. He set up many more auditions than NCAC had lined up for me in the previous couple of years. And he was sensitive enough to understand that as a new bride with a built-in family, I needed a little time to get my bearings.

Setting up house in Cleveland, adjusting to the kids, meeting their mother, helping the City Opera stay alive, going on a long, dreary tour, being shunned by my family, getting a new agent—the first three months of 1957 were one laugh after another. And I would not be going to New York to sing in the City Opera's spring season. The previous April, two days before Dr. Rosenstock's resignation from the post of general director, Morton Baum, chairman of the City Opera's finance committee, had announced the cancellation of the company's spring '57 season. I had been reassured by Julius Rudel that the spring season had been dropped in order to give the money men ample time to reorganize the company's financial structure. Julius had told me not to worry—we were definitely on for the fall. That was just as well for me, because it gave me a chance to get further acquainted with Cleveland and to really settle into our house.

Cozy, it wasn't. The house had been designed by President Garfield's son, who evidently had a headful of grandiose ideas. Unfortunately, none of them took Cleveland's climate into account. The rooms were huge, the ceilings were very high, and even with all the fireplaces going, it was almost impossible to keep that place warm. I was into the "layered look" in clothes long before it was fashionable. And indoors, to boot. I can't remember ever feeling warm in Cleveland except on July fourth—*if* the sun was shining.

I have to confess that I didn't do much housework, but then again, I wasn't allowed to. Peter had grown accustomed to having three maids and a laundress, and they'd grown accustomed to having a place to live. During the day, the ladies wore pink or green uniforms, and at night their uniforms were black-and-white. My most arduous household chore was finding things for them to do. The house may have been big, but at the rate we were furnishing it, each maid had one room to take care of. Two of them were openly rooting for Peter's ex-wife to make a comeback, and they let me know it would be peachy with them if I took a permanent hike. I didn't keep them around too long.

I don't know if the term was in use then, but if you think *culture shock* is a mild little reaction to new surroundings, try leaving a one-bedroom apartment in Manhattan for a twenty-five-room mansion on the outskirts of Cleveland. I had no idea how to come to grips with that house. When my father-in-law gave me the green light, I went out and bought oversized furniture to fill up some of those oversized rooms. Surprise, surprise: I couldn't seem to find a comfortable place to plop down during the day. And lonely? God, I was lonely. After the kids went off to school each morning, I'd go into my music room and play the piano for hours on end.

That was almost heaven compared to our social life. We did a lot of entertaining at home for a small circle of friends—a *very* small circle, many of whom were Pete's supportive office pals. The first friend I made in Cleveland was a woman named Fredonia Black, who'd studied singing with Estelle Liebling. Miss Liebling knew I was having a rough time in Cleveland and called Fredonia to ask her to look after me. Fredonia was a terrific, energetic lady who loved to sing and who loved the theater. She was about twenty years older than I, but you almost had to look twice to see that. She was a cute, perky blonde with a wry sense of humor. Fredonia and her husband were prominent members of Cleveland's social set. Bob Black was chairman of the White Motor Company, which was then one of the nation's biggest corporations.

Fredonia knew all the ins and outs of Cleveland society, and didn't particularly care for it. Through her, we met two other couples we liked: Don and Lee Pierce, and Lee and Eleanor Bayer. Eleanor was a writer and became my closest friend. She and her husband were both Jewish, and they shared my unflattering view of Cleveland's establishment. Eleanor later divorced Lee and married movie director Frank Perry, with whom she wrote *David and Lisa*. Eleanor died a few years ago. We also became friendly with Carol and Hank Greenberg. Hank had played baseball for the Detroit Tigers and had been one of the greatest home run hitters of his time. Newt and Anita Parks were the fifth couple in our little circle. Anita was up to her elbows in children—I think she had six—and was not happy with her marriage. She and her husband didn't get along very well, and their final argument took place during a dinner party at our house. I wound up being called on to testify at their divorce hearing.

Peter and I both looked forward in those days to the opening of two seasons: the Cleveland Orchestra's and the Cleveland Indians'. Peter was a real nut about baseball. He knew I'd always loved the sport and couldn't wait to take me to Municipal Stadium, where we would root, root, root for the home team—*Peter's* home team: the Boston Red Sox. That was the only team we ever saw the Indians play. Such behavior by a Cleveland newspaper executive could be considered odd only by those unacquainted with the unceasing—and usually unrequited—love Bostonians have for the Red Sox. They remain eternal optimists even though they know better. Come September, the Red Sox *always* seem to find innovative ways to lose. People who love the team blame its failures on nature or fate, and then impatiently await the following April. That's when Bostonians, wherever they may be, again start viewing the world through rose-tinted glasses. Let me put it this way: Red Sox fans are crazy.

Peter certainly was. What kind of man drags his wife and daughters to a ball game two hours before the first pitch is thrown? A Red Sox fan. My husband. The kids didn't mind, because we'd buy them all the hot dogs, popcorn, and little baseball doodads they wanted. As a true died-in-the-wool Red Sox fan, Peter felt it incumbent upon him never to be seen at a game without a beer in his hand.

The reason we got there so early was that Peter loved to see the Red Sox go through their warm-up drills. The first time we went, Peter called my attention to Ted Williams, Boston's great left fielder. By then, he was nearing the end of his long and brilliant career, but you'd never have known that judging by all the line drives he hit during batting practice.

Williams probably had played hundreds of games in Municipal Stadium, but before the start of fielding practice, he always went through the same little ritual. Williams would walk around left field and examine the turf like a gardener, looking for bumps, dips, divots, rises—he checked out his territory until he felt thoroughly comfortable and familiar with it.

I realized there was a lesson in that for me. My two stage screw-ups had taken place because I hadn't checked out all my props—the Valkyrie helmet in San Francisco and those golden slippers in New York. On other occasions, when a bed, a chair, or a table had been placed several feet from where it belonged, I'd had to make on-the-spot adjustments. Well, if a baseball player could prepare himself in a way that helped eliminate surprises, why couldn't an opera singer?

And so I started what I always called my Ted Williams Drill. I'd be out onstage an hour before every performance to check where each piece of furniture was placed and to make sure I had all my props. My props were important to me. That fall, when I sang *Traviata* at the City Opera for the first time, I had to stare into a hand mirror and sing about how awful I looked—and just as I did that, an offstage light caught the mirror and reflected so brightly into my eyes that I had to turn away, thereby ruining an important moment. Before the next performance, I solved that problem by using hair spray on the mirror until it turned cloudy.

The prop department always knew which mirrors and fans were mine. A small point, perhaps, but the use of familiar props gave me an extra edge of confidence. Edgar Joseph, the costumer, pinned a note to my Act I *Traviata* gown. It said SILLS' PILLS. I used a little pillbox in the opera, so they sewed a small pocket in the front of the gown to hold the box.

When the Cleveland Indians' season was over in late September, we had only a short time to wait: The Cleveland Orchestra's season began in October. Peter is a great enthusiast about symphonic music, and he and I shared a box at the symphony with Bob and Fredonia Black. We went every Thursday night. The Cleveland Orchestra performed through April, which dovetailed nicely with the start of the baseball season.

Aside from our small dinner parties, the ball games, and the concerts, our social life was restricted in the true sense of that word. Peter's Cleveland relatives saw us only on family occasions. Emery May Norweb, Peter's first cousin—his mother and her father were sister and brother—was president of the Cleveland Museum, and she was a very wealthy and powerful woman. Each year she gave a Christmas party for all the relatives, most of whom flew in for the occasion from other parts of the country. About sixty members of the Holden-Norweb clan would sit down at an enormous dining table and we'd be waited on by servants wearing white gloves.

When I went there for my first Christmas dinner, one of the guests came up to me and said, "For God's sake, pretend you've never seen me." Well, for God's sake, I had no idea who he was. Before the end of the evening, I finally remembered that the man had been a member of the Hour Glass Club, and that he used to stand next to the piano and sing very, very loudly.

Emery May and Peter and I were actually neighbors; her enormous house, like ours, was on Lake Erie. I point that out to underscore the fact that we saw her only at the annual family Christmas dinner and when the Metropolitan Opera came to Cleveland each year. Peter was a guarantor of the Met's tour, and we'd bump into her at a couple of parties honoring the Met's performers. That was it.

During this period a lot of Peter's friends became his former friends. I thought it was incredibly cruel of them to punish Peter because he'd married me. I took all those slights personally, and I shouldn't have. These people weren't sore at Peter because he'd married *me*; they were sore at Peter because he'd married a *Jew*.

I told you I was naïve about the kids? Well, I was far more naïve about anti-Semitism. I thought Peter's family and friends would avoid me at first because I was Jewish, but I was sure they'd become my friends once they got to know me. It never occurred to me that they wouldn't *allow* themselves to get to know me. Again, it wasn't anything personal. I wasn't Beverly; I was a Jew. For me, Cleveland was a five-year freeze-out in more ways than one.

I found myself pining for New York, but that only made me feel worse. My husband's work was in Cleveland, and I couldn't very well pressure him to leave just because I wasn't enjoying myself. Starting with the summer he turned eighteen, Peter had spent all his professional life working for the *Plain Dealer,* and he had every intention of eventually becoming the newspaper's editor-in-chief. I was just going to have to get used to Cleveland. My only alternative was to ask Peter to scuttle the goal he'd been working toward for almost twenty-five years. If I did that, I didn't deserve to be his wife.

Not coincidentally, I began reevaluating whether or not I truly wanted a career as an opera singer. I decided I didn't. I'd been at it long enough to know there were very few places to sing and that I hadn't really gotten anywhere. I was quite willing to confine my singing to the City Opera's short seasons and summer appearances at Cleveland's Musicarnival. I was twenty-eight years old, and I wanted to have a baby. If and when I became a mother, I wouldn't want to leave my child's upbringing to a succession of nannies while I went off to sing opera for months at a clip—and I'd probably never be confronted with that conflict, anyway. I had yet to set the opera world on its ear, and that no longer seemed very important to me. I looked into my heart and saw no ambition there.

That summer, I sang *Tosca* at Musicarnival and *Time* magazine did a piece about the performance. In the fall, when the City Opera reopened, Julius cast me as Sonia in *The Merry Widow* and Violetta in *La Traviata*. I'd been singing Violetta since that Charles Wagner tour six years earlier, but I'd never done the role in New York. I caused a mild stir among opera critics.

Julius, with John White overseeing the financial side of the business, performed admirably in his first season as the company's general director and principal conductor. Costs were down, attendance was rising a little, and the City Opera was at least temporarily on solid ground again.

When I returned home, I learned that Jean Morel, the wonderful, funny Frenchman who'd been my conductor for *Mignon,* would be conducting the Metropolitan Opera during its annual one-week visit to Cleveland. I couldn't wait to see him again, and I planned a big party in his honor. I did the whole bit—formal invitations, caterers, florists, musicians; nothing was too good for my Jean. I invited forty people. Our darling cousins Roy and Helen Bulkeley came, but even though many others had accepted, nobody else showed up. Nobody.

I'd put up with some hard times since coming to Cleveland, but this was the worst. Forget little emotions like anger, fury, or rage. After that night, and for all the rest of the nights I lived in Cleveland, I was a bitter woman. I felt utterly trapped.

NINE

It would be an understatement to say that I looked forward to leaving Cleveland to spend April of 1958 singing with the City Opera.

The season itself was going to be highly experimental despite the company's precarious financial condition. The City Opera was once again flat broke, and Morton Baum, our co-founder, made the rounds of foundations looking for grant money. Baum got a nice reception at the Ford Foundation. As was true of the Rockefeller and other foundations, the Ford people didn't issue grants to conduct business as usual. A specific new project had to be proposed by us and approved by them. Baum favored the idea of two seasons devoted entirely to American operas. Julius Rudel worried about the public's response at the box office, but the Ford Foundation and Baum prevailed. They gave the company $100,000 to be spent on our All-American 1958 spring season.

One of the highlights of that season would be the New York premiere of *The Ballad of Baby Doe,* a marvelous work by Douglas Moore. Then sixty-five, Moore continued to get better as he got older. In 1951, *Giants in the Earth,* only the third opera he'd ever written, had earned Moore a Pulitzer Prize in music. People who'd seen it told me *The Ballad of Baby Doe* was a modern masterpiece. Moore's opera chronicled the rise and fall of Horace Tabor, a fabulously wealthy Colorado silver baron who left his wife for Baby Doe, a miner's wife. Their love affair was scandalous and romantic, and they both came to an unhappy end. In 1899, three years after the United States abandoned the silver standard, a bankrupt Horace Tabor died in Baby Doe's arms. Horace's last request of Baby was that she never sell "the Matchless Mine" that had been the source of his wealth. In 1935, Baby Doe was found frozen to death at the entrance of the long-abandoned mine.

It's a beautiful love story, and Moore had written beautiful music for it. I wanted to play Baby Doe, but my chances of doing it were slim. *The Ballad of Baby Doe* had had its world premiere in Central City, Colorado, in July 1956. When it was being cast, I'd conveyed my interest in the role to Emerson Buckley, who conducted the opera's world premiere. He told me to forget about auditioning for it: he thought I was too big to satisfy Dr. Moore's conception of Baby Doe. Dolores Wilson, a small, perky protégée of one of the Rockefeller women, sang Baby Doe in that premiere. For whatever reason, Moore wasn't happy with her performance. He wanted a new Baby Doe for his opera's New York premiere, which would again be conducted by Buckley, one of the New York City Opera's resident conductors. The fact that the role had opened up again should have cheered me, but it didn't. Buckley and I had worked well together years before, but we'd had a big falling out. Buckley had said something to deliberately annoy me, and since I was still a quick-mouth then, I'd told him I thought men who grew beards were trying to prove something. Buckley had a full beard. I didn't think he'd be in my corner.

Dr. Moore and Buckley auditioned more than a hundred sopranos for the role of Baby Doe, and rejected them all. I learned that in a telephone call from Julius Rudel. Julius kept phoning me in Cleveland, urging me to come to New York and audition. Buckley surprised me when *he* called and invited me to try out. Julius then sent me Baby Doe's two big arias. I told him he was being ridiculous. In the opera, Baby Doe is described as a fluffy kitten on a satin pillow. Well, I hadn't shrunk since that original Baby Doe was cast. I was still five feet eight, which is hardly anyone's idea of a fluffy kitten.

Julius wouldn't take no for an answer, and then Peter got into the act; when *he* wouldn't take no for an answer, well, that was something else again. Peter cooked up an elaborate, completely trans-parent plan to get me to New York. His birthday was on February 6, and he asked me to celebrate it with him by flying to New York to see Lena Horne in *Jamaica,* a hit Broadway musical. I knew what was coming next: Since we'd be in New York, he thought I might as well audition for Dr. Moore.

Peter and I loved *Jamaica,* but I wasn't thrilled about the audi-tion part of the deal. I *still* had a lot of the street kid in me, and didn't like being put down without having a chance to answer back. I've already told you I was sensitive about my size, and when I was told that first time not to bother auditioning because I was too *large,* well, somebody pressed the wrong button.

So—I was too big for the part? Well, I'd show them *big.* I wasn't going to be a few inches too tall; I was going to be a *foot* too tall. The day before the audition, I went to Bergdorf Goodman and bought a white mink hat the size of a shako and a pair of shoes with spike heels. I wasn't trying to be theatrical, as I had been in my final audition with Dr. Rosenstock. Moore had probably agreed to hear me as a courtesy to Julius, but that didn't mean he'd changed his mind about wanting a tiny Baby Doe. Moore might turn me down, but he wouldn't *get* me down. I dressed up like a skyscraper to show Moore that *I,* not he, was boss of my destiny.

The audition was held at the City Center, and when I walked on-stage I must have stood about six feet five. I didn't show up with a chip on my shoulder—it was more like a great big brick. When I got to center stage, I said, "Dr. Moore, this is how big I am before I sing, and I'm going to be just as big when I finish. So if I'm too *big* for your Baby Doe, you can save my energy and your time by saying so right now."

I'd never met Douglas Moore until that moment. He had bushy, cottonlike white hair and the kindest face I'd ever seen. I could tell he was very surprised and taken aback—shocked, really—by my aggres-siveness. Moore walked up to the front of the stage and said, "Oh, Miss Sills, you look just fine to me."

I started singing Baby Doe's aria the Willow Song at a very brisk tempo, which is how I'd taught it to myself—I'd never heard it performed. While I was singing, Buckley suddenly walked down the center aisle and began conducting me, slowing me down. Don't ask me how, but at that moment I knew I had the job.

When I finished the Willow Song, Moore said, "Miss Sills, you *are* Baby Doe."

The chance to play her represented a big step up for me, and I was very grateful for the opportunity. Dr. Moore was a dear, sweet man, and Buckley and I really made music together. After the opera opened, I understood their caution about Baby Doe's size. The opera world has a longstanding tradition of allowing fans to greet singers backstage after a performance. Most people who came back to meet me were surprised—in some cases, startled—that the fluffy little kitten they'd seen onstage was actually a rather large cat. I was still the tallest kid in the class, but at least I could *play* petite.

Baby Doe was a difficult role. Baby's got a lot to sing, and her hardest aria comes at the very end. To sing the part, you need to sustain a high energy level all the way through.

She's also a wonderful dramatic character. Baby Doe is the classic Other Woman. It's hard to make her sympathetic, because audiences always feel terribly sorry for Horace Tabor's wife, Augusta. Augusta isn't the kind of woman who invites an audience to think *No wonder her husband left her*. Not at all. Moore wrote a wonderful aria for Augusta that lets you know she's a formidable lady from New England who, in keeping with the times, is strait-laced and uptight— but who's also very much in love with her husband. We performed *The Ballad of Baby Doe* during four of the next five seasons, and the women who played Augusta, Martha Lipton and Frances Bible, were awfully good.

Horace Tabor was played by Walter Cassel, who'd been sensational in the role when *Baby Doe* had premiered in Central City. Cassel, a great baritone, approached his role like a Method actor. Regardless of where we were, he always called me Baby, and working with him produced the most intense acting I'd done up to then. Each time Horace died in Baby's arms, I really *did* start crying.

Cassel also made me laugh onstage. Walter had a real problem with one rather insignificant line. When four dandies warn Horace Tabor that the silver standard is doomed, he gets angry and shouts, "You pussyfooting pipsqueaks." Walter came reasonably close, but never nailed it down. I'd be onstage with him when Walter would come out with "You pissy-footing popsqueaks," or "You possy-footing pupsqueaks." Walter and I both knew he'd flub the line, and each time he did, I could not stop laughing. The audience never reacted, because even in English it's hard to understand most words sung in an opera.

In any case, as soon as I knew I could handle the arias Dr. Moore had written for Baby Doe, my biggest challenge was to make her a real woman and a woman the audience would like. Over the years I've seen a lot of singers play Baby Doe as a fortune hunter who deliberately set out to snare Tabor. Maybe she did, but I saw that interpretation as a trap: As the opera progresses, it becomes very clear that Baby really *does* love Tabor.

I think Moore himself was a little ambivalent about Baby Doe. Moore wrote exquisitely beautiful, simple music for her—and you just don't do that for a scheming woman. I felt those two things gave me some leeway to portray Baby as a more likable woman. I found the key to my whole interpretation early in the first act, when Baby Doe sings, "I'm not good at judging people; live and let live is my motto." I tossed off the words with a small grin on my face, and made sure it didn't sound like a smart-ass remark.

After that, I softened Baby Doe as much as I could. I showed her as very reluctant to get involved with Tabor, which might not be historically accurate but nobody can prove otherwise. After she and Horace get together, Baby has the time of her life spending his money in typical *nouveau riche* fashion. I don't think that makes her wicked. Moore didn't think so, either, for he ends the opera with Baby Doe quite old and singing a long, heavenly aria about meeting Horace again in Beulah Land.

The Ballad of Baby Doe opened on April 3, 1958, less than two months before my twenty-ninth birthday. By then, being an opera singer had become second nature to me. I felt I could do any coloratura soprano role ever written, and I also thought I was a good actress. Nothing that subsequently happened in my career really surprised me, because I always knew what I was capable of doing. If that sounds egotistical, try to understand that when you're in the performing arts you need a certain amount of ego, a certain self-assurance, or else you'd never have the guts to face an audience. So I was never *surprised* by my capabilities, but until *The Ballad of Baby Doe,* I don't think I'd ever fully demonstrated them. We all thought Moore's opera was something special, but we weren't sure if we would do it justice. Instead of preparing *Baby Doe* at a leisurely, painstaking pace, we got it ready almost the way Peter and his colleagues used to put the Cleveland *Plain Dealer* to bed: with skill, economy, and great haste. Because Moore had delayed hiring his Baby Doe until mid-February, we had less than six weeks to prepare the opera. Even though we rushed like crazy, we never found time for a stage rehearsal of the opera's last scene, in which I sang Baby Doe's final aria. That was somewhat worrying, but on opening night, once the curtain went up, who had time to think about it?

I'd certainly had some fine nights as a performer, particularly whenever I sang Violetta in *La Traviata,* but at that point, nothing compared to the magic of my opening night performance in *The Ballad of Baby Doe.* For the first of perhaps a dozen times in my career, everything I did worked perfectly. I'd never experienced anything approaching that feeling before. Matters were clicking along magnificently, and then I suddenly found myself singing Baby Doe's final aria. I wanted to call timeout; I had no idea what I was supposed to do. A spotlight was shining straight into my eyes, and when I looked down at Buckley in the pit, he was motioning me to move toward the back of the stage. So I started walking backward, and then all of a sudden Buck motioned for me to sit down. I felt behind me with my foot, and sure enough, there was a stool. So I sat. I was singing nonstop while all this was going on, and I was very curious to see where it would all lead. I felt the answer before I saw it: Stage snow started falling on me. No one had bothered to tell me the opera ends with Baby Doe huddled down in a snowstorm. It didn't matter. The ending worked perfectly.

Everything had. I usually left theaters feeling a bit disappointed or angry with parts of my performance. Not *that* night. I felt I'd performed flawlessly—if I were a gymnast, even judges from Russia, Iran, and Libya would have given me a 10. No other soprano in the world could have matched my performance that night. I believed it then, and I believe it now.

Much of what I did vocally in my career was done purely by instinct. That was because nature had given me a voice and because Estelle Liebling was such a phenomenal teacher. However, if I wanted to analyze coloratura singing, I would suggest that there are three different categories for the coloratura soprano: the "impersonal, me-chanical" kind—hitting the notes—of which I consider the Queen of the Night in *The Magic Flute,* Olympia in *The Tales of Hoffmann,* and

Zerbinetta in Richard Strauss's *Ariadne auf Naxos* prime examples; the high, lyrical parts which demand endless breath control, arching legato lines, and sustained pianissimo singing, all in the very high soprano register, of which Sophie in *Der Rosenkavalier* and Baby Doe are two examples; and then, of course, the true *bel canto* coloratura with its equally long arching lines and the necessary breath control, but with a wonderful freedom to interpret sorrow, joy, despair, pride, and defiance through trills, runs, interval jumps, and so forth. My preference for the *bel canto* coloratura was predicated on this freedom to "act" with my voice and to color it differently for various parts. Why did I use a darker vocal quality for the slow part of the *I Puritani* mad scene than for the slow part of the *Lucia* mad scene? Not only because I was differently inspired by the music of Bellini than by that of Donizetti, but also because the character of Elvira and the situation of that moment in the opera dictated that approach to me. Rationally, I cannot explain the decision for the two different colors. The important aspect is that the vocal line of the *bel canto* style gave me the freedom to do this.

Of all of the roles I undertook, I consider the vocal delivery (not the characterization) of Zerbinetta the most astounding. Here was that so-called "almost mechanical" coloratura, and what made the challenge even tougher was the fact that Erich Leinsdorf, who had invited me to sing it in concert form with the Boston Symphony, talked me into doing the part in the original version. "High E's are bad enough," I said to Erich. "Now you want me to go up to F-sharps! I can't!"

"Just keep looking at me," Erich reassured me, "and you'll make it."

By God, he was right, and I don't have him alone to thank for it but certainly also the phenomenal technique Miss Liebling taught me. When that technique was absorbed by me first as a child and then as a young girl, I wasn't aware of what was happening to me. It came so gradually that it became second nature. In retrospect I would say that if I was able to do Zerbinetta, Queen Elizabeth, Lucia, Manon, and Louise, it was because the vocal chords responded perfectly to what I wanted them to do and because the breath control was my lifeline to whatever I wished to express vocally. This technique allowed me a much wider and richer range in the soprano repertoire than a lot of other singers with big international careers. In essence, I never considered myself a specialist.

The morning after the *Baby Doe* opening, we got a terrific review from *The New York Times,* but when I read through the music pages of the *Herald Tribune,* I was very upset to see they hadn't reviewed the opera. Very drily, Peter said, "Do you mind if I read the rest of the paper?"

He then handed me the *Tribune's* news section. "Here's your review," he said.

The *Herald Tribune* had run a rave review on the front page. There are a few moments in life when you realize you've become famous. That's one of them—when you make the front page of one of the most powerful newspapers in the country. The *Herald Tribune* is history now, but even today, when I make the front page of *The New York Times,* there's still a part of me that thinks: *My goodness, look at that!* I also feel that way when I see my name in crossword puzzles!

I did three performances of *Baby Doe* in eight days, and that was it for my spring season with the City Opera. In the fall, I went back and repeated *Baby Doe,* and also sang my two other biggies, Violetta in *La Traviata* and Rosalinda in *Die Fledermaus.*

The *Ballad of Baby Doe* turned out to be one of the most successful operas I ever did. It was the first major triumph of my career, and for a long time I thought it might be the only one. Although people began paying attention to me after *Baby Doe,* a full *eight* years passed before I experienced the same combination of artistic accomplishment and public recognition.

I was still very lonely in Cleveland, but I was learning to cope with it. I had a lot of time on my hands and structured my days with piano and singing practice and with learning how to cook. Relations with my stepdaughters continued to improve. Nancy and Lindley were like fire and ice. Nancy was terribly affectionate, but either unwilling or unable to come to terms with her parents' divorce. Lindley was almost the exact opposite of her younger sister. At eleven years of age she was self-contained and mature beyond her years. Unlike Nancy, Lindley couldn't be cuddled, but she liked talking to me and she was an engaging conversationalist. Lindley was a brilliant student, and it was fascinating to watch her grow up. There was still a gulf between me and the kids—that would never change—but at least we seemed to be making some progress.

I drove the children around town a lot in those days and also ran a lot of errands. I'd learned to drive in New York and considered myself a good driver, but for some reason I kept banging up Peter's station wagon. I simply couldn't park it without denting it. I finally found out why: Peter had had the station wagon custom-built three feet longer in back to accommodate his ex-wife's harp. I don't know if it happened by chance or design, but after I found out why the station wagon was so long, I almost systematically destroyed it, a fender at a time. I finally prevailed on Peter to get me a car of my own. He came through with a blue Buick convertible with a powder-blue top, which was very flashy for Bratenahl.

Peter and I had been happily and diligently trying to have a child of our own. In 1958 we each got the Christmas present we wanted: By late December, I knew I was pregnant.

The baby wasn't due until July 25, and Peter encouraged me to do my spring stint with the City Opera. In April 1959, I again sang *Baby Doe* and added a new role to my repertoire: the Coloratura in the world premiere of *Six Characters in Search of an Author*. Hugo Weisgall had written an operatic adaptation of the Pirandello play, and I thought the project would be a lark. It was more like an albatross. The direction seemed a bit strange, and at one point I found myself on a stepladder, quite unsure of what I was doing there. The conductor, Sylvan Levin, had been conversing with a couple of other cast members, and when he paused for a breath I asked him what my character was supposed to do while on the stepladder. Levin said, "Don't talk to me while I'm talking to someone else."

"I'll go you one better," I said. "I won't sing while you're conducting."

I stalked off the stage and out of the building. Levin could find himself another Coloratura; I quit. I was six months pregnant and didn't need to put up with nonsense, much less climb stepladders. Rudel and John White came after me and talked me back into the opera. I probably shouldn't have listened to them—the opera was a box-office and critical bomb. Douglas Watt's negative review in the New York *Daily News* was headlined SIX CHARACTERS IN NEED OF A COMPOSER. Still, I got warm praise. The conductor did not.

I returned to Cleveland in May, then was back in New York in June to record the City Opera's original cast album of *The Ballad of Baby Doe*. By then, I was seven months pregnant. My last performance with the City Opera had been on May 2, and at that point I'd gained very little weight and hadn't told anyone I was pregnant. When I showed up at our recording session wearing a maternity dress and looking enormous, most of my colleagues were very surprised. One of the orchestra members announced to everyone: "When this woman wants to have a baby, she has it in a hurry."

All of us were new to recording and frightened out of our wits. At that point, it was a great privilege to be asked to make a recording, and except within the opera world's inner sanctum, nobody had heard of any of us. Emerson Buckley, who conducted the session, warned us that because of the expenses involved, there wasn't enough money for retakes—we had to get everything right the first time. We'd sung *Baby Doe* a number of times, and I doubt that any part of the album was done in more than two takes. We were in and out of that studio as quickly as possible.

Our recording of *Baby Doe* did not set the opera world on fire. In fact, it didn't start selling until many years later, when Deutsche Grammophon purchased the recording and rereleased it with a new album cover that carried my name in big letters. They made a lot of money on *The Ballad of Baby Doe*. None of the singers got a penny more than the $320 we were originally paid for making the record.

I never really enjoyed making records because I missed the audience, the staging, and the stage timing. I also found that a recording studio's acoustics give little indication of what the engineers are hearing in the control room; I rarely knew how a take had gone until I actually went inside the control room and listened to it. As a result, I felt little personal connection with my recordings. I can't even say I did them for the money, because I routinely gave my royalties away to various charities. My records served only one purpose: to document my career. I think at least a few of them—*Manon*, the Mozart/Strauss album, and my recordings of Donizetti's three queens—will explain what all the fuss was about.

Of all my recordings, *Manon* seemed to me the closest I ever came to re-creating one of my stage performances in a recording studio. Instead of delivering a purely vocal performance, I sang

Manon as if I were onstage, using every nuance and every level of passion in my voice that an audience would hear in a full production.

Actually, until I retired, I hadn't listened to any of my recordings from start to finish. Peter has always said I can't stand the sound of my own voice, but that's not exactly true. I find it embarrassing hearing Peter play one of my records while I'm in earshot. Also, because I had approval rights on which takes would be used, I'd heard them in the studio, and that was enough.

The first time I really listened to my records outside a studio was during the summer of 1985, when I was signing albums in Tower Records on a promotional tour for EMI, which had remixed and rereleased a number of my recordings. I've still never sat down and listened to all the albums from beginning to end, but now I'm curious.

The one album I *have* listened to is *The Ballad of Baby Doe*. People often say I didn't come into my own vocally before 1966, but I think the *Baby Doe* album shows that I was there all along. In fact, if I'd been a European, I believe that album would have established me as a major artist. Because I was an American, nothing happened. In those days, most American singers were the Rodney Dangerfields of the opera world—we got no respect. I really believe my performance on the *Baby Doe* album is an extraordinary piece of singing. The high D pianissimos, the high E's, a fluid voice that's perfectly on pitch—it all comes through on that recording.

When we finished the *Baby Doe* album, I came right back home to have our baby. I was so large by then that I had to argue my way on board our flight from New York to Cleveland. I wasn't actually cutting it all that close. Our baby was due on July 25, but was in no hurry to arrive. I gave birth to our daughter, Meredith Holden Greenough, on August 4, 1959.

It wasn't an easy delivery. I was in labor for seventeen hours, and when I asked to see my baby, the doctors wouldn't bring her to me. They told me I'd given birth to a daughter weighing eight pounds eleven ounces, so I knew I had a good strapping kid, but they simply wouldn't let me see her. I thought that was strange and got very upset. They kept telling me: "You'll see her later." I hoped they were just trying to see that I got some rest after that long labor, but I knew better. Something was wrong.

Finally, one of the doctors told me my daughter had been born with hyaline membrane disease and yellow jaundice. Muffy—we never called her Meredith—was having trouble breathing and had been placed in an incubator. Hyaline membrane disease, a respiratory disorder, is still a leading cause of death among premature infants, but in many cases it can now be controlled with drugs. I've always found it very interesting that I never wanted to know any details of that ailment. When I finally saw Muffy for the first time, she had a fever of 105 degrees and was blond from head to toe. She was completely yellow and breathing very fast. Muffy survived hyaline membrane disease because she was such a big child; she went into that incubator at close to nine pounds and came out weighing seven.

Muffy's case of yellow jaundice, a blood disease, was equally life-threatening. Physicians measure the condition of jaundiced blood in terms of numbers. The specialist we brought in told us that if my daughter's blood measured minus 21, she would need a complete blood change. That's considered a drastic measure.

Muffy's blood reached minus 19 before she began responding to treatment. When I finally got my daughter home, eight days after she was born, her little heels had dozens of needle marks in them—that's where she'd been injected. I expected her to be delicate and sickly, but from the moment she came home, Muffy was a happy, resilient kid.

We were now a family in every way.

T E N

Muffy was an absolute delight—
a big, fat, bright, funny kid. I'd never seen a child as funny as Muffy.
She was constantly entertaining me, always finding ways to make me
laugh. Her stepsisters seemed to love her as much as Peter and I did.
To be accurate about it, I was *nuts* about my baby. I couldn't wait to
get her up in the morning just to see what she would do. My mother,
of course, designed Muffy's wardrobe and visited us often.

Despite my feelings about Cleveland, I was a very happy woman.
I immediately put my career on the back burner. I dropped out of the
City Opera's fall season, and in the spring of 1960, I sang just two
performances of *Baby Doe* and one as the Coloratura in *Six Characters*.

Emerson Buckley, my conductor in *Baby Doe*, was musical director of the Central City (Colorado) Music Festival, and around April
1960 he called me to ask if I'd sing for him at the summer festival. He
would be doing Donizetti's *Lucia di Lammermoor* and Verdi's *Aida*. I
agreed—I thought—to do Lucia, which is a wonderful role for a
coloratura soprano. Shortly before my birthday, Buck sent me the
score of *Aida*. I sent it back and said he'd made a mistake, and would
he please send the *Lucia* score. He wrote back that it was no mistake.
I had agreed to do *Aida* as far as he was concerned. Before then, I had

sung *Aida* in Salt Lake City and in Patterson, New Jersey. It was too heavy a role for my voice. But Buckley had all the confidence in the world that I'd make a great Aida. He reassured me that the theater was tiny—seven hundred seats. And besides, Central City was a good place to spend the summer with the kids.

I agreed to do the *Aida* sometime before my birthday. The connection is well established in my memory because of an incident that took place on that birthday. I was standing at a window watching a fire-engine-red station wagon come up our driveway, and Peter was sitting in a chair, reading. I turned to him and said, "You know, if there's one thing I hate, it's a red car."

That station wagon was my birthday present.

I knew I'd made a terrible gaffe, but I really *do* hate red cars. Peter had bought me the station wagon because I'd be driving the kids out to Central City for the summer; he'd commute from Cleveland to Denver each weekend. After I drove the kids to Colorado, and in order to justify my initial reaction to seeing the station wagon, I told him the car was dangerously underpowered and that I'd barely made it up the hills from Denver to Central City, about twenty-five miles away. I also told him the wagon's top speed was fifteen miles an hour—the car would have to be replaced. Peter decided to see for himself what the problem was, so he drove the station wagon from Central City to Denver—and was stopped for speeding. The officer who stopped us let Pete off when he told him: "My wife says the car won't go over ten miles per hour uphill."

I then said, "Well, the electronic windows don't work." Peter sat me down in the car, pressed four buttons, and of course all the windows worked. Sometimes I was amazed at the way he could control his temper.

Central City is a beautiful little town, and before Peter arrived I discovered a lovely jewelry shop downtown. A beautiful pair of earrings in the window caught my eye, and since I didn't have any money with me, I asked the shop owner to hold them until the weekend, when my husband would be arriving. When Peter and I visited the shop, the earrings were gone.

That Monday, I met the tenor who'd be playing Radames, the love of Aida's life. He was wearing *one* of the earrings I'd wanted to buy! I got even more upset when we started rehearsing. Central City's altitude is 9,000 feet, and after working with the tenor, I told Buckley

I was sure the man's voice wasn't strong enough to last five minutes. Buck told me I didn't know what I was talking about, and in a way he was right: The tenor didn't last even one minute. Our performance wasn't a fiasco, however. I had a knack for memorizing all parts of operas I appeared in, and when the tenor's voice gave out, I sang his role as well as my own. The audience never realized how screwed-up that performance was.

I didn't return to the City Opera in the fall. In fact, I didn't sing in New York again until the spring of 1962—two years later. My baby and stepdaughters needed me, and so did my husband. Peter was then in the midst of losing a family power struggle at the *Plain Dealer*. To me, it was obvious that Peter should have been made editor and publisher of the newspaper, but one of his less experienced relatives in Ohio was promoted over him. I thought I was going to have to work hard consoling Peter, but he didn't need any propping up. Surprisingly, he wasn't at all bitter or overly unhappy about being aced out.

If you ask me the name of the man who, aside from Peter, contributed more to my happiness than anyone else in the world, you'd be amazed at my answer: Sam Newhouse. Sam never gave us anything but wealth and pleasure. He bought the *Cleveland Plain Dealer,* and when I finally met him and Mitzi, his wife, I looked at Sam and thought: *This is an angel sent from heaven.*

Sam bought the *Plain Dealer* for $59 million, a substantial portion of which went to Peter. Peter was now a multimillionaire in his own right. We decided to move to Boston, his old bailiwick, and Pete had a wonderful job waiting for him on *The Boston Globe*. I looked forward to finding a house there, but Peter told me that wouldn't be necessary. His father owned a nineteen-room Georgian home in Milton, a Boston suburb. If I liked the place—and he was sure I would—Peter had already made arrangements to buy it for us.

So I went to Milton to look at the house with Peter. The place looked like an old English country home. The main entrance was surrounded by a wall of lilacs that must have been at least fifteen feet tall. The entranceway opened on to a large courtyard dominated by a huge Japanese cherry tree that in the spring shed its petals over everything. Peter's mother, a gifted horticulturist, had designed the house's extensive landscaping. She'd arranged her plantings in such a way that flowers would be blooming much of the year. The house had a lot of character. Its nineteen rooms were very spread out, weren't too big, and almost all of them had their own fireplaces. The kitchen windows faced the front courtyard and also the back of the house, where we had at least three acres of dense woods. I loved the place.

We moved from Cleveland to Milton in 1960. I was still simmering with bitterness when we left. Years later, when I went back to sing in Cleveland as Mrs. America Superstar, all of a sudden people were remarkably friendly to me. I was invited to be a houseguest here and to a party in my honor there—and I said no to everything. Except for my few buddies in town, I saw no one, and I went nowhere. And I made a point of not recognizing anybody. After performances, my standard line upon being introduced—or reintroduced—to the city's social jackals was "I'm sorry, I didn't get your name." I was interviewed by a lot of local radio, television, and newspaper reporters, all of whom asked me if I missed Cleveland. "What's to miss?" I answered. "I never had a friend in this city, and now that I'm well known, I have nothing but."

I really let Cleveland have it. The five years I lived there were the angriest, bitterest period of my life.

I was pregnant again when we moved to Massachusetts. I knew how much Peter and my father-in-law wanted a boy. Vose, Peter's brother, had never married, and his sister, Barbara, had two grown daughters. Peter and his father both wanted a son and heir who could carry on the family name.

Peter went to work as financial columnist for *The Boston Globe*, and I fell in love with Boston in a hurry. Sarah Caldwell had just started her opera company—at the time, she was using sheets for scenery and was putting on performances at the Donnelly Theater, which until then had been a run-down former movie theater. Soon after we got to Milton, I learned that John Alexander, my tenor buddy from the days of the Wagner tour, was going to sing in Sarah's production of *La Traviata*. Peter and I attended a performance and afterward we went backstage. Although I'd performed a few times with him at the City Opera, it had been several years since John and I had seen each other, and he didn't know I was living in Boston. Sarah Caldwell saw John give me a hug, and when she came by, Johnny introduced us and told Sarah about the *Traviata* he and I had done for Charles Wagner.

Peter and I were absolutely intrigued by what Sarah Caldwell had been able to do with twelve dollars' worth of sheets—that was just about the entire set of her *Traviata*. I told her: "I think what you've just done is a miracle. If we can help you in any way, we'd be happy to do that."

I meant financial help. When we lived in Cleveland, we'd contributed to the cost of bringing the Metropolitan Opera to town for a week each year. In Boston, Peter's family had long been patrons of the performing arts. Peter's mother had been one of the Boston Symphony's original donors, and his brother, Vose, who died in 1978, willed his considerable estate to the New England Conservatory of Music. I thought Sarah's tiny opera company was a perfect place for me to enter Boston's artistic community. The next day, Peter sent her a check for $250.

Johnny Alexander really must have gone on about me to Sarah. In May she telephoned to ask if I'd sing Rosalinda three weeks later in a production of *Die Fledermaus* she was planning to present. Arthur Fiedler, of Pops fame, would conduct. I said yes, and hung up feeling very flattered. Peter had heard the conversation and shot me a strange look. "What are you planning to wear?" he asked.

While talking to Sarah, I'd somehow forgotten that I was seven months pregnant and looked it. I immediately called her back and said, "I'm terribly sorry, Miss Caldwell, but I can't do *Fledermaus* with you because I'm pregnant."

"You weren't pregnant five minutes ago?" she asked. That was my real introduction to Sarah Caldwell.

My son, Peter Bulkeley Greenough, Jr., was born on June 29, 1961. Bucky weighed nine and three-quarters pounds and was a big, happy baby. I remember that my obstetrician was named Peter Robbins. Since we lived on Robbins Street and were going to name our son Peter Jr., we were sure nothing could go wrong.

When I was in Cleveland having Muffy, my mother had arrived from New York about ten hours into my very long labor. I must have looked awful when she saw me, and I was morbidly incoherent. Later Peter had told me how upset she was. I was determined not to upset her the second time. So I phoned her the moment I felt the first pain, and she got on a shuttle and arrived at the hospital about three hours later. It was late in June and very warm. They brought my mother in to see me. She looked absolutely beautiful. She had on a little white straw hat, white gloves, and a lovely linen suit. This time, though I was very hot and very uncomfortable and must have looked a sight, I was perfectly coherent and was able to assure her that everything was just fine. When she left, the nurse came over to me and said, "Who was that beautiful woman?"

"That was my mother," I said proudly.

"*That* was *your* mother?" the nurse exclaimed.

Those were the last words I heard before my son was born.

At the time of Bucky's birth Muffy was twenty-two months old, an adorable, inquisitive toddler. She did jigsaw puzzles on a four- or five-year-old level, and Peter had already taught her how to fold napkins for the dinner table. She seemed to figure things out very quickly. When we'd come back from grocery shopping, Muffy would put canned goods in their place by identifying the labels. Cans with a picture of the doggie went on one shelf; cans with pictures of string beans went somewhere else. When we did the laundry, Muffy would sit on the floor and sort all of it by color, which was rather remarkable for her age.

Muffy never was interested in boy or girl dolls. Her favorite toy was a stuffed mushroom with a face on it. Later on, she called it Punf, and he's still around. I also found her attention span remarkable. Muffy's favorite television show starred Bozo the Clown. I'd give her some cookies and she'd sit and quietly watch the whole program.

Probably because of all the things she could do, it worried me sick that Muffy couldn't say *Mama* or *bye-bye* or anything but *hot*. That came about after Muffy went near the stove one day—she was too short to see that I'd taken the teakettle off but left the burner on. I'd refilled the kettle and was walking back to the stove when I saw her little hand reach toward the burner. Without thinking, I whacked her hand away and yelled, "Hot! Hot! Hot!" I'd never touched or shouted at Muffy that way before, and for the rest of the day she walked around the house saying "Hot, hot, *hot!*" When Peter came home that night, she kept it up. Muffy was delighted that Peter and I were delighted. She didn't stop saying "Hot, hot, hot!" for days.

I was very worried about Muffy's hearing. We knew she had the intelligence to speak, and she was obviously a very bright child, yet not another word was coming from her. I'd already taken her to a doctor, who'd waved his keys in front of her and when Muffy grabbed them had said, "Obviously, the child can hear."

I rather thought it meant Muffy could *see,* so I decided to get her hearing tested. I made an appointment for her to be examined by Dr. Carlisle Flake, who was one of New England's leading ear specialists and a neighbor of ours on Martha's Vineyard. We had to wait two weeks to see him, and during that time I read a magazine article about an illness called aphasia. People with aphasia can hear, but can't assimilate sounds into words that have meanings. With that "hot, hot, hot" episode in mind, I took my daughter to Boston's Children's Hospital, where a doctor diagnosed her as suffering from aphasia. The tip-off, he said, was that Muffy liked to walk around on tiptoe in her bare feet—apparently, that was one of the symptoms of aphasia.

It was a very disturbing and confusing time, because while Muffy was being tested for aphasia, her intelligence was also being tested. Aside from not speaking, what else couldn't she do that other little girls her age could? I couldn't think of a single thing. Muffy was extremely well coordinated, and when she had her shoes on, she didn't walk on her tiptoes.

Finally the day came for Muffy to be examined by Dr. Flake. He disappeared into an office with her, and wasn't gone more than five minutes when he came back out to talk to us.

"Your daughter has a profound loss of hearing," he said. "You should get her outfitted with a hearing aid and into school. Get her educated as fast and as well as you can."

When I asked him about Muffy's possible problem with aphasia, he said, "Your child is not aphasic. She has no learning problem. Her only problem is that she can't hear."

He sent Peter and me to an audiologist and we quickly got Muffy a hearing aid. Today, the hearing aid she wears is a tiny little thing worn behind her ear and beneath her long hair. When she was a baby, the technology was not nearly so advanced. Her first hearing aid was the size of a big cigarette lighter, and it was strapped to her by a little harness. She and I immediately began an ongoing contest to see how often I could prevent her from destroying the hearing aid. Muffy was incredibly imaginative in her choice of places to hide it. One day I spent hours and hours searching for the thing and finally found it in one of my shoes. Muffy would never let me know where she hid it. She thought the two of us were playing the world's most wonderful game.

We learned about Muffy's deafness right around her second birthday. I was devastated by the news, but determined to help my daughter learn, and grow strong, and lead as normal a life as possible.

I remember a hot August day and the doctor suggesting we take her to the Sarah Fuller Foundation School. That's where Muffy met her first mentor, a terrific, funny young woman named Merl Sigel. Merl was Muffy's friend; my daughter held her hand as if they were contemporaries. Muffy stayed there for a year. She learned how to read the alphabet, how to pronounce the letter "B," and how to say words starting with *wh*. Muffy began doing all that when she was two years old.

Bucky was then two months old. I had a photographer come out to the house to take baby pictures of my son. The photographer told me he thought something was wrong with my boy. He couldn't get Bucky's attention. As he put it: "Your kid won't follow the birdie"— the fake canary attached to the camera.

After that, I started to watch my son very closely. He seemed to have spasms and peculiar moments when his eyes crossed very badly and when he lost control of his hands. I began worrying that Bucky might have some sort of nerve affliction. But then he'd calm down. Bucky was a cheerful and extraordinarily handsome baby, but it was almost impossible to make eye contact with him.

When Bucky was about six months old, I took him to the Children's Hospital in Boston. A woman doctor examined my son and told me: "There are so many things wrong with this boy that if I listed them as they are today, they would only be half of what you're going to be facing."

I looked at my fat, happy son and thought: *What could be bad?*

Bucky was retarded, they told us; they knew nothing about autism then. The doctor said Bucky would never talk and would never develop the control necessary to be toilet-trained. When Peter and I left the hospital, I said, "Well, the only good thing about today is that it's the worst day of our lives. From here on in, things have to get better."

Nothing got better for Bucky. My son's problems didn't really grow worse as he got older—it's just that we hadn't discovered the extent of his handicaps. My beautiful brown-eyed boy would lie motionless on my stomach for hours; at the time, we didn't realize his lack of interest in everything was an indication that he was autistic. I don't mean to imply that Bucky was a docile child, because he wasn't. If anything, he became hyperactive and quite self-injurious. One day he turned on the hot-water tap in the bathroom sink and then climbed into the sink and scalded his feet. When he was five he had his first epileptic seizure. Even if you've never seen one before, and I hadn't, you know what it is the moment it starts happening. When he began having seizures on a regular basis, we learned to put a spoon between his teeth and turn him on his side. It was years later, when he was twenty-two, that we learned that he was deaf, as well.

When Bucky was about eight months old, Oona McCarthy came to work for us, and she was a great source of comfort to our son. Oona set a personal goal of proving the doctor wrong by toilet-training Bucky, and she was able to do so. Oona, Peter, and I were the only three people Bucky recognized or even acknowledged. My son had some pleasures, but not many. Oona and I took turns watching him. In the backyard, we created a nice, safe environment for him to run around in, but it was really a prison with fences made of chicken wire.

We learned about Bucky's problems and Muffy's deafness within a six-week period. Peter was affected by the kids' problems, but he's a stoic; whatever happens, you just continue with your life.

I'm not a stoic at all. I was overwhelmed by the children's handicaps. My behavior changed. I would not leave the house. I stayed home and got terribly domestic. I took care of the children, I cooked, I made beds, and I tried not to think about the children's handicaps. My mother and my brothers telephoned every day. A lot of well-meaning friends called, and they all seemed to say the same thing: "I can't believe that *you* of all people would have a deaf child." That is not what I wanted to hear. I don't know *what* I wanted to hear.

I stopped flying to New York to see my mother and I canceled my weekly singing lessons with Miss Liebling. She and Mama were then neighbors—Peter had moved my mother into an apartment at 120 Central Park South, where Miss Liebling lived.

When I stopped coming to New York, Mama started flying up to Boston. She was a tower of strength. When Bucky's handicaps became known and it was clear he'd eventually have to be sent away to a special school, my mother's faith in God never wavered. "I know it's hard to see that your child is very sick, but you are lucky. Muffy can do everything except hear. And you have plenty of money, so your son will have the best care available."

Mama and my brother Sidney gave me identical advice about Muffy: Don't sit around and stare at her. In a rather forceful manner, my mother decided that very special things had to be done for my daughter. She insisted on Muffy's having art and dance lessons, and she made all Muffy's clothes. My two-year-old daughter had a wardrobe the likes of which has rarely been seen. My mother wasn't just another grandmother who brought presents; she was a grandma who *made* presents, and only for Muffy—and Muffy knew it. Grandma never gave Muffy a casual present; whatever she brought along always had a long story attached to it. Even before the child learned to lip-read, my mother would sit Muffy down on her lap and talk to her soothingly for hours on end. My mother had infinite patience and love. She didn't treat Muffy as if she was deaf.

Muffy couldn't wait to see Grandma-with-the-hat. My mother would put down her handbag and take off her gloves and coat, but she almost always forgot to take off her hat. In Muffy's first drawings, Grandma always wore a hat. My daughter idolizes my mother, who's given Muffy nothing but love, strength, and encouragement. They've always had a very special relationship.

In a sympathetic way, people have often commented on the irony of an opera singer's having a daughter who can't hear her sing. Believe me, that particular concern didn't enter the picture at all. I was a mother whose gorgeous daughter was deaf. My voice was the last thing I worried about Muffy's not being able to hear.

I was terribly depressed to learn about Muffy's deafness, and when I learned about Bucky's disabilities, I was simply crushed. How could this have happened to my children? Did *I* do something wrong? Did Peter? I worried that in looking at his first marriage, he'd see that he'd produced two healthy kids and one who was severely retarded. Why were two kids born healthy and one born retarded? Both Peter and I later became very active in the fight to prevent birth defects, and we learned that birth defects are never one parent's fault; when you make a baby, it still takes two to tango. If a problematic gene belonging to either or both of us had coupled with a different gene, our kids might have been perfectly healthy. But the genes didn't, and our kids weren't.

Was *anyone* at fault here? No one in either of our families could recall a single relative who'd been deaf. Peter's father died when he was ninety-six and never needed a hearing aid; my grandmother died at ninety-eight without a hearing aid, and my mother, now in her eighties, hears perfectly. So where did my daughter's deafness come from? It might have come as a result of her dual battle with hyaline membrane disease and yellow jaundice. It could have been caused by the high fever she experienced the first week of her life. Or maybe not. How do you account for it? You don't. You can't pinpoint the reason. In situations like ours, you do the best you can and make the most of the good things.

Peter was wonderful at that. He'd work all day at the *Globe* and call me up from the office to say, "Don't give her a bath. I want to bathe Muffy."

He never gave the child a casual bath. Muffy's papa would come home with four thousand rubber toys, and sponges that squeaked and tickled her when he rubbed them against her. Peter gave Muffy her first bubble bath. Who would give a two-year-old girl a bubble bath? Her father, that's who. Certainly not her mama; when mama bathed her, it was a question of how fast I could get her in and out and dried and dressed and brushed. When her papa bathed her, Muffy was Esther Williams starring in a Busby Berkeley spectacular.

Peter displayed the same discipline in regard to Muffy's clothing. Forget for a moment her grandma's handmade garments. I was busy buying baby things for Muffy to wear; Peter was busy buying her monogrammed sweaters. He was very anxious for Muffy to start reading as soon as possible, so everything he got her was either monogrammed or stamped with her name. Peter wanted Muffy to know that she belonged, and to have a sense of things that belonged to her.

Muffy has always been the pride and joy of Peter's life because she's a Greenough; she *fights* the way Greenoughs do. Muffy isn't a street fighter like her mother. Her approach is to be extremely proficient and do everything as well as she possibly can—she's a lady to the teeth. That child was never unpleasant or uncivil, but like her father, she's capable of a quick, strong flash of temper. I remember one day when we were at the beach—Muffy was a teenager—and she decided she wanted a wind-surfing boat, a Sunfish, for her birthday. Well, Peter launched into a whole song and dance about the Sunfish.

He told Muffy how dangerous those things were, that she'd get all wet, and that the idea was totally ridiculous. Besides, she could always rent a Sunfish for $4.50 an hour. Well, Muffy suddenly exploded, her temper flaring and volatile and lasting for maybe thirty seconds. Like Peter's.

The end of that story, of course, is that when we got home from the beach, Muffy was very shaken to see a Sunfish on our front lawn—Peter had already bought her the boat. Peter sees a lot of himself in Muffy. Thank God there's more of me in her, because without question I'm sweeter, funnier, and much more adorable than Peter. But there's no denying the wonderful relationship the two of them share. Peter has always encouraged Muffy to be adventurous, and even though I still worry too much for her, I know that Muffy is not fragile. She has gone on helicopter/hiking trips in the Canadian Rockies and a picture-taking safari in Africa, and with her sister Lindley and brother-in-law Paul has ridden down the rapids of the Colorado River. She even fell in once. She's tall, thin, blond, pretty, and very, very bright. She can't hear, but she can identify a number of sounds—such as my voice on the telephone or a police car's siren—by their frequencies. She can speak, and is a proficient lip-reader. Muffy earns a good living as a graphic artist and for a while had her own apartment in Manhattan. With Muffy, there were always joys to be shared because she had so many mountains to climb, and along the way she had so many triumphs. Our son could never have those triumphs.

But when I first learned of Muffy's deafness, I didn't know if she'd ever make it past a hill, let alone a mountain. As for Bucky— well, his potential was severely limited. For the past four years Bucky has been living at the Eden Institute in Princeton, New Jersey. The first time we were really able to make contact with him was when he was twenty-four—the Eden Institute taught him six signs of the sign language. Those were Bucky's first means of communication. It was the first time he had been able to focus his eyes on anything.

Bucky is twenty-six now, and to me he's still a lovable little boy. Peter and I visit him once a month, and sometimes when Bucky and I are out walking, he puts his arm around me. That always makes me think there's something inside Bucky trying to come out. When Peter takes us for a drive, Bucky and I sit in back because he has a tendency to reach over and grab the steering wheel or pull the keys out of the ignition. During some of these rides, the impenetrably vague look on Bucky's face has disappeared and been replaced by a lucid expression. For just a few fleeting moments every now and then, I suddenly find myself looking at a normal, extraordinarily handsome twenty-six-year-old man. I swear to you there are moments when my son's face displays absolutely normal intelligence. Medical textbooks claim that autistic kids live inside their own world, but here's Dr. Sills's diagnosis: I think autism is a severe disorder of the nervous system that causes wrong messages to be sent to the brain.

Bucky never climbed any mountains, but he negotiated some fairly steep hills. Autistic children are habitual in their movements and tend to be able to do repetitive tasks. There are a few wonderful organizations like the Dr. Scholl's company that do astonishing things for autistic people. The Dr. Scholl's company ships hundreds of cartons of the footpads it manufactures to Bucky's school, along with thousands of cellophane wrappers. Bucky and other residents of the Eden Institute stuff the footpads into the cellophane; Bucky gets a nickel for each one he does. The Dr. Scholl's people aren't picking up cheap help and exploiting the kids. They are there backing up a commitment to work with a portion of the population that most people regard as thoroughly hopeless. I don't know anyone from the Dr. Scholl's organization, but I'd like everyone there to know how much I appreciate their company's efforts on behalf of autistic children. They don't merely write a check; they set up programs and on a certain level actually bring young people like Bucky into their company. Peter and I were very proud when our son recently saved up enough money from his job to go on a vacation in the Pocono Mountains with some friends from his school. A small triumph, but a triumph nonetheless.

That was twenty-five years down the road, a road that's now a lot less bumpy for children like Bucky and Muffy. Even so, given the same circumstances today, I don't think I would have reacted any differently than I did. I've told you the rational side of my reactions. But on a more day-to-day level, when I first learned what Muffy and Bucky were up against, I went into shock.

Peter did his best to cheer me up. My husband invented something he called Adult Day: On Saturdays we'd leave the house in the morning and do whatever it was he'd planned for us. Adult Day would end with dinner out, usually at the Ritz-Carlton or a little Greek restaurant I liked. Sometimes we'd prolong the evening by going to the theater or a movie.

It helped, but it wasn't enough. Sarah Caldwell, in the meantime, had become a good friend. In February 1962, Sarah cast me as Manon in a production that also starred my City Opera colleagues John Alexander and Norman Treigle. Sarah's production was first-rate. She's always been an ingenious director and an excellent conductor—for *Manon,* she'd hired the Boston Symphony Orchestra, which performed beautifully. Norman, John, and I were a terrific team. Audiences and reviewers raved about *Manon* to the extent of speculating that perhaps the time had come for Boston to have an opera house of its own. It still doesn't have a real one.

I had a curious reaction to my return to opera. I loved to sing, and the best part of opera for me had always been the learning and rehearsing. Performing had been a sheer pleasure for me, as well, but it didn't feel that way when I sang *Manon.* In fact, after I learned about the kids' problems, I never felt such a pure excitement again. I enjoyed *Manon* for a different reason: For three hours a night I forgot about my own troubles and concentrated on hers. It was a great source of escape—that's what opera became for me. I couldn't wait to get to the theater and become somebody else.

After *Manon,* I continued walking around like a zombie. Julius Rudel kept writing notes and calling, and I finally agreed to sing two performances of *Baby Doe* for him that spring. Nothing magically therapeutic resulted. I was still deeply depressed and despondent. I rarely wandered out of my nineteen-room cocoon. Matters got bad enough for our doctor to tell Peter to devise a way to get me out of the house.

Peter did. On my thirty-third birthday he gave me fifty-two round-trip tickets for the Boston–New York shuttle. He wanted me to resume my weekly lessons with Miss Liebling, to start seeing my mother in New York, to get back into opera again—and to stop feeling sorry for the kids and for myself.

That wasn't easy to do. The way I did it was to put on a happy face. The public part of me became extra cheery; my innermost feelings were nobody's business but my own.

ELEVEN

Julius Rudel knew how low my spirits had sunk, and he continued sending me jokey little notes asking me to rejoin the City Opera. When I did, Julius camouflaged his persistent—he'd say pragmatic—pessimism and became a real pussycat. In the fall of 1962, Rudel cast me as Milly Theale in the company's two performances of *The Wings of the Dove,* Douglas Moore's newest opera. The year before, *Wings of the Dove* had had its world premiere at the City Opera. There was a lot of nice music in it, but *Wings of the Dove* wasn't well received, probably because it suffered in comparison to *The Ballad of Baby Doe.*

I also sang one performance of *Louise,* which the company was presenting for the first time. Working on that opera was like attending a reunion of my best friends in the business. *Louise* was conducted by Jean Morel—the man who *did* come to dinner in Cleveland—and featured John Alexander as my lover and Norman Treigle as my father. The chemistry among the four of us was remarkable. We all performed at the very peak of our abilities, and meshed so well that the audience probably thought we'd been singing *Louise* together for years.

Louise is a romantic opera about a Parisian girl who doesn't get along with her mother, defies her father, and runs away with her lover. Very contemporary. That's it for the story. Gustave Charpentier's music is magnificent. Louise's third-act aria, *"Depuis le jour,"* made an international star out of Mary Garden, who'd never been on an opera stage prior to the night she filled in at the Opéra Comique in Paris for some poor soprano who took sick. Louise's lover and her father also have beautiful music to sing. At the end of the opera, Louise leaves her father for her lover, and the final scene is so emotional that when the curtain came down, Norman and I were both in tears. The audience gave us a tumultuous ovation, but the next morning one of the newspapers called our performance "bland."

Over the years, my objection to the opera press in general has rarely had to do with reviews of my own performances. What always upsets me about critics is their failure to report the shared sense of something so unusual happening that no one who witnesses a particular performance will ever forget it. I still don't know why critics dash out of the theater before observing an audience's reaction. Do they think the public doesn't know what's good or bad? I always hear critics say, "I'm simply reporting from my own point of view."

Fair enough. But what kind of reporter ignores the audience's overall response to an opera but doesn't neglect to point out that after a particular aria, booing was heard? Sometimes you can walk into an opera house and feel the air charged with electricity. You know something extraordinary is going to happen, and it does—and the next day you read a perfectly good review in the newspaper, except that the critic has totally ignored the fact that he witnessed an *event*, not just another performance.

I'm not talking only about opera criticism here. I remember going to Avery Fisher Hall to see a performance by Itzhak Perlman, Pinchas Zukerman, and Isaac Stern in celebration of Stern's sixtieth birthday. Getting the world's three best violinists to play together was as momentous an event in classical music as putting together a pop concert featuring Stevie Wonder, Bruce Springsteen, and Barbra Streisand would be. The reviews the next day were fine, but none of the critics commented on the unique nature of the occasion or the extraordinary reaction of the audience.

I don't see many critics improving in that regard, either. In 1985, Gianna Rolandi starred in a City Opera production of *Lucia,* and on opening night she received a thunderous standing ovation at the end of the mad scene. There were 2,400 people in the audience, and at least 1,500 of them caused the opera to be delayed for several minutes because they were on their feet applauding. Not one critic mentioned it, which I felt was a serious omission. I wouldn't have minded if a critic had said that Rolandi had received a standing ovation but that from the critic's point of view, she hadn't deserved it—it's a critic's job to make judgments. But not to mention the reaction of people who are probably quite as knowledgeable about opera as the critic himself strikes me as a serious piece of misreporting.

I don't want to wander too far afield from *Louise,* because it was a turning point for me. I thought my performance in the opera was as good as my work in *Baby Doe,* meaning that for the second time in my life, I left a theater feeling no soprano in the world could have sung my part better. Norman and I were by then veteran performers with the City Opera, but aside from the string of *Carmen*s we'd done in Cleveland, we'd never performed together. Our work in *Louise* convinced both of us that we could make good things happen on stage. We were a natural team.

Life at home remained a struggle, but I was no longer benumbed by the kids' problems. I felt we were going through a rather tragic period, but nevertheless we were having some pretty good times. Peter had bought the first of a long parade of Welsh corgis. There are two types of Welsh corgis—Cardigans, which have tails, and Pembrokes, which don't. We almost always had Cardigans. I confess that I never loved any of the dogs, but I think that had to do with my upbringing. Let me put it this way: When I grew up in Brooklyn, Jewish girls never had dogs. I wasn't a dog person, and no matter how hard my husband tried to change that, he never succeeded.

Bumpy, our first Corgi, was given his name by Muffy—it was easy to pronounce and very descriptive. Bumpy looked like a foot-high fox and had the instincts of a sheepherder. He also had an ear—*two* ears—for music. I would practice three hours a day in Milton. When the dog heard me sing, he would come in from outdoors and settle himself under the piano. There he would stay. However, when I'd hit a very high note, Bumpy's ears would twang like a banjo. I *did* like Bumpy, even when he chewed up one of Gigi Capobianco's $400 alligator shoes.

Bumpy was mostly ignored by Bucky, but he hung around my

son. Whenever the dog thought Bucky was wandering off, Bumpy would sort of block his way and guide Bucky back to me. Bucky didn't seem to be unhappy. There was no way of knowing what or how he felt, but Oona and I made him as comfortable as possible.

When it came to Muffy, Oona was much more than a nanny or housekeeper. She was like Muffy's sister. And Lindley and Nancy were the best sisters to Muffy and Bucky that I ever could have hoped for. Nancy and Muffy were inseparable. Nancy taught Muffy origami and how to make things with her hands. When the four children watched television together, Muffy would be on Nancy's lap and Lindley would help me with Bucky. I think Lindley sensed my profound pain and anguish about my son. She's always been very sensitive. She and Nancy both had to make enormous adjustments in their lives—as, indeed, did I. There were times, however, when we weren't there for one another. Ours could hardly be called a typical American family—and the impact of my career was yet to come.

I went to school with Muffy at the Sarah Fuller Foundation School for deaf babies, which was in downtown Boston. We wanted Muffy to learn to talk. In addition to the training she got from Merl Sigel, we hired a tutor who came to our house after school and talked to Muffy all day long. The object was to get her to lip-read, and in order to do that, we had to train her to look at people's lips, not their eyes, which is the way we normally fix on people. I found that the easiest way to get Muffy's eyes directed at my lips was to buy great big rings—fake diamonds, gyroscopes, rings that contained little games in them—and keep my hands near my mouth. I was able to amuse her and draw her attention that way. I must have bought fifty of the silliest rings ever made in America and Japan, but they worked. Muffy began learning to lip-read.

In the autumn of 1962, when she was three, Peter and I enrolled Muffy in the Boston School for the Deaf, which was located about ten miles away in Randolph, Massachusetts. The school had an excellent reputation for being able to teach deaf children to speak. Deaf people who can speak are known as "oral deaf."

The school was run by the Sisters of Saint Joseph, which meant that my half-Protestant, half-Jewish daughter was going to be educated as a Catholic. When I brought Muffy to the school, I told Sister Mary Joseph, the head nun: "Sister, I'd give my right arm to hear my daughter say 'Mama.' "

I have to admit that at that stage, Muffy was a little bit spoiled and undisciplined. She was very cheerful each time she flushed her hearing aid down the toilet—deaf kids do that all the time. Since each hearing aid cost $300—and we also had to pay the plumber every time she flushed one away—I was much less cheerful than my daughter. I wound up sewing her hearing aid into a little harness she wore around her chest. She also loved brightly colored lipsticks—especially on her grandpa's walls. "Booful" was her appraisal of her artwork.

Muffy was a very clever kid. When she was naughty, she could tell by the expression on my face when I was about to scold her. On such occasions, my daughter would put a big grin on *her* face and simply turn off her hearing aid. Most of the time, I figured Muffy had enough trouble—I didn't have to discipline her, too, which is precisely how Peter had treated Lindley and Nancy.

In addition to Sister Mary Joseph, the other nun I met during Muffy's first day at school was Sister Dionysius, a strong lady who was six feet tall. I assumed Muffy would get all the discipline she needed and more. She wasn't boarding at the school, but it was clear to me that in the hours Muffy spent there, the sisters wouldn't allow themselves to be twisted around her little finger.

In December, my Muffy was an angel in the school's Christmas pageant. After it was over, the mamas were told to pick up their babies in the classrooms. So I went to Muffy's classroom, and there was "disciplinarian" Sister Dionysius holding my daughter way up over her head and crisply issuing her a stern order: "Is oo gonna give Sister big bye-bye kiss?"

So much for the discipline part; I thought my daughter would be ruined for life. When Sister Dionysius saw me standing there, she said, "Now, Muffy, give your mommy her Christmas present."

Muffy looked at me and like a little mechanical doll, she said, "Mama."

I fell apart. I was just undone.

That night we had a big Christmas dinner, with the Jewish grandma up from New York and the Episcopalian grandpa and his wife coming over from Concord, Massachusetts, plus Pete's brother, Vose, and sister, Barbara. After dinner we brought Lindley, Nancy, Muffy, and Bucky into the living room for the ritual of having the children hang up their Christmas stockings. While they were doing that, I remembered the last thing Sister Dionysius had said to me: "Be sure to ask Muffy who's coming to visit her on Christmas Eve."

I thought: *Oh, good, Muffy knows about Santa Claus!*

Well, we hung up the stockings, the other kids got bored and left, and there was Grandma sitting with her little glass of champagne, and there was Grandpa sitting with his *big* glass of champagne. I knew the proper moment had arrived. I said, "Muffy, tell Grandma and Grandpa who's coming to visit you tonight."

Muffy got down on her knees, crossed herself, and said, "Mother Mary, Joseph, and Baby God."

My father-in-law was drinking champagne and spit a mouthful halfway across the room. My mother sat there, staring at her precious granddaughter and looking stricken.

Peter and I started laughing so hard that I wound up crying. I couldn't take my eyes off my child on her knees. I'd been so sure I was going to hear "Santa Claus," which I knew would have tickled my mother. She didn't really approve of Muffy's encounter with Catholicism, but as a Jewish Christian Scientist, there wasn't much she could say.

Muffy was rather taken with the pomp and ceremony of the Catholic Church. Peter and I had different faiths, of course, but neither of us was religious in a conventional sense. The only religious holiday we celebrated was Christmas, and then only as an occasion to exchange presents. I kidded about having a half-Episcopalian, half-Jewish child, but I decided to let my daughter make her own choice of religions. Whatever she chose would have been fine with me. I believe the titles of all religions are man-made, and that we're all meant to have one religion. God doesn't sit up in heaven and say, "Well, there will be a Catholic religion," any more than he says there will be a Protestant, Jewish, Muslim, Buddhist, or Hindu religion. Man, in his usual manner of screwing things up, decided various religions had to be pigeonholed, but in the final analysis we all use God for the same thing: to get a little help—or at least ask for it. I recall one interviewer asking in what faith our daughter was being raised.

"In *good* faith," I said.

Later on, after we moved to New York City, Muffy came home from school one day and said, "A lot of girls don't have to go to school tomorrow. Is Joosh holiday."

I told Muffy she could stay home, too, because she was half-Jewish.
"I'm not Joosh," she said. "I'm Catholic."

"No, sweetie, you're Jewish."

"Okay, then I'll stay home," Muffy said. "Mama, what's a Joosh?"

The only formally religious thing I do is to light a little candle
every September 17, the anniversary of my father's death. I consider
myself religious, but I certainly don't need a temple to worship in.
I'm not attached to ceremonies. I think one practices one's religion by
how one behaves toward one's fellow creatures. The rest of it doesn't
matter.

I haven't adequately talked about Sarah Caldwell yet, probably
because that's not easy to do. Since 1957, when she founded the
Boston Opera Group, which later became the Opera Company of
Boston, Sarah has led a one-woman crusade to make Boston safe for
opera. She's rarely had two nickels to rub together, but that's never
stopped her from putting on ingenious operatic productions in college gyms and old movie theaters. Sarah is about five feet five inches
tall and, until recently, was very heavy. Beneath her somewhat disor-
ganized exterior beats the heart of a brilliant director and producer.
Many times, Sarah's demonstrated she can do more with $40,000
than anyone else could with $500,000.

Let me give you one example of her theatrical ingenuity. Toward
the end of my career, I sang the role of Norina in Donizetti's *Don
Pasquale*. I sang it at the Met and in Boston, and there's no question in my
mind that Sarah's production was one of the most brilliantly conceived I've ever seen. In one scene, Sarah wanted Donald Gramm,
who played Don Pasquale, to exit in a horse-drawn carriage, so she
had somebody build a cardboard horse drawing a cardboard carriage
with a seat inside it for Donald. When he sat down, scenery on
scrolls, cranked by two men, began moving behind him, and you saw
Donald riding through a town, cobblestoned street by street. The
whole effect was miraculous. In another scene, Sarah, in collaboration with her set designers, totally transformed a rickety, broken-
down room into an ornate Italian apartment in a total of twelve
seconds. Everything was literally breakaway—I'd never seen anything
like it.

I probably sang about twenty operas with Sarah, and none was
done conventionally. Sarah staged every opera as if she'd never seen it

before, and she probably never *had* seen it before, so there were no traditions for her to follow. Instead of just being charming, Sarah's version of *The Daughter of the Regiment* became a comic masterpiece and one of my favorite roles.

When we did Bellini's *Norma* together, Sarah wondered why the Druids would choose Norma to be their goddess if she looked and acted like everyone else. What was it about Norma that caused her to be referred to as the *casta diva*—the chaste goddess? Sarah thought Norma had some type of physical characteristic that none of the Druids had ever seen before. So Sarah decided Norma was an albino. Since the Druids had never seen a young woman with perfectly white skin and white hair, why *wouldn't* they consider her a goddess? And by God, the idea worked! I wore white, white makeup on my face, pink makeup around the rims of my eyes, and a long white wig. Sarah also came up with the idea that Norma occasionally had spells. She told me: "Think epileptic." But I just couldn't do that. I remember the two of us acting like crazy women at four in the morning, making all kinds of awful jokes as we tried to come up with plausible reasons why poor Norma would suddenly fall into a spell and undergo a complete change of behavior.

When we first got to Boston, I thought I'd like to be one of Sarah Caldwell's patrons and perhaps help manage her opera company—at that point, I didn't see myself continuing as a singer. When that changed, I sang as often as I could with Sarah. Her working habits were a bit odd, however. Sarah was at her most productive from ten o'clock on—P.M., not A.M. I remember Sarah rehearsing Donald Gramm and me in *Lucia* at three in the morning, which made it tough for her to be fully awake at eleven A.M., when the rest of the cast reported for rehearsals. Sarah frequently napped in the aisles during normal rehearsal hours, and the other singers, not knowing how late she'd worked with Donald and me, would be understandably miffed at her for not being alert. Or even awake. There was never a dull moment with that woman.

Sarah had a lovely house, but her real home was the theater. She slept, ate, and dressed in the theater, and usually didn't give a damn about how she looked. Sarah lives to create beauty and wit where none has existed before.

Not long after Treigle and I sang *Louise* in New York, Sarah brought us together to sing Gounod's *Faust* in Boston. She ran out of money before finishing the set, so we sang a long, very important scene on a bare stage, and even *that* worked. When I sang *Faust*, my career really was starting to move. In 1963, I sang *The Ballad of Baby Doe, La Traviata,* and *The Merry Widow* at the City Opera, and when the company went on its winter tour, I sang my first Donna Anna in Mozart's *Don Giovanni.*

Ludwig Lustwig, my manager, was very busy that year. I sang in Honolulu, at Robin Hood Dell outside of Philadelphia, at Lewisohn Stadium, and with the Philharmonic in New York. Opera impresarios throughout America now knew my name. To really impress them, I decided to sing the Queen of the Night in Mozart's *The Magic Flute.* I sang it first in Boston in January of 1964. Almost all of the Queen of the Night's part consists of two arias containing five high F's. I figured if I sang the role well, I'd impress the hell out of everybody— myself most of all.

That *had* to be the reason I did it, because I must tell you, the Queen of the Night is the most boring, pointless role I ever sang. The Queen of the Night sings an aria in Scene 1 of Act I, and then sings another aria in Scene 3 of Act II. Between arias, you sit backstage for at least an hour and a half.

The one redeeming feature of the role is its difficulty. At any given time, only four or five sopranos in the world are able to sing the Queen of the Night. How high is a high F? *Very* high. In addition to those five high F's, the Queen's two arias contain some rather difficult coloratura passages. And you can't be a pipsqueak soprano, because the only bird the character resembles is a ravenous vulture. You've really got to be able to sock those notes out there, especially in the second act, when the Queen sings her vengeance aria.

After I sang the Queen of the Night in Boston, I was invited to sing it in Lausanne, Switzerland, in May 1965. I remember Peter's scribbling a note in a scrapbook saying: "Bev's career goes international for the first time." Singing in Europe had never meant much to me, and singing the Queen of the Night meant nothing to me, but I accepted the engagement anyway. There are certain times in your career when you get invited to sing something that's in your reper- toire, and yours is not to reason why—you just go. Because of a timely coincidence, Peter came with me: The GATT (General Agree- ment on Tariffs and Trade) negotiations were then being held in Switzerland, and he covered them for *The Boston Globe.* We had a nice three-week vacation. The thing we liked best about Lausanne was a terrific Chinese restaurant. We were steered to it by a cab driver who told us every Chinese family in Lausanne ate there. I remember thinking: *All four of them?*

I'd be remiss if I didn't tell you that Lausanne's Mozart Festival was extremely prestigious—so much so that all the great singers fought to be in it. To me, it was strictly another engagement; at least that's how I felt when I got there. When I left, I felt somewhat different about it. On opening night of *The Magic Flute,* I hit all five high F's right on the button. The last of them is sung in the first third of the Queen's second-act aria. When I finished singing the final high F, the orchestra had to stop playing: the audience had broken into wild applause, and it seemed as though hundreds of people were shouting "Brava!" Those few minutes were incredibly exciting. I found then that American audiences aren't the only ones who applaud in the "wrong" places. European audiences do it all the time.

Because so few sopranos can sing the Queen of the Night, you can write your own ticket and live forever on that role. As soon as you perform it successfully a couple of times, you get an instant reputation. Every impresario puts you on his list, which is how you get to do Queen of the Night wherever you want. It's really astonishing—you can ask anything for singing the role, and you'll almost certainly get it. In the early days of my career, the highest fees I ever received were not for my Rosalindas, Violettas, and other roles, but for the Queen of the Night.

Although it didn't happen for about five years, the minute I was in a position to say goodbye to *The Magic Flute,* I did. I sang the Queen of the Night in Boston, Lausanne, New York, Tanglewood, Houston, and Vienna. I also was supposed to sing it in London.

In the summer of 1969, while I was in London to record an album, I heard that Covent Garden needed a Queen of the Night for its new production of *The Magic Flute.* My old friend Maestro Solti, who'd made a pass at me fifteen years earlier in Frankfurt, had since been knighted and was then director of the Royal Opera. I had Ludwig Lustig, my manager, write to Sir Georg about the possibility of casting me as the Queen of the Night. Solti replied that I'd have to audition, and since I was in London anyway, that seemed fair enough.

After I auditioned for him, Solti told me the Queen was mine. Sir Georg told me how pleased he was to see me—he couldn't have been kinder. I then called Lustig in New York and asked him to contact Solti and work out my contract with Covent Garden. When Lustig phoned Solti, Sir Georg said he'd not offered the role to me and didn't plan to. I've never had the opportunity to discuss the matter with Sir Georg.

I met Solti again in the mid-1970s, when I was walking past the Hampshire House in New York. Solti acted as if nothing unpleasant had ever taken place between us. We talked amiably about our lives, our children, and our careers. We vowed to see each other often, which of course we have not done. Solti subsequently invited me to sing with him in Chicago, but I was booked solid at that point. I regret that. Regardless of our couple of strange encounters, he's a great conductor.

A month after my first *Magic Flute* in Boston, I sang the three soprano roles in *The Tales of Hoffmann* opposite Norman Treigle in my debut with the New Orleans Opera. A month later, in March of 1964, Sarah Caldwell conducted me in my first and only performance as Adina in Donizetti's *The Elixir of Love,* which played more like a sleeping potion. During the City Opera's fall '64 season, I sang Rosalinda in *Fledermaus,* Marguerite in *Faust,* and Donna Anna in *Don Giovanni.*

In January 1965, I took the part of Constanza in Sarah's production of Mozart's *Abduction from the Seraglio.* In February, Sarah hired me to sing in the American premiere of *Intolleranza,* an opera about man's inhumanity to man. *Intolleranza* was written by Luigi Nono, an Italian Communist who had all the political sophistication of a snail. I'm probably being unduly harsh here; there's no reason to be critical of snails. The composer of *Intolleranza* was thoroughly shocked to discover that the majority of Harvard students were not Communists. To his credit—or, rather, to the credit of the Boston Opera Company— he was making full use of the lavish service at the Copley Plaza Hotel. All that might have been overlooked if *Intolleranza* hadn't been such a sophomoric piece of polemical garbage. Luigi and his opera were both Nonos.

In May 1965, Norman Treigle called. Norman and his wife and daughter were going to spend six weeks in Cincinnati that summer, where Norman was going to sing the four villains in *The Tales of Hoffmann.* Norman wanted to know if I'd do it with him. At the

Cincinnati Zoo. Norman wasn't kidding. Some Argentinian director named Tito Capobianco was set to direct *Hoffmann,* and Norman had gotten Tito to agree to use me if I wanted in. Treigle told me the performance would be staged outdoors but under a shed, and sure, we'd be singing over noises made by seals and elephants, but we'd have a good time. He found a terrific apartment hotel called the Vernon Manor, and persuaded me to come out there with the entire family. So I did. I took all four Greenough kids along, plus Oona and a college girl we hired as a full-time baby sitter. The apartment hotel was as comfortable as Norman said it would be, and it also had a huge swimming pool. Everything was hunky-dory until I went to meet the director.

Tito Capobianco is handsome and talented; his wife, Gigi Denda, is a tiny, ebullient choreographer who was once the prima ballerina at the Teatro Colon in Buenos Aires. When I got to Cincinnati, I immediately went to meet them—and I instantly saw that Tito was upset. I asked him if something was wrong, and he said, "No, nothing," and then turned to his wife and pantomimed the movement of a large, stiff zombie. Tito evidently had expected me to be tiny and didn't quite conceal his disappointment.

I was very angry with Treigle for not telling him I was a big woman. Tito had hired me on the strength of Norman's recommendation, and he wanted to kill Treigle for not telling him I wasn't a tiny, doll-like creature. Treigle told Tito to trust him, and they both sent Gigi to reassure me that everything would work out fine.

During rehearsals Tito kept asking me to do the strangest damned things. Instead of sending out a nice little wind-up doll in the first act, he and Gigi created a little ballet for Olympia. I didn't want to do it—I was sure I'd look foolish. I don't know how many times I told them: "I'm sorry, I can't do this." And I don't know how many times they told me: "If you don't feel like doing this particular thing we'll change it, but at least give it a try."

I was all apprehension and reluctance. In the second act, for the part of Giulietta, they wanted me to wear a long skirt slit up the side and a dress cut down to my navel.

"I sing," I said. "I don't show my legs or anything else."

Gigi and Tito talked me into showing my legs and almost *everything* else. Tito was always pressing me to do a very comic doll and a *very* sexy Giulietta. The movements filled me with dread, but I did them, and they worked. Norman and I had come to Cincinnati believing we already owned *The Tales of Hoffmann;* after working with the Capobiancos, we *knew* we owned it. Their production was nothing less than sensational. On opening night, however, I almost passed out before I started singing. The evening was hot and humid, and as the doll, I stood onstage inside a cylinder of nylon fabric, waiting to be wound up and let loose. There was no air inside that cylinder, and when the orchestra launched into the introduction to my aria, I began feeling faint. I came *very* close to passing out. In fact, the orchestra had to repeat the introduction before I was able to catch my breath and get going.

We wanted to bring the Capobiancos' production to the New York City Opera that fall, but when we broached the idea to Julius, he refused. Later that summer, Norman and I blackmailed, or at least coerced, Rudel into going along with our plan. Treigle and I were singing *Don Giovanni* on a City Opera tour in California, and before we went on, Norman said, "Let's sing this first act so well that Julius will want to throw up on the podium."

Sounds strange, I know, but after that first act, Julius *was* a little queasy—*Don Giovanni* really gets to him. Before Act II started, Norman and I had a short chat with Rudel, who complimented us lavishly on our first-act performances. Norman said, "Do you want Act Two to be as good as Act One, or do you want it to be lousy?"

Julius was a little mystified, so Norman made things crystal-clear for him. "Do we get the *Hoffmann* or don't we?"

We got the *Hoffmann* and the Capobiancos that fall. The production created a sensation. Tito became one of the company's resident directors. Not coincidentally, a year later I became an international star.

TWELVE

T*he Tales of Hoffmann* can be a showpiece for the bass and soprano because of the multiple roles each one sings. When Treigle and I re-created Tito Capobianco's Cincinnati production at the City Opera in the fall of 1965, Norman sang four roles and I sang three. (Stella, the fourth woman, doesn't sing.) *The Tales of Hoffmann* is an opera full of fantasy. Hoffmann, a young poet, falls in love with a famous opera star, Stella. He gets drunk and tells the story of Olympia, a doll who convinces people she's a woman; Giulietta, a woman who only plays at love; and Antonia, who will do anything, even die, so long as she can sing. Of course, these are all Stella. Norman's four characters—all of them incarnations of the devil—make sure Hoffmann winds up a very dejected young man. Composer Jacques Offenbach wrote *Hoffmann* with all that multiple role-playing in mind, which is part of the fun of performing the work.

One of the biggest chuckles I ever got from a New York review was from a piece by the then *Herald Tribune* writer. He suggested that NYCO was being "economical" and using one singer instead of the usual three sopranos. He should have done his homework.

The City Opera's *Hoffmann* was a great success on every conceivable level. After the fall season ended, we took the production on tour to Philadelphia, where Placido Domingo sang the role of Hoffmann. Placido, who was then all of twenty-four and quite chunky, had debuted with the City Opera that season in *Madama Butterfly*. Placido remained with the City Opera through the spring season of 1969, when the Met signed him up. (He did return several times in following seasons.) He and his wife, Marta, were a pleasure to get to know. All of us—Tito and Gigi, Norman and Linda, Placido and Marta, and Peter and I—spent the following few summers working and vacationing in Cincinnati.

In the fall of 1965, in addition to *Hoffmann*, I sang Rosalinda in *Die Fledermaus* and Marguerite in *Faust*. When our season closed on November 14, Julius Rudel played an extra in *The Merry Widow*, and then led the company, orchestra, and audience in a round of "Auld Lang Syne." The occasion was the City Opera's final appearance at the City Center. In the spring, we'd be moving uptown to New York's newest and most beautiful live entertainment complex, Lincoln Center.

In the works since 1955, when the New York Philharmonic and the Metropolitan Opera began seeking new homes, Lincoln Center was a spacious, three-theater complex on Columbus Avenue between 62nd and 65th streets. When you walk straight into the Center's large plaza, on your left is the New York State Theater, which we were to share with the New York City Ballet; in the center is the Metropolitan Opera House; and on the right is Avery Fisher Hall. Lincoln Center also contains the Vivian Beaumont Theater and the Mitzi Newhouse Theater, where dramatic works are staged; the New York Public Library for the Performing Arts; Damrosch Park, with its band shell for outdoor concerts; and, just north of 65th Street, Alice Tully Hall and the Juilliard School. God knows how much the entire project cost to build then and what it would cost to build now. I do know that the New York State Theater alone ate up fifteen million dollars. Its seating capacity is 2,735, about 500 fewer seats than we'd had at City Center. What a jewel of a theater it is.

In February 1966, Placido inaugurated the company's move to Lincoln Center by starring in the North American premiere of Alberto Ginastera's *Don Rodrigo*. I sang *Baby Doe* in a season largely devoted to doing old stuff we brought over from 55th Street. We needed lead time to build new sets, because the old ones didn't fit into this place

And so our real opening was going to take place in the fall, when the Metropolitan was due to have *its* opening.

Talk about coincidences. The Met was preparing the world premiere of Samuel Barber's *Antony and Cleopatra,* and we were getting ready to do Handel's *Julius Caesar.* Rudel chose that opera as a showcase for Norman Treigle, who'd been given the title role. Rudel also announced that Phyllis Curtin, who'd left the City Opera to join the Met in 1963, was being invited back to play Cleopatra.

When I heard that, I hit the ceiling. Julius's decision to cast Phyllis Curtin implied that no one in the company could sing Cleopatra, and I truly resented that. And so I marched into Julius's office and had it out with him. I told him that I understood he was our general director and that he had the right to choose any damn soprano from within the company to play Cleopatra—but the minute he said he needed someone from the outside to do the role, it was tantamount to his saying: "None of my little sopranos can sing the role."

I was not going to accept that, and I said so. I also told him—in fact, I swore up and down—that I wasn't personally campaigning for the role. If Julius gave Cleopatra to any soprano from the company, I'd drop all my objections. We had several good sopranos at the time, including Beverly Bower and Patricia Brooks, who could have done the role. I made it very clear to Julius that I wasn't feeling personally neglected; I was scheduled to sing Donna Anna in *Don Giovanni,* Constanza in Mozart's *Abduction from the Seraglio,* the three roles in *The Tales of Hoffmann*, and, God help me, the Queen of the Night in a new production of *The Magic Flute.* I said, "Just tell me you'll give Cleopatra to somebody who's in the company, but don't tell me none of us can do it."

Julius said, "Well, Phyllis *is* a member of the company."

"No, she's not with us anymore. She is now a member of the Metropolitan Opera Company," I said.

I'd known Phyllis Curtin for many years—she was the godmother of Norman's daughter. Phyllis had joined the City Opera two years before I did, and I'd often covered her in leading roles. Phyllis would sing the opening night of, say, *Die Fledermaus,* I'd sing the second or third performance, and there was no resentment on my part because I hadn't gotten opening night. Rudel had always been very fair about spreading around the opening nights.

Bringing in a soprano from outside the company was another

matter, however. A matter of principle. Julius just didn't see it that way, so I had a talk with John White, then the company's associate director. I told John that if Julius didn't give the role to me or one of our other sopranos, I was resigning from the company. John suggested that I see Julius at his home, not in the office, and so Julius and I made an appointment for breakfast at his place.

I again explained what I was feeling to Julius. Rudel wasn't going to be budged. I finally *did* take it personally. I told Julius that if I didn't get the role, I was resigning from the company.

"You're not going to resign," he said. "Where will you sing?"

"My husband intends to hire Carnegie Hall for me to do a New York recital," I said, which wasn't a bluff at all. Peter and I had talked about it. "And I assure you, when I sing at Carnegie Hall, my program will contain five of Cleopatra's arias—and you're going to look sick."

Julius wasn't looking sick at that moment. He was looking rather vexed.

"When do you plan to do all this?" he asked.

"The moment you tell me I can't have Cleopatra," I said.

Julius paused. "You know I promised the role to Phyllis," he said.

"I know you have," I said. "Perhaps you could promise her something else in the future. I think you should bear in mind that although I have a lot of replacements, I've got the bulk of the repertoire."

That was true. If I walked out, Rudel was going to have an almost impossible time replacing me in *The Magic Flute,* plus the three other operas I was supposed to do. I really felt I had Julius by the tail, but the argument wasn't about leverage—it was about doing the right thing.

Before our breakfast was over, Julius said, "Let me think on it."

He apparently called Phyllis and told her the truth, and then gave me the role. When that happened, I telephoned Phyllis, and we met for coffee at Francine's on West 56th Street. I remember sitting in a booth, explaining to Phyllis that after all my years of covering for her, I felt Julius's decision to invite her back had been unfair to me and to the rest of the company's sopranos.

She said, "Well, you know I can't agree, because I want to do that role. But there are no hard feelings. We'll always be friends. What's the point in *not* being friends?"

We did stay friends. Phyllis is quite a lady. And Julius was a gentleman. He wasn't at all upset with me. In fact, during the summer he came up to our place in Martha's Vineyard, along with his entire family, to help me prepare for the role. I remember the mob scene at breakfast during that visit. Our cook came in one morning, saw twelve places set, and remarked, "Mrs. Greenough, if I'd known I had to cook for so many, I'd have taken a job at Howard Johnson's."

Tito Capobianco, who'd directed me in *Tales of Hoffmann* at the Cincinnati Zoo, was going to direct *Julius Caesar,* and I knew that he and Gigi wanted me to play Cleopatra as very, very sexual. Her arias had to have a certain kind of ornamentation that Miss Liebling really couldn't provide, and I couldn't tell her that. Miss Liebling was one of the most famous cadenza writers in the world—there are books and books of her cadenzas—but I didn't want to sing cadenzas anyone else had ever done.

I'd kept up my lessons with Miss Liebling, but when it came time to prepare for *Julius Caesar,* I decided to work with a young man named Roland Gagnon. I'd met Roland at the beginning of 1962, when I returned to opera by singing *Manon* for Sarah Caldwell. Roland was Sarah's rehearsal accompanist, and starting with *Manon,* he'd been coming to our house every weekday morning from nine to eleven to work with me. Roland was then teaching at the New England Conservatory of Music and had earned his doctorate in organ music. He wrote a paper on Handel, in fact.

Roland Gagnon was then in his twenties, spoke beautiful French, and had one of the finest tenor voices I ever heard. He also had more hang-ups than you can imagine, one of which was that he couldn't, or wouldn't, sing in public. He was a handsome, slender Canadian exactly my height and had a big, dark moustache that I couldn't persuade him to shave off. There was something about Roland that made you want to take care of him. He'd always arrive in the worst possible humor, and instead of saying "Good morning," he'd be gruff to Oona and say, "Well, for Chrissakes, where the hell is the coffee and where the hell is *she?*" Oona, for some reason, loved Roland and would say, "Don't talk fresh. Mrs. Greenough is getting dressed, and since you're in such a fine humor, I hope she's late."

Then she'd give him coffee and the newspapers, and would treat him like one of the children. It got to be an Abbott and Costello routine for both of them, because Roland would act foul even when he didn't feel that way. He really became another member of the family. If Roland was there for dinner, he got dinner; if not, his plate was removed. Milton is ten miles south of Boston, and on snowy nights he'd sometimes stay over. All the kids got to know Roland very well, and because he was so moody, they all ignored him. Except Muffy. She fully accepted Roland the way she accepted Bumpy, our dog. And it was terribly funny to see her impose herself on Roland. If he was in the library playing the piano, she would simply sit down next to him. He was so shy and introverted, yet he accepted that as perfectly normal.

I'd been working with Gagnon for three and a half years when *Julius Caesar* came up, and by then I was used to taking criticism from him that I took from absolutely nobody else. If I was convinced something was good, I didn't care what anybody told me, I was right—unless Roland said otherwise.

Roland wrote all the ornamentation for everything I sang from the moment we began working together in 1962. I know Miss Liebling was hurt by that, but Roland was simply too talented *not* to use. When Julius and I started working on *Julius Caesar* the summer before its premiere, Roland taught me how to sing Cleopatra. He wrote all the ornamentation and showed me how to throw myself into a role musically, to convey as much dramatic intensity with my voice as I did with my body.

When he and I began preparing the ornamentation for Cleopatra's arias in *Julius Caesar,* I told him I felt that every time Cleopatra was with Caesar, she should caress him vocally. So that's what we went for: the most sensual kind of ornamentation imaginable.

On the first day of rehearsals, I showed up ready to play Cleopatra like an operatic Elizabeth Taylor, and Norman was prepared to do a Shakespearean Caesar à la John Gielgud. Tito told us both to forget it. When Norman asked him what he intended to do, Tito said, "I'm going to do it baroque."

"What's baroque?" Norman asked.

"Slow motion ballet," Tito said.

Norman and I panicked, of course, but Tito and Gigi had done their homework and were very sure of themselves. Tito had cut the 242-year-old opera from five hours to three hours, and he and Gigi had researched it thoroughly; they had discovered that performers had once done the opera with balletic movements. There'd be no simple walking for us. "Make no gesture," Gigi told us, "except as if you were waving feathers." She felt I would have no problems. I wouldn't have dared to try that approach with any other directors. By then, Norman and I had great confidence in the Capobiancos. With Gigi and Tito, there was never an "easy" way. Whatever we did with them, we gave everything we had.

As opening night approached, *Julius Caesar* became something special, although not for Norman and me. Rudel had invited Maureen Forrester, the great Canadian mezzo-soprano, to play the role of Cornelia, the widow of Pompey. That was a smart move, because twenty years ago, no one could touch Maureen in this repertoire—it was almost like having the heavyweight champion of the world come in and strut his stuff. It was exciting to have her join us. Maureen Forrester was a Name; nobody knew who the hell Norman Treigle and Beverly Sills were. All the attention was focused on Maureen, to the extent that *Time* magazine did a feature on her before *Julius Caesar* opened.

Meanwhile, the international press had come to New York to review the opening of the Metropolitan Opera. Less attention was being paid to the Met's world premiere of Samuel Barber's *Antony and Cleopatra,* starring Leontyne Price, than to the opening of the world's greatest opera company in a brand-new house. The opera press corps was in town to check out the acoustics and design of the Metropolitan Opera's new home. Although we were only fifty yards away from the Met in Lincoln Center, absolutely no one knew what the New York City Opera was up to.

That point really hit home one afternoon when I was out walking and bumped into Rosalind Elias. Rozzie, who was singing at the Met, is cute as a button, with big saucer eyes and a perky little nose. As always, she was almost beside herself with enthusiasm. "Boy, there's so much *excitement* in New York!" Rozzie said. "We've got Leontyne opening our house and you've got Maureen! Who's singing Julius Caesar?"

"Treigle," I said.

"And who's the Cleopatra?"

"Me, you dummy. Who'd you think it was?"

"How the hell should *I* know?" Rozzie laughed. "That's the best-kept secret in New York. All we hear is Forrester."

I was *so* unsavvy in those days. I just presumed that everyone knew Norman and I were starring in this opera, and here even a longtime colleague hadn't heard about us. I went back to Julius and told him it was pretty obvious the public had never heard of Treigle and Sills, and he agreed with me. The City Opera had a one-man public relations department, and his press releases usually got lost when *The New York Times,* for example, had to choose between doing a story on the City Opera or the Met.

"I'm going to get myself a public relations person," I said to Julius.

"You *should,*" he told me. And so I did. Whenever I sang with Erich Leinsdorf and Sarah Caldwell in Boston, I'd gotten into friendly conversations with Edgar Vincent, a New York-based publicist. Edgar was reputed to be the opera world's brightest, classiest P.R. man, and I'd certainly come to regard him as such. Edgar represented several famous conductors, and he'd suggested me for jobs with clients of his, like André Kostelanetz. We had once discussed working together, and Edgar had told me that to do public relations on a national scale for me, he would need something special to publicize. I called Edgar eight days before the opening of *Julius Caesar.* He agreed that the time was finally right for us to begin working together.

I'd contacted him too late to publicize my appearance as Cleopatra properly, but Edgar said, "We're going to have a ball." And for the rest of my career, we certainly did. Edgar became a mentor, manager, *Sunday Times* crossword puzzle consultant, and above all, my friend. He's a gentleman with an impeccable code of ethics. Edgar never overstated the function of a publicist. Operatic careers, he said, were not built on press hype. Edgar couldn't sing or act for me, nor could he persuade opera critics and audiences to like me—that was *my* job. His job was to let it be known where I sang well, got good reviews, and won public approval. Edgar supervised every aspect of my career, and he and his associate, Marjorie Samuel, who handled day-to-day matters, did a wonderful job for me.

The Met opened its season before we did, and unfortunately, Barber's *Antony and Cleopatra* was not very well received. The opera house itself, however, got rave reviews for its acoustics and architectural beauty. I still prefer Philip Johnson's New York State Theater, the City Opera's home, especially because of its spectacular three-tier promenade. The international press corps decided it might as well see what else was going on at Lincoln Center, so its members walked across the plaza to see our *Julius Caesar*.

I don't know what they expected, but I know what they got. Norman was noble, Maureen was marvelous, Tito and Gigi's staging was superb, and all the work that Roland and I had put into Cleopatra paid off. At the end of the second act, Cleopatra sings a long, difficult aria, *"Se pieta,"* in which she laments that she's ready to die if God won't take pity on her and allow her to love Caesar. Roland and I decided I would sing it in what's called *fil di voce,* as in *filigree.* It was a risky thing to do, because you have to sing very high and very soft for a very long period of time, which takes a lot of breath control and tremendous technique. You have to sing that aria as if you're not breathing; the audience must *never* be aware that you're actually taking time out to breathe. *"Se pieta"* is about eight minutes long, and I sang another of Cleopatra's arias, *"Piangero,"* the same way.

I must say that Julius was extremely cooperative. Just before the start of our opening performance he said, "To do 'Se pieta' like that, you're going to need incredible breath control. Are you sure you're going to have it?"

"No, I'm *not* sure," I told him, "but it's certainly worth a try."

"I'll go right along with you, and if you're in trouble and you want to start moving, we'll go," he said.

Well, the opera started, and I made it through *"Piangero"* and then, when I began *"Se pieta,"* an absolute hush came over the audience. People were hanging on every note. I think *"Se pieta"* was the single most extraordinary piece of singing I ever did. I know I had never heard myself sing that way before. It was very different from the usual coloratura fireworks—it was all control and pianissimo singing. When I finished the aria, I saw Gigi in the wings. She was weeping. The curtain began coming down very slowly, and the deathlike silence continued—and then a roar went through that house the likes of which I'd never heard. I was a little stunned by it: The audience wouldn't stop applauding. Treigle and I hated to break character by taking curtain calls between acts—why work so hard persuading the audience to believe in our characters if Bev and

Normie were going to take bows every time the audience liked what we sang? So I didn't come out for a bow, but the people wouldn't leave their seats. They just sat there applauding and applauding as if it were the end of the opera.

I had another aria to sing in Act III, and when the final curtain came down, I just knew I'd never performed like that before. I hadn't gone into the theater thinking: *Okay, fellas, lean back. I'm going to give you a piece of singing like you never heard before.* What happened is simply that the role of Cleopatra was tailor-made for me. Vocally, there were just no hurdles in it that I couldn't handle, and handle brilliantly. And I knew it. In most operas, there's always a section that troubles a singer for one reason or another. However significant or however trivial, it just sits there and you can't get it out of your head, and when you reach that moment in a performance, you've gone through all kinds of preparation and worry. I didn't worry about *any* part of *Julius Caesar.* When I finished, I didn't have a single correction to make in my performance. I went home totally happy. I remember going backstage and saying to Peter and my mother: "I want to hear somebody do what I just did."

"You never will," my mother said. I took that for what it was worth, which was plenty: Mama had listened to my voice since I was three, and she wasn't above coming backstage every once in a while to say, "I think you should work on your high E's, honey."

The next morning I took the shuttle back to Boston; Oona had taken care of Bucky and Muffy for several days and had to be relieved. I read the New York papers on the plane, and I'd gotten sensational reviews. There was no question that my performance in *Julius Caesar* was going to change my life. I'd finally been in the right place at the right time. At the age of thirty-seven, I became an "overnight" star.

Someone once asked me how you can go to sleep virtually unknown and wake up a superstar. I think that happens in any field the first time you prove you can do one thing better than anybody else in the world. I'm sure lots of ladies subsequently may have sung Cleopatra as well as I did in 1966, but at the time, nobody else could have equaled my work that night. Four days after my first Cleopatra, when I walked in the New York State Theater's stage door, I stopped to look in the message box at the switchboard.

The five-inch box was jammed. I had invitations to sing in literally *every* major opera house in the world—except, of course, the Met. That's when the craziness of my career began.

Our fall season ended on November 13, and the following year I sang in Austria, Mexico, Peru, and Switzerland, and in a number of cities throughout the United States.

How did I feel? Well, I was no longer a young girl, so the attention I was getting didn't knock me over the way it might have ten years before. My main concern in life was the fact that I had two children with severe problems. The career was really rather incidental at that point—it was nice to have, but not essential. I'd survived so much in my personal life that I didn't see how a career could make a great difference to me. As a matter of fact, when you don't need the money and you have a very satisfactory marriage, it's difficult to muster the drive necessary to establish a great career. I know I didn't have that drive when we first moved to Boston. I was then thirty-two, thrilled to have escaped Cleveland, and content to live my life as Beverly Greenough, wife and mother. Things didn't work out that way.

I guess what I'm trying to say is that I never expected to have a career of such enormous proportions. While it was happening—and even at the height of my career—all the attention I attracted was a little hard to believe. I'd often think: *Who, me?* That was the extent of my identity crisis. I really can't think of an aspect of my career that I *didn't* enjoy. To me, becoming famous meant that I could pretty much pick and choose whenever and wherever I wanted to sing. I loved performing, and I never lost that love or questioned it.

When I worked with Roland Gagnon on *Julius Caesar,* I became Cleopatra. That was the first time I lost my own identity while onstage and realized I could become any character I played. It was a joyous, healing experience for me. All those hours and years of working with Roland, and rehearsing and performing, were my escape from being Beverly Sills. And when I first met Roland, I *needed* an escape.

My son's handicaps were terrible to see. A few months after my appearance in *Julius Caesar,* it became clear that we weren't doing Bucky a favor by keeping him home. My son was always isolated and alone, with no one his own age or size to play with or relate to. Since he was autistic, he rarely did either of those things. When the girls had friends in to visit, I had to separate Bucky from the children, because his behavior and the noises he made were bizarre. Bucky cannot speak at all, and as a child, his frustration was so great that he became dangerously self-abusive. Caring for Bucky and keeping him safe each day was a twenty-four-hour job, and Oona and I were wearing very thin.

When he was six years old, we sent Bucky to the Dr. Franklin Perkins School in Lancaster, Massachusetts. Peter and I both knew that our son was leaving home forever. A few weeks after Bucky left, I sang the three soprano leads in *Il Trittico,* which is made up of three one-act operas by Puccini. In *Suor Angelica,* I played an unwed mother who's become a nun and who learns that her son died two years earlier. My mother was in the audience and tells me she never saw me give a more moving performance. That was probably the most personally painful opera I ever sang. I performed *Il Trittico* on March 8, 1967. I never sang it again.

In the summer, the Treigles and the Greenoughs joined the Capobiancos in Cincinnati, where I spent most of July singing *Traviata* and *Die Fledermaus.* Julius realized he had a very special team in Norman, me, and the Capobiancos. That fall, he put us all together in *Le Coq d'Or,* which Norman was very anxious to do. Julius asked me to select an opera I wanted to sing the following spring. I suggested *Manon,* and he liked the idea.

Rimsky-Korsakov's *Le Coq d'Or* is based on a Russian fairy tale about a shrewd, lazy king who's given a golden rooster that crows whenever the king's armies are needed. Treigle played old King Dodon, and I played his adversary, the Queen of Shemakha, who's vowed to conquer King Dodon through her beauty.

When Norman and I worked with Tito and Gigi on *The Tales of Hoffmann* and *Julius Caesar,* we'd followed what I thought would be our standard operating procedure: At our first rehearsals, the Capobiancos had talked to both of us about blocking, lighting, special effects, and so forth. This time, the Capobiancos concentrated almost 100 percent on Norman, and when they weren't directing him they were working with Muriel Costa-Greenspon, who played a comic character called Amelfa. There seemed to be a plot and a plan for everybody but me. I kept saying: "I feel I should be doing something here." And Tito would say, "No, no. Sometimes less is better." That wasn't like him at all. Usually, when Tito saw that I was uncomfortable he'd drop everything, find out why I was having trouble with a particular moment, and then solve the problem. Not this time. Tito ignored me completely, which is the most insulting thing a director can do to a performer. Yet the Capobiancos were like family; they would *never* do that to me. But they *did*! The only thing Tito said to me was: "Think Mae West."

I said, "How can I think Mae West? I have nothing to *do*."

"Just make the lines funny," he said, and continued to skip over me. Everyone else was moving except me; Tito kept me planted on the stage as if I were a tree. He kept saying: "Stay there. Don't worry."

"How can I *not* worry?" I said. Norman was being given a million pieces of stage business; I was given none.

"I sing in this opera, too, you know," I told Tito. "When do *I* come into the picture?"

Things remained like that until five days before dress rehearsal, when I stopped everything and told Tito: "Listen, we have to have a talk—I can't go on like this."

I really said that.

Well, Tito and Gigi and Norman looked at each other, and I could see they were all in on something together. Tito said, "We're going to have a rehearsal this afternoon for you alone."

"Well, *finally*," I said.

Tito left me with Gigi, who took me into a dance room and told me what they'd cooked up for me in Act II: a twenty-five-minute, comic hootchy-kootchy belly dance, to be done while I was singing a long aria.

"Forget it!" I told Gigi. "I can waltz, but that doesn't make me a dancer."

"You can do it," she said.

"You're crazy," I told her. "Let me ask you something. Knowing what you had in mind for me, why didn't you and Tito give me at least two weeks to learn this instead of waiting till five days before dress rehearsal?"

Gigi told me Tito thought I'd be *very* anxious to dance after sitting still for so long. The reason everyone else had been given blocking directions was to free me up for a week—I was through going to rehearsals. From then on, I was to work out in a dance room with Gigi every day.

"What are you planning to do with me?" I asked.

"You'll see," she said.

We worked three hours that first day, and by the end of it, I was frightened to death. While singing to this old king about how beautiful my body is, I'd be doing stomach rolls, hip rolls, and shaking my fanny at the audience. My big worry was that people would think I was actually trying to be sexy. Gigi kept saying: "Keep in mind it's a trade-off: For every two sexy movements, you're going to do one funny, absolutely ridiculous movement. The audience will be caught off guard and will understand it's a takeoff. They'll love it."

I was going to be wearing a little bra and harem pants and a five-tiered headdress decorated with sequins and crystal beads—when the lights hit it, the thing looked like a chandelier. When Gigi showed me the costume, I figured that with just a little despair and dieting, I'd be fine. "This is a pushover," I told her. "None of this will really be suggestive."

"Don't bet on it," she said. "Tito's going to have the scene back-lit."

Back-lighting would emphasize and accentuate every inch of me. "You can't do that to me, Gigi," I complained. "I'm too big to get away with that. *Everything* about me is too big."

"But that's the whole point," she replied. "If you were perfectly formed, if your figure was thirty-four–twenty-three–thirty-four, *then* we'd have a problem. You're not built like that, so we won't have a problem—*if you behave right!*"

I wasn't quite sure what she meant by that, but I trusted Gigi, so I behaved right. Tito and Gigi's concept of the Queen of Shemakha worked out brilliantly and was one of the major reasons why *Le Coq d'Or* turned out to be a real crowd-pleaser. Our opening night performance caused critics to trot out their fanciest adjectives; we had a big, big hit on our hands.

For whatever reason, our third performance wasn't nearly as good as our first two had been, or at least I felt that way when I came offstage after Act II. I asked Gigi for her opinion and she said, "Everything's fine, Beverly."

I think that's the only time I've really gotten ticked off at Gigi. "You're one of the very few people I trust, so don't ever lie to me. If it's rotten, I expect you to tell me so," I said. "I'm going to ask you again: How's it going tonight?"

"Rotten," she said.

I never had the same kind of problem with Julius Rudel. He

usually thought the operas I did with the Capobiancos were going to be real stinkers. Before *Julius Caesar,* Rudel took a long look at Tito's balletic approach to the work and told Gigi: "They all look like faggots and queens." Before *Le Coq d'Or,* he told her: "This is a Mickey Mouse show, a disaster." In all fairness to Julius, whenever our little team proved him wrong—which was every time he questioned us—he'd acknowledge the fact, sometimes graciously, sometimes grudgingly. After *Julius Caesar* he told me: "God watches over a fool like me."

The following season, the spring of 1968, Tito and Gigi directed me in *Manon.* While we were in rehearsal, Rudel told Gigi: "The style is wrong. Why is everyone moving around with handkerchiefs? It looks ridiculous."

Julius never addressed such comments to Tito or me, because we would have screamed at him. In point of fact, the Capobiancos' production of *Manon* was hauntingly beautiful and effective. The sets, by Marsha Eck, were reminiscent of Fragonard paintings, and designer José Varona provided the cast with vivid early eighteenth-century costumes.

Rudel the impresario was an eternal worrywart; Rudel the conductor was a marvelous ally in the pit. Julius was one of the few conductors I ever sang with who was interested in helping me create dramatic theatrical effects. We seemed to be on a wavelength all our own. I could have my back turned to Julius and take a five-second pause without ever having mentioned it to him, and we'd always begin together again. It was uncanny.

Sometimes, when I was tired, I'd look down to the podium and Julius would smile at me and nod his head reassuringly, and I'd know that he was ready to provide me with whatever I needed, be it a change in pacing or timing. Years later, as company director, I came to understand fully the frustrations he faced. When the final curtain came down, all the tumult and shouting was directed at the singers. Of course, when he conducted, Julius got the opportunity to take the final bow, but the audience's greatest applause was always reserved for the singers.

Manon was another major step forward for me. I'd done it first with Ponselle in Baltimore on a kind of semiprofessional level, and hadn't sung it again until I came to Boston and did it with Sarah

Caldwell. I thought Manon would be a good role for me; my voice was perfect for French repertoire and I spoke the language fluently. I loved the role vocally, but I never liked the character until Gigi and I sat down and talked about her for several hours.

I'd heard a lot of Manons, including Victoria de Los Angeles's portrayal, which was one of the most famous. I thought De Los Angeles had all of Manon's early innocence but never quite came into her own as a believable member of the Parisian demimonde. Hers was certainly a beautifully sung version, but still, I'd never seen a portrayal that totally appealed to me. As I noted earlier, from the moment they walked onstage, most singers played Manon as a slut, and I didn't agree with that interpretation at all. They also failed to imbue her with the sophistication that helps Manon become the talk of Paris. You have to make the audience *very* aware of how far this woman has come. Manon is first seen as an awkward little girl carrying a basket with her lunch—bread and grapes. By the start of the third act, she's become a glamorous courtesan who does a dance with her walking stick, wears expensive jewelry with ease, and sends noblemen off to find still more bracelets for her.

In the Saint-Sulpice scene, when Manon goes to lure her former lover away from the monastic life, Gigi and I decided that Manon's approach should be sensual rather than romantic. When I sang to Des Grieux, I'd almost wrap him up in a chiffon scarf I was wearing. At the end of the duet, Des Grieux buried his face in the scarf, as if my perfume had simply overwhelmed him. Tito's concept of the scene for Manon was very physical and sexual. Des Grieux was the romantic until after their duet. When the curtain came down, he was actually kissing Manon's breast. Tito staged it as pure lust. One night while we were doing that scene, a woman seated behind *Newsweek* critic Hubert Saal turned to her husband and shouted, "Sam! Sam! She's driving him crazy!"

Michele Molese, the tenor who played Des Grieux, did a pretty good job of driving *me* crazy. He also did a good job of driving himself crazy. I'd first sung with Molese when he played Hoffmann in *The Tales of Hoffmann*. One night when he thought he was singing badly—and we were lying together on a couch in the midst of a passionate scene—Molese whispered, "I'm going to be a used-car salesman."

I told him: "*Tomorrow* you'll be a used-car salesman; tonight, you'll sing *Hoffmann*."

When we did *Manon* together, Molese and I had a scene in the second act in which Des Grieux and Manon are in bed together. I have no idea why, but even in dress rehearsal, whenever we got to that scene, Molese would start biting and nibbling away at me. In no uncertain terms I told him to cut it out. Molese heatedly denied doing anything wrong.

Well, he did it to me on opening night, and this time I asked Julius to step in and tell him to stop. Molese told Julius I was imagining things, but Gigi and everyone else in the wings had seen what he was up to. I finally hired the company's photographer, Beth Bergman, to take some shots of Mike and me during a performance, and once again he began giving me love bites. Beth's photos clearly established that, but when we showed him the pictures, he *still* denied doing anything wrong. He claimed he was only acting. Molese was a fine talent who stayed with the New York City Opera until the end of 1973 and returned only occasionally thereafter. Mike never really hit it big, but after he left I often worked with tenors who'd leave me muttering, "Where are you, Molese?"

The City Opera's spring 1968 season included *Manon,* and again my faith in the Capobiancos was rewarded—the opera was a spectacular success. Miss Liebling, then ninety, had been in ill health for several years, but Peter made a point of picking her up and driving her to my opening nights at the City Opera. Miss Liebling was never more pleased with me than when I sang French repertoire. The next morning, after New York's various media reviewers had praised our production to the skies, Miss Liebling sent me a bouquet and a note that said "See? Teacher."

That didn't mean Miss Liebling had mellowed. In the fall, I sang Marguerite in a new production of *Faust*. The morning after *Faust* opened, Miss Liebling telephoned me at seven o'clock to say that my trills in the Jewel Song had been slow and sloppy, and that she expected me at her studio at ten. Teacher was right. We worked for forty-five minutes, and when I left, my trills were no longer slow or sloppy.

Gigi recently reminded me that the Metropolitan Opera had hired Renata Scotto to do nine performances of *Manon* the year following the City Opera's production. After seeing our *Manon* sell out in the spring and again in the fall of 1968, the Met acknowledged that our production would be a tough act to follow, and canceled their own. Scotto sang a different opera instead.

I think the Capobiancos enabled me to come as close to a definitive Manon as I could. People came to see my performance from all over the world, and except for Rolf Liebermann's production at the Paris Opéra, I was invited to perform the role all over the world.

A couple of years before—the summer prior to doing *Julius Caesar*—I'd made an alleged debut with the Metropolitan Opera in a concert performance of *Don Giovanni* at Lewisohn Stadium in New York. After *Manon,* I expected Rudolf Bing to invite me to sing next door at the Met, but that didn't happen. Crushed, I wasn't. Before the end of the year, my list of international appearances included engagements in Chile and Argentina. I still wasn't very well known in Europe, but that was about to change too.

THIRTEEN

During the first week of January 1969, Edgar Vincent got a somewhat frantic telephone call from Thomas Schippers, the American conductor, who was living in Rome. That April, to commemorate the one hundredth anniversary of Gioacchino Rossini's death, Schippers was scheduled to conduct six performances of the composer's *The Siege of Corinth* at La Scala in Milan. Tommy had a problem: Soprano Renata Scotto, who'd been cast in the lead role of Pamira, was pregnant and had just canceled. Schippers needed a soprano who spoke Italian and who could learn the role fast.

Edgar certainly *did* know a soprano who could solve Tommy's problem. When Schippers called me, I told him yes, of course, I'd be more than happy to step in. This was not a great sacrifice on my part. La Scala is to opera what the Palace Theater was to vaudeville, what Yankee Stadium has been to baseball, what Lourdes is to people who believe in miracles. La Scala is *the* official shrine of international opera. If you sing well at La Scala, God smiles on your career. Every Italian—and every opera singer—knows this.

So I signed up to sing Pamira. Dramatically, the role was unsatisfying—no acting was asked for or needed; *The Siege of Corinth* was one of the few stand-up-and-sing operas I ever did. When you finally get the chance to sing at La Scala, however, you tend to take it, regardless of what's playing.

Schippers reassured me that Pamira would be a powerful part. He'd inserted a lot of music from Rossini's earlier version of the opera, *Maometto II*, into *The Siege of Corinth*. Tommy said I'd love it. I asked him when and where he wanted me to show up. He wanted me to fly to Rome in early February to begin working on the role with him.

Edgar then accomplished what he considers some of the finest work he ever did on my behalf: He helped me to back out gracefully from prior commitments to sing with the City Opera, with Eugene Ormandy, and with the Boston Symphony in four performances and a recording of Beethoven's Ninth Symphony. Erich Leinsdorf graciously released me from the Boston Symphony engagement. The City Opera was no problem, either. Julius Rudel and John White couldn't have been happier for me. Eugene Ormandy, however, was less than thrilled. I was supposed to sing four concert performances as well as make a recording of Mendelssohn's oratorio *Elijah* for him. I was canceling a very important engagement. Gene—who was still "Maestro" to me in 1979—decided to ponder the question of which was more important: an engagement at La Scala or an appearance with Ormandy and the Philadelphia Orchestra. When I first told him about it, he didn't offer instant reassurance that he'd release me from my contract. I went down to see him in Philadelphia.

I desperately wanted to sing at La Scala. "Maestro," I said, "I'm an opera singer, for God's sake, and it's La Scala, for God's sake. For God's sake, let me *go*!"

He finally did, but only on condition that I come up with a suitable replacement for myself. Edgar took care of that: He found Jane Marsh, a soprano who'd just won the prestigious Tchaikovsky competition in Moscow—the competition that had made a star of Van Cliburn.

In the meantime, Schippers sent me a copy of the score. He wasn't mistaken about Pamira; on a purely vocal level, it was indeed a dream part, a *phenomenal* part. As is true of the best *bel canto* operas, Schippers's hybrid was filled with coloratura fireworks—*torrents* of high notes. And Gagnon ornamented my arias like you can't believe. My God, what a job he did. When Gagnon read the score he told me that one aria, *"Dal soggiorno,"* would make me or break me. It was a very high, sustained piece of singing, and I was either going to win or lose right there. We worked hard and long on it.

Peter accompanied me on a night flight to Rome, but when we got there we discovered that Schippers was busy conducting concerts and couldn't see us for three days. Peter suggested a quickie vacation in Taormina, on the Sicilian coast. Instead of staying overnight in Rome, we flew on to Catania, the destination of that bungled World War II paratroop mission Peter had investigated. From there, we drove a few miles up the coast to Taormina and checked into the San Domenico Palace, a monastery that had been converted into a beautiful hotel. We'd been flying all night, and right around five o'clock I told Peter I was bushed and needed a little nap before dinner. I woke up at eight P.M. feeling thoroughly refreshed. "That nap was just what I needed," I told him.

When we walked into the hotel's restaurant, an American couple we knew from Boston approached us at the little bar just off the entrance. The man said, "Hi, Bev. Gee, we missed you yesterday."

I didn't know what to make of that, so I gave him a polite smile and kept moving. When we walked into the dining room, the headwaiter came up to us and said, "Your usual table, Mr. Greenough?"

I looked at my husband. "What's going on here, Peter?"

He started laughing out loud. Peter just could not contain himself. "You certainly *did* need that little nap," he said. "You were asleep for about twenty-seven hours."

"You're kidding," I said.

He wasn't kidding.

"You were supposed to wake me up for dinner."

"I did." He laughed. "Aren't you hungry?"

I *was* very hungry. And I was very upset. I'd lost an entire day out of my life, and it was all Peter's fault. It took me a while to see any humor in the situation. I think I finally came around when the waiter served our first course.

Peter is a bit of a practical joker, which is why he absolutely *loved* our first meeting with Tommy and Nonie Schippers. A couple of days after my big sleep, we visited them at their duplex apartment in Rome. Nonie was the daughter of Mike Phipps, one of the largest stockholders in U.S. Steel. I was still admiring the apartment's furnishings when Nonie came down the staircase bearing a tray of tea and cookies. When she got downstairs, she tripped over a rug and sent everything on the tray flying. She picked herself up and said, "How's that for an entrance?" We were instant friends.

Tommy was from Kalamazoo, Michigan, and his Dutch parents had nicknamed him Skip—he was a very All-American kind of fellow. He and I were about the same age, and he'd been performing almost as long as I had. Tommy was six when he gave his first piano concert, and as a teenager he performed piano and organ concerts throughout the Midwest. When Schippers was seventeen he won a national contest to conduct the Philadelphia Orchestra, immediately after which he was hired by the Metropolitan Opera as a coach-pianist.

Schippers became a resident conductor of the New York City Opera in 1952, and in the spring of 1955—six months before I joined the City Opera—Tommy was lured away by the Met. Ever since then, he had had been a brilliant fixture on the world opera scene. Eileen Farrell was about the only singer I knew who didn't like Schippers. Once when he was conducting, she came out onstage, looked down into the orchestra pit, and said, "Ah, I see that Pippers is in the shit again!" Funny, funny woman. Wonderful, wonderful conductor.

Tommy and Nonie and Peter and I got very chummy. After I'd worked a week or so with Tommy, my husband and I returned to Boston. On February 20, I opened the City Opera's so-called spring season in *Manon*. After popping down to San Antonio to join Treigle and Alexander in *Faust,* I gave the second recital of my career in Cincinnati. Roland Gagnon was my accompanist and was very clear about letting me know that if and when I started doing recitals on a regular basis, I'd best start looking for another accompanist; he hated performing in public.

Shortly after the Cincinnati recital, Peter and I flew to Milan and sublet a ten-room apartment. I was going to be away over Easter, five weeks in all, and I wanted the kids, my mother, Roland, and Gigi to fly over and stay with us—Tito was too busy then. The apartment was very pleasant and came complete with a nice Italian maid and cook, who liked the idea of having the American prima donna stay with them. We usually had a lot of company, and because the place was so big, we always had some laughs guessing who'd turn up at the breakfast table.

One morning when I woke up early, I walked into the kitchen and there was Gagnon, drinking a cup of coffee and reading an Italian newspaper. He acted as if we were home in Milton.

"Good morning," I said. I sat down and poured myself some coffee. "How are you?"

"Fine," Roland said.

I absolutely refused to ask when he had arrived or why. I'd invited Roland to fly over as my guest for opening night of *The Siege of Corinth;* he'd shown up three and a half weeks early. Why had he come so early? By the end of the day, Roland told me he'd gotten nervous. He was worried that he and I weren't working every day, and that all the ornaments he'd written were being battled over, which happened to be the case. Schippers had hired a gentleman by the name of Randolph Mickelson to do the ornamentation. I told Tommy and Mickelson I would not give up one note of my ornamentation. Mickelson and I had knockdown battles over that, because I was insisting that Mr. Gagnon get credit for my ornamentations. The way it worked out, I think Mickelson got a program credit for some type of musical preparations, and nobody got credit for ornamentations. Roland didn't care, which is why nobody has ever heard of this gifted man. An awful lot of people have taken credit for work he did. He cared only that I sang his ornamentations and sang them well.

Three or four months before I was hired by La Scala, Hubert Saal had begun interviewing me for a major *Newsweek* article that had a chance to become a cover story. Saal was taking a made-in-the-U.S.A. approach, but that changed when I got the La Scala engagement. At that point, *Newsweek* decided to tie the article to my La Scala debut and go with a cover story.

For the first time in my career I felt a great deal of pressure. I had a lot at stake here. If my performance as Pamira was a fiasco, I could kiss the *Newsweek* cover story goodbye. The same thing would probably be true of any chance I had to win a European following. If I sang badly, every opera impresario on the continent would know all about it the next day. When you flop at La Scala, you don't just fall on your face, you fall down a manhole.

On top of all that, I felt terribly uncomfortable going in as Scotto's substitute. Callas was gone from La Scala, Tebaldi was in America, and Scotto was then the reigning queen of Milan's great opera house. She was a tiny, beautiful Italian woman, and here was I, a big, unknown American. Renata was a special favorite of the costume lady, who treated me as an interloper.

A well-publicized incident took place between us. The woman had cut and sewn a gold costume for Renata, but because of my hair color, I didn't go for the gold. I thought silver would be a far better color for me. Costume and set designer Nicola Benois agreed, so I asked the wardrobe lady please to redo the dress in silver. Even though she told me not to worry, she did nothing about it. I tried to explain to the woman that Renata and I had talked, that we were friends, and that it was a happy occasion for both of us. The costume lady remained resentful. And the gown remained gold.

On the day of our first dress rehearsal, I carried the costume onstage and had the wardrobe lady meet me there. In front of the rest of the cast and the chorus, I asked her quite loudly: "Did I not tell you four or five times to make this costume in silver?" Yes, that was true, she conceded. I borrowed the pair of scissors she wore like a pendant and cut the gown in half. I told her to make it in silver, at which point the chorus broke into applause and began *cheering*. Italians love their pasta *al dente* and their divas temperamental.

Apart from that woman, the people backstage were helpful and efficient. La Scala is big business. By opera standards, the theater is almost stadium-sized—it is the largest in Europe, seating 3,600 people. La Scala's management behaves like IBM executives assessing a small company that makes good home computers—they credit the little guy's enterprise, but understand that *they're* the aristocrats of the business. La Scala was a little too impressed with itself. While the sets for *The Siege of Corinth* were tasteful—and certainly Benois is a great designer—they were also old-fashioned. I thought we could have done something a little more imaginative.

I needed all the help I could get. Gigi joined me in Milan, and she did my makeup and also gave me suggestions on the staging. The idea was for me tactfully to convey several of her ideas to Sandro Sequi, the director. Gigi definitely helped make a rather static opera more interesting. Roland prepared me well, and I was in top shape vocally. Of course I couldn't very well bring him into the little rehearsal room with Thomas Schippers—that's not the way it's done. I thought that when we started rehearsing onstage, Roland and Gigi would get a chance to watch what I was doing. That's what we did: They showed up at the theater four or five days before opening night, and the two of them checked me out. They liked what they saw and heard.

I was very comfortable working with Schippers and with the two other featured singers in the production. Bass Justino Diaz and mezzo-soprano Marilyn Horne were world-class talents, and fellow Americans, to boot.

I'd never bumped into Marilyn before. When we met in Milan, Marilyn's first words to me were: "We might as well get it out in the open—I prefer Sutherland to you."

I burst out laughing. Joan and I were never rivals. And we were totally different performers. Joan has a terrific sense of humor and I knew she would have found the remark as funny as I did.

Marilyn Horne has a *great* voice, but never has gotten the attention she deserves. Unfortunately, that's the common fate of mezzo-sopranos. Except in *Carmen* and a couple of other operas, mezzo-sopranos are always the second leads. They rarely get the last curtain call. When you make a career of standing next to a formidable soprano like Sutherland and hearing the crowd cheering for her, it can bother you—and I think it bothered Marilyn a lot. Let's face it: The pitcher gets the credit for winning or losing a baseball game, but he certainly needs support and, often enough, sensational play from the rest of the team. Well, on the Sutherland-Horne team, Joan did the pitching.

Marilyn and her daughter had taken an apartment in the same building my family and I were staying in, and I spent a good deal of time with her. Every day we walked to the theater together, had lunch together—we got along very well. Until opening night. Edgar Vincent had come to Milan to handle press coverage of my La Scala debut, and an hour or so before I went on, he was in my dressing room showing me some publicity pictures taken at the dress rehearsal.

Suddenly, Marilyn barged in, absolutely furious. Marilyn was singing the part of Neocle, the soldier Pamira's father wants her to marry, and she was wearing all her armor. Someone in La Scala's publicity department had told her that Edgar was not only handling my publicity, but was also in charge of picking out pictures to be run alongside *The New York Times* review of *The Siege of Corinth*. Marilyn called Edgar a son of a bitch and threatened to punch him in the face if my picture appeared in *The New York Times* and hers didn't. Edgar tried explaining that he was working for me, not for the *Times,* and was not in any position to select what the *Times* would or would not publish. Marilyn didn't believe him. She was convinced Edgar was planning to cut her out of any *New York Times* photos. Marilyn bellowed a bit more and then stormed out. Horne was still more upset later when *Newsweek* published a cover story on me during the La Scala engagement, even though Marilyn was mentioned prominently in the article.

Despite all that nonsense, it was a joy to sing with Marilyn Horne. Neither one of us was known to the La Scala audience—she had debuted there a short time before in Stravinsky's *Oedipus Rex,* which didn't properly show her off. It was fun to take on that public and show them a thing or two about singing Rossini.

Besides the run-in with Marilyn, I had one other unpleasant experience before that first performance. Claques—paid cheering sections made up of two or three dozen people—are still alive and well throughout the European opera world. Nowhere, however, are claques as accepted and well organized as in Italy. The way you get a claque to clap for you is to pay off its leader. If you don't pay off, the claque will boo and whistle every time you open your mouth, which can turn a performance into a nightmare. And so at most opera houses, particularly in Italy—and *most* particularly at La Scala—everyone pays off. Intriguingly enough, once your claque begins getting paid off, its members become your fiercest partisans, your most loyal allies. The various claques then compete with one another to see who can scream longer and louder for the singers they both love and victimize. It really is crazy.

The following season, I sang *Lucia* at La Scala. On opening night, the head of the claque came backstage and demanded an extravagant amount of money from me. If I didn't pay, his people would boo, whistle, and hiss at me all through the opera.

"I belong to a very powerful 'family' in New York," I said, lying through my teeth. I was so icily angry that the guy didn't *dare* doubt me. "Do you understand me? Do you understand what I mean by *family*? One sound out of you, and I would suggest you leave Milan. Do I make myself clear? Do you understand what I'm telling you?"

He understood; we were speaking Italian. The man was thoroughly shaken. My father's family, the Silvermans, were certainly a powerful bunch.

During the run of *The Siege of Corinth,* Schippers decided that before every performance, the four Americans—Schippers himself, Diaz, Horne, and I—should each put the equivalent in lire of about $10 into a single envelope, and let the claques themselves decide how to divide it up. We did that and weren't bothered again.

Our opening night was magical. Roland had been right about the "*Dal soggiorno.*" When I began singing it, that wonderful hush from the audience was there again. Schippers was the kind of conductor that sopranos dream about; when I hooked on to a high D pianissimo, Tommy just let me sit on it until I'd had enough. When I came off the high D, the audience *sighed.* It was an incredibly exhilarating moment. There were times in my career—and that was one of them—when I felt like a trapeze artist doing dangerous somersaults without a net underneath. When you execute those somersaults flawlessly, the audience feels the same sense of triumph the performer does. Moments like that are memorable and damned exciting.

The Siege of Corinth was a success of blockbuster proportions. *The New York Times* heaped lavish praise on the four Americans involved. The *Times* ran a photo of Horne and me next to its review. *La Stampa,* Italy's leading newspaper, noted that "Two American interpreters of Rossini brought *bel canto* again to La Scala." Italian critics called me "the new Callas," "La Sills," "La Fenomena," and "Il Mostro"—which means either "the incomparable one" or "the monster"; take your pick.

Even though there'd been friction between us at La Scala, Marilyn and I seemed to leave it all behind in Milan. Whenever she and I saw each other at Lincoln Center, we'd embrace, have a nice little talk, and then go our separate ways. In 1975, when I was getting ready to do *The Siege of Corinth* in New York, I made sure Marilyn was offered the role of Neocle. She declined.

I did receive a shock a few years ago, however, when Marilyn came out with her autobiography. In it, she stated that she was the person who suggested me to La Scala in the first place. That's just not the case. If Edgar Vincent hadn't recommended me to Schippers, I wouldn't have been at La Scala. For that and everything else I shall always be indebted to him. He did everything for me except sing.

When I returned home from La Scala, a great hoo-ha had descended on the land. To quote my daughter's first words, I was now hot, hot, hot. I received offers to sing all over the world.

Although Ludwig Lustig was nominally my manager, I sifted through all the proposals with Edgar. One day he looked at me and said, "If you really want a career, Beverly, why are you living in Boston? Have you thought about moving to New York?"

Well, no, I *hadn't* thought about moving to New York. I was very happy in Milton, and so was Muffy. Peter had his job as financial columnist of *The Boston Globe,* and *he* was happy. We had no need, or plans, to move.

I was very pleased by what had happened at La Scala, but thrilled? No. When I got back from Milan, I was a month short of turning forty. I was married to a very well-to-do, generous man, so I didn't need any money. I *did* need the escape that jumping into a character's skin for several hours a night continued to afford me. I also began experiencing a much more positive urge to take on more difficult *bel canto* roles, which greatly displeased Miss Liebling. She wanted me to stick pretty much to French repertoire like *Manon,* and told me that way I'd be able to save my voice. But what was I saving it for? Better to have ten glorious years than twenty safe and ultimately boring ones.

I wanted to live dangerously, I suppose. Even though my career had blossomed late, I didn't envision myself doing much singing past my fiftieth birthday. For some reason, Pete and I had hit on fifty as the magic number for my retirement. To sing "safe" repertoire implied that *careful, noncontroversial,* and *easy* would take the place of *risky, provocative,* and *challenging,* which was the approach I'd always chosen in my career. I didn't feel as if I were in a marathon. It was never my ambition to sing longer than anyone else.

That became a sore issue between Miss Liebling and me almost immediately after I returned from La Scala. For five years Tito Capobianco had been trying to get me to look at a score of Donizetti's *Roberto Devereux,* a rather unpopular opera about the ill-fated love affair between Queen Elizabeth and Lord Essex. Ill-fated for Essex— she eventually had his head chopped off. I was never remotely interested in the opera, but Tito was insistent. Tito had given Roland a tape of a Montserrat Caballé concert performance of *Roberto Devereux,* and he asked me over to his apartment to listen to it. No offense to Madame Caballé, but I still wasn't interested in what I heard. A third of the way through, I told Roland to turn off the tape. Callas had sung Donizetti's *Anna Bolena,* but she hadn't bothered with *Roberto Devereux,* and I could understand why.

Roland told me to read the text. He then began sending me letters about Queen Elizabeth. I told him *Roberto Devereux* was filled with historical inaccuracies. Roland said, "So what?" He wanted me to sit down and visualize the dramatic possibilities. Gradually, he got me to see that Queen Elizabeth was a fascinating character and that I'd been glossing over some incredibly dramatic lines without bothering to think what they meant. The line that finally convinced me to play her comes when Elizabeth, having been scorned by Devereux, condemns him to death and says, "It would have been better for you to incite the wrath of God than to incite the wrath of the daughter of the terrible Henry the Eighth." When I read that in Italian, it was a sentence that sat on a page, but when that line is sung to Donizetti's music, well, it's like a cannon shot. There were so *many* moments like that. Elizabeth had given Devereux her ring, which he was to send to her if he was in trouble; he never did. She says, "I gave you the ring of royalty and you behaved like a beggar!" Not too many operatic characters deliver text like that. And when I put the text together with the music, the dramatic possibilities seemed sensational.

Miss Liebling felt that *Roberto Devereux* would take a terrible toll on my voice, and not only advised against doing the opera but refused to work on it with me. I was relieved by that, because I wanted to work on *Roberto Devereux* with Tito, Gigi, and Roland. With those three, I knew I'd have people constantly asking me to give more, not telling me to be careful and go easy. I didn't have *time* to take it easy. I felt as if I'd been told: "You've only got a limited time to live. *Go* for it!" That was pretty much the truth in terms of my operatic career, so I *did* go for it.

I asked Rudel if he'd let me sing *Roberto Devereux* at the City Opera. Julius thought that would be fine. He scheduled the premiere for our fall 1970 season. A little more than a month after I got back from La Scala, Peter and I flew over to London to record *Roberto Devereux* with Robert Ilosfalvy as Devereux and Beverly Wolff as Sara. We recorded the album for Westminster Records, which hired the Royal Philharmonic Orchestra, conducted by Charles Mackerras, to provide us with heroic accompaniment.

I was now in great demand, and I began performing all over the world. Airlines loved me—I started flying close to 250,000 miles a year. I wish there had been frequent-flyer plans then. Not long after the *Devereux* recording, Peter, Muffy, my mother, and I spent three weeks in the Philippines. Eugenio Lopez, who was the czar of Filipino industry at the time and whose brother was vice-president of the country, had brought me there to sing six concerts.

That visit provided me with my first close-up, personal experience with a dictator. We not only met Ferdinand and Imelda Marcos, we got to know them. There we were, in Malacañang Palace, having dinner with them. I saw the all-pervasive poverty. Did I see the corruption? No—you never do. Did I see the power? Oh, yes, I saw the power. When we arrived at the Manila airport, we were met by eleven cars, all with bodyguards. I guess they thought we needed them. When we drove to our hotel, the lobby was filled with armed soldiers. We had one entire floor of the hotel to ourselves. One day Miss Sills wanted to go shopping, so President Marcos's soldiers bounced everyone out of a huge department store in order to allow Miss Sills to shop at her leisure.

When I arrived in Manila, I decided that as a courtesy, I'd wear Philippine gowns for my concerts. Pitoy Moreno was the Dior of Manila. He made me three gowns, each of which was weighed down with beads. Imelda showed up wearing gowns made by Givenchy. She looked beautiful; I did not. Philippine-style gowns, with their "butterfly" sleeves, do not look wonderful on ample women.

We really had to learn not to admire anything out loud, or else it would be given to us. The first time we realized that was when my mother commented on a pearl ring worn by the wife of a government official. The next day, the ring, accompanied by flowers, was sent to her hotel room. One day I expressed an urge to see Corregidor; the next day, a 150-foot yacht, complete with musicians, showed up to take us there. At a museum, I noticed a lovely fish plate; when we got back to New York, the plate was in a crate of farewell goodies. The Marcoses were kind and friendly to us, and now I'm very embarrassed about it.

When we returned home, we moved from Milton to a cooperative apartment on New York's West Side. It was a very sudden move. Peter decided that with the sale of the *Plain Dealer* and a trust fund that had matured for him, he wasn't going to work anymore. He had been getting some funny comments about being the millionaire financial columnist. Although he laughed them off—"Obviously, my advice must work"—they rankled.

My mother panicked when I told her Peter was retiring. "Don't you dare let him do that. The two of you will never survive," she said. "You can't be together twenty-four hours a day. Get him out of the house."

I tried. I really did. The truth of the matter is that Peter immersed himself in philanthropic endeavors—all dealing with handicapped children—and was busier than ever. Just before we went to the Philippines he'd said, "Ah, the hell with it. If you want to, let's move to New York."

Peter bought a nine-room co-op on the West Side, a ten-minute cab ride away from Lincoln Center, for $100,000. Friends told us we were nuts to pay so much for a West Side apartment. It is now worth more than a million dollars.

When we got back from the Philippines, I was *really* home again.

FOURTEEN

We must have been living in New York for at least fifteen minutes when rumors began circulating that I'd married an eighty-year-old millionaire who'd bought Westminster Records for me so that I could record anything I liked. *Opera News*—I began to call it *Opera Snooze*—actually printed that choice bit of nonsense, and at first it struck me as funny. I told people that Peter wasn't that chintzy; instead of buying me Westminster Records, he'd actually bought me Westminster Abbey. But I stopped laughing when I realized the magazine really was being rather vicious. Peter took no notice of the item until he saw how upset I was. "Calm down," he told me. "We have lawyers. We'll sue."

That's just what I wanted to hear. I threatened to sue *Opera News* for God knows how much, and they quickly agreed to print a retraction. I still don't know why the magazine printed that nonsense in the first place. Had the editor bothered to call my husband, he would have learned that Peter was a conservative fifty-four-year-old who never invested money in my career; he wanted me to be able to say I made it on my own. Peter showed up at my premieres, but if I sang nine performances of an opera like *Thaïs*—which Peter called *Thighs*—I assure you he'd miss eight of them. Peter's always been his own man. At one opera, a woman sitting next to him thought he wasn't applauding loud enough for me. Peter almost bit her head off. "I'm her husband, not a cheerleader," he snapped.

My husband traveled with me only when it fit into his plans. When I started singing in San Francisco again, Peter came along because our close friends Walter and Ellen Newman live out there; he and Walter go off fishing together, and Ellen and I shop. I was one of the few leading sopranos whose husband wasn't hanging around the dressing room.

I liked that about Peter. It reinforced my feeling that he didn't love me for my high notes. Our relationship has always been that of Peter and his wife, not Peter and his wife the opera star. If you look at singers who have good marriages, you'll generally find that their husbands work in another field. You'll also find that their singing careers aren't the focal point of their families' existence. Eileen Farrell, for instance, was married to a policeman until his death in 1986. She lives in Maine and has never given a damn about becoming a superstar. She has always known she is a great singer, and that has been enough for her. Before her retirement, Eileen had one of the world's greatest dramatic soprano voices. The woman sings like a goddess and talks like a sailor.

Birgit Nilsson's husband also remained aloof from his wife's career. He was content to stay home in Sweden, and never interfered in her business negotiations. Birgit was a tough Swedish cookie and liked to bargain for herself. Once, when she felt Rudolf Bing wasn't offering her enough money to appear at the Met, Birgit took great pleasure in telling Bing: "When the birds are not happy, they do not sing." Whenever I preceded her into a city, she used to send me reviews of my performances. Once she sent me a clipping in which another soprano was compared unfavorably to me. In the margin, Birgit noted, "We always get our best reviews when we don't sing."

Opera singers sometimes marry men who do become involved in their careers. In the case of Joan Sutherland and Richard Bonynge, it's worked out very well. Richard is her mentor. Joan trusts him completely, and should. He's an accomplished artist in his own right.

Peter's only involvement in my career was to manage my money. I couldn't have found anyone better suited to do that. Peter has devoted much of his life to the study of business and finance. The one agreement Peter always insisted on was that no matter how little or how much I made, we were to live on his money. There was never any question of "Well, if you're not interested in buying that, Peter, I'll spend my money." Everything we bought, we bought together— with Peter's money.

Everything I made went into various trust funds. This was not a sacrifice on my part, because it didn't change how we lived. If we found ourselves in Milan and I wasn't singing at La Scala, we had the same hotel suite and the same limousine we would have had if I were singing—everything was the same, except I didn't have to work nights. I never felt any pressure to earn as much money as I could. When Peter gave me a ring inscribed I DID THAT ALREADY, he was reminding me that just because I had a success at one opera house, I didn't have to repeat it at another. I didn't have to do anything I didn't want to do.

Moving to New York was a snap for Peter and especially for me, since my mother and brothers were there. Muffy had a much tougher time adjusting. By then, it was just the three of us; Lindley was away at Bennington, and Nancy, who'd enrolled at Barnard, had her own apartment in Manhattan. Muffy's life was seriously affected by the move. She'd been very happy in Milton. Every morning, she'd be picked up by a station wagon and driven to the Boston School for the Deaf, and in the afternoon there was plenty of room outside the house for her to play with her dogs. The peaceful structure of her life was completely undone when we carted her off to New York. From the moment she arrived, Muffy hated Manhattan. She hated the dirt and the buses and the crowds, and it took her a while to get used to all that.

Muffy also had to make a big adjustment at school. We started her off at the Lexington School for the Deaf, a wonderful public school for children from all over the city. She initially had a lot of extra work to do, because as an oral deaf person, she hadn't been taught sign language. The Lexington School taught what's known as "total communication"—both speaking and signing. From my own point of view, that's a bit of a misnomer. It's *extremely* difficult for deaf children to develop and master speech skills while also using sign language—total communication it isn't. In most cases, when deaf people talk *and* sign, you can't understand what they're saying; sign language remains their primary means of communication.

Muffy stayed at Lexington for a very short while. The school's faculty felt she was ready to move faster and face stiffer academic challenges. Beverly Grunwald, the late wife of *Time* magazine's editor-in-chief and a great pal, suggested we apply to Nightingale-Bamford, a private school for girls on East 92nd Street.

I was very impressed by the school's headmistress, Joan McMenamin. The girls called her Big Mac, and she was a hearty, terrific, no-nonsense lady. I liked her, and I liked the school. The girls wore uniforms, and I liked *that*. It took away the moronic competition of little girls trying to outdress one another, which wasn't my style or my daughter's. Muffy was used to wearing a uniform to school and then coming home and changing into jeans, so at least that aspect of her life in Milton was restored. Muffy was the only deaf student at Nightingale-Bamford, and although her classmates initially made an effort to include her in things, she was rather lonely.

Muffy didn't have all her dogs to play with anymore, because we had to give two out of three of them away after moving to the city. New York seemed to make all the dogs go crazy. Until we moved there, Puli, our Hungarian dog, had never heard a doorbell; he was an outdoor pet. Whenever the doorbell rang, the dog got frantic and would dive under a bed—the doorbell changed his whole personality. We wound up giving him to a friend in Great Barrington who owned a farm.

Bumpy, the Corgi, went to Vermont with Lindley.

We had a toy poodle named Gigi whose specialty was to leap into the toilet bowl and then splash around and scream like crazy until one of us came to rescue her. She was almost the same color as the beige carpeting in our new apartment, and managed to get stepped on by the three of us several times a day. We kept her awhile, then gave her to a lingerie buyer.

Soon we had another in our long line of Welsh Corgis. While I was recording in London, Peter had bought the dog in the countryside nearby and justified the purchase by saying it was best to go to the breed's "roots"—I thought they came from Wales. He left for home two days ahead of me, and I subsequently found out my husband bought Corky a first-class seat and sat next to it on the flight back to New York. The Pan Am stewardesses loved Corky. They were the ones who blew Pete's cover.

Muffy thought Corky was the most beautiful dog in the world. She said he smelled like strawberries. I thought Corky was a lunatic and smelled exactly like a dog, but as Peter said, if Corgis were good enough for the Queen of England, why not for me?

I can only tell you that Corky caused the single most severe, most prolonged fight Peter and I ever had. When we moved in, our co-op apartment was in dire need of a new kitchen. Peter told me to spare no expense in remodeling it, and I took him at his word. The kitchen wound up costing us $25,000, which was an extravagant price, especially in those days.

One day I walked into our solid gold kitchen and saw Corky *eating* it. He was a little pup with sharp teeth, and his favorite food was the kitchen. He literally ate it up inch by inch. I tried everything I could to stop him, including smearing the baseboards with hot Chinese mustard in hopes it would burn his tongue. Corky *loved* the mustard. I thought maybe he wouldn't like the taste of rat poison, but I never got the chance to find out. One evening I found Corky chomping away on a corner of a custom-built mahogany cabinet. He'd chewed away the corners of *all* our custom-built, overpriced mahogany cabinets. Well, I yelled at the dog and he bared his teeth at me, and that was the final no-no. I marched straight into the bedroom and told Peter: "That dog has just bared its teeth at me. Either the dog goes or I do!"

Peter stared at me and *thought* about it. My husband now claims he immediately said, "Okay, the dog goes," but that's not the way I remember it. We actually fought about the dog almost all night long. Finally, at around four in the morning—and by then I was screaming at Peter—he said, "You know, most people fight about sex, money, or their children. Here we are fighting about a damn dog." Except he did not say "damn."

He gave in and let me win. But I really lost, because when we gave Corky away to a Congregational minister on Martha's Vineyard, Muffy was distraught. Not too long after that, I came home one afternoon to find Peter and our daughter looking so cheerful and happy that I thought: *My, what a nice little family we are.* And then the doorbell rang, and I opened the door, and in toddled a little . . . Welsh Corgi. Before I had a chance to open my mouth, Peter said, "You're not going to believe it, Bev. This one is a lady, a real Southern lady, and you know what good manners Southern ladies have."

He was *serious.* I could see that my daughter was in love with the puppy, so I accepted what was obviously a conspiracy—and a *fait accompli.* This Corgi's name is Laurie, and every once in a while she still goes nuts and runs around the house knocking everything down, but she's never chewed up the furniture or bared her teeth at me. Laurie's okay. I pretend she's somebody else's dog. She's crazy about me. See what I mean about Corgis?

We'd barely settled into the new place when I began preparing for the City Opera's fall season. Julius realized that the *Newsweek* cover story and all the favorable fallout from my La Scala debut had made me a big drawing card, so he slotted me into five operas. That fall I sang Constanza in Mozart's *Abduction from the Seraglio,* Marguerite in *Faust, Manon,* my last *Baby Doe,* and the title role in the City Opera's first-ever production of *Lucia di Lammermoor.*

By then—and to Julius's credit—he'd go along with whatever opera Tito, Gigi, and I wanted to do together. As a child, I'd seen Lily Pons sing *Lucia,* and I'd loved all the trills and fine little high notes she hit. She sang spectacular coloratura stuff, and that's what sent audiences wild. I also loved the way she looked. Pons was beautiful, and one of the first sopranos I ever saw who wasn't a big fat lady and who actually looked like a young woman about to be married. But she didn't act the role plausibly. *Lucia* contains opera's most famous mad scene—it takes place just after the new bride stabs her husband to death—but Lily never acted like a mad, tragic heroine. She always performed the mad scene with her hair perfectly coiffed, and wearing a white satin gown with a red velvet sash across it to represent blood.

I sang my first *Lucia* in Fort Worth in 1968, and in January 1969, I sang it again in Edmonton, Canada, and in Boston with Sarah Caldwell. I knew that if I did *Lucia* with the Capobiancos we had a chance to set New York on its ear. Julius may have allowed us to do the opera, but he was his usual skeptical self. Rudel called *Lucia* a Scotch *shmatte,* which is Yiddish for "rag" or "cheap piece of clothing." He refused to conduct the opera, so Charles Wilson, who'd been with the company since 1962, took over in the pit and did a superb job.

By then, I'd made some mistakes and learned from them. In Fort Worth and Edmonton, I'd sung the mad scene dressed in a revealing, off-the-shoulder nightgown, which is what most sopranos wear. When I read Sir Walter Scott's book *The Bride of Lammermoor,* I realized that Scotland was cold, its castles drafty, and its teenaged girls modest—I needed a warmish, heavy-looking nightgown. The idea wasn't to get audiences thinking *They're really being true to the book*. My approach simply made sense, even if you'd never read the book. Gigi pointed out that when you look at a wedding party and see men wearing capes over heavy clothes, and then see a woman in a grayish-blue, dour-looking nightgown rather than some flimsy little thing, the mood stays unbroken. You continue to make audiences feel that the castle is cold, and that those huge fireplaces aren't there for aesthetic reasons. And when Lucia comes down a flight of stairs and says she's shivering, you don't think it's because she's not dressed warmly enough; you go along with the idea that she's having a strange chill, that she's turning ice-cold from madness.

When I sang the opera for Sarah, she decided Lucia didn't have time to change out of her wedding dress before killing her husband, which was fine, but she had me stab him with his own sword, which wasn't so fine. In the book, Lucia stabs her husband with a small knife thirty-nine times, and that makes perfect sense if we're talking about a mad, hysterical woman. But there's no way Lucia could stab someone thirty-nine times with a sword—it's too big and unwieldy. The murder takes place offstage, and Sarah liked the idea of Lucia emerging from her bedroom in a bloody wedding dress and dragging a bloody sword. She was right—it *was* dramatic. But by having Lucia kill Arturo with a sword, we lost an edge of her madness. There were a lot of beautifully thought-out ideas in Sarah's production that I carried with me for a long time, but that wasn't one of them.

When we decided to bring *Lucia* to New York, Roland, Gigi, Tito, and I sat up late every night studying the various cuts that had been made in the opera over the years. When I'd performed the traditional version of *Lucia,* Enrico, Lucia's brother, had come off as a total scoundrel. Enrico dupes his sister into marrying a wealthy man she doesn't love by forging a letter showing that her lover, Edgardo, has been unfaithful. When you do the opera totally uncut, however, you see that the brother is a desperate man who loves his sister but doesn't know what else to do: Unless Lucia marries this enormously wealthy and powerful man, her family will be in ruins. With all the text restored, it becomes obvious that Raimondo, the chaplain of Lammermoor, is the real villain of the piece. Raimondo sees where *his* fortunes lie, and using his religious authority, he—not the brother—

finally talks Lucia into marrying Arturo. On her wedding night, when she discovers Edgardo has never been unfaithful to her, Lucia goes mad and murders her new husband. Raimondo, the opera's only hypocrite, could have prevented all that. With all the traditional cuts restored, *Lucia* becomes a different opera. And a better one.

When Tito, Gigi, and I took a fresh look at *Lucia*, we realized what Donizetti had in mind when he wrote it. We saw that from the very start, Lucia is a very weird child who's had hallucinations about rivers of blood and who's fairly demented even before her brother and the chaplain push her over the brink. We saw that Edgardo, her lover, has been so tortured by her brother that's he's almost as crazy as she is. We all felt that the opera had not really been plumbed to its depths, so that's what we resolved to do.

We presented every single note Donizetti wrote—the first uncut *Lucia* performed in New York in more than a century. Tito put in some wonderful touches. Just after Lucia's wedding, Edgardo bursts into the castle, rips off the chain he'd given Lucia, and throws it to the ground. Throughout the opera, I'd clutched that pendant a lot, so the audience was very aware of it. A few minutes after the mad scene starts, Lucia gets down on her hands and knees, and without any words being said, we know what she's looking for and see that she can't find it. Tito set that up beautifully. Roland wrote me a beautiful mad scene cadenza, and I sang parts of it to different characters, as if I were speaking to them. I also began moving as if I couldn't see anybody—as if my reality had become a dream. The only time I seemed aware of what I was doing was when I referred to Edgardo; for the rest of it, I was gone, catatonic, lost in a world of madness. I also received wonderful support from my mad scene flautist at City Opera, John Wion. John memorized the entire mad scene, cadenza included, and he played it while standing next to the conductor. He never took his eyes off me.

Lucia di Lammermoor was a huge success. On opening night, had you asked me what my favorite role was, I would have said Lucia, because when the curtain came down, I was in tears. She really got to me. Afterward, Julius Rudel came by and said, "I should have known you'd make a piece of lace out of a Scotch *shmatte*."

From then on, life became a merry-go-round. A few weeks after *Lucia,* Roland was my accompanist for a couple of recitals I did in

Chicago and New Orleans. Outside the Chicago Auditorium, I saw a SOLD OUT banner partially covering a billboard that advertised a recital by "Opera's Newest Superstar—Beverly Soils."

I began appearing on a lot of television talk shows, and I have Johnny Carson to thank for that. It was Carson who first told me: "If you come on *The Tonight Show,* you'll humanize opera. *Show* 'em you look like everybody else, that you have kids, a life, that you have to diet." I thought: *Smart man!* After going on with Johnny, I did my first *Dick Cavett Show* that December and then appeared with Mike Douglas and Merv Griffin. I intended to do just what Carson advised: I wanted to popularize opera and demonstrate to people that opera singers aren't unapproachable aliens. Prior to going on the shows, my husband had always said, "Just wind her up and she'll sing." After I started appearing on television, Peter underwent a change of heart. "Just wind her up and she'll talk," he said.

I much preferred singing. In January 1970, I sang *La Traviata* in my debut at the Teatro San Carlo in Naples. I wanted to perform there because San Carlo supposedly was the finest opera house in the world. I wasn't disappointed. The acoustics were perfect, and when you walk into the place, you're walking into the seventeenth century.

I liked everything about San Carlo. The backstage crew were funny, accommodating, and very, very sweet. I never sang with a single artificial flower on stage. The crew always chipped in for live camellias and said it was their "homage" to me. Everything San Carlo promised, it delivered, including the great Alfredo Kraus to sing Alfredo in *La Traviata.*

I wanted all the crazy, traditional cuts that had been made in the opera to be opened up, and that was fine with Margherita Wallmann, who was a well-known stage director. Margherita was more than willing to go along with my interpretation of Violetta. I played her as a woman who knows she's doomed from the moment the audience first sees her. That's never done in Italy; Violetta, a consumptive, always comes out lively and sparkling, which beats the text to a pulp.

She also allowed me to play the first-act party scene the way I saw it. Violetta, the Baron's mistress, becomes furious when he arrives late for her party—he's been out gambling. To get even with him, she begins flirting with Alfredo, a young man who's just walked in. At the end of the party, it's customary for the Baron, who's presumably annoyed, to kiss Violetta's hand and leave. But I thought: *The Baron expects to spend the night with her—he* always *spends the night with Violetta—so where's he going? After all, this is his mistress. He's got a proprietary interest here. He's just spent a fortune on a party for her, so wouldn't he hang around, smoking his cigar and waiting for everyone to leave?*

That sent the rest of the singers into a tizzy—the idea of having someone smoke a cigar on stage *always* makes singers nervous. But the director thought it was a nice touch, and went with it.

The way I played the scene, Violetta has done everything but slap the Baron's face for humiliating her by showing up late. I had her extend her hand haughtily to the Baron, who tries to hold it; she pulls her hand away. He nods in understanding and then walks off, furious. *She* does the dismissing.

When I exited in the second act after *"Amami Alfredo"* the audience applauded. Since Violetta doesn't appear again in Act II and the baritone has his big aria, I had at least ten minutes until curtain calls. I went to my dressing room, kicked off my shoes, took a powder puff and made huge polka dots of powder on my face to absorb the sweat, took off my belt, and stretched out on the chaise. The door burst open and the director of San Carlo yelled, "You must go out and bow. Kraus cannot continue. They will not stop applauding."

"Are you crazy?" I yelled back. "Bow in the middle of an act? If I did that in America my career would be over."

"Well," he said, "if you *don't* do it here, your career will be over!"

I went out, no shoes, no belt, with powder all over my face. Alfredo Kraus broke up onstage. I looked a mess and the Neapolitans loved it.

I even liked the claque at San Carlo. A couple of days before the opening of *Traviata,* just after a dress rehearsal, the head of the claque came backstage to talk to me. He said he didn't want any money from me. "You don't need me," he said. "I go home and put on my smoke-air," meaning smoking jacket. Peter and I went to a restaurant after the opening night performance, and the same man was there with about fifteen of his cronies. Peter noticed they were all drinking coffee, so he sent six bottles of wine to their table.

The next day, one of the Neapolitan critics said, "It took an American to teach us how to sing Verdi"—which really tickled me, because I'd been wary of the reception I'd get. La Scala and the Teatro San Carlo have a rivalry as bitter as the one between the old New York Giants and the Brooklyn Dodgers. When it comes to opera, whatever the Milanese love, the Neopolitans detest. Callas had been adored in Milan, but not in Naples. The rivalry between the two cities' opera fans is really intense.

While I was still in Naples, the head of Deutsche Grammophon, Karl Faust, called up and invited Peter and me to fly over to Hamburg to discuss a possible recording contract with his company. Herr Faust, a charming man, offered me a fortune to record Handel's *Messiah* and *The Creation* by Haydn, with Karl Richter conducting the Boston Symphony Orchestra. I turned him down. I'd worked with Richter once, and I had no wish to do so again. In 1968, when I debuted at the Teatro Colón in Buenos Aries, Richter had conducted Norman Treigle, Maureen Forrester, and me in a horrible production of *Julius Caesar*. The Capobiancos weren't invited down, and Richter refused to make any cuts, so we began each evening's performance at seven and ended at one in the morning. By midnight, I'd be saturating myself with coffee for enough caffeine to keep me awake. Audiences were bored stiff, and so were we. Richter, who's dead now, drank a lot during performances; he was not pleasant to work with. I told Herr Faust I'd record for Deutsche Grammophon if he hired Erich Leinsdorf to conduct. I didn't think that was a big favor to ask, since Leinsdorf was then the Boston Symphony Orchestra's music director. Herr Faust told me Leinsdorf was tied up with other projects, so I suggested we postpone the recordings, but he said he needed them immediately.

Herr Faust made one last impassioned pitch for Richter. "He's the greatest conductor of Handel's music in the world," he said.

"I won't ever sing with Richter," I replied.

Herr Faust and his associates went into shock; Peter and I returned to Naples.

I'd signed a three-year contract with La Scala, and a couple of months after my *Traviata* in Naples, I returned to Milan to sing *Lucia*. Why mince words? The production turned out to be provincial, cheap, tawdry, poorly directed, and poorly conceived. Our premiere was conducted by a white-haired fellow named Nino Sanzogno. During a subsequent performance, I realized that Sanzogno had been replaced by a bald conductor who hadn't even bothered to introduce himself to me before we went on. He turned out to be the rehearsal pianist, so at least he knew my mad scene cadenza.

On opening night, the tenor had a rough time and was booed. During our second performance, just after I sang my first aria, a tenor I'd never laid eyes on came onstage. He walked over, *shook hands with me,* told me his name, and then began to sing. He, too, was roundly booed. Lucia doesn't see Edgardo, the principal tenor, again until after she's agreed to marry another man. When Edgardo came onstage again—right, another tenor! The young man was frightened to death and could barely be heard. Which wouldn't have mattered, because the audience was in no mood to listen. Mercifully, there are no tenors around during Lucia's mad scene. In the La Scala production, while Edgardo sang his final aria, Lucia was carried onstage after her death. I sneaked a peek: *Another* tenor! That did it. I quit. I told La Scala's general director that his opera house was unworthy of its great name.

The one funny moment of this horror story took place when I began rehearsing the flute cadenza in the mad scene. Sanzogno told me I wouldn't be permitted to sing it with the ornamentations I was using, which had been written by Roland Gagnon.

"Why not?" I asked.

"Non è scritto cosi," he said. ("It's not written that way.")

"How *is* it written?"

"Here, look," he said, showing me the music.

What he showed me was not Donizetti's untouched version, as Sanzogno believed, but Estelle Liebling's cadenzas. After I pointed that out, Sanzogno never said another word about my cadenzas.

After our triumphant *Siege of Corinth,* I should have paid attention to what Tommy Schippers told me about La Scala: "Don't come back here unless you're in a new production, with a conductor you like and a cast you want," he'd said. "Unless all that's spelled out in a contract, you'll be making a big mistake, Beverly."

He was right. When La Scala is good, it's very, very good, and when it's bad, it's horrid. La Scala may be the only opera house in the world that never has mediocre performances. La Scala has nights of glory and nights of despair. There's no in-between.

After *Lucia di Lammermoor,* I was supposed to sing *Roberto Devereux* at La Scala, with Tito Capobianco directing and Luciano Pavarotti in the role of Devereux, to be followed by a new production of *I Puritani* with Luciano. Well, after that *Lucia,* the first thing I heard from La Scala was that they wanted my next opera to be the new *I Puritani* instead of *Roberto Devereux.* I had some misgivings, but I was willing to go along until Luciano phoned me and said, "They're *not* giving us a new production. It's the one I did in Bologna with Mirella Freni."

When I heard that, I telephoned La Scala and said, "Forget it—I did that already. You promised me a new production. You either give me a new production of *Puritani* or else count me out."

La Scala told me a new production wasn't in the cards, so I said fine, and I cancelled. I told the management that as far as I was concerned, our contract was nonexistent. I never sang again at La Scala.

A couple of years later I accepted an invitation to sing *Traviata* at La Fenice in Venice. Several people in the business told me I'd like La Fenice better than La Scala or San Carlo. I did. It was spring, Venice was gorgeous, the Cipriani is a glorious hotel, Peter stayed with me the whole time, and during our stay I had my forty-third birthday. It seemed as if not a day passed without Peter going to Nardi to buy me a little bauble. In all the years we've been married I've never returned, or wanted to return, a single piece of jewelry he's bought me. I admire my husband's taste in everything he does.

We'd taken a rooftop suite at the Cipriani, and the hotel had a heated swimming pool. Our stay was like a honeymoon. To celebrate my birthday Peter gave me a dinner dance at the hotel. I loved every minute of that visit.

I agreed to sing *Traviata* at La Fenice because Tommy Schippers was conducting, Gian-Carlo Menotti was directing, and the sets were designed by the man who'd decorated Onassis' yacht, so you can imagine the decor—Violetta's little country house looked like the palace at Versailles.

There were no claques at La Fenice, and I found that refreshing. The only sour note during our rehearsal period was sounded by La Scala's *intendant*, who visited me in my dressing room one day. He came right to the point.

"You owe La Scala two productions," he said.

"I owe you nothing," I replied.

"I can prevent these performances in Venice from happening," he said.

He had to be kidding. When I'd done *La Traviata* at San Carlo, the production had become the rage of Italy. I'm not being immodest when I tell you that people were coming to Venice from all over the country—and were literally fighting over tickets—to see me at La Fenice. I don't think Italians are necessarily more knowledgeable about opera than American audiences, but they certainly are more passionate. At the end of one of our performances, a woman seated near the stage tearfully called out: *"Che bella morte!"*—"What a beautiful death!"

"You must be crazy," I told the man from La Scala. "Do you really think you're going to keep me off this stage? Are you that foolish?"

He wasn't. I didn't hear from La Scala again.

Our opening night—in fact, all our performances—went like a dream. Venetians are incredibly friendly. When Peter and I went to restaurants, people would come over to our table, draw up chairs, sit down, order coffee, and begin talking to us.

Nonie Schippers, like Peter, didn't come to another performance after our premiere—Peter spent those evenings with Muffy. Tommy and Nonie had taken a small villa on the same little island occupied by our hotel, so after the opera Tommy and I would hop into a gondola and share a ride back. For whatever reason, we'd always start singing at the top of our lungs. The conductor from Kalamazoo and the diva from Brooklyn harmonized such operatic classics as "You Are My Sunshine," "For Me and My Gal"—you name it, we probably sang it. I usually ate dinner at around four in the afternoon, and by the time we got back to the Cipriani, the hotel's kitchen would be closed. In the afternoon Tommy and I would therefore buy the equivalent of pizzas, wrap them up, and eat them in the gondola while we were singing and screaming and shrieking our way back home. The men who operated those little boats knew they were dealing with a pair of lunatics, but sometimes they joined in the singing.

FIFTEEN

Although he did so unintention-
ally, Sir Rudolf Bing played a big part in helping me become America's best-known opera singer. After my successful debuts at La Scala
and the Teatro San Carlo, I really expected him to invite me to sing at
the Metropolitan Opera. He did and he didn't. Bing offered me a
Lucia on October 15, 1970—the same night I was scheduled to open
in the City Opera's premiere of *Roberto Devereux*. When I respectfully
declined, as he knew I would—the premiere was a well-publicized
event—Bing offered me a second *Lucia* in December, when he knew
I'd be making my debut at Covent Garden in London. I suppose that
was Bing's way of getting himself off the hook, for by then, newspaper
and magazine writers were all over him for pointedly ignoring me.

I'd heard that Bing got very annoyed when one of his board
members asked why I wasn't singing at the Met. Bing said, "Can't I
spend five minutes of my life without hearing that woman's name?"

I didn't complain about not being asked to sing at the Met. I've
always tried to be cheerful, because I think people who whine are
boring, and I never *could* tolerate bores. There was a part of me that
wasn't cheerful at all, but I'd been cheerful for so long that it had
become a way of life. I was always the wisecracker, the girl who'd say

something snappy to relieve tensions, and I never changed. And I always enjoyed performing, which I think accounted for a major portion of my public appeal. Audiences like to watch performers having a good time doing something difficult. People love to say, "My God, she makes it look so easy."

I've always been a good communicator, and I think people identified with me. I was a nice-looking woman, but not beautiful, so women liked me, and I was a funny woman, so men liked me. And I never took my singing career too seriously, and everybody liked *that*. Opera fans knew I had a wealthy husband and appreciated the fact that I didn't *have* to work, so I was out there busting my tail for the sheer fun of it. I suppose I secretly wanted people to think of me the way I thought of John F. Kennedy. He was a very rich man who didn't have to go into politics to earn a living, but did because he so obviously enjoyed it. He also had an easy acceptance of unhappy events in his life. I used to think of that quality as a special kind of grace.

Why did Bing keep me from singing at the Met? I don't know, although it's true he had two fine sopranos in Joan Sutherland and Montserrat Caballé. It's also true that I'd become the prima donna of a rival company that was a one-minute stroll from his office, and perhaps that had something to do with it. Perhaps it didn't. At that stage, Bing and I experienced a clash of personalities. He once told a reporter: "Not every great singer can sing at the Met"—to which I responded, "Not every great singer wants to."

The press lined up solidly behind me, which only stiffened Bing's resolve to exclude me from his company. I was continually approached by reporters who wanted to do interviews on the subject of "poor little Bubbles" from Brooklyn being blackballed by an Austrian-born autocrat. I declined scores of such requests. When the subject came up in interviews relating to a specific production, my pat answer was to say that I'd revolutionized American opera by proving you can have a big international career without once setting foot on the Met's stage. I stayed away from criticizing Bing on a personal basis, but a few months after I returned from Naples, he finally made that impossible.

One night on the *Dick Cavett Show,* Bing exhibited astonishing contempt for the people he hired.

"Opera singers are poor, pitiful creatures; they tremble before they go onstage," he said. "Their success is only due to some abnormality of the vocal chords, a kind of throat disease. Most of them come from humble backgrounds, and fame is not easily digested by someone who can barely read or write."

Now *that* was cute, especially coming from a man whose involvement in opera didn't begin until he ended his career as a floorwalker in a London department store. Cavett called and asked me to appear on his show the next night, and I agreed, with one proviso: We'd spend no more than ten minutes of the half hour discussing Bing.

It was a pithy ten minutes. Almost as soon as the program began, Cavett facetiously asked if I agreed with Bing's assessment of opera singers.

"It's distressing to hear him refer to what he has to sell in such scornful terms," I said. "If you don't feel that what you're selling is the greatest thing in the world, you're in the wrong profession. Every singer I know can read his fee on a check and can write well enough to endorse it."

Bing had told Cavett: "In my twenty years [as the Met's general manager] I have never once set foot in a singer's house. I haven't been to the movies in ten years."

I don't know why Bing claimed not to have seen any movies in ten years; Peter and I had sat in back of him at a screening of *Midnight Cowboy*. Bing probably didn't remember that, because he slept through the movie. What's more, a newspaper story had just appeared about a party he had attended at Rozzie Elias's home.

Bing had already announced he'd be leaving the Metropolitan Opera in 1972. A year after his retirement we met in San Antonio, where I was singing *La Traviata*. Bing came backstage and said some nice things to me, I said some nice things to him, and we buried the hatchet. Temporarily, as it turned out.

I must tell you that although every American opera singer wants to appear at the Metropolitan Opera, it no longer seemed so imperative after the acceptance I received at La Scala and San Carlo. Once back in New York, I had more immediate matters on my mind.

The most pressing of these was the series of "Great Performers" recitals I'd signed up to do. As I've already mentioned, Roland Gagnon was dead set against touring, and his temperament wasn't really suited to constant repetition of a concert program; he needed new things to keep him interested. It takes about six months to put together a recital program, and although you may try something very difficult when you're feeling terrific—or take out the toughest piece if you're feeling poorly—the recital program stays pretty much intact.

When Roland told me he'd rather stay home and take care of his cats than travel around as my accompanist, I went to Edgar Vincent and said I needed an accompanist who was upbeat and funny and friendly, because our relationship was necessarily going to be a close one. We'd be a team. When I went out on a concert tour, it would be me and my accompanist. That would be it: no manager, no publicist, no secretary; just us. My husband might come along once in a while, but only if a friend he wanted to visit lived in the city where I was singing.

Edgar introduced me to Charles Wadsworth, now the artistic director of the Chamber Music Society of Lincoln Center. Charlie had accompanied soprano Shirley Verrett, another of Edgar's clients, and they'd gotten along very well.

The moment we were introduced, Charlie and I had a kind of instant rapport. Without anything's being said, I knew he relished his time alone as much as I did mine, and that he wasn't ever going to want to hang around me on tour. Charlie knew I liked him, and when we were on the road we never felt the need to invite each other to dinner or a movie. Charlie had phlebitis, and during our tours he'd spend his afternoons lying in bed with his leg propped up on a pillow and watching a ball game or old movie on television. We never spent time with each other beyond our two-hour rehearsals and our performances. We usually traveled to recitals together, but he didn't always return with me. After a concert, no matter where we were, if there was a red-eye flight back to New York, I was on it. Whether Charlie was on it was a matter of his own choice.

Charlie's a funny man who looks a little like Jimmy Carter, only younger and a bit more handsome. He's got blond hair, prominent teeth, and a very prominent smile. We share the same birthday, although I'm older than he is, or at least I was when we met. By now, maybe he's caught up with me.

Charlie had accompanied some of the most famous concert singers in the world, and he had very strong ideas. Nevertheless, he never clashed with Roland, who continued to work with me. In the beginning, Roland and I picked the program, did the basic work together, and then I polished it with Charlie. Roland and I would set *tempi* and phrasing, determine where I'd breathe, and so on. Charlie usually sat in with us and would offer very positive suggestions. He would say things like "Why don't we try to expand on this phrase a little, because I have a great big flourish underneath that would give you the kind of sweep you're trying to get."

However such a matter was decided, the conclusion was always a happy one. Neither man ever wound up saying: "Well, if you want to do it *his* way . . ." Charlie and Roland had a healthy respect for each other.

Only a few days after I got back from Italy, Charlie and I did our first recital together in Great Neck, New York, and on February 1, 1970, I made my New York City recital debut at Philharmonic Hall. I loved that program: Vivaldi, Mozart, Strauss, Fauré, and a Schubert group that began with "Ave Maria" and ended with *"Der Hirt auf dem Felsen"* ("The Shepherd on the Rocks"). Later on, when Charlie and I started doing up to fifty performances a year, I began to include contemporary songs in each of my concerts.

After singing two *Hoffmanns* with Treigle in Orlando, Florida, and a concert in Carnegie Hall, I almost bit off more than I could chew. On February 19 and 22, I sang *Lucia* with the New York City Opera, and on February 21 and 23, I sang Donizetti's *The Daughter of the Regiment* with the Opera Company of Boston. Offhand, I don't know of any other soprano who's sung two different leading roles four out of five nights in two cities. It's called pushing your luck. I once sang on three different continents in three weeks. I had to keep a notebook, with entries made well in advance, about which gown to wear in which city. Between operas, concerts, recordings, TV shows, and interviews, I was *very* busy. I was often very tired, but that never detracted from my enjoyment. My husband, the noted Yiddish humorist, called me a *meshuggeneh*—a crazy woman. He even pronounced it right.

I originally planned to sing only *Lucia* during that period, but when Sarah Caldwell offered me any opera I wanted, I saw a chance to act out one of my Lily Pons fantasies. *The Daughter of the Regiment* had been Pons's baby, and I had always wondered what it would be like to sing it myself. In addition to that, I had to follow my one unbreakable rule: Sarah always came first. Whenever I got the opportunity to work with that woman, I fit it into my schedule. Sometimes it was a tight fit, but that only spiced things up for both of us.

The *Daughter of the Regiment* that I did in Boston was vintage Sarah Caldwell, which is to say it was brilliant. Before my career was over, I'm sure I sang the role of Marie at least a hundred times, often in productions that cost a fortune, but none touched hers. The *Daughter of the Regiment* that we did in 1970 was the most spectacularly imaginative production of that opera I've ever seen.

The Opera Company of Boston, S. Caldwell, proprietor, was eternally homeless, so Sarah was always scrambling around to find places to perform. I'd gotten used to singing for her in former churches and movie theaters, but this time, she really outdid herself: Sarah rented the gymnasium at Tufts University.

When you came into the gym, the first thing that caught your eye was a huge banner hung over center stage. It showed a picture of Napoleon with a finger pointed at the audience. It read: NAPOLEON A BESOIN DE VOUS, a takeoff on the famous Uncle Sam poster of World War I.

The gym seated a couple of thousand people, and Sarah introduced them to her newest invention: audience-participation opera. The portion of our audience that was seated in the bleachers became members of the kind of card section often seen in football stadiums, but never in opera houses. Sarah and her staff placed sheets of red, white, or blue paper on every seat in the bleachers, along with instructions about when to hold them up. When I made my entrance from the back of the gym—banging away at a drum and singing an aria that began with a cadenza based on *"La Marseillaise"*—the bleacher section held up its cards to form a huge French tricolor. The rest of the people in the gymnasium went a little wild when they saw that.

I don't think anyone but Sarah could have transformed that gym into a great place to watch an opera. *The Daughter of the Regiment* takes place in the Tyrolean Alps, so Sarah built a paper mountain that went up a side wall of the gymnasium. At one point, the Marquise, Marie's aunt, asks a French soldier to escort her to her home in the Alps. They both walked up a flight of metal stairs, decorated with gold ribbons and bows, and through a door on the second floor that was surrounded by the facade of a French château. It was the men's locker room.

Simple things like getting singers onstage and off presented special problems, but Sarah came up with special solutions. Muriel Costa-Greenspon, who played my aunt, was driven up to the platform we performed on by a horse-drawn buggy that came rolling down the center aisle. Who *cared* if the horse misbehaved? We were in a gym, after all, and there was plenty of sawdust on the floor. The crowd loved it.

Aside from automatically admiring everything Pons sang, and almost everything Donizetti wrote, I liked the role of Marie because she struck me as such a funny kid. Marie's a teenager raised since infancy by a regiment of French soldiers who found her on a battlefield. She starts out as a tomboy whose rich aunt—who's actually her mother—learns of her whereabouts and takes Marie home with the intention of molding her into a sophisticated lady. Marie isn't interested, thank you. She misses the military life and all her adoptive fathers. Will she ever be allowed to return? Not to worry. Just before the final curtain, Marie learns the Marquise is her mother, and both declare their undying love for each other. Then Marie marries the regiment's newest soldier, formerly the enemy. *They* declare their undying love for each other. Everyone lives happily ever after. *The Daughter of the Regiment* is unlike most *bel canto* operas I sang. The soprano doesn't go mad. No heads are chopped off. No one commits suicide or murder or otherwise expires at the end. It's a very cheery piece.

I decided to take the gaiety one step further: I played Marie as a lovable klutz, and I got away with it. The first time the audience saw me, my uniform was buttoned all wrong, my sleeves were two inches too short, I wore the ugliest knee-length boots you've ever seen— black with horrible gold buttons—and I had my hair frizzed out like Little Orphan Annie's.

I carried around a pile of props because my Marie was always ready to deal with any situation. If the soldiers sang the regimental song, she had a little flag to hold up. If they wanted a drink, she was ready with a cask of wine and several tin cups. Whenever the regiment's soldiers went on a march, their daughter, the little drummer girl, took out her sticks and played her snare drum. Badly. The girl could not keep time, and I'm not too sure she could *tell* time. Because she was such a lousy drummer, the regiment was always out of step—a general indication of the way they did everything. Like their beloved Marie, the regiment's soldiers also had a tough time deciding which buttons went into which buttonholes. The French Army's 21st regiment was rather pathetic, but its members didn't think so. *They* all thought the 21st was a crack unit. True, they couldn't march without tripping over each other, but they had plenty of *esprit de corps.*

Every soldier in the regiment adored Marie and would do anything for her, and she'd do anything for them, including laundry and peeling potatoes. You never could tell when one of the troops would get mud on his tunic, so Marie always carried a clothesline just in case. Various items were clanging and banging and hanging off her at all times and at all angles.

The way I played her, Marie never had a prayer of becoming a sophisticated woman. The second act opens with a dance lesson, which is there to show how graceful Marie's become. My Marie wasn't graceful. When I started dancing with the ballet master, I accidentally stepped on his toes and knocked him down. When the dance was over and he ordered me to do a low curtsy, I wound up flat on my backside. An *awkward* child. And an angry one, as well. Marie wanted to be back at the barracks with the guys; she had no use for this overly effeminate ballet master. When he showed me how a proper young lady should use her fan, I hit him with it. It was a touch of slapstick in an opera that lent itself to that kind of humor.

Next came the daily singing lesson with Marie's aunt. Muriel Costa-Greenspon had a great comedic gift for playing stuffy, pigeon-brained characters. Donald Gramm, one of the most wonderful bass-baritones of his time, played Sergeant Sulpice, the regiment's commander and Marie's main father figure. Donald was a close friend and had been a long-time colleague at the City Opera. In 1966 the Met made him an offer he couldn't refuse, and he'd since become an international star.

Sergeant Sulpice came onstage toward the end of my singing lesson—he and the Marquise, Marie's aunt, had a little romance going. The sergeant was waiting for us to finish the last song of my lesson.

Sarah had staged it perfectly. As the Marquise and I sang, we waited while a metronome on the piano clicked back and forth eight times. On the ninth swing, Muriel and I paused, and the metronome rang out with the sound of a cuckoo clock. And then we sang for eight beats and again paused on the ninth. We did that all the way through the song. When it was over, I was supposed to shut off the metronome by attaching the arm to a safety hinge.

On opening night, the metronome became unhinged. I couldn't seem to shut it off, and while fussing with it, I apparently did something to make the metronome go cuckoo on *every* beat. The audience started to crack up. It took less than half a minute to shut that little monster up, but when you're onstage and something screwy happens, every second seems to enjoy a long and happy life before moving on.

I waited for the audience to stop laughing before delivering my next line of dialogue. Just as I turned to speak—*precisely* at that moment—the metronome started cuckooing again. The audience immediately went crazy, and I wasn't feeling too sane myself.

Gramm, who played pompous men better than anybody else, turned to me and, in character, said, "I will fix it." I liked Donald's approach to the problem. He walked over to the metronome, gently picked it up, gently placed it on the floor, and then kicked down savagely and smashed it silent. The audience gave Donald a rousing ovation. I curtsied to him and sat down.

And then the metronome went cuckoo again.

I'd never seen a crowd of proper Bostonians come down with a case of mass hysteria. I wasn't quite sure what to do next; none of us was. I also was having a hard time keeping a straight face. In hopes of getting some moral support and perhaps an idea of what to do while waiting for the crowd to calm itself, I looked down at Roland Gagnon, who was conducting the orchestra. But Roland was not on the podium. He was on the floor, laughing like a lunatic.

That did it for me; I was gone. I just threw back my head and started *roaring*. Muriel was in worse shape than I was, but Donald was Donald; nothing could make my Donald break character. *Nothing*. The man had a will of iron. Gramm surveyed the chaos around him and quickly took charge of the situation. He strutted up to the metronome, slammed it to the floor, and stomped on it. With his foot still on the totally devastated machine, Donald turned to the audience and bowed gallantly.

The bleacher section celebrated Donald's victory over the wounded metronome by holding up its cards and again unfurling the French tricolor. The crowd was *screaming*. All this incredible joy and excitement was focused on Donald, who was absolutely eating it up. In character. The crowd continued its ovation until Gramm sensed we could resume the opera.

When Donald took his foot off the metronome, it said, "Cuckoo."

I'd had all the pandemonium I could handle. I picked the damned thing up and handed it to a musician, who heaved it way under the performing platform. Regardless of the craziness—or perhaps because of it—I think my first *Daughter of the Regiment* might have been my best. It was definitely the most memorable of my career.

Over the next several months I appeared in concerts and operas all over the country. When I'd started performing in the mid-fifties, the American opera scene was pretty much restricted to New York, San Francisco, and Chicago, with occasional performances put on in Baltimore, Philadelphia, and New Orleans. That all changed by the start of the 1970s. In Texas alone, I sang in Austin, Dallas, Fort Worth, Houston, Laredo, McAllen, San Antonio, Waco—you name the town, I sang there.

Opera became popular in Texas the same way it did in a lot of previously isolated regions of the nation. It started with money. In the case of Texas, it was oil money, and it made a lot of people very rich, very fast. That kind of money creates a following for the arts, because after using it to buy houses, private planes, cars, and jewelry, people have to spend it on other things. And for other purposes, such as creating a social hierarchy. That's one reason why a number of rich Texans quickly amassed incredibly valuable art collections, which led in turn to building museums where those collections went on loan for everyone to see. Museum donors give parties and create educational programs for their children, who wind up knowing more about the arts than their parents do.

Opera benefited in much the same way. Small groups of wealthy people began plunking down hard cash to pay for visits by leading opera stars. During those visits, the donors would put on lavish parties because they wanted to show off their wealth and fancy clothes. Musicians steeped in opera, many of them World War II refugees from Europe, were hired to teach, direct, and produce operas. That's how opera companies sprang up all over the country. This is a good old American tradition, and it works, and I'm not ridiculing it, either.

After World War II, the donors who helped set up these brand-new opera companies traveled to Europe, saw La Scala and other theaters, and suddenly realized their own theaters left a lot to be desired. Next thing you knew, cities like Houston, Seattle, and San Antonio had built opera houses of their own. As soon as you have a beautiful theater, you can lure fine conductors and musicians to come live in the area. And that's how you build up the cultural life of a city.

Aside from my commitment to Sarah Caldwell in Boston, my primary allegiance was to the New York City Opera Company. In September 1970, I returned there to sing several roles during the company's fall season, which had now grown to more than two months long. I sang *Lucia* on September 10, and *Manon* on September 25. Miss Liebling was too ill to attend the opening of *Manon*. That night, while I was singing the role she most liked me in, my beloved teacher passed away.

I learned about her death after the performance, and the news made me numb. I'd always known the day would come when Miss Liebling wouldn't be with me, but that did nothing to lessen my sense of loss. For the very first time, I felt that life was going by too fast. I chided myself about not spending enough time with Miss Liebling during the last year of her life. She'd been sick, and Peter and I had visited her, but I was all wrapped up in my career. After Miss Liebling died, there were times when I'd sing especially well and I'd think: *Teacher would have liked that.*

When I was ten years old, Miss Liebling had arranged a Portuguese folk song for me as a birthday present, and I ended all my recitals with it. The first four lines of the song still come to mind instantly, whenever I remember Miss Liebling, which is quite often:

Tell me why you bid me leave you.
There are tears in your eyes.
Tell me why you wish our parting.
Is not my love worth more than sighs?

Three weeks later I debuted as Queen Elizabeth in *Roberto Devereux*, which hadn't been staged in the United States since 1851.

Forget the singing itself for a moment; in terms of characterization alone, Elizabeth was the most ambitious undertaking of my operatic career. Until then, in every opera I'd sung, I'd played a young woman, and I'd always looked like myself. Oh, I might have worn a wig to change my hair color, and there had been the heavy white makeup for *Norma,* but that was about it. For *Devereux,* I had to become Queen Elizabeth in the autumn of her life. Gigi Capobianco created my makeup, and at first she fashioned a putty nose for me, but it usually fell off by the end of Act II, so we did it with makeup instead. Gigi also made a latex bald pate for me, and gave me stark, chalk-white facial makeup that she lined with streaks of black to show Elizabeth's age.

We also remodeled my body. Because Elizabeth was no longer young, the gown I wore contained boning that flattened me on top. The gown itself felt like lead; it weighed fifty-five pounds and was far too heavy for our female dressers to work with. Instead, Edgar Joseph, the head costume man, and his assistant, Joe Citarella (who now holds that job) both had to help me into it. If the gown was tough to put on, it was tougher to get around in. Spending three hours at a time in that costume was no picnic.

I'll tell you right now that Tito Capobianco, Gigi Denda, and Roland Gagnon were the best collaborators God ever put on this earth. When those three worked with me on a role, no other singer could be as well prepared. *Devereux* was Tito's production, Tito's staging, Tito's everything. It was as if he had laid out a banquet, and when you examined each dish you saw that he'd cooked up something special for the most sophisticated palates in the opera world. Gigi gave me Elizabeth's every gesture, every step, and every subtlety—we lived Elizabeth every waking moment. Peter bought me a huge collection of books about her, and Gigi and I practically memorized them. *Devereux* never became static, for Tito and I always experimented with new approaches to different scenes and different lines. Both of us would have gotten bored if I'd simply shown up and performed my role the same way over and over and over again. It was important to keep trying to perfect it, because that meant I was still creating. People who saw me do *Devereux* a dozen times never saw the same performance twice.

I'd always been interested in the dramatic content of operas and felt I had a theatrical flair, and Tito encouraged me to pull out all the stops. He was very willing to let me ham it up, and then he'd tone me down. In doing so, Tito brought me through one stage of development.

Roland took me through another stage by introducing me to a new way of singing. He showed me how I could achieve various dramatic effects through the use of text—Tito couldn't do that as a director, but Roland could as a vocal coach. Instead of using my body to express an emotion or attitude, I could convey the same thing by the way I sang a *word*. Once I caught on to that, it opened up a whole new world for me. Onstage, less was better. I didn't *need* a lot of sweeping physical gestures; my delivery of a line could accomplish the same thing. That may not sound revolutionary, but the way Roland worked, it was.

I couldn't have asked for a juicier, more dramatic role than Queen Elizabeth. Bette Davis played the same part in the 1939 movie *The Private Lives of Elizabeth and Essex*. Miss Davis's Devereux was Errol Flynn; mine was Placido Domingo, who, despite his City Opera successes in *Don Rodrigo* and *La Traviata*, was still relatively unknown. That would soon change: *Devereux* was the final role on his City Opera contract, after which Placido became a star at the Met. I sometimes wonder what Bing would have done for singers if he hadn't continually raided our company over the years. In his book, *The Met*, published jointly by the Metropolitan Opera Guild and Simon & Schuster, Martin Mayer points out:

> Through the Bing years, the City Opera was a more important source of new American artists for the Met than all the European houses and the auditions put together. Any list would have to include Dorothy Kirsten, Judith Raskin, Tatiana Troyanos, Shirley Verrett, Ruth Welting, Maralin Niska, John Alexander, Kenneth Riegel, John Reardon, Placido Domingo, José Carreras, Cornell MacNeil, Sherrill Milnes, Richard Cassilly, and many others.

Placido returned to the City Opera as a tenor in 1974, when he sang Don José in *Carmen*. But he'd come back a year earlier to make his debut as an operatic conductor with *La Traviata*. As might be gathered from that, Placi was a fine musician, a skill that always separated him from the rest of the pack.

He was also a real trouper. In the second act of *Roberto Devereux,* Elizabeth puts her hand on Essex's shoulder and forces him to his knees, and then slaps him across the face. All through rehearsals, the fake slap I gave Placido was singularly unconvincing, and we both knew it. Placi didn't blink an eye about going along with the obvious alternative—if I really had to whack him, then so be it. In the first act, I wore a big imitation crest ring on my right hand, and during the intermission I was supposed to switch the ring to my left hand. One night I forgot to do it and nearly killed Placido. When I was getting close to the moment Elizabeth slaps Essex—and while I was singing—I heard people in the wings screaming "Change the ring!" I didn't know what they were going on about. Seconds before I was about to deliver that slap, I suddenly flashed on the ring, so as I lifted my hand for the blow, I slipped off the ring and *then* slapped Placido.

Those slaps were merely solid. I once smacked a tenor so hard his moustache landed up on his eyebrows. That was no accident. The singer, who was playing Essex, absolutely refused to wear a wig. There *I* was, spending two hours a night to get into makeup and walking around in a fifty-five-pound costume, and he couldn't see his way clear to wear a *wig*? Did he really think Queen Elizabeth had fallen for a man with a *crewcut*? On top of that, the tenor also happened to cross the stage at a very dramatic moment in my aria, thereby destroying it. Because it takes longer to sing about something than talk about it, a good deal of time is required to build to an operatic climax. If something disruptive happens two-thirds of the way toward building that climax, you can't stop and say "Let's start over." This tenor was the kind of singer who stands onstage and instead of listening and reacting to what's going on, concentrates only on the next line he has to sing. Too bad, because he has a beautiful voice. Between the man's unwillingness to wear a wig and his inattentiveness onstage, I got so mad I couldn't see straight. I had no compunction at all about slapping him.

The second act of *Roberto Devereux* is a fountain of overpowering emotion. In most scenes, Elizabeth has her entire court around her and is a nonstop study in anger. Elizabeth is constantly flailing around, hitting her dress, snapping at everyone—her fury knows no bounds. How *dare* Devereux dump the Queen for another woman! His *head* will roll! The only standing ovation I ever received in the middle of an opera occurred at the end of the second act of *Roberto Devereux*.

As soon as I'd seen that her big last-act aria was a soliloquy, I realized I could give Queen Elizabeth another dimension. What I did was to turn her into a very old woman. She keeps up a tremendous front when anybody's around, but I crumbled her in that aria; I absolutely shattered her. When that aria is over, the audience knows the depths of Elizabeth's fear and loneliness.

In the third act, Donizetti gives Elizabeth *her* mad scene. It comes at the end of the opera, when Elizabeth hears the cannon shot signaling that Lord Essex's execution has just been carried out. Her wrath is awesome. The Queen attacks everything and everybody, and instead of having her sing those lines in beautifully pear-shaped tones, my Elizabeth screamed and ranted. She wailed about the fact that her best friend, Sara, a Donizetti invention, had been her rival all along; she seethed at having been politically maneuvered into executing Essex. Roland and I were not looking for pretty singing. Elizabeth was full of shrill sound and unbridled fury. She'd lost the only man she'd ever loved. Elizabeth was far too tough to break down and cry, but the death of Essex marked the end of her own life as a vigorous woman, and she knew it all too well. The Queen of England had suddenly become a bitter, heartbroken old lady. She'd continue to be the most powerful woman in the world, but the rest of her days would be filled with frustrated, relentless rage.

Roberto Devereux contained one of the longest endings, and certainly the wickedest, I've ever come across in an opera. Elizabeth was the hardest role I ever took on. As much as I may have loved Manon, Lucia, Baby Doe, Violetta, Cleopatra, Marie, and several other ladies I played, I loved playing Queen Elizabeth the most. *Roberto Devereux* was both the greatest artistic challenge and the finest achievement of my career.

SIXTEEN

In the first half of the nineteenth century, Gaetano Donizetti wrote more than seventy operas, three of which had become favorites of mine: *Lucia di Lammermoor, The Daughter of the Regiment,* and *Roberto Devereux.* After the success I enjoyed in *Devereux,* Roland Gagnon proposed that I take on Donizetti's two other Tudor queens, *Maria Stuarda* and *Anna Bolena.* Roland thought that singing Donizetti's three queens was a goal worth shooting for, as opposed to merely selecting my repertoire on a scattershot basis. He began talking to me in terms of leaving "documents" behind. Roland had an idea I'd eventually occupy my own little niche in opera history, which initially struck me as pretentious and improbable.

Roland didn't give a damn what I thought. He wanted me to become the first soprano in modern opera history ever to sing the three queens. I know that I'd been rather surprised to discover that Maria Callas hadn't tackled *Roberto Devereux,* especially since she liked Donizetti—Callas enjoyed major triumphs in *Lucia* and *Anna Bolena.* She might have had the same feeling about *Devereux* that I did at first: Unless you put the text and music together, as Roland did for me, it's hard to have a good idea how that opera will play.

When I decided to go after Donizetti's two other Tudor queens, I had no problem talking Julius Rudel into doing them at the New York City Opera. Rudel had already blocked out the company's spring and fall 1971 seasons, so he penciled in *Maria Stuarda* for spring 1972.

I had plenty to keep me occupied until then. On December 23, 1970, two months after I performed *Roberto Devereux* in New York, I debuted at London's Covent Garden in *Lucia*. I received an odd welcome there. When I went to Covent Garden for my first costume fitting, I noticed that the elderly lady in charge of wardrobe had a huge picture of Joan Sutherland hanging in her office.

Joan Sutherland is a prima donna in the best sense of the term— she's a wonderful, polite woman who's not modest about her singing, and indeed she doesn't need to be. Joan doesn't walk around saying "I'm simply amazed at what's happened to little ole me." She's well aware that her voice is big and beautiful and thrills people by its sheer technical virtuosity. Joan strives for vocal perfection, which is why she's sometimes been accused of having mushy diction. Believe me, Joan can speak clearly, but she'll sacrifice anything for purity of tone.

I approached my roles differently: I'd sacrifice *any* pure tone to make a dramatic point. I never really listened to my voice until last year, when my albums were reissued on compact discs. My assessment is that I knew exactly what I was doing, and that I was often a risk-taking, exciting singer. I think my most singular quality was the way I used text. And it didn't hurt to have a unique voice that people could identify very easily, in the same way they could immediately identify the Beatles or Frank Sinatra.

The same is true of Sutherland's voice, of course. But in a sense I felt that we were in different businesses. Her approach was purely vocal; mine put much more of an emphasis on the dramatic content of an opera. We were apples and oranges. Trying to decide who was better was as ridiculous as trying to compare Sinatra and Crosby or Matisse and Picasso.

When I saw that photograph of Joan Sutherland, I told the wardrobe lady: "Oh, I see you're also a fan of the great lady." She remained silent and glared at me, so I walked away. But I got the message. In terms of costuming, wigging, and the like, it would be a great overstatement to say that I was greeted warmly at Covent

Garden. I realize that the British are a reserved people, but this went way beyond reserved. This was called cool and distant.

I suppose I had Fleet Street to thank for that. Before I stepped foot in England, London's daily tabloids were full of sarcastic Miss America Superstar stories. They also claimed that about 150 members of my "claque" were flying over to make sure I got a proper reception at Covent Garden. Some claque. The Friends of the City Center and members of the New York City Opera Guild were going on an opera tour of Europe, and their first stop was London and Covent Garden.

The English press was after me before I opened my mouth. Peter had bought me a gorgeous leopard coat—this was before we were all made aware of endangered species—and the newspapers ran photos of me in that coat with snide captions. I had a lot of friends in London, including Estée Lauder and Fleur Cowles, and I think the newspaper reporters felt I was far too comfortable in *their* city. Everybody seemed to be telling them what a hotshot I was, and they just weren't going to sit still for that. Not for a *moment.*

The television people were much friendlier. I did an hour-long BBC profile in which I was interviewed by Bernard Levin, one of England's most distinguished journalists. When the show was broadcast in the United States several years later, it won an Emmy.

I've always loved London, and after recording *Roberto Devereux* with the Royal Philharmonic in 1969, I recorded as many of my albums there as possible. Every summer, Peter, Muffy, and I would check into a big suite at the Connaught Hotel, and I'd spend more than a month in London, working, seeing friends, shopping, and watching tennis at Wimbledon. I had a love affair going with the English public. During the month or so I was in London for my Covent Garden debut, you couldn't walk past a record store without seeing blown-up photos of me that EMI had supplied to its dealers. Every record I'd ever made became a best seller. I didn't do any record signings, and in a way I think Englishmen liked that about me. I really felt embraced by them.

John Tooley, Covent Garden's general director, is a very charming man whom I've gotten to know much better since I became his counterpart at the City Opera. In 1970, when I debuted with his opera company, I didn't know him at all. John came backstage to visit me just once, on opening night. Birgit Nilsson was singing there on alternate nights, and she used to leave funny little notes for me. The first time I opened up the dressing room closet, I saw the kind of big flannel robe my grandmother wore, with felt slippers beneath it. Birgit had pinned a note to the robe that read "Don't laugh at this—you'll need it." She was right: The dressing room was freezing. In a drawer she left a note that said "Put your rear on the toilet seat slowly. It might shock the high notes out of you."

Birgit was right about that too. When Tooley came backstage to say hello, I jokingly told him how Birgit and I felt about the "loo." Tooley may have been taken aback, but he smiled. He said he'd never received any complaints about it.

I debuted in an old production of *Lucia,* and the costumes were terrible. The sets were designed for a singer who had a totally different interpretation from mine, and the stage was badly lit for my mad scene. As had been true of my La Scala *Lucia,* I started with one tenor and finished with another; the first one canceled out after opening night, and I had no rehearsal with the second. Once again, I'd been a dummy. I should have told Tooley: "If you want me, bring Tito and Gigi in to direct *Lucia,* and give me a new production. Otherwise, forget it."

My one stroke of luck was working with conductor John Pritchard. John was helpful and supportive, and if I hadn't known he'd be in the pit every night, I doubt if I would have finished the engagement. Professionally speaking, Covent Garden was a nice place to visit, but I was glad I didn't live there.

My debut attracted a lot of attention. All my performances sold out, at the highest prices Covent Garden had charged since Callas's final appearance. Unfortunately, I had a lousy opening night. My singing was fine, but I just could not use those sets. I'd been told that all the critics sat together in one box, as if they were part of a coffee klatch. An EMI recording engineer heard one of them say, before the opera began: "I wonder how much her husband had to pay to let her sing here?"

Stanley Sadie, London's leading music critic, gave me a great review, but writers for the city's pack of tabloids went at me tooth-and-nail. They didn't really attack my voice. Their put-downs were more along the lines of "Who said this woman is such a special actress? We have Miss Sutherland's *Lucia.* Why did we have to bring Beverly Sills over?"

The audience couldn't have been kinder, but several critics were put off when my so-called claque made the enormous "mistake" of sending flowers up to the stage when I came out for my last bow. I wound up with very little respect for English opera critics. Later, I was asked to bring over the City Opera's production of *Roberto Devereux,* but I wasn't interested. I am not a masochist.

After the first couple of performances of *Lucia,* my family went back to the States, and I was alone in London for a while. *Very* alone. One of the things I always loved best about being an opera singer was the chance to make new friends every time I went into a new production. When I sang at Covent Garden, I never saw anyone from the cast. I was definitely the outside superstar; I wasn't included in anything. London's artistic and operatic communities treated me the same way many of the city's newspapers did—as an interloper.

Not long after I opened at Covent Garden, conductor Lorin Maazel called and asked me to fly over to Berlin and sing a *Traviata* for him between performances of *Lucia.*

"Why would I want to do that?" I asked.

"Because I'm conducting it and we're friends," he said. "My God, the Deutsche Oper is my house. And you never do anything in Europe. It's not going to hurt you to sing in Berlin."

Well, I went, and Lorin was right; it *didn't* hurt me to sing in Berlin. It didn't help me, either. The production had been designed for another soprano—what else was new?—and the costume I had to wear was blood-red. I told Lorin: "With my hair, how can I wear a red gown?"

Lorin called in the designer, who said, "I'm sorry, but with the set we're using, I can't give you any other color."

So I wore the gown—you can't be too choosy when you're doing instant opera. I flew to West Berlin on a Monday night, and I practically had to force Lorin to let me rehearse with the rest of the cast on Tuesday. Lorin said, "We both know the music, so let's not bother with rehearsals. We'll just have fun." I sang *Traviata* on Wednesday night, and was back in London on Thursday.

I wasn't happy about that *Traviata,* but I suspect my dismay had less to do with the production than with being a Jew in Germany. In previous visits, Peter and I had encountered several ex-Nazis and anti-Semites. In 1968, at a cocktail party held at the American consulate in Hamburg, an elderly German woman backed Peter and me into a corner and informed us that the Nazis would have won

World War II if their V-2 rockets and jet planes had become operational a year earlier. Peter, who's fluent in German, replied that he'd been a bomber pilot during World War II, and that his only regret was that he'd missed dropping a bomb on *her*. In Frankfurt, I mentioned to a cabbie that the city seemed to have a great many fur shops. "That's because there are still too many Jews around," he replied. Peter told the guy to stop the taxi, didn't give him a tip, and cursed him out in German.

Before I left Berlin, Maazel introduced me to Egon Seefehlner, a dear sweet man who was the head of the Deutsche Oper. Egon took me on a tour of West Berlin, which, except for the big bombed-out church that sat in the middle of town, seemed like a brand-new city. It was, of course. By the time Germany surrendered, Allied bombing raids had reduced Berlin to rubble. When we were driving around, Egon said, "Would you believe I'm the oldest thing in this city?"

Seefehlner offered me *Roberto Devereux,* no holds barred, damn the expenses and full speed ahead. And if I didn't want to do *Devereux,* that was fine too. The Deutsche Oper receives an enormous subsidy from the German government, and Egon was ready, willing, and able to finance a new production of whatever opera I wanted to sing.

I thought about that offer every moment I was in West Berlin. It was ten degrees below zero the night I sang *Traviata* there. The Deutsche Oper is housed in a gray concrete building. If I did an opera in West Berlin, and if Peter didn't come with me, as I knew he wouldn't, I'd be lonely and unhappy. I wouldn't be happy even if I worked with the Capobiancos and could persuade Gigi to stay with me for the whole run. Tito would leave after the first night, and then the *two* of us would get depressed. I finally started thinking: *I can get a* Devereux *anyplace I want—why do it here? I'm only going to get homesick.*

I was homesick already. Singing in Europe held no special thrill for me. Herr Seefehlner was quite gracious when I told him I couldn't see my way clear to coming back to Berlin.

Before I finished my run in *Lucia* at Covent Garden, John Pritchard and I flew to Paris, where he conducted a concert I gave at the Salle Pleyel. That was some night. We'd prepared a program of arias, many of which were French, and the audience went wild. And

talk about rave reviews! I must say that one of the few disappoint-
ments of my career was never to have sung at the Paris Opéra.

In December of 1970, just before I flew to London, President
Richard Nixon appointed me to the Council on the National Endowment for the Arts. I'd been invited to sing at the White House several
times, but I didn't like Nixon's politics, and I'd always come up with
a plausible reason to avoid showing up. I still don't know why
Nixon's people kept after me, but they did. I must have turned down
at least eight invitations before his staff mousetrapped me. I'd signed
to do a concert at Washington's Constitution Hall on February 1,
1971, and when I returned from London, a White House aide called
and said that since I'd be in the capital on February first, would I sing
at a White House gala the following evening? Peter and I had a long
talk about it. Instead of causing a political furor, it seemed smarter to
accept the invitation. I told myself I was honoring the office of the
President, not the man who was occupying it. I didn't quite convince
myself that I was doing the right thing.

Was *I* in for a shock: President Nixon turned out to be far more
charming and likable than I'd imagined. My whole family came
along—Peter, Muffy, Mom, and my brothers and their wives. Sidney
was excited about visiting the White House and would have gone
regardless of who was President. Stanley had some misgivings about
going—he wasn't fond of Mr. Nixon's politics, either—but he came
all the same.

The first thing Nixon told me was that his Aunt Ollie was deaf,
and that at the age of eighty she'd gone to Africa to do missionary
work. He'd been well briefed, and seemed genuinely interested in my
daughter's welfare, or at least he had the politician's ability to make
me *think* he was genuinely interested. On a certain level I didn't care
about any of that; the gesture itself was all that mattered. I felt very
flattered that the President of the United States had spent time
finding out about me and my family.

My mother was more excited about our visit than any of us.
Again, Nixon had been well briefed about our family, and he obviously had a superb memory. When my mother reached the President
on the receiving line, he talked to her at great length about her three
children and what they'd accomplished. Mama looked at him and
said, "Mr. Nixon, only in America could my children be invited to

meet the President of the country." Boy, did *he* find a new fan that night.

Make that two new fans. Contrary to his depiction in the press, Nixon was a delightful conversationalist, and he carried himself with the kind of dignity and presence we want all our Presidents to possess. He struck me as very formal, but he also had a healthy sense of humor. This may sound strange in light of what we later learned about Nixon, but he seemed to have great respect for the office of the President and for the White House itself. Before the evening's festivities began, the President and Mrs. Nixon took all of us on a quick, twenty-minute tour of his favorite rooms. Nixon took great pains to tell us stories about the wallpaper in one room, the furniture in the next, and he spoke generously of the improvements Jacqueline Kennedy had made during her time in the White House.

I still can't equate the voice on those Watergate tapes with the confident leader who was so courteous to me that night. Nor can I understand why, knowing they existed, Nixon didn't just destroy the tapes. If that wasn't part of a death wish, tell me what is. I guess that if I'd never met Nixon, the Watergate affair—the entire mess he made of his presidency—would never have upset me as much as it did. In trying to make sense of the whole thing, my only conclusion is that our Presidents live such isolated, overprotected lives that they lose touch with reality. They forget that ordinary people, *real* people— honest-to-God American citizens with no overriding political goals or ambitions—live beyond the White House gates. With a little help from their friends and flunkies, our Presidents sometimes act as if they believe more in monarchy than democracy.

In retrospect, before Watergate surfaced and brought him down, Nixon probably got much better media treatment than he deserved. His wife didn't. Pat Nixon was greatly maligned by the press, which created a kind of Iron Jaw persona for her. What a pity and what a distortion that was. Pat was bright, friendly, very well read, and always beautifully dressed. Because Nixon made that speech in the 1950s about his wife not having a mink coat but only a good Republican cloth coat, Mrs. Nixon acquired the image of a frump. The image wasn't the reality, and reporters knew it, but didn't bother doing anything to correct the public's impression of her.

I got to know her pretty well. Pat used to come and see me whenever I sang at the Chandler Pavilion in Los Angeles and she and her husband were at their home in San Clemente. She always brought me a basket of flowers and strawberries. A couple of Secret Service agents would whisk her into the theater through a doorway very close to my dressing room, and we'd sit and talk for about twenty minutes before my performance, chatting about our children, our homes, people we both knew—girl talk, really. She liked watching me do my makeup. I didn't find her shy. I think Pat just felt there was a formal protocol that went along with being the First Lady. She had certain duties to perform, and she performed them very well.

Compared to every other recent First Lady, Pat Nixon always seemed remote and unemotional. She wasn't, and you'd know that after talking to her for five minutes. I hated the way she was treated by the press, and even her daughters, Julie and Tricia, got pummeled in print. The media is much rougher on Presidents' daughters than on their sons. I remember all the snickering and giggling that went on when Lynda Johnson started going out with actor George Hamilton. What was so funny? I never got the joke. I didn't find it strange when the Johnson girl began to put on makeup and wear her hair prettily. How many mothers have longed for that day when their daughters look in the mirror and say, "Gee, I gotta do a little bit more with my makeup and my hair"? Think what your reaction would be if a handsome movie star began courting *your* daughter. If it happened to mine, I'd think it was rather nice. Later on, when Julie Nixon married David Eisenhower, the press tore into her *and* her husband. I don't know how Pat Nixon managed to hold her tongue while all that was going on. *I* wouldn't have.

The night I sang at the White House, Mrs. Nixon invited me to bring Muffy around for a real tour of the place the next time we were in Washington. Some months later, when my daughter and I were down there again, I called Pat's social secretary. I told her we'd like to come over for a tour, but I didn't want to disturb Mrs. Nixon. I just wanted to see if we could avoid standing on those long lines.

When we got to the White House, Muffy and I were given the standard VIP tour. We were walking along a balcony when Mrs. Nixon spotted us—she had just come out of a room with some people from Thailand. Pat left her guests for a moment, came over to greet us, and asked us to wait while she finished saying goodbye to them. A couple of minutes later we were seated in her apartment, being served tea and cookies and hearing all about her daughter

Tricia's wedding, which had taken place a few days before. Pat gave Muffy a piece of her daughter's wedding cake that she'd preserved in a beautiful tiny box, and then took us on a tour of *her* favorite White House rooms. Pat never turned her face away from Muffy when she was speaking, which made it easy for Muffy to lip-read. I'll never forget her kindness to my daughter that day.

The performance I gave at the White House almost turned into a fiasco. I'd prepared a program of eleven songs, but I don't think I'd gotten through three of them before I popped the zipper on the back of the white silk gown I was wearing. A few minutes later I suddenly realized the back zipper was open all the way down to my waist. I grabbed the front of the gown just as gravity was about to turn my recital into a striptease. Without saying anything, I backed out of the East Room, leaving three hundred people wondering if I'd lost my marbles. Moments later I returned wearing a long red velvet evening coat—the only reason I had it with me was because Pat had told me the East Room was drafty. As soon as the concert ended, I was able to joke about what happened, but believe me, for a few seconds there, I knew I had a shot at making a little history of my own in Washington. In front of my mother, yet.

Shortly after President Nixon left office, President Ford invited me to sing at the White House. The contrasts between the Fords and the Nixons couldn't have been more apparent. When you visited the Nixon White House, the atmosphere was very formal and official, and you never forgot for a moment where you were. Nixon was always aware of traditions that had to be followed. When he and his wife were before the public, Nixon kept things quite impersonal between them. Despite the fact that Pat was a kind, open woman, I didn't feel there was a lot of warmth in their relationship, at least not in public.

The Ford White House was run on a much more informal basis. Gerald and Betty Ford had a very happy, healthy relationship, and weren't the least bit intimidated by the White House. I became very fond of Betty, and Gerry was always fun to be with because he has a terrific sense of humor, much of it devoted to putting himself down. He is really a sweet, strapping, down-to-earth man who is far more handsome in person than he ever appears to be on television or in photographs. Ford was quick to confess he didn't know much about the arts and always left the cultural part of White House evenings to Betty. Since he was President, he couldn't bow out entirely, though.

Gerry has a gift for malapropisms. I became aware of that when I entertained at what turned out to be a hilarious state dinner in honor of England's former Prime Minister Harold Wilson and his wife, Mary. To start with, Annie Douglas, Sylvia Kaye, and I all showed up wearing identical sequined Norell gowns. Our only saving grace was that we'd ordered them in different colors: Annie's was white, mine was green, and Sylvia's was brown. When the three of us looked at one another, we just about fell down laughing. I mean, you expect *some* exclusivity, because Norell gowns cost a fortune. One reason they're so expensive is that each sequin is hand-sewn. You may lose a couple in the course of a dinner dance, but no more than that.

Before we all left that night, Annie Douglas got hold of some White House stationery. The next day she went out and bought some brown and green sequins, and enclosed them in letters she sent to Sylvia Kaye and me. The letters, supposedly signed by Betty Ford, castigated us for forcing the First Lady to "clean up after us." She ended by writing: "Here are your damned sequins, and stop trying to pass your dresses off as Norells—Annie Douglas is the only one of you who showed up in the real thing."

By the time the first course was served, it was painfully evident that Mrs. Wilson was suffering from intense jet lag. She didn't stop fidgeting all night. Mrs. Wilson tried every trick in the book to stay awake. I really felt sorry for her, because I'd gone through the same thing many times. When you have jet lag and social obligations that don't permit you to sleep it off, you're talking real torture. We were all trying to be polite and pretended not to notice. I was seated on the President's left, Mrs. Wilson was seated to his right, and on my left were Senator Strom Thurmond and Babe Paley. Babe always ate like a truck driver, and all us chubbier ladies were jealous of her because she wore a size Toddler Two and weighed maybe ninety-three pounds. As usual, Babe's attention was riveted on her plate. She was really packing it in, but every couple of minutes she would come up for air, look at me, and say, "Jet lag is the worst damn thing in the world!" And then go right back to stuffing herself.

Mrs. Ford was at the next table, seated between the Prime Minister and Cary Grant. At the start of the evening, Cary Grant had come up and introduced himself by taking my face in his hands and saying: "Lady, I love you." I thought I'd never recover from that. I spent the whole evening staring at that incredible man, which is probably how most women reacted when meeting him. Carol Burnett once told me that upon learning she'd be sitting next to Cary Grant at a dinner, she'd primped all day and changed her makeup five times. When the big moment arrived and she was introduced to him, Carol became completely undone. How's this for flustered: Carol greeted Cary Grant by saying, "You're a real credit to your profession."

President Ford had his hands full with our table, because we were all being inattentive and giddy. I think we got him totally disoriented. About twenty minutes before my recital started, I excused myself and walked over to the East Room, where I warmed up with Charlie Wadsworth. Just before the Fords and their guests started filing in, Charlie and I went into a little anteroom. We waited in there and listened as the President introduced me to his guests.

Ford started out by saying, "There is no more beautiful sound than that of a well-trained human voice," and I thought: *Now that's a nice beginning.* He then said, "Our artist tonight has made it big, even though she's from Brooklyn." At which point Danny Kaye started laughing and shouted, "What do you mean, even *though* she's from Brooklyn?"

Everybody started in with some good-natured heckling, but the President continued on, rather like a soldier unaware he's strolling in a mine field. Throughout the evening, there'd been a lot of talk about cancer and operations, because Betty Ford, Annie Douglas, and Happy Rockefeller, who was also there, all had recently undergone well-publicized cancer surgery. Everyone had been commenting about how gutsy those ladies were and how terrific they looked, which was quite true. The subject was obviously on Gerry's mind because he went on to say that Miss Sills was "as much at home in a Verdi ballad as she is in a Strauss operation." That did it: The entire audience got hysterical.

Ford turned to his wife and said, "Didn't I tell you that *you* should make the introductions?"

He finally got to the end of his speech and asked everyone to welcome that wonderful opera singer "Beverly Tilsit."

When I walked out, I said, "Mr. President, from here on in, wherever I sing, I want you to come along and warm up the audience for me."

Peter and I became frequent guests at the Ford White House, and I didn't always have to sing for my supper. I remember going to a

White House dinner in honor of Prime Minister Lee Kuan Yew of Singapore. The President introduced me by saying, "Prime Minister Lee, I want you to meet Beverly Sills. She's our most famous professional."

Betty said, "*Opera star!* Dammit, Gerry, she's an *opera* star!"

I think that was my favorite moment with the Fords. Whenever Betty corrected his little gaffes, Gerry would laugh at himself, and you could easily sense the great bond of humor and affection that existed between them.

After the Carters came to the White House, I was invited to sing there often. After my first appearance, Betty Ford phoned Kay Shouse, the great lady and benefactor of Wolf Trap, and said, "Beverly *can't* sing for them. She's *our* opera singer."

Six months after my debut at Covent Garden—and almost a year before my first stage performance in the role—I went back to London to record *Maria Stuarda*. Roland and I had worked hard on the opera, and I had a ball recording it, mostly because my hilariously irascible pal Eileen Farrell sang Queen Elizabeth.

Eileen's voice was heard throughout London, and not just on records. Eileen has a bawdy sense of humor. One day we went shopping for cashmere sweaters in the Burlington Arcade, and a bespectacled salesman brought out the largest sweater he had. Eileen took one look at it, unbuttoned her jacket, and said, "Now, honey, how can a pair like these squeeze into *that*? Show me a sweater for a *real* woman—none of this junior-sized crap."

We went to the theater together one evening, and a woman from Dallas came up to me, complimented me lavishly on what I was wearing, and said, "Wha, Bullets Durgin, Ah've never *seen* you lookin' so swell!"

Eileen and I do not merely giggle; we're cacklers. She called me Bullets for the rest of the evening, and we nearly were asked to leave the theater. She insists that her initials, E.F., don't really stand for Eileen Farrell, but don't inquire what they *do* stand for, because she'll tell you. Easy she isn't. The real Eileen Farrell is a warm, affectionate woman, fiercely loyal to her family. If you ask about them, Eileen will talk five hours straight about her son the lawyer, and her daughter the doctor.

God, I bounced around that year. My journals are a little spotty, but I know I gave more than eighty-five performances in 1971. Peter, Muffy, and I ended the year in Israel, where I'd agreed to do eight concert performances of *Abduction from the Seraglio,* with Julius Rudel guest-conducting the Israel Philharmonic Orchestra. Except for performances at the New York City Opera—I got $500 per for those—I was then receiving about $10,000 a night. I decided it would be wonderful if Muffy and my mother came along to Israel with Peter and me. My mother was thrilled. Before we left, she said, "I hope you're donating these concerts. No nice Jewish girl takes money out of Israel." I was not about to argue with her.

On our first day in Tel Aviv, Peter, Muffy, and I went for a long walk, and we noticed little kiosks next to all the bus stops. The kiosks were covered with posters announcing my concerts. I can't read Hebrew, but my name and appearance dates weren't written in Hebrew—those I *could* read, and they added up to fourteen concerts, not eight. I immediately called Abe Cohen, the manager of the Israel Philharmonic.

"What's with the fourteen concerts, Abe?" I asked. "I only agreed to sing eight. How can you ask me to do fourteen in twenty-five days?"

Cohen laughed and said, "Well, Bev, the price is right."

I'd gone to Israel because I was curious about the country, as I think all Jews are. But just as I feel no ties to my mother's Russia or my father's Rumania, I don't feel I have roots in Israel. I'm an American woman. My roots are in the United States. But I love people who shake their fists at the heavens and say they will not be defeated, and so I love Israel.

While I was there, I became intensely aware of my heritage as a Jew, and that was certainly true in a musical sense. Whenever I turned on the radio, and even when Peter and I went to the Wailing Wall, I'd join in the singing we heard. My husband would say, "What is that? Where did you learn that?" I had no idea where I'd heard those songs, only that I knew them.

I never stopped laughing in Israel. Aside from my concerts, all I remember is sitting at tables, laughing and eating. I think they feed you in your sleep over there. When you go to a Jew's home, there's an incredible excess of food and nonstop conversation, the decibel level of which sometimes seems deafening. It's all part of a crazy sense of humor that's built into being Jewish. I can't define it, but I can give you an example of what I'm talking about. I had a friend who took her mother to the unveiling of a tombstone, which is a traditional religious ceremony held a year after a Jew's burial. When the veil was lifted, the people in attendance got their first look at a very large tombstone that had been placed atop the grave. My friend's mother said, "Look at the size of that thing! Now that's what I call really *living*!!"

My visit to Israel didn't change my religious beliefs. I believe in God, but I've never been religious in the sense that I think you have to go into a building—whether it's a synagogue, church, mosque, or cathedral—to pray. I don't believe God is interested in real estate. Culturally, yes, I'm very Jewish, and I felt that very keenly in Israel. One of my concerts took place in the community hall of a kibbutz. It was freezing in that place, which I hadn't anticipated. I'd brought along a light dress, and the harpist lent me her sweater, but I still had to sing with my coat on. The hall was so cold that my breath was visible all the while I was singing. The audience had known there wouldn't be sufficient heat; they all wore overcoats, hats, scarves, gloves, and boots. At the end of the concert, their applause was muffled because of their gloves, so they began stamping their feet. That was a moment I'll never forget.

One of the great experiences of my life took place about four years later, when I sang with conductor Zubin Mehta and the Israel Philharmonic *and* the Los Angeles Philharmonic at the Hollywood Bowl. It felt as if only a week had passed since I'd last seen the Israeli musicians. We spent at least half an hour hugging and kissing before we could get down to rehearsing.

By then, I shared Zubin's passion for the Israel Philharmonic, whose members are fantastic musicians. They're also expert debaters. Our rehearsals, in fact, often seemed like one long running argument, and neither Zubin nor I could act like moderators and put a lid on it. Every musician in the Israeli Philharmonic had a strong opinion about tempo, dynamics, each other—*everything*. Naturally, I joined in, and between my Brooklyn Yiddish and Mehta's hilarious Indian Yiddish, our rehearsals resembled a Marx Brothers comedy. I'd say, "I need to take this passage a bit slower," and before Zubin could say, "Fine," the first violinist would get up from his chair and say, "You can't take that passage slower. There's a violin line underneath it, and if you take it slower, you'll destroy my line."

His line? *I* was the soloist, or so I thought. We wound up doing opera by committee. I sang a long aria from *Abduction from the Seraglio,* which begins with an almost endless orchestral introduction featuring five soloists. Each of them had something to say about how the aria should be approached. When the debating was done, however, we ended up making beautiful music together.

If you can imagine the sound of those two orchestras playing together at the Hollywood Bowl, you'll understand why I was reminded of a Deanna Durbin movie I once saw called *100 Men and a Girl,* only in this case it was more like 200. I don't really know how I got through the concert itself, because it was an overwhelmingly emotional event for me. I was in love with the Israel Philharmonic, and I still am. Someone once asked me if my husband was Jewish. I replied, "When you're in love, the whole world is Jewish."

That's how I felt that night.

SEVENTEEN

People in show business are often asked to lend their names to charitable causes. We're always assured that we won't be called on to donate time or money—just the use of our names. I always refused such requests. I already had stationery with my name on it, and felt that if a cause wasn't worth more than my name, if it wasn't worth my time or money, why bother?

In 1971, officials of the March of Dimes asked me if I'd consider becoming national chairman of the Mothers' March on Birth Defects. The Mothers' March is a nationwide activity wherein mothers actually go out and ring doorbells to raise funds to help prevent birth defects. The March of Dimes people weren't asking me for the use of my name on their stationery. They wanted me to help them raise money, and to speak publicly about my personal experience with the nightmare of children born with birth defects. I asked for a little time to consider their request.

Obviously, I knew I'd have to talk about my own children, and I didn't know how my daughter would react to that. So I sat down with Muffy and discussed it with her. She was then all of twelve years old, but Muffy understood the need to battle against birth defects, and thought I should take the job. And so in 1972, I became national chairman of the Mothers' March on Birth Defects. When I assumed that office, Muffy traveled with me a great deal and allowed her photograph to be taken. She also appeared with me on a PBS program in which she acted as interpreter for deaf viewers.

By 1958 the March of Dimes had become the only organization that ever set out to cure a disease—polio—and actually did so. After Dr. Jonas Salk's and Dr. Albert Sabin's vaccines eliminated polio, a good deal of debate ensued about whether or not the March of Dimes, having fulfilled its purpose, should simply disband. The organization decided to continue, and its new focus became the elimination of all birth defects.

When I became national chairman, I found the going very rough at first. It was difficult for me to talk to parents of thalidomide babies who'd been born without arms or legs. It was difficult to visit intensive care units and see a dozen or more premature babies, few of whom would survive.

What I did enjoy were the breakfasts that were arranged for forty or fifty parents of handicapped children. I'd usually meet with them on the morning of a fund-raising banquet at which I'd be making a speech. Many of the couples I met were filled with despair, and I simply tried to bring a measure of comfort to them. They were all going through the same things Peter and I had gone through. The first thing you think is: *Why did it happen to me?* That only produces self-pity, immobilization, and an inability to do anything positive for the child. What helped me most with my children—especially with my son—was my mother's telling me that my children were created in God's image and therefore were perfect. She enabled me to take the next step, which was to ask: *Why did it happen to my children?* The next step after that was to begin working toward the day when we *will* know why my children were born with birth defects.

This is not an easy subject to talk about. I've had very emotional meetings with parents. You finally get down to the level of what a calamity it is to see a young human being unable to enjoy the full measure of the joys of living. My daughter—the proudest accomplishment of my life—has been able to overcome her handicap. She lives a normal life. My son doesn't, and never will.

For obvious reasons I'm bound to the March of Dimes for the rest of my life, but I'm also bound to the organization because of the near-miracles it's responsible for. I've held in my hands two-pound babies who would have had no chance of survival ten years ago. Premature birth is the leading cause of infant mortality, but with the aid of March of Dimes funds, Dr. Robert Creasy, then of the University of California, San Francisco, developed a program that can identify women who are at high risk for delivering their babies prematurely. Such expectant mothers are trained to recognize early signs of pre-term labor, and are treated with newly developed drugs that can halt their labor. The March of Dimes has set up a number of clinics throughout the country that offer Dr. Creasy's program.

I've also seen a March of Dimes grantee develop a test that can detect PKU (phenylketonuria) in a single drop of a newborn baby's blood. The symptoms of PKU—severe mental retardation and growth deformities—can now be successfully treated with a special diet begun the moment a baby is born. There are now close to two hundred disorders that can be detected or ruled out before a baby is born, and the list is increasing. We are rapidly approaching a time when most birth defects will be both diagnosed and successfully treated in utero—before the babies are actually born.

Which brings me to the subject of amniocentesis, the simple procedure of withdrawing a small amount of the amniotic fluid that surrounds the fetus and analyzing it for disease and genetic defects. Amniocentesis is a touchy issue with Right-to-Lifers. They claim that if there's the slightest chance a child won't be born normal, amnio-centesis encourages women to have abortions. I have actually heard some "far" Right-to-Lifers describe amniocentesis as a "search and destroy mission." The fact is, only about 2 to 3 percent of women who undergo amniocentesis have abortions. If amniocentesis had been developed when I was pregnant, and if I had known what was in store for my son, I still would have chosen to have him. He's mine, and I don't love him any less for what he is. But that's my decision to make, no one else's. I do not approve of indiscriminate abortion, but neither do I approve of people setting themselves up as judges. Only God is qualified for that job.

When I began working with the March of Dimes, I made sure that wherever I sang, I'd do a series of media interviews on behalf of the organization, and if the local chapter could arrange a fund-raiser, I'd be available as a guest speaker.

None of this interfered with my career. My performances were selling out wherever I sang, and that was especially true at the New

York City Opera. As a result, Julius Rudel was now amenable to letting me sing whatever I wanted. In 1972, I wanted to sing the toughest roles in my repertoire: Queen Elizabeth and Cleopatra, plus Mary Stuart in *Maria Stuarda,* the second of Donizetti's three Tudor queens.

Stuarda was the queen I liked least. I think Donizetti himself was far less interested in Mary Stuart than he was in Queen Elizabeth and Anne Boleyn. He gave Elizabeth a final scene of fury the likes of which I have never seen in any other opera, and there's a *great* mad scene in *Anna Bolena.* He left Mary mentally intact and in control of the situation, and at the end of the opera she calmly puts her head on the chopping block. Mary Stuart was the weakest character and had the weakest music of the three queens. I found it truly odd that Mary, who was known to think with her heart and not with her head, didn't have a single love scene with the tenor. Sopranos *always* have a love scene with the tenor. That's what tenors are *for.*

The opera's one flash of Donizetti's genius is a powerful denunci-ation scene in which Mary Stuart calls Elizabeth a vile bastard—audiences always get excited when the two ladies shriek at each other. Aside from that, *Maria Stuarda* was the easiest of the queens to sing, because Elizabeth is onstage for the first half of the opera and then disappears, after which Mary Stuart comes in.

If Roland and I hadn't decided to go after all three queens, I'd never have done *Maria Stuarda.* It's possible, I suppose, that Donizetti felt the same way I did about Mary Stuart: You had to go through her first in order to get to *Anna Bolena.*

I was all geared up to sing *Anna Bolena* that fall. In fact, I planned to sing all three queens the following season. Starting in 1970, when I made my debut in *Roberto Devereux,* Roland, Tito and Gigi, Julius, and I had carefully planned and orchestrated my pursuit of the three queens. *Devereux* had been televised, and it seemed likely that *Bolena* would be televised, too.

One day during the spring 1972 season, Julius called me up and said, "Beverly, I'd like to do something special for Norman in the fall."

"Fine," I said. "What do you want to do?"

"A new production of *Hoffmann.*"

Given the New York City Opera's finances, I didn't even have to ask what that meant: Goodbye, *Anna Bolena.*

"It's really going to be hard for me to leave the queens just when I'm about to finish them," I said, but I didn't kick up a fuss. After we did *Julius Caesar* together, my career had taken off and Norman's had just sat there. Anyone who ever heard Treigle sing knew he was one of the greatest operatic talents of his time. But Norman never got the recognition he deserved. That was another piece of petty stupidity on the part of Mr. Bing. Keeping me out of the Met had ceased being a real sore point, because I'd made out just fine by myself. To keep Norman out at a time when the Met was relying mostly on Cesare Siepi for its bass roles was a terrible injustice. Norman's talent was absolutely hair-raising, which made his inability to achieve worldwide prominence doubly hard for him to swallow.

Norman was a high-strung, chain-smoking, deeply religious man. He was unpredictable onstage in the best sense of that word—he never played any role the same way twice. As a result, when we performed together, neither did I. Whenever Norman and I sang together, the wings of the stage were packed with colleagues watching us perform.

Norman tried not to allow his frustration to show, but Julius, the Capobiancos, and I all knew his lack of success was eating away at him. So why *shouldn't* he have a *Hoffmann* that might vault him to stardom? I could wait a year for *Anna Bolena,* and in the meantime I could record it.

And so, in August 1973, Peter and I went back to London and I recorded the last of Donizetti's queens for EMI. Paul Plishka sang Henry VIII, Shirley Verrett sang Jane Seymour, Stuart Burrows sang Lord Richard Percy, and Julius Rudel conducted the London Symphony Orchestra.

Peter, Muffy and I spent a lot of our summers traveling, and one of my favorite cities to visit—and sing in—was Buenos Aires. Except for its frequent military coups—the country's dictators seemed to have a shorter shelf life than a pound of butter—I love almost everything about Argentina: its people, its culture, its artists, its shops, its restaurants, and above all, its nonstop sense of gaiety. Buenos Aires' air is barely fit to breathe, but the city's veil of smog can't diminish its beauty. It is also one of the world's safest cities. You can walk anywhere at night and never have to worry about being mugged.

In 1968, the first time Peter, Muffy, and I went down there, Tito and Gigi Capobianco, who are native Argentinians, came with us. I knew about five words of Spanish. Tito said he would "help" me with the language. For instance, he taught me that when I wanted to compliment an artist, I should say "Never in my *puta* life have I seen such a lovely painting." After getting a couple of very strange looks, I realized Tito was teaching me every dirty word in the Spanish language.

The Teatro Colón in Buenos Aires is bigger than the Met. Glitzy, it's not. The Teatro Colón is a little worn at the edges, but it's as comfortable as your favorite old easy chair. Every claim the management made about the theater's acoustics turned out to be true. Compared to most of the world's famous opera houses, the Teatro Colón's acoustics are *fabulous*.

I'd usually do six or seven performances over a three-week period—after two weeks of rehearsals—and I was paid a fortune. Argentine audiences are unique in their behavior. If they like something, they scream like crazy. If they don't, they remain almost eerily quiet. When Norman Treigle and I did that horrible five-hour *Julius Caesar* with Karl Richter, the audience didn't care for Treigle's performance. Norman was totally unnerved when his arias were greeted with dead silence.

Argentinians are opera nuts. Scores of people would follow Peter and me down the street in Buenos Aires, laughing and talking to us, and every once in a while ducking into a store to bring us something to eat. Whenever I was there, the city's record shops silk-screened my photo on banners and hung them across the streets.

During the summer of 1972, Alfredo Kraus and I sang *Lucia* at the Teatro Colón. It was the Capobiancos' production, and I squeezed in my performances between shopping trips with Gigi—first things first. We all had a terrific time until a couple of nights before our closing performance, when a new military junta overthrew the old military junta that had been in power for about six months. The next morning, the city's main streets were lined with armed soldiers and guard dogs. Muffy, who wasn't quite thirteen, was very frightened and started crying when all these guard dogs began barking and trying to lunge at us. We took the world's shortest walk that morning. I had no idea who was for or against what, or who was in or out of power—we were totally in the dark. All I knew was that Buenos Aires was filled with teenaged soldiers running around with rifles or huddled around machine guns. What was to prevent any of those kids from getting trigger-happy? I wanted out.

The new government sent along word that we'd all signed contracts to perform, and therefore we *would* perform. They ordered us to go ahead with our performance because they wanted it broadcast on radio, as before. The new government was determined to show all of Argentina that it had nothing to worry about. Turn on your radio and you still get the opera.

The American Embassy very thoughtfully sent cars to take us to and from the opera house. The Teatro Colón seats almost 4,000 people; when I walked out onstage that night, there were no more than 350 people in the audience. Most of the musicians were either late or absent, but the entire cast and chorus were on time. And scared out of our minds.

Argentina's new rulers told everyone that life would go on as usual, but to use a word Tito taught me, that was a load of *mierda*. When we went to pick up our pay, we discovered that the rules had been changed on us. I'd always been paid in dollars that were deposited in Buenos Aires' Banco de Boston and then transferred at the end of the engagement to the New England Merchants National Bank in Boston, which is where I banked. It was a simple transaction, and perfectly legal and acceptable.

Suddenly, it wasn't so acceptable. The coup occurred on a Thursday night; on Friday morning the banks were open for business; Argentinians really *are* accustomed to military coups. When Peter and I went to the bank to transfer my performance fees to the New England Merchants National Bank—we planned to leave Buenos Aires on Monday morning—our man at the Banco de Boston told us: "The government says you can take two thousand dollars out of the country, but the rest has to be left in the bank. The government would prefer that you invest it in Fiat of South America."

I was then probably the highest-paid opera singer in the world, and a lot of money was at stake. I said, "I don't want to invest in Fiat."

Peter said, "Beverly's *not* going to invest in Fiat. We're going to get that money out of here. That's all there is to it."

"But they'll confiscate your money at the airport," the banker said. "They probably won't do a body search, but they'll be looking for that money. It would be a great mistake to lie to them."

"What do you suggest I do?" I asked.

He had given the matter some thought. "I suggest you go to Ricciardi and buy the biggest diamond ring you can find, one that costs as much as the Teatro Colón owes you. And don't pay for it in dollars. When you find out how much it costs, I'll covert your money so you can pay for it in pesos."

Ricciardi is the Tiffany's of South America. I knew that Birgit Nilsson almost never took money out of Argentina—she bought all her jewelry at Ricciardi. The quality of its gems was unquestioned, and its prices were competitive with those of the rest of the world's finest jewelers.

We did what our banker advised. We went to Ricciardi, and I fell in love with a gorgeous ten-carat diamond ring. We got an excellent price on it, too, because the conversion rate from dollars to pesos was extremely favorable—coups have a way of driving up the exchange rate. I was happy and the new government was happy: I had spent my earnings in Argentina. A couple of my friends invested in Fiat of South America. They later regretted it.

After we left, the Teatro Colón became a national opera house—only Argentinians were allowed to sing there. Even though the government has changed hands many times since then, when I left Buenos Aires in 1972, I knew I'd never return. That was the first time I'd ever felt frightened and unprotected overseas. Up until then, an American passport had always seemed to guarantee that you'd be treated with courtesy and respect. Since then, there's been a continuous decline in the power and prestige of an American passport. In fact, when Americans travel overseas nowadays, there are so many mad dogs on the loose that you almost have to *hide* your passport.

We had no problems buying that gigantic rock, which I planned to sell—and convert into dollars—as soon as I came home. Three minutes after I had that ring on my finger, however, I was completely attached to it. When we returned to New York, Peter saw how I felt about the diamond, and never raised the question of selling it. My mother, however, had a very interesting reaction to the whole episode.

"You can't go out and buy yourself diamond rings—I've never heard of anything so dumb," she told me. "Your husband has to buy you your jewelry. Women do not buy their own jewelry."

My mother is *so* wise.

I didn't tell my husband about that conversation. Peter and I used to see his Boston tax lawyers twice a year. When next we visited the law firm of Goodwin, Procter and Hoar, I told our attorney that we had to discuss the diamond ring I was wearing.

"What about it?" he asked.

"Well, I've decided to keep it," I said. "But in my family, women don't buy their own jewelry."

"What kind of family do you have?" he said.

"A Jewish family, where men buy the jewelry," I said. "I think my husband should pay for this ring."

Peter started laughing, and the lawyer thought I was joking. I wasn't. When I told the lawyer how much the ring cost, he said, "That would seriously upset Peter's cash flow."

"Well, he can pay for it on a time basis," I said. "But at some point, I want to be able to say my husband bought me this ring."

"Beverly, what difference does it really make? That's like robbing Peter to pay Peter."

I didn't laugh. My husband did. The more Peter laughed, the more we both confounded this conservative Boston attorney.

I still have that ten-carat diamond ring. As I said before, I've always held on to every piece of jewelry my husband bought me.

In the fall, Norman Treigle and I worked hard preparing the City Opera's new *Tales of Hoffmann.* Norman's depression seemed to disappear, which made the rest of us very happy for him. Tito and Gigi did the staging, Julius was our conductor, Ming Cho Lee did the sets, and José Varona designed the costumes—it was like a big family reunion.

On opening night, to the detriment of everyone else in the cast, Norman turned in the most extraordinary, egotistical, self-serving performance I've ever seen on an opera stage. He wasn't merely being a ham and upstaging everybody by doing cheap schlocky stuff. Norman was doing all kinds of inventive balletic movements and was never where he was supposed to be. Treigle was lean as a noodle and a great dancer, and in the first act he did things to me onstage the likes of which I'd never run up against. There's a big sextet in the Venice scene in *Hoffmann,* and we were supposed to end it standing tush-to-tush; instead, Norman wrapped his arm around me in a grandly dominating fashion.

When I came offstage at the end of the first act, Tito rushed up and said, "Fight back! Don't let him get away with this!"

During intermission I sat in my dressing room feeling total distress. For Norman. I thought to myself: *If he wants this so badly, I'm going to give it to him.*

I didn't fight him, and Norman continued his wild *tour de force.* During the second intermission Gigi Capobianco came into my dressing room and said, "I'm counting on you to do something to make him stop."

I told her no, I wasn't going to do battle with Norman. He wanted the night, and I was giving it to him.

Treigle carried this strangest of performances to his final moment onstage. As the evil Dr. Miracle, he had to play a violin and coerce Antonia, the deathly ill daughter of a dead opera star, to sing until she, too, was dead. When I keeled over, Norman crashed the violin and threw it on my body, and all I can tell you is that when the curtain came down, I knew I'd seen an astonishing performance. Crazy, yes, but definitely astonishing. Even though I was onstage with him, I felt less like a performer than someone who had the best seat in the house. I was absolutely fascinated.

We all got lovely reviews, and Norman got the lion's share of compliments—it was his night, no question about it. Basses don't have too many of those. There are maybe six operas that showcase a bass, and *The Tales of Hoffmann* is one of them. Norman had his moment of glory, and I was happy for him.

Our next performance of *Hoffmann,* a matinee, took place three days later. Just before the opera started, I walked into Treigle's dressing room and said, "Norman, I'm very happy you had your triumph the other night. I'm going to show you that it was a present from your old friend Beverly, because today, I'm gonna eat you up alive."

I couldn't do anything to him in the first act, when I play a wind-up doll and sing an aria. But after that, Norman never knew where I was onstage. I improvised all my movements so that every time he turned to me, I was someplace else. Since *Hoffmann* is a weird opera, anyway—most of the characters aren't human—you can get away with a lot of eccentric behavior. I did to Norman what he had done to me, and he was totally befuddled. The sextet that was supposed to end with us standing backside-to-backside? We sang that on a platform, and at the end of it I walked off the platform, and because of the way I positioned myself, Norman was forced to sing the end of the song with his back to the audience. I nailed him all night long, and he *loved* it! Norman recognized what I was doing, and he was almost as fascinated by my performance as I'd been by his. By the end of the Venice sextet, Norman was staring at me as if he were seeing a marvel. He was totally helpless—as helpless as I'd been a few days earlier.

That night, after the performance, Peter and I had everybody over to our place. At one point during the evening, Norman took me aside and said, "Thanks for the other night."

"Don't mention it," I replied. "And don't try it again, either."

Noman laughed and said, "I won't. It takes too much out of me."

The Tales of Hoffmann was the last opera Treigle sang with the company at Lincoln Center. When the season was over, Norman dropped out of the New York City Opera. The following spring, he appeared in a City Opera production of *Mefistofele* in Washington, D.C. In February 1975, at the age of forty-seven, this brilliantly talented, tortured man died alone in his New Orleans apartment.

Norman Treigle was a great artist who went unrecognized, and I am still haunted and mystified as to why he never got the acclaim he deserved. Audiences went wild over his *Mefistofele*. His devil in *Faust* was definitive. His four villains in *Hoffmann* will never be equaled. Unlike Norman's critics—and he had damned few of those—I'm not making any statements I can't back up. I was *there*. I *witnessed* his brilliance. I still believe that a superstar is anyone who can do one thing better than everyone else in the world. In the case of my own career, one role—Cleopatra in *Julius Caesar*—raised me from obscurity to stardom. Norman, however, probably sang a half-dozen roles that no other bass in the world came close to equaling. So maybe my definition of superstardom is wrong. Maybe one has to be in the right role in the right place at the right time. Maybe Norman's timing was off, somehow. Or maybe he just had bad luck—or no luck at all.

The other side of the coin—instant superstardom—can also shake a singer down to his roots. In January 1972, I sang my first *I Puritani* opposite Luciano Pavarotti in Philadelphia. Luciano's career was then just beginning to take off. The first time I stood on stage with him and heard him sing, I thought: *My God, this man sings so beautifully*. I never heard Caruso live, of course, but I can't imagine

My swan song at the New York State Theater—balloons, confetti, and a million dollars raised for the New York City Opera.   © BETH BERGMAN 1987

On opening night of *Julius Caesar* (opposite), the second-act curtain was coming down, the audience was going bonkers—and the next morning I was a star. I still get goose bumps thinking about that moment. © BETH BERGMAN 1987

Walter Cassel and I in *The Ballad of Baby Doe,* my first major breakthrough. I found it hard to say good-bye to Baby after each performance. © BETH BERGMAN 1976

Norman Treigle and I doing our very special loony tunes in *The Tales of Hoffmann.* © BETH BERGMAN 1972

Julius Rudel and I look so calm here. The camera lies. From the moment of that final curtain call of *Julius Caesar*, things were never calm. © BETH BERGMAN 1984

Marilyn Horne and I in *The Siege of Corinth*, otherwise known as The Bobbsey Twins Meet La Scala. Our Milanese designer was very big on feathered hats.

Lucia's mad scene (opposite) in performance at the New York City Opera. I really miss her.

© BETH BERGMAN 1976

Pavarotti and I singing *Lucia*. Luciano is a sweet and adorable pal—I don't see him nearly as often as I'd like.

COURTESY SAN FRANCISCO OPERA—
PHOTO: CAROLYN MASON JONES

When I sang *La Traviata* at Naples' Teatro San Carlo, the gown I wore as Violetta made me look like a large Victorian lampshade.

In the Met's 1978 production of *Don Pasquale*, my Norina was a coloratura cut-up reminiscent of Lucille Ball.
J. HEFFERNAN

When Tito and Gigi Capobianco told me how to play the Queen of Shemakha in *Coq d'Or,* they said, "Think Mae West." © BETH BERGMAN 1987

It was one of my dreams to portray all three of Donizetti's queens: Anne Boleyn (left), Queen Elizabeth (middle), and Mary Stuart. PHOTO BY JACK MITCHELL

I still regard my Queen Elizabeth in *Roberto Devereux* as the crowning artistic achievement of my career.
© BETH BERGMAN 1973

Placido Domingo and I played our characters much the same way Bette Davis and Errol Flynn portrayed them in *Elizabeth and Essex*.
© BETH BERGMAN 1976

No, this is not Miss Sacher Torte of 1977. Try *The Merry Widow,* a.k.a. Sonia, Zenia, or Anna.   PHOTO BY JACK MITCHELL

Elvira, the heroine of *I Puritani* (opposite), was traditionally depicted as a silly adolescent, but I played her as tragic and made it stick.   © BETH BERGMAN 1987

I sang Massenet's *Manon* in almost every major opera house in the world.
© BETH BERGMAN 1987

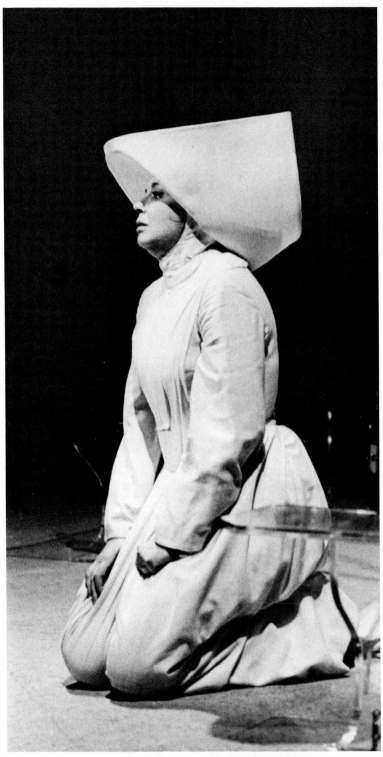

Suor Angelica was one of three one-act operas in Puccini's *Il Trittico*. Angelica broke my heart, and after a single performance, I never sang her again.
© BETH BERGMAN 1987

Hairstyle courtesy of egg-beater, I sang the role of Juana, the mad queen of Spain, opposite John Bröcheler in *La Loca,* an opera that was not the happiest of experiences.
PHOTO BY ROBERT CAHEN

Joan Sutherland, director Tito Capobianco, and I during rehearsals for his 1980 San Diego Opera production of *Die Fledermaus.* Tito said, "We'll make history with this production," and we did.
PHOTO BY ROBERT CAHEN

At home in Manhattan, and on the phone as usual—probably to a prospective donor for the New York City Opera.   © HANS NAMUTH 1987

The powers that be at Lincoln Center. From left to right, my male harem consists of Jerome Robbins, Zubin Mehta, James Levine, Nat Leventhal, and Peter Martins.

being more touched by a voice than I was when Luciano sang Arturo to my Elvira.

Before the end of 1972, Luciano and I sang *Lucia* in San Francisco. I'm not exaggerating when I tell you that our engagement out there created civic pandemonium. Luciano had become a superstar in the blink of an eye, I was at the top of *my* game, and together we knocked San Francisco for a loop. Every night we sang, the opera company had to turn thousands of people away. The crowds outside the opera house were almost as big as those inside.

Since the opera house could accommodate only a fraction of the people who wanted to see us, Luciano and I gave free concerts in Golden Gate Park, and at least 30,000 people showed up for each of them. Meanwhile, back at the San Francisco Opera House, audiences were going absolutely bonkers every night. Excitement and ovations like you can't believe.

Cyril Magnin, my San Francisco father figure, gave me his car and driver for my six-week stay, and sometimes after a performance, Luciano and I would be driven back to his hotel, where we'd eat supper. Luciano stayed at the Huntington because his room had a kitchen, and I stayed at the Mark Hopkins because my room *didn't* have a kitchen. I never could eat past three o'clock on the day of a performance, so by midnight, if you accidentally held up a hand in front of me, you might lose it.

Luciano would prepare a late supper for us, usually a salad and pasta. True story: Luciano tested the pasta for doneness by ladling out a handful and then throwing it against the ceiling. If it stuck, it was ready; if not, he let the pasta cook a little more.

It always took a while for us to wind down. We were definitely not going out to glamorous parties or even unglamorous parties. San Francisco is damp at night, and Luciano would keep a scarf wrapped twice around his head. I'd usually wear a mink cape with a great big hood on it. We'd sit there in his hotel room, waiting for the adrenaline to work its way out of our systems. We'd talk about our families, our dreams, about money, about his European background—it was all very relaxed and pleasant. When we finally felt like normal human beings again, I'd walk a half block over to the Mark and go to sleep.

If it sounds lonely, it was. Even though artists can be eaten alive by acclaim, the perks that go along with being a great star are often overrated. True, when you reach a certain level you can have the

limousines, the four-room hotel suites, the great food, the champagne—
but none of that finally costs a thing, because it's all a tax write-off.
You can have all that. And almost as soon as you get it, you stop
thinking about it. The human soul is so resilient. In 1953, when I
first came to San Francisco, I took a trolley to the opera house, lived
in a flophouse, cooked in my hotel room, did my own hair, and used
lipsticks down to the very last bit. All I dreamed of was becoming an
opera star.

Back then I didn't realize that the trappings of stardom would
include chauffeurs and jewels and furs and maids. When all that
came, I was working so hard that those things became necessities, not
amenities. In order to look the way people expected me to, I needed
hairdressers and manicurists to come to my house or my hotel room
when I was on the road. I had to dress theatrically, and shopping was
a problem. When I'd walk into a department store I'd be recognized,
and I'd spend more time signing autographs than buying clothes.
Time was the one luxury that was always in short supply. And so
people at stores like Saks Fifth Avenue and Bergdorf-Goodman would
select five or six gowns for me and send them over to our apartment,
and I'd pick and choose what I needed. In retrospect, yes, that kind
of service is something special. At the time, however, I didn't feel I
was being pampered. I felt only that I was attending to one part of
my job as efficiently and as quickly as possible.

After a while, you don't notice the expensive amenities. They're
there. Sometimes you don't even want them: When Peter didn't come
with me on a trip I always stayed in small hotel rooms where I could
see all four walls. The thought of staying in a suite by myself
frightened me.

The psychological side of stardom is incredibly difficult to deal
with if you don't have a stabilizing force in your life. My family
always brought me down to earth. I had three stepchildren and two
children of my own, and they all had problems I had to help solve. I
had a husband who put up with my career, but wasn't wild about
how much time it kept us apart. I had a mother who wouldn't permit
me to become a legend in my own mind, and thank God for that. I
am my mother's daughter, and to this day she demands, in a very
dignified and positive way, a certain mode of behavior and respect
from me. If I tried to alter my relationship with Mama to accommodate my outside life, well, that was simply unacceptable.

My "circus" was different from Luciano's. I often felt like Olive Oyl with one arm being pulled by Popeye—my family—and the other by Bluto—my career. Luciano's circus was less complicated but far lonelier. His wife traveled with him in the beginning, but when their children were old enough to go to school, she stayed home to raise them. You get very lonely without your family around. You crave attention and company, and pretty soon the need for company gets bigger and bigger, and that's why a lot of superstars travel with an entourage. They're frightened to be left alone.

I don't know if Pavarotti travels with a large entourage. I do know he's reached a plateau that's so lonely and rarefied that it may be putting him through hell. The truth of the matter is that the press now devotes more space to photographs of Luciano and his handkerchief than to writing about his voice and his performances. The press frequently sneers at the hype devoted to a superstar, but the press itself is responsible for all the hype. Pavarotti, meanwhile, still possesses one of the great voices of our time.

There's something terribly poignant about Pavarotti. Luciano and I recently had dinner together after a *Tosca* he sang at the Met. We held hands and I reminded him of a night in San Francisco during our *Lucia* run when we performed together at the Fol de Rol, an annual ball at which artists entertain to raise money for the San Francisco Opera. Luciano and I sang the *"Libiamo"* from *La Traviata*. The audience gave us a great ovation and wanted us to repeat it, so we did. When they wanted us to sing it a third time, we waltzed to the *"Libiamo."* When they *still* didn't stop applauding, I told Luciano: "I think they want to see blood from our throats."

"No," he said. "There is nothing left for us to do except to be clowns."

Opera is an extremely disciplined art form, and every excess a singer indulges in has a direct effect on the voice. The Pavarotti that people talk about now is such a contrast to that chubby, funny guy who used to take walks with me in San Francisco, who'd sit in my dressing room and tell jokes during performances, and who'd cook us spaghetti afterward. In the early days, when Luciano got fat, I think he was tortured by all the jokes made about his appearance. On the surface, he's now adopted a very cheerful attitude about his weight, but it's probably a source of great sadness to Luciano that he can't control his appetite.

I suspect it's sadness that makes him overeat in the first place. Any excess in life is a substitute for something that's missing. The number of opera singers who are womanizers, boozers, nymphos; the singers who consistently cancel; the singers whose suicide attempts— successful or unsuccessful—are hushed up; all bear witness to the incredible strain of performing the art of opera. Even Joan Sutherland, that lovely lady with the voice of the century and the most serene of performers, is not immune to the strain. At a 1986 concert at Avery Fisher Hall, I noticed Joan nervously and constantly kneading the side of her green chiffon dress. I'd never seen her do anything like that before. Once you reach a certain plane, there is no avoiding the pressure. I may have handled it with humor, but that doesn't mean I didn't feel the pressure. Believe me, I did.

EIGHTEEN

In the fall of 1973, I finally completed my quest of Donizetti's three queens by singing *Anna Bolena* at the City Opera. From start to finish, Anna Bolena is a marvelous character to play. As was true of Queen Elizabeth in *Roberto Devereux,* Donizetti gave Anne Boleyn great lines and great vocal flourishes, especially toward the end. Tito Capobianco was his usual innovative self. At one point, a child dressed as the eight-year-old Elizabeth was brought onstage to remind audiences that Queen Elizabeth was the daughter of Anne Boleyn and Henry VIII. Julius particularly admired Tito's ability to integrate the sets from all three Donizetti queens, thereby cutting way down on production costs.

Anna Bolena was a challenge on the order of *Roberto Devereux.* I presume Callas was drawn to the opera for its dramatic content. *Anna Bolena* appealed to me for the same reason, but I also felt the opera was an almost daunting test of vocal virtuosity and stamina. Anna's mad scene takes up the last twenty-five minutes of the opera, and unless you really pace yourself all night, you just can't perform it properly. A sympathetic conductor, such as Julius Rudel, would bring me along slowly so that I'd have plenty of steam left for those last twenty-five minutes. It's a very dramatic scene. Anna hears people in the streets rejoicing over the marriage of Henry VIII to Giovanna (Jane Seymour) and denounces them as an evil couple. She sings that the only thing missing from their festive day is her own blood, which will be spilled soon enough. Her mind gone, Anna finishes her aria just before being led to the chopping block. If the real Anna had had to sing that mad scene, she probably would have died of exhaustion.

I liked Anna a lot. Her costumes were very beautiful and didn't weigh fifty-five pounds each. And because Anna was a young woman, I didn't have to spend two hours putting on makeup, nor did I have to walk like an old lady and wear a great heavy crown with wigs attached to it. The singing was as demanding as Queen Elizabeth's, but less abusive of the voice. No matter how angry Anna got, it was a young woman's anger, so her singing was more florid than Queen Elizabeth's. Her two final arias—one sounds like "Home, Sweet Home" —feature a lot of pianissimo singing, which was my forte. Anna leans back on a staircase and dreams of the happy moments of her youth, and it's a kind of musing that spins out slowly; you can take your time. When she begins contemplating reality, Anna collapses and weeps; she's horribly frightened of being executed. She's a heart-breaking character and, in her own way, very easy to play. Her final rage is the rage of a powerless young woman who knows she's doomed. At the end of *Roberto Devereux,* Elizabeth was similarly irate, but her final aria was much tougher to sing, because her voice was that of a furious, heartbroken old lady who was still the most powerful woman in the world.

By then, I'd made a somewhat radical departure from operatic tradition: I never warmed up before a performance. Because of the constant demands made on my voice, I wanted to preserve it as much as I could. Technically speaking, that was heresy. I remember some colleagues, among them Richard Tucker, singing for two and a half hours straight before a performance. Most singers have their own peculiar little exercises. Some men practice primal screaming. Norman Treigle used to walk around backstage singing "Money, money, money." Tenor Jon Crain would sing "Gina Lollobrigida"—he claimed the thought of her warmed up his voice and everything else. A few of the men always have fun singing "Forn-i-ca-tion."

I think some of the men—especially the tenors—sang about fornication more often than they performed it. A number of tenors, like prizefighters, abstain from sex the night before a performance, and sometimes longer than that. This might be an apocryphal story, but it certainly ran rampant throughout the opera world during the 1960s. Franco Corelli, a tenor, was then so popular he was singing just about every fourth night at the Met. Supposedly, a very distraught Mrs. Corelli one day confronted Rudolf Bing and told him: "My husband won't have sex with me for three nights before he sings and is too tired to have it for three nights afterward. Since he's singing every fourth night, I want you to know that you have ruined our sex life."

On the other hand, opera certainly has its share of studs, and they don't seem hampered by a lack of energy. I've heard plenty of tales about intermission quickies, but frankly, I doubt them. Knowing how exhausting the art form is, I cannot believe that any male star I sang with was lunatic enough to lock his dressing room door and play around during a performance.

When it came to warming up, the women I knew were a lot more conventional than the men. Nilsson would begin singing scales a good hour before curtain time, and strange noises could be heard through the door of her dressing room. She squeaked through her nose, possibly to push her voice into resonance. I don't exactly recall Eileen Farrell's routine but I do know that, before performances, she'd start giving out with belches that sounded like rolling thunder. Like Eileen, most singers get very nervous just prior to a performance. I was a little odd in that respect. I couldn't *wait* to get out there, and the waiting never shook me up. I always had lots of people in my dressing room until about five minutes before I went onstage, and some of them even smoked a lot.

In my early days of studying with Miss Liebling, I'd do about thirty minutes of vocalizing before each performance. She gave me progressions of trills and arpeggios that warmed up my voice evenly. When I first started my career, I heard sopranos whose roles contained a lot of high C's pounding out high C's while warming up; they'd sometimes leave half the performance in the dressing room. Miss Liebling's approach was much sounder. We had terrible battles when I later stopped doing vocal exercises before performing, and sometimes I saw the wisdom of Miss Liebling's method. *Traviata*, for example, stays in the middle register for quite a while before you get to the big aria, and then you start reaching for the high notes right away. If I didn't warm up beforehand, she felt I wouldn't have enough time to hit those notes easily. She probably was right—for *Traviata*.

I felt different about much of my *bel canto* repertoire, especially the Donizetti queens. All three share an interesting characteristic: The first arias you sing start off high, and the last arias—in *Lucia, Roberto Devereux, Maria Stuarda,* and *Anna Bolena*—are all drawn-out killers. I felt that after fifteen minutes onstage, I was just as warmed up as if I'd spent half an hour warming up in my dressing room—and I was a lot fresher. I must say that Miss Liebling's method was sensible, though, when it came to singing in a cold theater; at such times, my voice didn't acclimatize nearly as quickly as it would have if I'd warmed up. But I didn't even give in on that point. Once I set out on a path, it's very hard to pull me off it.

In the fall of 1973, I flew out to California to sing *La Traviata* in San Francisco. When Kurt Adler, the San Francisco Opera's general director, had invited me to appear as Violetta, we couldn't agree on a conductor. I finally said, "Why don't you do it yourself?"

Adler was more nervous than anyone in the cast. He did a lot of yelling, mostly at the chorus. Our rehearsals were filled with tension. The big problem was Kurt himself—he simply buried his head in the score and kept it there. He almost never looked up at the stage, and the absence of eye contact with our conductor was driving everyone nuts. During our dress rehearsal, the first act seemed more like a funeral than a party. I decided to break the tension in a way that would also break Kurt's habit of not keeping an eye on his singers.

That dress rehearsal happened to be on Halloween. At the start of the third act, I came onstage wearing one of those Groucho Marx get-ups—eyeglasses, a big plastic nose, and a moustache. The chorus and the singers already onstage broke up, but at least five minutes passed before Kurt became curious as to why everyone was laughing. When he finally looked up, he started laughing as hard as everyone else. I walked over to the edge of the orchestra pit and said, "You ought to look up here every once in a while. You're missing all the fun." After that, Kurt looked up at us a *lot,* and his nervousness about conducting again disappeared completely.

I again took part in the company's annual Fol de Rol, the benefit ball at which, the year before, Pavarotti and I had sung the drinking scene from *Traviata.* The event has a long history of attracting the opera world's biggest guns, all of whom could be counted on to try things no one expects them to do. Lily Pons once turned up in a scanty costume and sang "Diamonds Are a Girl's Best Friend." At one Fol de Rol, Placido Domingo conducted the orchestra. This time around, Joel Grey, the evening's master of ceremonies, and I sang *"La ci darem la mano,"* a famous duet from *Don Giovanni,* and then did a soft-shoe to it. Joel later sent me a picture of us tap-dancing together. He signed it "The Bantam of the Opera."

At seven A.M. on a Sunday, the day I was to perform my fifth and final performance of *Traviata* in San Francisco, I got a telephone call from my husband, who was in New York. We'd been building—and building and building—a house on Martha's Vineyard. We'd designed it together, and it was ready at last. After the matinee, I planned to take a red-eye flight to Boston. Peter would pick me up at the airport and drive us to our new house. On Monday, we'd unpack all the crates and furniture that had been stored at the Martha's Vineyard airport for almost a year, before being delivered to the house in the last few days.

Knowing I had a performance that afternoon, Peter had waited as long as he could before telephoning me. "I have terrible news for you," he said.

This is what flashed across my mind: Something has happened to our son.

"Last night our house was burned to the ground by an arsonist," Peter continued. "Nothing is left."

I wanted to laugh with relief that Bucky was unharmed, and then I almost cried in despair over our loss. We'd worked long and hard on that house. The only thing to do was to rebuild it. A couple of days later I told the contractor: "We'll just keep doing it until we get it right." We've just had our twelfth summer in that house.

The two arsonists were caught. One of them shot himself. The other is still in jail.

When I finished my appearances in San Francisco, I joined the New York City Opera in Los Angeles for performances of *Anna Bolena* and *Maria Stuarda,* plus the company's premiere of *I Puritani,* which we'd bring back to New York for the spring 1974 season.

The one time I'd sung *Puritani*—with Pavarotti in Philadelphia— had been the result of a last-minute decision to go into a makeshift production with practically no rehearsals. Instant opera. Luciano and I walked on stage together, opened our mouths, and brought down the house. But the role of Elvira hadn't interested me. Bellini wrote exquisite *bel canto* music for her, but an Italian's view of love among the Puritans just didn't turn me on.

As was so often the case, I changed my mind about the opera after Tito and Gigi Capobianco sat down and showed me how rich a character Elvira was, or could be. For most of the opera, while the Puritans and Cromwell are warring with the Cavaliers and Stuarts, Elvira is so thwarted in her love for Lord Arturo that she slips in and out of craziness. Tito and Gigi convinced me that the key to Elvira was to find a way to play her without making her look silly.

I wound up having a lot of fun with her. Every time I played Elvira, I gave her a different mental ailment. One night she'd be catatonic; another night she'd be hysterical.

We premiered *I Puritani* in Los Angeles because the production was paid for by our Southern California angels, Lloyd Rigler and the late Lawrence Deutsch. Deutsch and Rigler were the men behind Adolph's meat tenderizer, and they were extremely generous patrons of the arts. They provided us with an ample budget for our production of *I Puritani*. The sets were stunning, and as always, Tito had certain dramatic moments in mind when he conceived the production. He gave me a stunning entrance for Elvira's very famous mad scene. With an elegant painting of trees serving as a backdrop, Tito had me come onstage from the top of a tall, steep staircase. He put the rest of the stage in darkness. All the audience saw was a very slight figure approaching from a great distance, and in total madness. Elvira was in her own world.

Each of the stairs was about seven inches high. I wore ballet slippers, and Gigi taught me how to curl my toes around each step in such a way that my body didn't bounce on the way down. Have you ever seen dancers who can glide around and look as if they're on roller skates? That's what Gigi showed me how to do. The way Tito staged it, the audience saw a very hazy light on a figure off in the distance that seemed to be walking on air. The moment I finally hit the stage, I began singing a *cabaletta* in which a demented Elvira sings "Come to me, my beloved," when there's no beloved around.

After our dress rehearsal, Peter and I joined Julius Rudel and his wife, Rita, for dinner at the Scandia restaurant. During the meal,

Julius began talking to me about my future. He told me he wanted out of the administrative end of running the company. Would I be interested in taking over those duties after I retired? I told Julius I'd think about it, but in the meantime, I wasn't planning to retire for several years.

I Puritani was a major success. On opening night, when I made my entrance atop those stairs, a total hush fell over the audience. Nobody coughed. It was the kind of silence every singer dreams about.

Although I enjoyed performing operas that were becoming associated with me—I sang Traviata, Lucia, and Daughter of the Regiment dozens of times in early 1974—I continued to look for new roles to add to my repertoire. In June, Sarah Caldwell invited me to play Rosina in Rossini's The Barber of Seville. Normally, Rosina is a perky girl who belongs to what I call the bow-on-the-behind school of acting—a soubrette. I decided to make her a bit wiser than she's usually portrayed. Donald Gramm, who'd teamed up with me in Sarah's hilarious Daughter of the Regiment, played Bartolo, and once again we ran into some unexpected silliness. At one point, he and I were both up on a balcony, and I had to throw a letter down to the stage for my lover, Lindoro, to pick up.

When I released the letter, it sailed like a paper airplane. Instead of landing on the stage, it ended up in the orchestra pit. Donald and I both stared at it in shock. That letter plays a very important part in the plot. In it, Rosina tells Lindoro that she loves him and arranges a time and place to meet him. If Lindoro doesn't get that letter, he and Rosina don't get together. If he and Rosina don't get together, you might still wind up with an opera, but it won't be The Barber of Seville.

I had no idea what to do next. Luckily, Donald did. After spending a few seconds sizing up the situation, Donald pulled a Kleenex out of his pocket. Speaking very loudly, he said, "Want another letter?"

"Sure," I replied.

"Here," he said. Donald waved the tissue around for everyone to see. The audience quickly got in on the joke, and by the time I dropped the Kleenex onto the stage floor, everyone was roaring with laughter. As was true of Sarah, there was never a dull moment with Donald. Because he was sure audiences wouldn't catch on—and they never did—he loved to slip in a few puns on stage for the sheer pleasure of making me laugh. That kind of thing happens much more often than you'd suspect, and not just in foreign language operas. In *The Ballad of Baby Doe,* there's a scene in which townsmen loudly rumor that Horace Tabor has secretly bought Queen Isabella's jewels and presented them to Baby Doe. Jack Harrold was playing Chester A. Arthur to my Baby Doe. When President Arthur overhears the rumor, he's supposed to turn to me and say, in astonishment: "Queen Isabella's jewels?"

Jack's sense of humor was very much like Donald's. One night he whirled around and said, "Queen Isabella's Jewish?"

Nobody in the audience caught it.

In the fall of 1974, I performed a kind of operatic pentathlon—I sang all three Donizetti queens at the New York City Opera, plus *Lucia* and *I Puritani.* One night when I was singing *Maria Stuarda*— and while I was holding a very long, high note—I experienced the worst, most violent pain I'd ever felt. I dropped the note immediately, and the audience gasped—but not as loudly as I did—because I was famous for that high note. It was as if someone had slashed the bottom of my stomach with a sword. I sat down on a bench that was onstage, and after about fifteen seconds, the pain passed and I finished the rest of the performance without further problems.

The next morning I called my brother the doctor. Sidney suggested I see the chief of gynecology at a hospital in New York. He's a very shy man, so I'll respect the doctor's privacy. After I underwent a series of tests, he and my brother agreed I could go ahead and fulfill the rest of my singing commitments for 1974. After the City Opera's season ended, I was scheduled to sing the Capobiancos' production of Donizetti's *Lucrezia Borgia* in Dallas and *The Daughter of the Regiment* in San Francisco, and then rejoin the City Opera during its annual visit to Los Angeles in November.

I would then return to New York, and on December 1, I'd have a hysterectomy. My brother and his colleague decided it was better for me to be safe than sorry. I didn't argue with them. I was forty-five years old, and Peter and I certainly didn't plan to have any more children.

On a Friday, the day before I left for Texas, the gynecologist examined me in his office and found some polyps and removed them.

He'd let me know the biopsy results on them as soon as possible. The next morning, off I went to Dallas.

Soon after I got there I took part in a short rehearsal of *Lucrezia Borgia,* or at least I tried to. I was in terrible pain, and I began hemorrhaging. Tito sent me back to the hotel, and Gigi stayed with me.

On Monday morning I received a telephone call from my brother. Sidney said, "The tests were positive. Peter is on his way to Dallas to pick you up and bring you back to New York. We've got a few problems."

That was not a cheerful day. My mother and Sidney met us at the airport and the four of us drove directly to the hospital. I didn't ask Sidney or the other doctor too many questions. They didn't volunteer too many answers. Sidney kept saying we had to wait until they could see everything.

My operation took place on October 24, 1974. My brother assisted with the anesthesia. I was lucky. I had a tumor the size of a grapefruit, but the doctor removed it entirely. He said that "while he was in there," he had looked all around, and everything else was clean. I would not require further treatment.

Between the operation and a rather drastic loss of blood, I dropped a ton of weight quickly. My weight's always fluctuated, but until then, I had never had to worry about more than a fifteen-to twenty-pound weight gain, which I could starve off fast enough. I'm a big, tall woman, and when I trimmed down to play slim-waisted glamour pusses in operas like *Manon, Le Coq d'Or, La Traviata,* and *Anna Bolena,* my playing weight was about 155 pounds. After my operation, I probably weighed about 125 pounds. I don't think I'd weighed 125 pounds since I was four years old.

I didn't enjoy recuperating at all. My friends were obviously shocked by the way I looked. My hair was pulled back very severely, my face was drawn, I was in pain and taking painkillers—I was *sick.* People had gotten used to thinking of me as the mouth, always talking and with the TV always on, and all of a sudden every noise jarred my nerves. I'm a voracious reader; a stack of books was piled up next to me, all of them untouched. I couldn't move. I floated in and out of awareness, but I could see that I scared the hell out of my friends. They did the same to me. I remember hearing one of them in the hallway saying: "There's a very high mortality rate for ovarian cancer."

There *is* a high mortality rate for women who contract ovarian cancer, and I felt I was in grave jeopardy for the next five or six years. I'm aware of it still—you're *always* aware of it. It's something that will stay with me forever, because my father died of cancer, and around a dozen of his relatives also died that way. Since my operation, I've had three facial cancers removed, one of them a melanoma on my upper lip that left a little cave. The doctor told me: "I can fix that up if you're unhappy with it."

I told him: "No, thanks. Just leave me be."

I suppose one reason the illness came as such a total shock was because I'd always felt invincible. I guess all of us feel that way. Cancer is something your best friend has, the same way other people have retarded children.

When word got around how sick I was and how much weight I'd lost, I began thinking that the longer I waited before resuming my career, the more certain people would be that I was dying. I couldn't stop focusing on the idea that people thought I was on my deathbed. I just was not going to let that happen.

A few days after my operation, I told my doctor: "I'm going out to San Francisco to do *The Daughter of the Regiment*."

"Good for you," he said. "When is it?"

"Opening night is November twentieth." That was less than a month away.

He started laughing. "That's not even worth discussing," he said. "You're not going to be able to get out of bed until after Thanksgiving."

That's what *he* thought. I knew I was a quick "heal." When we lived in Milton, I'd had surgery for gallstones and, nine days later, had sung with the Cleveland Orchestra.

My mother had once told me that after she'd had her babies at home, she'd bought some binding tape and strapped herself up. By doing so, she'd firmed up her stomach muscles almost immediately. So I asked my mother to buy me the biggest Ace bandage she could find, and she bound me up in it. It looked as if I were wearing the world's largest diaper.

The next day, when the doctor came around to examine me, he said, "My, my, what are we playing? Medieval witch doctor? What is this?"

I told him I felt as if I had no insides left, and that I didn't want my stomach muscles to get flabby. After explaining what that Ace bandage was all about, I told him: "Sooner or later I'm going to have to sing. I was up and walking the day after I had my babies, and I just don't see that this is any more drastic."

"Well, it is," he said. "You've lost too much weight and too much blood."

"Is it too soon for me to walk up and down the corridors?"

"That you can do," he said.

Six days after my operation, I began walking, and doing breathing exercises, and humming for about two hours a day. I was out of that hospital in two weeks and did a dress rehearsal of *Daughter of the Regiment* in San Francisco on November 17. My brother said the operation had affected my brain. My doctor was furious.

Peter thought I was insane. He came with me to San Francisco because he was frantic about what I was doing. In retrospect, my going back so soon was a dumb move. On the one hand, I was afraid people would think I was going to die, but I'm afraid when I got to San Francisco, I only convinced people that I *was* dying. I went from a size sixteen dress to a size ten, and in a photograph taken of me for the 1974 San Francisco Opera Calendar, I look like a cadaver. No question about it: That is the face of a very sick woman. It's a face that frightened me. It frightened a *lot* of people. The talk of San Francisco was how weak I was and how careful I had to be backstage.

To be blunt about it, I was in agony. The opera company's dresser followed me around with a pillow, but even when I sat down, the pain was almost unbelievable. I was wrapped up like a mummy with that Ace bandage, but it didn't help much. When I stood up, let alone when I sang, the pain was close to unbearable.

As noted earlier, Marie is a very energetic young lady, so I had to cut out just about all my stage business. I had very little stamina. At least I took care of myself. I didn't go out once between performances. I stayed in bed in my room at the Mark Hopkins and had all my meals sent up to me. I went no place and saw no one except Peter. I felt weak and washed out.

For a long time afterward, I didn't understand why I had put myself through that ordeal. I *did* tell myself I had been worried people would think I was dying if I didn't immediately spring back into action. The plain truth is that if I had canceled, *I* would have worried that I was dying. Lying in that hospital bed was a constant reminder of my own mortality, and I simply wasn't prepared to deal with that. Having realized all that, I'm still glad I did what I did. I sang all my performances. I beat the pain.

After *Daughter of the Regiment* I went to Los Angeles to join the City Opera in *I Puritani*. *I Puritani* is a nice, easy, stand-up-and-sing opera. Mindful of my recent surgery, Tito had cut out a lot of my stage business, so I thought the engagement would be a snap. I had another thing coming. One night at the end of Elvira's big mad scene, I was supposed to faint dead away. Thank God one of the men in the chorus caught me before I hit the floor—though the audience never realized it, I was *not* acting.

When the City Opera finished its run in Los Angeles, Peter, Muffy, and I went down to Puerto Vallarta for a month. We were joined there by Ellen and Walter Newman, whom we refer to as our West Coast family. I've never seen Peter as warm and as unguarded as he is with Walter. Peter's got his fishing cronies on Martha's Vineyard, but with them he always seems very much in command. With Walter, there's a total sharing. We travel with the Newmans more than with any other couple. Ellen is like a sister to me, and her brothers Donald and Jerry, and her father, Cyril Magnin, have been family to us for twenty years.

We rented a beautiful house in Puerto Vallarta that had a pool and a tennis court and an awfully nice staff. The Newmans brought along their sons Bobby and John, and on New Year's Eve, which was also Bobby's twenty-first birthday, we gave a big party for about 125 people and had a hilarious time. Bobby was a wonderful boy, and he and Muffy had a very special relationship. They just took to each other and were best friends.

I recuperated very quickly, and I had a lot of energy. Fear can be a great motivator. I was extremely nervous about standing up and singing again. I'd done it in San Francisco and Los Angeles, but it had been painful. I wanted things to get back to normal as quickly as possible.

A few months after we got back from Puerto Vallarta, I was walking along Fifth Avenue when I saw my gynecologist coming out of Tiffany's. I went up and hugged him, and we talked for a bit. He had recently remarried and had just bought his wife a present. In the most pleasant way possible, he said, "You have an appointment with me next week. Don't cancel it—I know you."

I told him I'd be there and asked how things were going for him.

"Fine," he said. "You know, Beverly, I think about you a lot."

"I think about *you* a lot too," I said. "Every twelve minutes, in fact, I think about you."

"Why every twelve minutes?"

"Because every twelve minutes I have a hot flash," I told him.

At that point, I *did* have hot flashes every twelve minutes. Peter said that every time I had one, he could feel it across the room. I cannot tell you how many times I'd get all dressed up and be on my way out the door to dinner when I'd have a hot flash and suddenly I'd be bathed in sweat; my hair and gown would look as if I'd come in out of the rain. Those hot flashes would last a couple of minutes— just long enough to ruin how I looked and felt. I'd have to walk back to the bedroom, take off all my clothes, jump into the shower and start all over again. That condition only persisted for a couple of years. Given the alternative, it was a cheap enough price to pay.

NINETEEN

In 1972, just after Sir Rudolf Bing retired as general director of the Metropolitan Opera, his successor, Goeran Gentele, asked me to lunch for the purpose of inviting me to finally make my debut at the Met. I was then still involved in singing Donizetti's three queens, so Mr. Gentele and I agreed to put off my Met debut until the spring of 1975.

I didn't want to duplicate any of the roles I'd sung at the New York City Opera, and I was a little at a loss for the proper vehicle for my Met debut when Edgar Vincent came up with an intriguing idea. Since my role as Pamira in La Scala's 1969 production of *The Siege of Corinth* had brought me international acclaim, why not give New Yorkers a chance to see what Milanese opera fans had liked so much? To make the event even more novel, we decided to go with the same production, the same cast, the same conductor, the same director, and the same set designer. All was joyful when Tommy Schippers and I began discussing the project in 1972, but later that year, his wife, Nonie, was diagnosed as having stomach cancer. She died the following year. Such beautiful people, and such horrible luck. Tommy also died of cancer, in December 1977.

Tommy was happy about conducting *The Siege of Corinth,* and from our La Scala cast, Justino Diaz wanted in. Marilyn Horne wanted out, and Shirley Verrett replaced her.

Gentele liked Edgar's idea. In 1972, Gentele died in an automobile accident. Schuyler Chapin, his successor, enthusiastically endorsed our agreement.

Edgar and I had a long talk about how we should treat my debut at the Met. I wanted it made clear that I was not *defecting*. I didn't want anyone thinking my appearance at the Met meant that I was saying goodbye to the New York City Opera. The way I accomplished that— and Edgar wasn't too thrilled about it—was to say that I was going to be a guest singer at the Metropolitan Opera, just as I'd been a guest singer at every other great opera house in the world. I also said the New York City Opera would continue to be my home, and that my Met schedule would be made to accommodate my City Opera schedule, not vice versa. Therefore, I would finish my seasons at the City Opera, and sing at the Met only when it didn't interfere with what I was doing across the plaza.

We scheduled my Met debut for Monday, April 7, 1975. Our rehearsal period couldn't have proceeded more smoothly, and there was a good reason for that: Shirley Verrett, Justino Diaz, Harry Theyard, who'd replaced La Scala's Italian tenor, and Tommy Schippers were all my friends. We ate together, we joked together, we laughed—we were colleagues.

Every aspect of that production was handled beautifully. The set was lovely, my costume was made just the way I wanted it—I didn't have a single unpleasant moment. The people who ran the Metropolitan Opera were very good to me, and I was very good to them. My opening night performance was a benefit for the Met. Orchestra tickets cost $60, and parterre boxes went for $500, the highest prices in Met history up to that point. My debut became an Event. All five performances of the *Siege* sold out well in advance. The Metropolitan Opera had to turn down seven thousand ticket requests.

The irony is that my friends were far more excited about my Met debut than I was. One day during rehearsals we all went down to the Met's lobby to pose for the cover of *Opera News*. Tommy Schippers came over to me and said, "You really should have this cover to yourself. This is going to be an historic event."

I said, "Oh, come off it, Tommy. I'm just going to sing and have some fun."

Nobody believes me when I say this, but my debut at the Met was not an extraordinary event in my life. Too many years had gone by. I was forty-six. Singing next door was no longer on the checklist of things I *had* to do. I didn't think I'd get a special kick out of singing at the Met, and I didn't. It was just too late for that to happen.

On opening night, people sent me so many flowers that the Met's backstage looked like a funeral parlor. I kept up my usual routine. My dressing room was full of friends until just a few minutes before I went onstage.

The one extraordinary memory I have of that evening was the moment when my foot hit the stage. When I made my entrance, the crowd greeted me with one of the greatest roars I've ever heard. My claque was out in full force: my mother, Peter, Muffy, my brothers, my sisters-in-law, and a number of my friends, including Maria Jeritza, Robert Merrill, Risë Stevens, Annie and Kirk Douglas, and Sylvia and Danny Kaye. Danny acted like a cheerleader the whole night—he has a great whistle. I think the audience and I felt that a longstanding wrong had been righted. When the final curtain came down, the audience gave me an eighteen-minute solo ovation. It was as if they and I had both showed the Met something.

Mine may have been the only dry eyes in the place that night.

Don't take that to mean that I'm hard-hearted. I'm not, and I can prove it. I belong to an exclusive club in New York City, and if polled, 100 percent of the members would tell you that I'm a softie. I suppose I *should* point out that the club consists of only two members—me and Arlene Francis.

Arlene and I met fifteen years ago and quickly recognized that we shared the same terrible personality trait: Neither of us could stand it if everybody didn't love us. No matter how venomous a critic or colleague might be, we'd only say nice things, *sweet* things by way of reply. We didn't want to offend *anyone*. Butter wouldn't melt in our mouths. We felt like the biggest *nebbishes* in the world.

We founded our club to remedy that situation. We meet two or three times a year for lunch at one of the best restaurants in New York, usually Le Cirque or La Grenouille. At one club meeting, I'm the chairman and she's the president. If I pay the check, she gets to be chairman of the next meeting. Arlene and I once shared a secretary, Carol Butz. Carol comes along as recording secretary, but never gets around to taking notes.

When we sit down to lunch, we start off by ordering the most expensive bottle of red wine in the house. Since Arlene, Carol, and I don't drink hard liquor, and since red wine loosens the tongue more than white, in no time at all we become *very* talkative. We finish the wine with the breadsticks, and by the time our nonfattening lunches arrive, we're happily lambasting the people who've abused us since our last meeting. Lunch lasts exactly two hours. At the end of it the three of us kiss each other goodbye. We walk out feeling immensely better, and can't wait for the next club meeting.

Some critics don't fare too well at our meetings. I know it's not considered wise or good form to denigrate critics, but I think I can count on one hand the number of critics actually qualified to judge an operatic performance. Music critics really *do* need some formal education. Yet newspaper editors exercise very little care when hiring music critics, possibly because it's an unrealistic position. To do right by the job, a music critic needs expertise in conducting and singing, needs to know how to play at least a few instruments, and should have the command of a couple of languages besides English. Much less time is spent reviewing the qualifications of music critics than of sportswriters, and that's understandable, but only up to a certain point. In the last two years, more people have attended performances at Lincoln Center than events at all the neighboring athletic stadiums combined. We're not talking about a moribund art form here.

I *do* believe criticism is necessary, but criticism is not a defined art form. It's just one person's opinion. God did not put special gifts in certain eyes and ears. A critic may have read more about opera than most of the other people in an audience, but that's about it. A critic's art lies also in his or her writing ability, and there isn't even too much of that around these days. Critical writing that's boring is just as unacceptable to me as critical writing that's uninformed.

Don't get me started on critics.

After my Metropolitan Opera debut, I went on tour for the Met and performed *The Siege of Corinth* in Boston, Dallas, Detroit, Atlanta, Memphis, and Minneapolis. In the fall of 1975, I sang Marie in the City Opera's first production of *The Daughter of the Regiment,* and I also sang *I Puritani.* Now that I was working regularly for both the City Opera and the Met, I didn't seem to have a moment to myself. I no sooner finished the City Opera's fall season than I was back at the

Met for another *Siege*, after which I flew to Los Angeles for City Opera performances of *Daughter of the Regiment, Lucrezia Borgia,* and *La Traviata*. I ended 1975 in Palm Beach, singing an instant *Traviata*. The trip didn't turn out to be a waste of time, mostly because of a memorable conversation I had with Rose Kennedy.

I had first met her in Boston in 1965. Mrs. Kennedy was then heavily involved with the Mater Dei Guild for the Blind. One day she called and asked if I'd help plan and sponsor a fund-raising luncheon for the guild. She called me because I was a Greenough, and my husband's family were known to be very philanthropic. Peter's father had headed the North Bennett Street Settlement House, and Peter's mother had always been very generous to the Boston Symphony.

After Mrs. Kennedy telephoned me, we met for tea at the Chilton Club to plan the luncheon. We naturally wound up talking about our children. Mrs. Kennedy told me about Rosemary, her mentally re-tarded daughter, and I told her about Bucky, who was then four years old. Mrs. Kennedy, a very religious woman, said that God gives children with severe problems to the people He loves most. I remem-ber saying: "I wish He didn't have such a love affair with me."

After that, we saw each other at a number of charity events in Boston and Washington. In 1975, soon after my appearance in Palm Beach was announced, I received a note from Mrs. Kennedy saying that she and Mrs. Laddie Sanford, a friend, wanted to give a luncheon for me while I was performing there. We again talked about our children. Rose invited me to come to her house the next morning.

I did. It was a beautiful day, and we went for a walk along the beach. Mrs. Kennedy put on dark sunglasses and a huge straw hat to keep the sun off her face. She wore a sweater over her skirt and blouse, and had stockings on, but took her shoes off. I'd shown up in a shirtwaist dress and no hat—in those days I wasn't worried about getting wrinkles from the sun. I walked barefoot along the beach.

Since I'd first met Mrs. Kennedy, her son, Bobby, had been assassi-nated, and after that the family continued to suffer one blow after another. Some of her grandchildren have also lived or died tragically and, in their own way, quite as violently as their fathers.

Toward the end of our walk, I asked Mrs. Kennedy how she'd been able to remain so strong in the face of all the tragedies her family had endured. She talked more, then, about the belief she'd touched on before. Certain people, she said, are born with an invisible little black mark on their foreheads. These people often endure tragedy, but only because God loves them so much and because He feels they can bear much more than other people. She said such people—and she counted herself as one—are put on this earth to be constantly tested by God.

And then she lifted her right hand up toward the heavens and told God: "I will not be defeated."

I told Mrs. Kennedy I was going to steal that line from her, and she said I was free to take it. She then invited me to go to Mass with her the following morning.

I said, "Mrs. Kennedy, I don't think it would be such a good idea; it would only confuse God."

She laughed. Rose Kennedy is a splendid lady.

In January 1976, I was back at the Met. I'd agreed to sing *La Traviata* with Placido Domingo and Sherrill Milnes, and with James Levine conducting. When I showed up for rehearsals for *Siege of Corinth,* which would open the season, I learned that Milnes and Levine had become involved in the Met's new *Aida,* and Placido was nowhere in sight. Placido and Sherrill had been replaced by tenor Stuart Burrows and baritone Ingvar Wixell. They were both excellent singers, but I felt the Met had broken its word to me.

It was Prima Donna Time. I told Schuyler Chapin: "Either Sarah Caldwell conducts *Traviata* or you can look for a new Violetta."

My pique was partly calculated. I'd never worked with director John Dexter, and I had no grand illusions about his directing me from scratch. I planned to integrate parts of the *Traviata* I'd done with Sarah in Boston. And so the Great Barrier came down. Sarah Caldwell became the first woman ever to conduct an opera at the Met.

I was allowed to design my own costumes, so I liked the way I looked, but I found the production itself very hard to work with. Everything was big, big, big. You simply can't create an intimate mood when you're supposed to be in a small summer home in the country and you find yourself in a place the size of a palace. Those settings were all old stuff. When you're in a situation like that, you finally stop fighting and you just stand in the middle of the stage and sing. Which is exactly what I did.

On the whole, my experience at the Met—I sang fifty-seven performances there—was personally pleasant. The chorus, the crew, the wardrobe and wig people—Nina Lawson is a dream—were wonderfully talented and enthusiastic about their work. But now, having spent six years on the other side of the footlights, I look back and realize the Met has long been almost destructively arrogant. Sometimes, the event following a Met performance seemed more important than the opera itself. And despite what many of its benefactors thought, good opera and Met opera were not always synonymous. Good opera is the result of unceasing hard work, of always trying to become better. Smugness and complacency can only result in second-rate performances. And sometimes good manners and plain ordinary common sense were notably absent. I was invited to attend the company's one hundredth anniversary celebration, and although I was in the box with some of the other "artists in attendance," you wouldn't have known it from the program—my name was missing. Instead of apologies, chagrin, or embarrassment, I was confronted with the explanation that my name had been deliberately omitted because I had sung so few times with the Met. I wonder why Marian Anderson was included—she sang only one opera there.

During the run of *La Traviata* at the Met, I got a call out of the blue from Carol Burnett and her husband, Joe Hamilton. She said, "Bubbles?"

I said, "Yeah?"

"This is Carol Burnett."

I said, "Sure."

"This *is* Carol Burnett."

God knows what kind of practical joke I was expecting, but there's no mistaking that voice. "Hi, Carol," I said, and we started talking as if we'd known each other forever.

She said, "I want to do a television special with you at the Metropolitan Opera—you're the only one I want to do it with, and if you don't do it, I won't do the special."

I told her I had no idea what we could do together.

"What are you worried about?" she said. "I pay writers thousands of dollars to come up with ideas. What can you do besides sing?"

"What can I do besides sing? Nothing. Well, actually, I can tap-dance, but I haven't tap-danced since I was seven."

Joe broke in and said, "Wouldn't you know it? The one thing you can do, Carol can't. What else can you do?"

I couldn't think of a single thing, at least not for a television show. "Well, we've watched you on TV," Joe said, "and you seem funny."

"I can't tell jokes," I said.

"You don't have to," he answered. "I'll tell you what—Carol and I are coming into New York. Why don't we get together?"

I agreed, and then talked to Edgar Vincent about the idea. Because of Edgar's great desire to preserve my image as an opera star, he'd always been very careful of how I was presented on TV. The closest I'd ever come to doing the kind of thing Carol wanted to discuss was when Johnny Carson and I did a Jeanette MacDonald/Nelson Eddy skit on *The Tonight Show* in 1974. I wore a stunning prima donna gown, Johnny dressed up as a Canadian Mountie, and we sang a memorable, if not exactly brilliant, version of "Indian Love Call."

When we finished the song, Carson asked, "How'd I do?"

"You have a *great* voice," I told him. "Unfortunately, it's just not suitable for singing."

Johnny laughed. "Listen," he said, "on this show, *I'm* the comedian."

I had a good relationship with Carson and still do. From my earliest appearances on *The Tonight Show,* in the early seventies, Carson always encouraged me to try interesting things. For instance, he'd get a harpist for me and I'd sing something by Rachmaninoff or Rimsky-Korsakov. Or I'd do some Spanish songs with his guitarist.

Carson has a reputation for being aloof, but he used to come visit me before the show went on. He was very relaxed with me, and we became good friends. After my appearances on *The Tonight Show,* Kirk and Annie Douglas usually would put on a little supper party, and Peter and I would go to their home with Johnny and Joanna, who was then his wife.

I was one of the first opera singers Carson had on *The Tonight Show,* and I liked the fact that he was extremely protective of me. Before one broadcast, Carson went up to his friend Don Rickles and said, "Beverly's going on first, and when you come out, don't fool around with her. If you try anything funny, I'm not going to help you out."

"Don't worry," Rickles said. "My mother called me today from Miami. She read that Beverly was going to be on the show and said that if I got fresh with her, she'd fly in and beat me up."

Later on, I hosted the show a few times, which didn't faze me in the least. Carson's staff was very good about making sure I knew how long each segment would last and when to break for commercials. One night my guests were Eydie Gormé, Dinah Shore, and Carol Burnett. By then, the four of us had become one another's best friends. As it turned out, we got into a fight about who was whose *best* best friend. The argument got so crazy that at one point Eydie wasn't talking to Carol, Carol accused me of betraying her, and none of us was talking to Dinah. We called her Little Mary Sunshine because Dinah never swore, and we got in some digs at her because she was then going out with Burt Reynolds. Rather than try to stop the carrying on, I participated, and I think all of us forgot we were on television. It was a very funny evening.

I always had an easy, good time on *The Tonight Show,* especially doing the Nelson Eddy/Jeanette MacDonald spoof. I'd never tried anything like that on TV, and it couldn't have worked out better.

Which is why I was so eager to find out what Carol Burnett and Joe Hamilton were cooking up. Before the end of January they came into New York and we all sat down at a round table. The show they outlined was going to be called *Sills and Burnett at the Met.* Carol's production company would rent out the Metropolitan Opera for several days, and she, Joe, and her writers had come up with a string of comedy sketches, songs, patter, and a big, incredible tap-dancing finale that Carol and I, complete with top hats and canes, would perform with an all-male chorus line.

I told Carol: "I really *was* seven the last time I tried to tap-dance. *I* can't tap-dance."

"Don't worry about it—your feet aren't even gonna touch the ground," Carol said. "We're gonna have chorus boys from one end of the stage to the other, and they'll carry us both—that's why we're hiring thirty-two of them. Believe me, they'll make us look good."

Joe then delivered the clincher. "There's no way we're going to put you on the stage of the Metropolitan Opera and not have you sing an aria," he said. "We'll have all this comedy going, and then everything will come to a complete stop. Bob Mackie's going to make you a sensational gown, we'll have a full orchestra in the pit, and you'll come out and sing whatever aria you want. You're a great opera star, and you're going to have your Metropolitan Opera moment. You don't have anything to worry about."

I thought: *Okay, I'm protected. As long as I get a chance to sing an aria, the audience will know I'm doing the rest because I'm having a good time.*

I agreed, and we went to work. CBS would televise *Sills and Burnett at the Met* on Thanksgiving Day of 1976. We taped the show on March 8th and 9th, and the Met was packed solid on both days. God, we had fun. We opened the telecast by coming out in football jerseys, and soon afterward I changed into my gown and sang *"O luce di quest anima"* from Donizetti's *Linda di Chamounix*. In one comedy sketch, I played a dowdy Miss Bushkin vying for a role with a fancy Broadway star named Miss Friebus. In another, I sang Catherine the Great in an overdone costume that included a huge crown and an ermine-trimmed ten-foot train—Carol's character was Catherine's official train-shlepper. Every time I opened my mouth to sing, goblets, mirrors, and chandeliers shattered all over the stage.

Toward the end of the telecast, Carol was perched on a spinet and singing "Stormy Weather," when I was abruptly rolled out atop a grand piano, singing *"Un bel di."* We then did a medley of songs dedicated to the pain of unrequited passion. After that, it was time for our finale—tap-dancing, high kicks, and all those terrific chorus boys to make us look as though we knew what we were doing.

And then it was over. When Carol and I stood there on that stage, taking our bows, I realized that the show we'd just finished meant much more to me than my debut at the Metropolitan Opera. I know that might be hard to understand, but the Met debut was exciting only because the kid from Brooklyn had finally made good. Every dog has its day, and I'd had mine. By excluding me for so many years, the Met itself had robbed me of any intense feeling about appearing there. I'd done La Scala, Fenice, San Carlo—it had all happened already.

But I have to tell you that when that TV special was over, and I stood there with my arm around Carol, I thought: *I'm never going to be any happier than I am at this moment.* To me, that television special stands right next to my Queen Elizabeth in *Roberto Devereux*. The first time I sang *Devereux*, I thought to myself: *I pulled this off! I did something everyone said I wasn't going to be able to do.* I'd felt the same way about *Julius Caesar* and *Manon*—I'd made something extraordinary happen. When I finished with Carol, I thought to myself: *By God, I did it! I have just had one of the most exciting nights of my life on stage. And I love this woman Carol Burnett!*

Carol and I cried and cried when it was over. And then we went to the 21 Club for dinner and we bawled some more because we knew we'd have nobody to play with the next day. After that, we telephoned each other three times a day. We talked about doing another TV special, but I think we both were just looking for an excuse to work together again. We still talk about doing another TV show, but at the age of fifty-seven, I'm not exactly looking to make a comeback.

Carol and I have stayed very, very close. We've known each other for ten years now, and we still talk at least once a week. She's a phenomenon. The nice thing about Carol is that when you visit with her, she's never on—she doesn't do *shtik*. She's a delightful, soft-spoken woman with striking good looks. On television, this great comic actress always liked to make faces and mug a lot, so people got the idea she was kind of homely, but Carol's really beautiful. I've never known anyone who wasn't totally captivated by her.

I've been lucky to have had good friends. I met Gigi Capobianco in 1965, and she's been with me through the heights and depths of my life. This tiny, graceful former prima ballerina is still a source of artistic inspiration and giggles, a rare combination indeed. I still share my innermost thoughts and feelings with her, and if I were in trouble I would phone her first. Dinah Shore and I have been close for about fifteen years, but I don't see her or talk to her nearly as often as I'd like. Our friendship has a different rhythm: Dinah and I can pick up the telephone and simply resume our previous conversation, even if it took place four months before. There are a couple of things in our relationship that we take for granted. For instance, Dinah doesn't necessarily call me every time she comes to New York, but whenever I go to Los Angeles, it's a given that I'd better call her and that she'll cook dinner for me. While Danny Kaye is also a great cook, Sylvia Kaye is the one who keeps our friendship alive.

I suppose I have an odd assortment of close women friends. Liz Smith, a funny lady, is someone I can call up at any time and talk to about anything. Shirley Lord, *Vogue*'s beauty editor, is also like that. She's a warm, affectionate, and loyal woman.

Barbara Walters is another confidante. Like Gigi and Carol, we're contemporaries, and I admit that Barbara and I love to gossip—we tell each other everything. Barbara's a brilliant woman whose whole life has been show business. Her father was Lou Walters, who ran the Latin Quarter, and I think kids who grow up even on the periphery of show business acquire a kind of sophistication and a gift of gab that the average youngster doesn't have. Barbara had a retarded sister who died in 1985, and we both work on behalf of adult villages for retarded people.

The difference between Barbara's public image and her private reality is astounding. Barbara's a great romantic. I really believe the reason she put off getting married again for so long is that she enjoyed the chase so much. She's got a terrific sense of humor, and she's very much the good Jewish daughter: You never hear Barbara use dirty words. *Never.* Sometimes we'll meet a couple of friends for lunch, and if they start using the language a lot of so-called sophisticated New York women use, she gets terribly uncomfortable. I've seen Barbara give such warm and sincere after-dinner talks in her own home that it's hard for me to equate that woman with the tough news correspondent I see on television.

In May of 1986, when I was in San Francisco doing some fund-raising, I called Pete to tell him I was taking the red-eye flight home. "No, you're not," he said. "Barbara is marrying Merv in Los Angeles tomorrow and she wants us there. What dress do I bring out for you?" I was so pleased and happy. Merv Adelson is a handsome, soft-spoken, gentle, strong man. Just what my friend needed. Pete and I love him.

When I arrived in Los Angeles, I called Barb. She wanted me to read a poem at the wedding—Elizabeth Barrett Browning's famous sonnet "How do I love thee? Let me count the ways." I read the poem, and her daughter Jackie sang to her. Later at the dinner, Merv got up and said it was the only party they would ever attend where Jackie sang and Beverly spoke.

It was Barbara who got me my own television show, though inadvertently. Barbara interviewed me in December 1975 on *Not for Women Only*. Several months later, when she left NBC for ABC, the producers of *Not for Women Only* asked me to take over the show. I had to turn them down—my singing career was still going full-blast, so there was no way I could do five shows a week. NBC mulled that over and decided to offer me a one-hour weekly interview show. That I could do. But not immediately. The network wanted me to kick off the show in September, but agreed to wait a month because I was going to spend September in San Francisco.

In 1975, Cyril Magnin gave me a very special gift: an opera

production. I could sing whatever opera I wanted, wherever I wanted, provided it premiered in San Francisco. Cyril would pay for it.

I knew just the opera I wanted to do: *Thaïs*. Since Mary Garden had taught *Thaïs* to me when I was a teenager, I had always known it was a role I was going to play. I liked the character a lot. Thaïs is a courtesan in ancient Egypt who becomes a religious convert through the efforts of a monk named Athanael. Sherrill Milnes, the world's reigning baritone, wanted to sing Athanael. Good role: In the third act Athanael realizes he loves Thaïs, and tells her so—just as she's about to die. I love Massenet—Manon had been a wonderful role for me—and the music he wrote for *Thaïs* is quite enjoyable and not terribly demanding in a vocal sense. Tito agreed to stage *Thaïs,* and I had a very good feeling going into it.

I told Cyril: "Look, let's do it in San Francisco with the idea that if I want to take it to the Metropolitan Opera, the Met won't have to pay anything for it."

Cyril thought that was a good idea. I'm not sure Kurt Adler agreed, but Cyril was such a major supporter of the San Francisco Opera that Kurt knew he just about had to go along with it. When I phoned Anthony Bliss at the Met, I said, "I can give you a brand-new *Thaïs* with Sherrill and me. You can have the production for nothing. Interested?"

Tony was *very* interested, and scheduled *Thaïs* for the spring of 1978. We opened in San Francisco on September 10, 1976, and by the next afternoon, every performance was sold out. Tito staged the opera brilliantly, and Sherrill was marvelous. *Thaïs* was one of the best presents I've ever received.

One night during the Met's run of *Thaïs* was scary, though. Tony Bliss came to me before the performance and told me there had been a threat on my life. The kook who wrote the letter claimed I was a whore who had seduced a priest and that I was going to get it. Sure enough, when the curtain rose, I could spot the police in the house because their shields reflected the stage lights.

Nothing happened, though, until later. I left my dressing room with my friend Kitty Carlisle Hart, who was my guest that night. Just as we were about to emerge from the stage door and get into my limousine, a flushed-faced, wild-eyed character came up to me and started muttering about what a dreadful woman I was. The language he used was incredible.

Wham! A gang of policemen landed on him and dragged him off, kicking and screaming. The police pushed Kitty and me into my car and told us to get out of there. We sat back in the seat and shook for a few minutes afterward.

I returned to New York from San Francisco on October 2 and immediately started taping my TV interview show. *Lifestyles with Beverly Sills* was broadcast Sunday mornings on NBC, right before *Meet the Press.*

I think the two most memorable interviews I did were with Mikhail Baryshnikov and Yul Brynner. Baryshnikov had not yet been interviewed on American TV and agreed to come on my show only if I submitted a list of questions to him beforehand. That wasn't because he was afraid I'd ask him anything unpleasant. Misha's English was quite limited then, and he was worried that he wouldn't understand my questions. They weren't at all complicated. When I started to consider what I wanted to know about this man, I realized that we were both performers, and that we both felt enormous pressure not to make mistakes onstage. In my case, it was missed high notes; in his case, it was missed steps.

And so that's what we began talking about. I told him it's obvious to everyone when a singer misses a high note, but in ballet, a dancer would have to fall down before I knew something terrible had happened. In his funny, garbled accent, Misha said, "That may be true, but it doesn't make me feel any better." After that we moved away from our prepared questions, and Baryshnikov talked about goals that he sets for himself and how furious he gets when he's practiced a step for weeks and weeks, finally perfects it, and then goes onstage and blows it.

Before Yul Brynner came on, his people sent me a long, long list of no-no's that began with instructions not to ask him about his family and not to ask him to perform in any way, shape, or form. Fine. When Brynner sat down, he said, "You know, my sister Vera sang with you in the New York City Opera."

I knew Vera Brynner quite well, and told Brynner that she was a very charismatic singer. That loosened him up. When we talked about *The King and I,* I told Brynner I'd always felt he made such magic with that line "Is a puzzlement" that he could have done the entire sequence without music—almost as a poem. He said, "Maybe I *could* do that."

When we broke for a commercial, he startled me by asking for a stool. "Put a camera on me," he said. "I want to try 'Is a puzzlement' as a poem."

Well, we ran for a stool, and when we got back from the commercial, Brynner sat down and performed it as a poem, and he was incredibly moving. When he finished, he said, "You're right. That's a very interesting concept."

After that, I just figured, to hell with all the no-no's, and we had a terrific interview. *Lifestyles* ran for a couple of years, and since then I've been offered a lot of talk shows, but I've just been way too busy to give television another shot—until lately. In the late fall of 1985, when the City Opera's season ended, I went out to lunch with Barbara Walters and mentioned that I'd seen 105 of the company's 140 performances that year.

Barbara's mouth dropped open. "You'll go nuts if you keep that up," she said.

I explained that it was necessary for me to attend all the premieres and check out the cast changes and generally let everyone in the company know that I'm around and watching and listening. Barbara told me I had to use other parts of my brain or I really *would* go batty. She called her manager, Lee Stevens of the William Morris Agency. Next thing I knew, I was having lunch at the Four Seasons with Shad Northshield, who produces *Sunday Morning* for CBS television. In the summer of 1986, Charles Kuralt welcomed me on the show as his new cub reporter. I appear every other week or so, and I've interviewed Jimmy Breslin, John Brademas, and Franco Zeffirelli, among others. The job's been as refreshing as Barbara anticipated. Sometimes I think she knows me better than I know myself.

TWENTY

When Jimmy Carter was elected president in 1976, I sang at his inaugural party and, later on, at a White House Governor's Ball. Peter and I wound up seeing the Carters on a number of occasions and got to know them very well. I liked Carter a lot. He was a deeply religious man who became President at a time when the nation's religious and family values were changing—toppling, in fact—with nothing to replace them. Carter stayed very true to himself and his beliefs, and although his popularity waned, voters had more trouble with him than he had with them. For most of his four years in office, I think the public just couldn't seem to cope with a genuinely good man, and perhaps an incorruptible one, in the White House.

Slick, he wasn't. Carter sometimes used language almost biblically, which is why he caught flack for telling *Playboy* that he sometimes looked at women "with lust in my heart." Any other politician would have said, "Sure, I look at pretty women," and no one would have thought twice about it. He also caused a stir when he seemed to have asked his daughter for advice on what to do about nuclear weapons. All Carter really did was explain the bomb to Amy, as I once heard Peter do with Muffy. Any other politician would have said, "Is there something wrong with talking to my child about her future?" But Carter didn't have that kind of political savvy.

Jimmy and Rosalynn Carter had a good marriage, and I always liked seeing them together—they were very close and comfortable with each other. Not coincidentally, the Carter White House reflected that; it was peaceful and informal. The ambiance during his administration was definitely not one of high living. The photos I have of my visits to the White House during his term in office are indicative of the Carter style. When I look at photos of my White House singing appearances during the Nixon and Ford years, I'm seated with three or four instantly recognizable people. In the Carter days, I'm seated at large round tables with people I'd have trouble identifying now. Carter and his wife would send along those photos with short affectionate greetings. I have one picture of President Carter and me dancing together, and on it he wrote: "You're just beautiful," and signed it "Jimmy."

Rosalynn Carter was just as bright as her husband and perhaps a bit tougher. I once attended a Washington Gridiron Club dinner at which various members of the capital's press corps kiddingly slaughtered and then skewered the Carters for their Southern drawl. Jimmy was off in Oklahoma dealing with some kind of oil disaster, so Rosalynn was called on to act as a last-minute replacement for the President.

When the time came for Rosalynn to respond to all the good-natured ribbing, I remember her standing at the microphone, looking absolutely chic and beautiful, her hair shining, her eyes alive with mischief. Did she do a number on those people! She started off by saying: "Ah just had the best *tahm* tonaht. Ah just *love* to come nawth and heah how funneh yew Yankehs tawk." She demolished that crowd. You could not stop laughing. When she was done with them, those reporters were squirming in their seats, but they loved every minute of it. Rosalynn Carter is a masterful, brilliant woman.

Early in 1977, Tito Capobianco finally got an opera house of his own: Tito was appointed general director of the San Diego Opera Company. I'd made my San Diego debut in 1970 in his production of *The Tales of Hoffmann*, the first opera Tito, Gigi, Norman Treigle, and I ever worked on together. I was back there again in 1973 for a *Daughter of the Regiment* and in 1976 for *Norma*. I never lost my appreciation of the way Tito directed me. It was very important to me to keep refining my roles, because that meant I was still creating instead of simply repeating the same thing over and over again—which would have been too boring. With Tito, that was out of the question, anyway. He was always looking for ways to improve my performances.

The *Norma* he gave me in 1976 was totally different from the first ones I'd sung with Sarah Caldwell in Boston. Whereas Sarah made Norma into an albino because she felt Norma had to look different from the rest of the Druids, Tito turned her into a female Solomon—or "Mother Bubbles," as some of the more irreverent members of the tribe referred to me. They had T-shirts made that read SOME OF MY BEST FRIENDS ARE DRUIDS. Norma is a very long role, and when I sang it I was reminded of what Birgit Nilsson had once said about singing the role of Isolde: "You need a comfortable pair of shoes." *Norma* wasn't vocally tiring, but by the end of it, my feet would be killing me. Birgit, incidentally, had once attended a performance of *Manon* I was singing, and afterward she said, "My God, Beverly, it's a French *Götterdämmerung!*"

During his first year as head of the San Diego Opera, Tito gave me a new production of *The Merry Widow,* which we then brought to the New York City Opera and which was telecast on PBS in the spring of 1978. *The Merry Widow* is a pretty, almost foolproof operetta. People seeing it for the first time are always amazed that they know and love the music but never realized where it came from.

Tito also engaged me to sing *La Traviata,* which I'd done the year before at the Met. I started singing *Traviata* when I was twenty-one, and I'd always thought Violetta was much younger than Alfredo. When I first saw *Camille,* I loved Greta Garbo, but she seemed older than Robert Taylor, and I simply couldn't understand how it was possible for a woman to be in love with a much younger man.

My philosophy changed as I got older and the tenors got younger. I sang *La Traviata* more often than any other opera—I was still singing it in the final year of my career. As the years went by, I was more and more influenced by Garbo's performance in *Camille.* Suffice it to say that an older woman/younger man relationship no longer seemed like a mystery. In August 1976, when Tito directed me in a live telecast of *Traviata* at Wolf Trap, our only national park for the performing arts—it's located about twelve miles outside Washington,

D.C.—tenor Henry Price was *many* years younger than I. Didn't bother me at all. Miss Liebling had always said that before I sang the first note of an opera, I must decide how old I was going to play the character. In my mind—and this is the way I played her through the end of my career—Violetta never got past twenty-eight. Alfredo was always twenty-three.

After I sang *Traviata* for Tito in San Diego, I was back with Sarah in Boston to sing my first Gilda. As a child, I'd loved Verdi's *Rigoletto*. *"Caro nome"* was one of the first arias I memorized by listening to Mama's Victrola. I'd been well rewarded for it: Gilda's most famous aria had won me my spot on *Major Bowes' Capitol Family*. In 1957, I sang a concert version of *Rigoletto* in Chicago, but after that—and, actually, before it as well—I have to confess I'd studiously avoided Gilda. I loved playing strong, dramatic women, and Gilda was a bore.

When Sarah first approached me about the role, I told her how I felt about Gilda. Sarah then lectured me—actually, she screamed at me—and said, "There are no boring roles. There are only boring *singers!*"

She then made Gilda come alive for me. The secret to playing Gilda is to understand that everything she sings about has already happened to her. She's a storyteller, so you have to be one yourself. After she's been abducted and deflowered by the Duke, she wants to tell us how it all came about. Gilda literally tells a story in almost every scene. She turned out to be quite a spirited young woman. I should have taken her on sooner, but better late than never.

I think the only role I wanted to do but didn't was the Marschallin in Richard Strauss's *Der Rosenkavalier*. The Marschallin fascinates opera-goers, and one reason is that any woman of any age can play her. Close your eyes and I think you can imagine what Manon or Queen Elizabeth looks like. You can't do that with the Marschallin. She's been played by sixty-year-old women and by gorgeous young singers, too. A lot of bona fide opera mavens expected me to give the role a try, but by the time I wanted to sing the Marschallin, my career was just about over. It would have taken me at least ten or fifteen performances to really begin nailing down the character. I just didn't feel I had the time.

I didn't, either. I was still singing at the Met, the New York City Opera, and regional opera companies, performing concerts and recitals all over the country, doing fund-raisers for the March of Dimes,

Lifestyles for NBC television, and serving on the board of Wolf Trap. That and running a family *and* three homes—in New York, Martha's Vineyard, and Key Biscayne. Wonder Woman or wonder *why* woman?

In August 1977, I also began serving on the board of the City Opera. That came about as a result of a palace revolution.

It all began with a highly emotional telephone call I got from John White, our managing director. John, who'd been with the company since 1946, told me that our new board of directors had decided to fire him. When I asked him how he knew that, John read me the contents of a so-called White Paper that had been presented at the board's last meeting. The board's White Paper was a plan to reorganize the company along corporate lines, with a number of vice-presidents in charge of such activities as marketing, publicity, technical affairs, and so on. Our new chairman was a forty-three-year-old multimillionaire coal dealer named John S. Samuels III, and he'd brought in a group of bright executives. The new board had decided to radically overhaul the company's almost mom-and-pop approach to fund-raising and administration.

White told me that the board planned to fire him first, and then go after Julius Rudel. The board reportedly was upset with Julius for accepting so many guest conducting jobs. Its members felt he wasn't devoting enough time to City Opera.

"Can you do anything?" John asked.

I thought I could. I was still the company's prima donna, and as such, I had a lot of clout. I told John to sit tight.

After we hung up, I found out that the board did indeed plan to fire John White. I didn't know John Samuels at all; I'd never even laid eyes on our new board chairman. I called David Lloyd-Jacob, a board member I did know, and said, "Look, I don't know what's going on with the company, but if you want to maintain my services, John White can't be fired. If he is, I assure you I'll call a press conference and create more trouble than you can possibly imagine."

Lloyd-Jacob said he'd get back to me as quickly as possible. He obviously talked to Samuels, because when he telephoned a little later, he said, "Beverly, we'll certainly accede to your wishes on one condition: that you join the board."

I agreed, and a few days later I was invited to meet Samuels at his duplex apartment on Fifth Avenue. Samuels surprised me. He was erudite, knew a lot about opera, more about ballet, and had great taste. He introduced me to his wife and to his children, one of whom was a schoolmate of Muffy's at Nightingale-Bamford. Samuels reminded me of Jay Gatsby.

Toward the end of our meeting, Samuels said, "I'd like to make a proposal to you. People at the City Opera have told me you don't plan to be singing with the company past 1979. Would you like to talk a little about that?"

I said, "Well, yes, I want to stop singing while people are still saying it's too soon, rather than, 'Will that woman *ever* quit?'"

"I think that's smart," he said. "You should always get out while people are still fighting for tickets rather than when you have to give them away. Have you thought about what you're going to do after you retire?"

I told him I really hadn't.

"After a career like yours, you certainly can't sit around and do nothing."

"Oh, I'm not worried about doing nothing," I told him. "I'm sure something will come along."

"It *has*," Samuels said. "I think you should consider taking over the New York City Opera."

"John, you already have a man who's running it."

"We can talk about that at a later date," he said. "I just want to plant a seed in your mind."

When I got home, I called Julius and told him about my meeting with Samuels. Julius reminded me about our discussion at the Scandia restaurant in Los Angeles.

"Look, let's be practical," he said. "I want to do more with conducting and less with the administrative side of things. How about joining me as co-director of the company?"

I told him I wouldn't give him a firm answer until after he had taken time to really think about such a move and talk it over with Rita. Julius did, and his offer stood. If I stepped in as his co-director, Julius would be free to take any number of guest conducting appearances he'd been offered throughout the United States and in Europe, and the board would not feel that the company was "neglected."

Peter and I discussed whether I should take the job, and if so, when. I had promised Peter I'd retire when I was fifty. There was no need for me to turn my career into a marathon to see how long I could last.

I needed to spend more time with my husband and especially with my daughter—Muffy's the one who paid the greatest price for my career. I have visions of her as a little girl saying "Bye-bye, Mama." Muffy always accepted my career unquestioningly, almost as if it were inevitable.

Muffy had grown up and become a very pretty, self-reliant young lady. She remained at Nightingale-Bamford throughout high school, and in order to graduate, she needed a second language. When you've barely mastered a first language, it's kind of silly to think about a second, or so I thought. Well, for her second language, my daughter studied Latin—and even spoke some. It was so funny to hear her. The nice thing about Latin is that, in the way of pronunciation, what you see is what you get. Muffy had no lip-reading problems at all. She would have had lots of trouble reading lips if she'd taken a language like French, where "oh" can be *au, ot, eau,* or *eaux.*

During the years I was away singing, Peter was home helping Muffy with her schoolwork. The day she graduated, my daughter went up to Peter with her high school diploma and said, "Papa, I'd like to tear this in half, because half of it belongs to you."

Even though Muffy had done things like winning a twist contest with John Lindsay's son at a school dance, she was rather lonely at school. The first time she really joined the crowd was after she entered the National Technical Institute for the Deaf, which is affiliated with the Rochester Institute of Technology. She stayed there for about a year, but, as had been the case at the Lexington School, she again told us she needed more of an academic challenge. So she came back to New York and enrolled at Pace University in Westchester County.

Over the years, she and Bobby Newman, the son of our friends Walter and Ellen, had kept in touch. They often wrote to each other, and Muffy was very happy when he was accepted to Harvard Business School. She considered him the brother Bucky never was able to be. After Bobby came east in the fall of 1979, they both were very excited about seeing each other, and I heard a lot of talk about the football and baseball games they attended together. And then one day Bobby's dad called to say Bobby had passed out and was in a Boston hospital.

Bobby had a malignant brain tumor and died before he was twenty-five. I remember the three of us flying up to visit Bobby in the hospital. He was having trouble seeing and asked if he could just hold Muffy's hand. Ellen and Walter and Peter and I remained outside while our daughter and their son talked quietly inside his hospital room. My husband strongly believes Muffy's never quite gotten over Bobby's death.

My daughter needed me. Peter had gotten used to putting up with my career. Although I feel I could have talked him out of holding me to a firm retirement date, I really had no compulsion to continue singing.

I'd allowed myself to be booked for five years' worth of concerts in order to avoid turning my last couple of years of performances into an endless series of farewell appearances. In spite of my resolve to stop singing, it was hard to ignore the fact that those bookings added up to fees of about $7.5 million. I told Peter we had to be nuts to throw away that kind of money. Want to know my husband's exact response to that? Peter said, "Keep your eye on the ball, Bubbly. You're getting out."

We fixed on October 1980 as my retirement date, because I'd already given Tito the go-ahead on a project of his that would take place then: Joan Sutherland and I had agreed to alternate appearances as Adele and Rosalinda in a *Fledermaus* that Tito would stage for us in San Diego. I was so devoted to Tito that I would have gone along with practically anything he asked me to do. Tito was trying to make the San Diego Opera a major company, and I guess he wanted to make history, because Joan and I had never been on the same stage before. When the news was announced, you'd have thought Stalin and Roosevelt had agreed to alternate in the roles. Tito knew what he was doing. *Historic* was the one word Joan and I heard over and over again.

In the meantime, I accepted Julius's offer, the board approved, and we settled it: Following that *Fledermaus,* I would become co-director of the City Opera. We tried to keep that information secret, but rumors started circulating, so on January 10, 1978, I announced my retirement effective in the fall of 1980.

Eight days later, I opened at the Met in *Thaïs.* Tito directed it, my English friend John Pritchard was the conductor, and Sherrill Milnes again sang Athanael. All through our rehearsal period, I saw almost no one from the Met, and that didn't sit well with me. The same was true for the performances after opening night. So the night of the fourth performance, at about five minutes to eight, I picked up the telephone and called the rehearsal office. Different theaters have different names for it, but there's a number you dial that's the 911 of the opera world. I said, "Hi, this is Beverly Sills. I'm not feeling well," and I hung up.

By two minutes of eight, my dressing room was so crowded that I really *wasn't* feeling well. Why did I do it? I guess I just wanted to be sure *somebody* at the Met cared whether or not a performance took place that night.

For the most part, I was now doing cream-puff roles: Norina in *Don Pasquale,* Rosina in *The Barber of Seville,* and, for a change of pace, Adele in *Die Fledermaus.* The high notes were still there, but the stamina wasn't. In the fall of 1978, Donald Gramm, Alan Titus, and I starred in the City Opera's premiere production of Rossini's *The Turk in Italy.* I had a lot of fun in that opera because my character, Fiorilla, was a little minx. I played her like Sophia Loren in *It Started in Naples*—a girl who just loves men, and who walks down the street in a tight skirt, swinging her pocketbook and her body as if she knows everyone's eyes are on her.

About a week before Thanksgiving 1978, Julius asked me to come over to his place and said he needed to speak with me at once. When I arrived, Rita looked as if she'd been crying, and Julius was terribly upset. He'd been feuding with John Samuels over a number of issues, and he was fed up.

"I've made up my mind—there's no way I can work with Samuels," he said. "It's not the board. It's him. I think Samuels is going to try to get me fired. I've been offered the job of music director of the Buffalo Philharmonic, and I'd like to take it."

Julius proposed that I start working with him as co-director immediately, which would allow him to take the Buffalo Philharmonic job. I said okay, and then Julius set up an appointment to advise Samuels of the situation.

Samuels came over to Julius's place, and apparently Julius kept him waiting in his foyer for a good twenty minutes. Finally, Julius told Samuels he'd been offered the Buffalo Philharmonic and had accepted—and that I'd agreed to step right in as co-director of the City Opera. Samuels said he didn't think it was a good idea for Julius to sign on with the Buffalo Philharmonic, although he couldn't advise him against it. At the end of their conversation Samuels said, "We'll just have to let the chips fall where they may."

A week or so later, Julius decided to resign from the City Opera as of June 20 the following year, when his contract was due to expire. After Julius informed the board of his decision, Samuels got back to me and told me the board wanted me to take over as general director as soon as Julius left, which was well before my planned retirement date.

All this took place while I was rehearsing and getting ready to open in *Don Pasquale,* my last opera for the Met. We opened on December 3. On December 12, the City Opera announced that a press conference would be held the next morning. We were all very hush-hush about the purpose of that press conference: Julius was going to announce his resignation as general director and the fact that I would succeed him on July 1.

On the night of December 12, I sang in a performance of *Don Pasquale,* which Julius attended. Afterward, when my chauffeur was taking us all home, I saw a copy of the *Daily News* sitting alongside him. The front page of the *News* had a picture of me with a headline saying I was replacing Julius as head of the City Opera.

Harold Schonberg of the *Times* had been scooped by Bill Zakariasen, who apparently had discovered what would transpire at the press conference the next morning. Schonberg hastily wrote a story based on a short conversation he had with John Samuels, the only NYCO official he was able to reach. Samuels implied that Julius was being forced out. The early edition of the *Times* headlined the story: CITY OPERA OUSTING RUDEL AND INSTALLING MISS SILLS AS DIRECTOR. In its second edition—after hearing from us—the *Times* ousted the word *ousted.*

At our press conference Julius and I made it clear to everyone that he wasn't being pushed out and that we were still close friends. In spite of that, the *Times's* story caused a lot of people to think I was responsible for Rudel's resignation. One more time: no way. There's no question that Julius's resignation affected our relationship, however. In the beginning, any and every artistic and administrative change I made was taken as criticism of Julius's regime. When I found out the company's finances were in disastrous shape, the press naturally implied that the company's former administration hadn't taken care of business. That was bound to have a negative effect on our relationship, and for a while it did, but Julius and I were never enemies. In fact, exactly one year after the day he resigned, Julius sent me a sweet, affectionate letter thanking me for letting him out of prison.

I had a lot to learn very quickly, so in the spring of 1979, after I began acting as co-director of the company, the only role I sang at the City Opera was Fiorilla in *The Turk in Italy*. I didn't have the luxury of spending much time around New York. As a fiftieth birthday present, Cyril Magnin had commissioned Gian-Carlo Menotti to write an opera for me, and Larry Deutsch and Lloyd Rigler had paid for the production. The opera was *La Loca*. I was supposed to perform it in San Diego in June of 1979 and bring it back to New York in the fall for my farewell appearance with the City Opera.

The idea of *La Loca* was actually conceived by Tito Capobianco in 1976, when I began discussing my retirement plans with him. Tito thought the story of Juana, the mad, tragic queen of Spain, had the makings of a great opera and would be a perfect vehicle for my farewell performance in an opera. Mssrs. Magnin, Deutsch, and Menotti all agreed with him. The only problem was that Menotti, a gifted composer with two Pulitzer Prizes to his credit, was a bit lax when it came to meeting deadlines. *La Loca* wasn't finished when we started rehearsing it. *La Loca* wasn't finished when we *performed* it.

It was a very tense and crazy enterprise, believe me. Starting in December, Menotti, who had an apartment in New York, would call up and say he had a few pages ready. Roland Gagnon would go over there, and sometimes there *were* pages to pick up—sometimes there weren't. When there were, Roland and I would work on them. I learned *La Loca* four pages at a time. I didn't have a clue as to what to do with poor Juana, because I had no idea where Menotti was taking her.

Menotti arrived in San Diego about the same time we did. Tito literally locked the composer up in his hotel room, and every day we'd get a few more pages. He didn't finish *La Loca* by the time we opened, which is why we rehearsed on the day of the opera's premiere. The fact that I chose his work to be my final new role should at least have motivated him to complete it on time. On opening night, Calvin Simmons, who conducted *La Loca,* still didn't have an orchestra score. He conducted from a vocal score.

Tito and I played opera doctors and helped transform Menotti's hurried effort into a truly powerful work. I think Menotti owes us a great debt, although I doubt he'll ever acknowledge that. I could well have said, "Mr. Menotti did not finish the work that he promised me. Therefore I shall be singing *La Traviata* in my final performances in San Diego." Instead, Tito and I stuck with it and concentrated on patching up an incomplete opera.

In spite of all our problems, I was very attracted to the character of Juana. The daughter of Ferdinand and Isabella, Juana was stripped of her crown and was imprisoned by her husband, and then her father, and finally her son, who called her La Loca, the crazy lady. Our biggest argument with Menotti concerned the mad scene, which takes place at the end of the opera, when she's in prison. Tito and I both thought her mad scene was ludicrous, and to make matters worse, Menotti hadn't yet gotten around to finishing the music for it.

Juana is by then a wretched gray-haired woman living in filth with her poor little girl—and all of a sudden she begins singing a marvelous aria about herself at her youngest and most vital. Tito came to me and said, "This doesn't belong in the mad scene. This belongs right in the beginning, when Juana's being dressed for her wedding."

Tito was absolutely right. This particular aria is a buoyant folk song with lines like "On the third horse, without bridle, without spurs, a red sash around his hips, rode my faithless gypsy lover . . . carrying kisses on his lips." It's a wonderful song, a terrifically energetic aria, and it ends very flirtatiously. A woman wasting away in prison would *not* sing this aria. Why was it there? Probably because Menotti hadn't written any music for the mad scene. Gian-Carlo got so frantic that he took a lovely aria he'd written for the beginning of the opera and tried to stick it on the end. I told Menotti I wouldn't sing it in the prison scene. Tito and I insisted on putting it in the opening.

There was text for the rest of the mad scene, but a lot of it was just plain silly. Juana had been through such a long ordeal, and Gian-Carlo had written words for her like "Catch it, catch it."

I asked him, "Catch *what*? What is Juana trying to catch?"

Menotti said, "Well, she imagines things. Words tumble from her mouth."

"Not *those* words, Gian-Carlo," I told him. "I wouldn't sing them even if there *were* music for them. They're ridiculous."

Tito and I contrived a different mad scene, and I did much of it in pantomime. I had to speak dialogue instead of singing text, but Tito thought I could do it, and so did I. Juana's mad scene turned out to be a real *tour de force,* and aside from my Queen Elizabeth in *Roberto Devereux, La Loca* was the best piece of acting I've ever done. I wound up loving the role, but there's no question that doing it was an ordeal.

I like Gian-Carlo. When he directs an opera, he gives you a beautiful setting; the characterization has to come from yourself. I first worked with him when he directed me in *Traviata* in Venice. He's a professional charmer with a million stories to tell, but it's very hard to know the real Menotti, and by now even Gian-Carlo may have forgotten who that is. He's extremely likable, but when he feels he's been wronged he makes no bones about it in public. At an opera seminar sponsored by the Gettys in Venice in 1985, Gian-Carlo, addressing every major opera director in the world, said that contemporary works have no home of their own. Then he looked right at me and said, "Of course, my works *used* to have a home at the New York City Opera, but under the present management, that is no longer the case."

I couldn't stop laughing long enough to respond. But I also had to bite my tongue. I know he thinks I'm angry at him, but I'm not. When *La Loca* finished its run in San Diego, Menotti promised to complete the music during the summer so that when I brought it to New York that fall, it would be done. He also said, "There are certain things I'd like to contribute in the way of stage directions."

"If the work is finished before we do it in New York, I can't imagine that Tito wouldn't sit down and talk to you about it," I said.

When we brought *La Loca* to New York for my farewell appearance with the City Opera in the fall of 1979, Menotti still hadn't completed the music for it. He subsequently finished it, and has invited me to come see the opera in Germany and at the Spoleto Festival in Charleston, South Carolina. I wasn't able to go either time, and I always tease him about it. I say, "Gian-Carlo, I've already seen *La Loca* done perfectly. Why would I want to spoil it for myself?" I've never listened to his completed score.

La Loca premiered in New York on September 16. The final performance of *La Loca,* on November 16th, was also my final performance for the New York City Opera.

Julius had selected the repertoire for the company's 1980 spring and fall seasons, and although I was actively taking part in the selection of singers, attending meetings, and raising money, I was still singing. I'd committed myself to doing a number of concerts and three operatic engagements during 1980. I sang *Fledermaus* in Boston, Miami, and San Diego.

Tito's idea—for Joan Sutherland and me to alternate in the roles of Rosalinda and Adele—never came to fruition. In October, I was working at the City Opera and taking red-eye flights back and forth to San Diego. Every time I arrived there for the rehearsals, I was too tired even to *think* about switching roles—instead of rehearsing, I went to bed. I think Joan was equally relieved to drop the second role, because I'm not so sure she was ready to take on another role she hadn't done before. It was all in fun, anyway. Would anyone seriously cast Joan Sutherland as Adele? No, of course not. I suppose the same thing could be said of me, but I'd played Adele once as a lark, and with Tito and Gigi directing, I'd had a good time of it.

I had to create a different Adele in this production because of the way Joan played Rosalinda. I'd always played Rosalinda as a real Viennese *hausfrau,* a middle-class woman who, when it came time to attend a fancy ball, dressed gaudily and was out of her element. My Rosalinda was a pretentious lady who made Adele wear a uniform, but because Rosalinda didn't know what she was doing, Adele's uniform was all futzed up with ruffles and bows and looked plain silly.

Joan, however, plays a very grand Rosalinda, so there's no place for a silly little maid, because Joan's Rosalinda is a tasteful, beautifully gowned woman. I suddenly was placed in the position of being a rather straight maid. No way I was going to do *that,* but I also knew I couldn't play Adele as the slapstick character who unconsciously destroys rooms instead of cleaning them. I decided to play Adele *dainty.* I made her into a ditz who spends eternities plumping up pillows because her mistress just adores big, fluffy pillows. I'd work on a pillow for a good ten minutes, put it down—and then sit on it. In the ball scene my Adele nipped at booze and was really loaded by the end of Orlofsky's party. Her Laughing Song was Miss Ditz out on her first toot. I was still fixing and changing till the very end.

Joan and I had a good time, and I suppose in a way we *did* make history: there probably are more pirated tapes around of our *Fledermaus* than of any other single operatic performance. It was also a big disappointment for those who were determined to show we were rivals. We genuinely liked each other and we still correspond. At

Christmas, Joan sent me a book on needlepoint. (I still can't do it.) Her husband, Richard Bonynge, conducts at the New York City Opera. Ricky and I are crossword puzzle nuts, and when he debuted at the City Opera he found a puzzle book on the podium from me.

That was the last opera I ever sang. I did not, however, regard it as a sad occasion. I was terribly anxious to get back to New York and begin devoting all my time to my job as general director of the City Opera. A couple of weeks later, after the company's farewell gala in my honor, I was able to do just that.

TWENTY-ONE

When Julius Rudel resigned as the City Opera's general director, I invited him to stay on as principal conductor, and he accepted. Relations between Julius and board chairman John Samuels continued to deteriorate. John and Julius just never hit it off, and there's no explaining it. They almost seemed to take pleasure in irritating each other. For reasons known only to Mr. Samuels, he was slow in signing Julius's new contract, which only added to the bad blood between them.

During the first six months of 1979, when Julius and I were co-directors of the City Opera, he maintained day-to-day control of the company, and I had no problem with that. I was still singing, and because of the company's precarious financial condition, I also spent a lot of time out of town raising money for the City Opera. That was the main reason I'd been asked to join the board in the first place. I had gone to my first board meeting in August of 1977, and by the time Julius announced his resignation, I'd already brought in more than a million dollars.

Between trips, I began trying to familiarize myself with how the company's administration functioned. If you like life in an under-ground bunker, you'd love working for the City Opera. Our offices are in the basement of the New York State Theater. They're airless, institutional, and overcrowded. Long, narrow corridors. Old linoleum on the floors. Bad lighting. Nobody had promised me a rose garden, and I wasn't looking for one. All I wanted was a place to sit down, but every inch of office space was already occupied. Julius's sofa became my headquarters.

Julius kept up a cordial front, but he'd been running the company autonomously for twenty-one years, and it wasn't easy for him suddenly to start sharing power with me. That was our agreement, however. Before accepting the co-directorship, I'd told him I wasn't going to just sit in a chair so that he could tell the board: "See? I have a co-director. Now let me tell you what I'm going to do."

I got to select several operas we'd present over the next few seasons, beginning with Sarah Caldwell's production of *Falstaff* for fall 1979. Donald Gramm played Falstaff, and Sarah directed the opera and was going to conduct it, but had to cancel when she got sick on opening night.

Julius and I tried to avoid stepping on each other's toes, and we generally succeeded. Still, there came a time when I knew I was crowding him, in a couple of senses of the word, so I moved across the corridor to the sofa in John White's office. It was a difficult situation, but we handled it as best we could.

The thing that puzzled me most was the manner in which the company's finances were managed. I kept asking Julius: "How deep in debt are we?"

Rudel would say, "I've never been able to understand financial things—John does all that."

So I'd walk back across the corridor and talk to John White. Whenever we ran short of money, John would pick up the phone and somehow come up with what we needed. It soon became obvious to me that without John, there wouldn't be a City Opera. In addition to raising money, John negotiated contracts with the unions and all the artists, and made critical decisions regarding sets and costumes. Julius chose the artists and repertoire, but even there John had enormous input and influence. He and Julius let me know that although we were getting along by the skin of our teeth, we were still getting by, which is about all a nonprofit organization can hope for. As both a board member and co-director of the City Opera, I had yet to get my first look at the books. Whatever shape we were in, I couldn't do much about it, anyway, at least not immediately. I was just about to embark on *La Loca,* and added to that were my concerts and my appearances with the City Opera; my time was pretty much spoken for.

I should have made time. I *definitely* should have made time.

Before I became general director of the City Opera, Mary Garden had been the only other prima donna ever to head up a major opera house. In 1921, while still singing, Mary ran the Chicago Lyric Opera straight into the ground. In one year, she managed to lose a million dollars, a rather stupendous sum back then.

I promise you I'm not sensitive about it now, but when I formally took over for Julius, I couldn't believe the treatment I got from a lot of people in the opera world. It wasn't a matter of their thinking they were about to observe the Peter Principle at work—people didn't really doubt that a singer could be an impresario. Instead, what I got was a lot of criticism that, at its heart, was anti-female—here was a woman doing a man's job, and she obviously was going to fall on her face. The put-downs had a snide tone to them that was hard to miss; overnight, I had suddenly become a dumbbell. I'd never had people openly question my intelligence, and yes, I bitterly resented that.

Peter G. Davis of *New York* magazine and Robert Commanday of the *San Francisco Chronicle* took potshots at me, and later on, after I replaced our public relations director, Sheila Porter, it's my feeling that her brother, *The New Yorker*'s Andrew Porter, seemed less objective about the company. Donal Henahan of *The New York Times* was one of the few music critics to urge opera-goers to give me time. Don't shoot the piano player yet, he wrote. I'll always be grateful to him for that.

I felt like the woman in that song by Sting: every breath I took, every move I made—people were watching me. And clucking their disapproval. Whatever I did that was different from what Julius had done was reported to him as an act of treason, which didn't exactly do wonders for our friendship. We're close again, but it took years for that to happen, and I blame some of that on New York's so-called intelligentsia. When I decided to employ a secretary other than the woman who had served with Julius, word filtered back to me for months about how I was tearing down everything Rudel had spent his life building up. That kind of thing threw me for a loop.

My first couple of months on the job brought a series of personal and professional tragedies. When I took over in July, I hired Roland Gagnon as my music administrator. One weekend in August, Roland and I were supposed to fly together to Lake George, New York, to check out a singer in a local opera production being staged there. Roland said, "It's stupid for both of us to go, Beverly. What's the big deal? I'll go listen to the guy, and if he's any good, he's going to have to come down here and sing for you anyway. And if he's not any good, why bother making the trip?"

I reserved a room for Roland at a hotel in Lake George, and over the weekend, the hotel manager called and asked if Mr. Gagnon had changed his plans—Roland hadn't shown up. That was very unlike him. I telephoned Roland's apartment and didn't get an answer. Then I called his building's superintendent, who told me he hadn't seen Roland around that weekend. I asked him if he'd go into the apartment to check on whether Roland might be ill, but he couldn't do that without permission from the police. I called the police, and they broke down the door.

Roland was dead. The police found him in his bed. He had died of a cerebral hemorrhage, probably while he was sleeping. I loved Roland, and even though he was younger than I, he'd been my musical mentor since 1961. I was devastated by his death.

I threw myself into the job with a vengeance, and if I was looking for comfort, what I found only added to my distress. I had no idea the City Opera's finances were in such bad shape. When I took over completely in July 1979, John Samuels, our chairman of the board, told me the company was financially viable. At the time he stepped down as general director, Julius also said the company was financially healthy. Both men left me with the impression that we were probably about $800,000 in the hole, which is a manageable deficit for this particular nonprofit organization. Raising a million dollars to close our deficit didn't seem at all impossible to me. But then, when I got my first look at the books, our deficit looked more like $2.5 million. I immediately brought our financial records home and had Peter look them over.

When he was finished, my husband turned to me and said, "You're bankrupt."

"What do you mean?" I asked.

"You've got subscription funds being spent as they come in, and they're being spent to pay off debts," Peter said. "You don't have any future operating funds, and that's the *real* killer. The day will come when you won't have enough money to open a season. Somewhere along the line you're going to come to a screeching halt."

My husband estimated the City Opera's accumulated debts to be close to $4 million. I asked him what he thought I ought to do about it.

"Call an emergency board meeting, put the City Opera in Chapter Eleven, and resign," he said.

"I won't do that," I answered. "I'm not letting the company go down the drain."

"You can't save it, honey," Peter told me. "Face it: It was a mistake to take the job. Be realistic."

"I'll raise the money."

"And who'll mind the store? Who'll supervise your artistic product? Where's your payroll going to come from?"

"I'll think of something, Peter," I said. "I'm not quitting."

In my first weeks on the job without a co-director, every bit of financial information I came across was uniformly bad. Shortly after I moved into Julius's former office, John Samuels and I were taken to lunch at La Caravelle by a member of the Ford Foundation. The foundation was unhappy with the City Opera. Some months before, the Ford Foundation had given us a matching grant of $250,000, based on $250,000 in pledges made to the company. They'd discovered that the pledge money had never come in, nor would it, because some of the "donors" had been asked to make "soft pledges." A soft pledge means the donor just pledges the money, but won't have to pay it. I subsequently got in touch with all the people who'd made those pledges, and several of them honored their pledges, and several of them didn't. Larry Deutsch had died of cancer, and Lloyd Rigler honored Larry's pledge. Beginning in 1958, when it had underwritten our season of American opera—the season in which I sang *The Ballad of Baby Doe*—the Ford Foundation has been a major corporate sponsor of the City Opera. I certainly didn't want to bend those people's noses out of joint. Soft pledges instantly became a thing of the past.

From the moment I became general director, I found myself constantly in a life-or-death pursuit of money. Dozens of creditors were jumping on me at the same time, and I wasn't sure I could handle the situation. I don't know how many five-minute phone calls I made to come up with funds we needed immediately. At the height of our fall

1979 season, our advertising agency sent us a bill for $200,000 and told me they'd stop placing ads for us until they got their money. They wouldn't take monthly payments because, in the past, the company had always fallen behind on its payments. Well, that meant another overnight trip somewhere to come up with a quick $200,000.

The donors who came to my rescue were friends I could level with about the company's predicament. Sidney Harman of Harman Kardon—we go back so long that he still calls me Bubbles—said, "I'll help you because I love you, but I think this money is going down the drain."

When I went to see Lucille and David Packard, of Hewlett-Packard, David said, "Bev, you've got an impossible task."

Lucille said, "But she looks so *tired,* David. Let's help her."

They did. I cannot recall being turned down for a major gift either by an individual or a corporate head. I was back in New York a couple of days later with that $200,000, but it didn't benefit the company at all. Our advertising expenses had already been budgeted; they just hadn't been paid. Paying off overdue bills isn't called stability; it's called survival. Given our deficit, I really felt as if I were trying to resuscitate a corpse.

The process was nerve-racking. We owed everybody. We owed the New York City Ballet some money. We owed Lincoln Center a *lot* of money. The company had borrowed nearly $400,000 from Lincoln Center. I found out about that particular debt when Marty Segal, who was then chairman of the Lincoln Center board, and Leonard Block, the treasurer, took me to breakfast at Orloff's restaurant. Both men told me they felt it would be unfair to Lincoln Center's other constituents if the City Opera didn't at least pay interest on the loan.

"What's the point in asking me for interest?" I said. "If I had any money, I'd be paying the debt, not the interest."

Leonard Block said he understood the bind I was in, but still, we really *had* to come up with interest payments.

"Look, I don't think it's a good idea for me to announce that the New York City Opera is going out of business because its parent organization, Lincoln Center, is *putting* us out of business," I said. "Let me do this with you: Forget the interest—you can't deal with us as if we're a profit-making organization, because we're not. I recognize and acknowledge the debt, and I'll pay it off. Why don't we make a plan? I'll pay you two thousand dollars a week."

Both men smiled politely. "At two thousand dollars a week, Beverly, we won't be around when that loan finally gets paid off," Block said.

"You're right," I answered. "But next week you'll be two thousand dollars richer than if you start dunning me for interest."

Block burst out laughing. "I don't know if you're a con artist—I don't know *what* you are," he said, "but we'll try it."

The following week, I sent Lincoln Center our first $2,000 payment. I made sure they always got their check on time. When we had more money to spare, I paid Lincoln Center $5,000 a week. It took several years, but we repaid the debt in full. A week after I sent Lincoln Center its final payment, Leonard Block donated $100,000 to the company. He is some special man!

Eventually I came to realize there was one unforeseen benefit of working in such a pressure cooker of a job: It gave me absolutely no time to dwell on the thought of never singing again. I don't think that would have been true if I hadn't been pushing myself so hard. Later, when I had retired from singing completely, I would think about it only at odd times, usually when listening to other sopranos singing roles I'd done. It was even more of a shock to see other women in my costumes. One of the moments when my retirement really hit me came while the company was rehearsing a revival of *Anna Bolena*. I was walking across the stage on my way to the women's dressing rooms, and without thinking, I went over to one of the chairs and moved it so that the audience would see me at a better angle. I had resumed walking across the stage when it suddenly registered that I was not going to be sitting in that chair. I'd crossed that stage dozens of times since my retirement without doing anything like that before.

My retirement from the operatic stage did not have any traumatic effect on me. You don't go to sleep with a voice and wake up the next day without one—the voice is still there. But it's resting, and it's entitled to a rest after all those years. The fact is, no one can sing as well at fifty-seven as he or she could at forty-seven. Could I go into a studio tomorrow and record some simple little art songs? Yes, and I probably could also get through some fluffy opera roles. But I would feel under pressure to maintain the standards I always set for myself, and at this point in my life, I don't choose to go into the arena and face the bull again. It's a relief *not* to be singing.

*   *   *

In my first couple of years on the job, I was so busy raising money that my involvement in the company's productions consisted of little more than running in and out of the theater and asking: "Is everything okay?" Every opera we presented from the fall of 1979 through the fall of 1980 was either an old production, a borrowed production, or one that had been chosen by Julius. I had my own opinions of how certain operas should be staged and how they should look, but I was loath to interfere with a project that had been started before my time, especially since I knew I wouldn't be around for many rehearsals. In the spring of 1980, for example, we had a new production of *Don Giovanni,* which Julius had planned a long time in advance. He conducted it, and he had chosen the designing and directorial teams.

I didn't see the set designs until the day they were shown to builders for the purpose of submitting bids. The late Hans Sondheimer, who'd lit every City Opera production I appeared in, showed me the designs, and I told him the production couldn't work. The sets were too cluttered, and there were too many moving parts, including some kind of hydraulic device that moved a statue on stage. Drops and scenery would be flying in and out—it seemed a bit much. The simpler you do Mozart—which is to say, match the look of the opera to its sound—the better off you are. I was *very* worried about the functional aspects of the production's two staircases, because I knew they'd prevent the principals from singing out front. I'd sung about fifty Donna Annas, thirty Donna Elviras, and I'd even played Zerlina, so I *knew* the two staircases would be a problem. I still couldn't bring myself to butt in. Julius got what he wanted.

One of my goals, you see, was to show the world that you don't have to be a bastard to run an opera company. I was going to accomplish everything with a great big grin. I actually did that for almost nine months. The turning point for me was that production of *Don Giovanni*—that's when I realized I had to wise up and stop being nice, cheerful Beverly.

Carlos Chausson had been cast in the role of the Commendatore, and Julius told me he wanted to mike Chausson's voice. I told him no—we did not have sophisticated enough sound equipment. Our amplification equipment took a while to warm up, and then it would *explode* into sound.

Without telling me, Julius went ahead and told the stage manager to mike Chausson, anyway. In the graveyard scene, when the Commendatore began challenging Giovanni, the whole house suddenly erupted with sound so loud that it nearly knocked me out of my chair.

When the opera was over, I went backstage and screamed at the stage manager for having ignored my orders. While I was yelling at him, I heard another member of the stage crew say, "She's pulling a Rudel."

I felt absolutely miserable. My goal of running an opera company with a smile always on my face was obviously naïve.

Trading places with Julius wasn't as easy I thought it could be. For instance, I'm sure it wasn't a thrill for Julius to have to ask my permission to have extra rehearsals. In the meantime, Julius's conducting career continued to flower. Since stepping down as the City Opera's general director, Julius has conducted at the Met, the San Francisco Opera, and the Vienna Staatsoper.

A few weeks after he conducted *Don Giovanni,* Julius sat down with me and told me he wanted to resign as our principal conductor. I was totally taken by surprise and tried to talk him out of leaving, but I couldn't. Julius had received a lot of offers to conduct other orchestras, and felt that if he didn't accept them, he'd never get where he wanted to be as a conductor. He said, "I once did you the favor of releasing you from a number of performances with the City Opera so you could make your debut at La Scala. Now I want a similar favor: I want you to release me from my contract."

He also told me that people we both knew were coming to him with tales of intrigue and trying to put a wedge between us. He felt we'd both be better off without having to endure that.

The next day I wrote Julius a six-page letter telling him, among other things, that he and the City Opera had always come first in my professional life, no matter how much money I was offered elsewhere. He knew I considered him a great musician and a close colleague— why else would he have been asked to conduct records of mine and so many of my performances outside the City Opera? I told Julius I would accommodate our schedule to fit his any way he chose. I wouldn't hold him to his contract, but I wanted Julius to reconsider leaving the company.

His mind was made up. Julius told me he'd conduct my farewell benefit performance that October, plus Kurt Weill's *Silverlake* and

Otto Nicolai's *The Merry Wives of Windsor,* but nothing more after that. He was about to conduct *The Tales of Hoffmann* at the Met, he had a long-term agreement to conduct at the Chicago Lyric Opera, was about to debut in Buenos Aires and Prague, and he also had to attend to his job as music director of the Buffalo Philharmonic. He was booked solid. Julius had put in thirty-five years with the City Opera, and it was time to move on.

In my first year as general director, I raised $5 million for the City Opera, which was $1.5 million less than what we lost. It finally dawned on me that moving out of the old City Center theater on West 55th Street had been a horrible mistake. Had we remained there and been able to persuade the city to renovate the theater, which it has since done, we wouldn't have run into money troubles. When we left the City Center, we were still mounting one new production a year for only $8,000. When we moved to Lincoln Center, we had to build two completely new productions a year at a cost of $65,000 each. We're now at the point where we're building three new productions a year that cost $200,000 each.

The various hidden expenses of moving to Lincoln Center finally began to catch up with us toward the middle of the 1970s. I was able to tide the company over, partly because I could draw crowds, but also because friends or corporate sponsors were willing to pick up the tab for new productions I appeared in.

If we hadn't moved to Lincoln Center with the New York City Ballet, we would now have our own, year-round opera house. Our overhead would be low, we'd have a place to perform Christmas operas for children, and we'd have the time to work with our young singers all year long. Speaking as a general director, we should have stayed put, although I'm very certain that if we had, my singing career never would have taken off.

Don't doubt me on that point. The 55th Street theater was dingy and out-of-the-way, and Lincoln Center was getting all the attention. Had we stayed at City Center, New York City would have become a one-opera town; everyone would have gone to Lincoln Center to hear the Met. That is because even a beautiful diamond requires the proper setting. The international press would never have covered the *Julius Caesar* that made me famous had it been performed at City Center. The theater's backstage area and wing space were so limited that our sets literally had to be cardboard cutouts. I remember the City Opera's doing *Manon* back in the early fifties. The soprano who sang it was as good as anyone who ever sang the role at the Met, but does anyone beside me remember her name? It was Eva Likova.

I'll tell you what would have happened if the City Opera *hadn't* moved to the New York State Theater. The Met would have invited me to sing there five or six years sooner than it did. There's no question in my mind about that. I would have come in, and probably debuted in *Traviata,* and had a nice career. I think I'd have been the house singer—the lady who goes in and performs after the big star does the premiere. In the late 1950s and 1960s, the Metropolitan Opera predominantly featured foreign divas. The Met had Callas and Tebaldi, and with Sutherland and Caballé coming up, what did they need me for? I would *not* have hung around the Metropolitan Opera year after year. Instead, I would probably have stayed home, spent my husband's money, bought myself a house in Europe, and enjoyed my life in a totally different manner. The only thing that kept me singing so long was the scope and excitement of my career.

Me and my hoo-ha career. I'd helped the company grow, but when I stopped singing in 1979, our attendance plummeted. I made up my mind that the New York City Opera would never again rely on one singer the way it had relied on me. John White had included at least one performance of mine on *every* City Opera subscription plan. Because tickets to my performances were quickly snapped up at the box office, the one sure way to see me perform was to buy a subscription. That was smart marketing, yet in a sense it destroyed the company's ensemble ethic. We'd always taken pride in our no-star system, but after my career went into high gear, that was no longer true. By 1975, journalists were asking me how the City Opera could still claim it didn't have a star system. My only reply was: "I've now been singing with the City Opera for twenty years. Would you like them to fire me?" One claim the company still could make, however, was that it created its own stars and didn't import them as the Met did.

When I stopped singing, I knew we'd feel it at the box office. My response was to try to make the public aware of the company's roster of extraordinary, if unknown, artists. I set out to show opera-goers that instead of being presented with established superstars—as was true next door at the Met—they could discover their own at the City Opera. It wasn't an easy sell.

My retirement may have contributed to a drop in our attendance, but it really had nothing to do with the company's financial mess. Opera lovers applauded when the City of New York announced that our rent at Lincoln Center would be $1 a year. So did I, until I became head of the City Opera and discovered that it cost the opera and the ballet companies almost $40,000 a week to keep the New York State Theater clean and air-conditioned and/or heated. That's more than $2 million a year. When I took over, the city was giving the New York City Ballet and the New York City Opera a combined total of $300,000 a year to maintain the theater. No *wonder* we were broke.

One day I was going through a list of New York City grants to the arts, and saw that the Metropolitan Museum of Art got $10 million a year, the American Museum of Natural History received $6 million a year, and way down at the bottom was the New York State Theater with $300,000. I had no quarrel with the museums' getting their share, but they weren't facing extinction. We were.

I went to see Mayor Ed Koch and told him about our problem. I also told him that because we were called the New York City Opera, I had no chance of raising money for the company outside of New York. We could no longer afford the luxury of having our company called the New York City Opera. I told the mayor I was going to change our company's name to the American National Opera, which would give us a chance to solicit contributions from all over the country.

Mayor Koch is a very bright, decisive man. Ed said, "Wait, wait, wait. What are we aiming for?"

"We're aiming to get more money," I said. "We can't afford to maintain this theater, Ed. To tell you the truth, it's falling apart. We need new seats—they're in dreadful shape—and the walls are paneled with some kind of carpeting that's turned completely grubby."

In 1982, Mayor Koch got the city to increase its annual outlay to $1.3 million, which wasn't nearly as much as we needed, but it was a beginning.

The New York State Theater's most serious problem was its acoustics, which were just plain lousy compared to any of the world's great opera houses. From the day I started running the company, my first priority was to survive; my second was to improve the theater's acoustics. Given our hand-to-mouth way of life, however, I didn't think I'd ever get it done. But then Les Samuels, a philanthropist and our company's guardian angel, volunteered to pay for all the necessary renovations. We're not talking chopped liver here: The cost of dramatically upgrading our acoustics would be $4 million. Samuels didn't even swallow hard. He made arrangements for the money to be donated to the company through the Fan Fox and Leslie R. Samuels Foundation.

I was focusing so hard on our monetary plight that I almost forgot why I had wanted the damn job to begin with. I was there to produce operas. The first one I got involved with was *Silverlake,* which we presented in March 1980. Julius had chosen the project and had started working on it with Broadway producer/director Harold Prince. In 1976, Hal had come in and directed the American premiere of an opera by Josef Tal called *Ashmedai,* and it was a smash. His staging was nothing less than brilliant. I'd known Hal for a long time, and I really looked forward to working with him, because the man is a genius. Hal Prince has one of the most creative minds I've ever come across.

He's also warm, affectionate, and caring. Hal is a very good-looking man of medium height, who's built very compactly and who keeps himself in fine trim. He's almost totally bald and wears glasses, but they're usually perched on top of his forehead—I still don't know how Hal manages to balance them there, but he does. Before I became general director of the City Opera, I actually had a social life. I'd met Hal at parties and I'd seen Stephen Sondheim's *Company, Pacific Overtures, Sweeney Todd,* and several other Broadway shows he'd directed. I also saw the *Ashmedai* he'd done for Julius, and I'd never seen an opera staged like that. The staging was totally original from start to finish. As experienced as Hal was, he didn't have a frame of reference for doing operas, so he never borrowed a thing from other operatic directors. I'm sure he occasionally had been to the opera, but I can't believe it had been his favorite form of entertainment.

Hal's art is stagecraft. He gave us a whole new concept of lighting. Hal knows how to light and isolate different parts of the stage at once so that he can actually create five or six different moods without resetting the scenery. He gets something going on in every nook and cranny of the stage, and then orchestrates it into a smooth, unified flow of action. The man is also a joy to work with. When he tells the cast or crew: "Hey, guys, you're really special," they glow.

After Julius and Hal had decided on the musical score of *Silverlake,* I stepped in and worked with Prince on the production. *Silverlake* is a Kurt Weill opera about a poor man who steals food from a grocery store and is fired on by a policeman, Officer Olim. Olim feels sympathy for the so-called thief, and when the policeman wins the national lottery and becomes a millionaire overnight, he invites the man he has wounded to live with him in his castle. The opera raises a question as to whether or not the clerical, bureaucratic mind can ever be defeated.

Silverlake was the first opera I cast. The singer who played the lead character, Officer Olim, had to look very unusual. The opera takes place in a period very similar to post-World War I Germany, and maybe I subconsciously thought of him in *Cabaret,* but for whatever reason, Joel Grey's face immediately popped into my mind. He was perfect for the part, and I knew he'd accept—not because of the fun we'd had at that San Francisco Fol de Rol, but because he'd already been directed by Hal. I knew Joel would leap at the chance to work with him again.

Hal really *is* that good. *Silverlake* would have set us back at least six times what it actually cost if Hal hadn't come up with the idea of using huge Plexiglas doors on casters to form the walls of various rooms. When we needed to change rooms, we merely had to move the doors into a different configuration. We never actually changed scenery until the last act, when the stage was covered by a shimmering silver lake. Joel was wonderful; Julius was terrific; the opera worked—*that's* why I'd taken the job.

On opening night Hal gave me a plant that I placed on a little wooden stand in my office. Within a week the plant died. That really *bothered* me. One of its leaves was still green, so I clipped it off, chucked the plant in a wastebasket, and then planted the leaf. I took very good care of that leaf. I watered it every day, and left it under a lamp at night—I made sure everyone knew that lamp had to stay on at night. I then pasted the headline of a newspaper article about me across the bottom of the pot. The headline reads: "I WON'T BE DEFEATED" —BEVERLY SILLS' INDOMITABLE SPIRIT IS INFUSING NEW LIFE INTO THE NEW YORK CITY OPERA.

Everyone who worked in our underground warren thought I had

lost my mind over that leaf. But pretty soon they all started coming by to water it. I know this will strike you as a little crazy, but everybody really started rooting for that little leaf to live. I don't know how long we kept it up, but one morning when I walked in, another little shoot had come up through the earth. A couple of days later another one appeared, and then another after that, and eventually that leaf became a lovely, healthy plant that's alive and well in my basement office of the New York City Opera. You don't have to tell me how dumb it was for a group of intelligent people to identify with a leaf, but we did. That leaf survived. The New York City Opera would survive. It *had* to. I wouldn't *allow* our company to die.

TWENTY-TWO

In the fall of 1980, I chalked up more hits than misses. We did Romberg's *The Student Prince,* and I invited Jack Hofsiss, who'd staged *The Elephant Man* on Broadway, to direct it. Everything about that production seemed perfect, down to the last shiny button. It sold out quickly, and when we brought *The Student Prince* down to Wolf Trap in Virginia, it sold out there too. Julius had purchased from the Miami Opera a production of Bizet's *The Pearl Fishers,* which he'd never used. I took it out of mothballs, and we had ticket lines out to Amsterdam Avenue. We also did a new production of *The Merry Wives of Windsor,* which got wonderful reviews. That same season, however, I put on a triple bill of one-act American operas that I'd commissioned. *An American Trilogy* fell flat on its face.

In terms of selecting our repertoire, my first full season as general director of the City Opera came in the spring of 1981. The company's performances of *Don Giovanni* were a smashing success, primarily because Sam Ramey and Justino Diaz agreed to alternate with each other in the roles of the Don and his sidekick, Leporello. Ramey and Diaz played off each other so flawlessly they drove audiences nuts.

The first production I did from scratch that season was Verdi's

Attila. To get it funded, I picked up the phone and called Bill Fisher, a longtime friend and supporter of the City Opera who lives in Marshalltown, Iowa. Bill's father invented the pumps that are used to move oil, water, and other liquids underground. Bill Fisher and his wife, Dorothy, believe that supporting the arts is a privilege. Bill is an extremely rich man who realizes that the future of City Opera depends on how financially stable we can become. Every year he supports us through donations made by the Gramma Fisher Foundation, named after his mother, his children's "Gramma."

I've always felt that what sets the City Opera apart from the Met is not only our repertory concept, but also our willingness to present new operas, historically neglected masterpieces, and virtuoso works of somewhat limited appeal. *Attila* fits into the latter category, almost to the point of being an oddity. I can produce operatic standards like *La Bohème* and *La Traviata* every year without worrying about attracting audiences, because there really *are* people who'll happily see eighty-six productions of each. *Attila* has never been a big box-office attraction, and to produce it successfully you need a great bass, which we had in Sam Ramey.

Bill Fisher said he'd fund *Attila* if I'd share it with at least two other opera companies; since it's rarely performed, he wanted *Attila* to be seen in at least three cities. One of them had to be Chicago, because Bill was also a major supporter of the Chicago Lyric Opera, whose general director, Carol Fox, was a close friend of his. I wanted Tito Capobianco to direct *Attila,* and since Tito was head of the San Diego Opera, we quickly agreed on San Diego as the third city to present the new production.

Carol Fox had never been a fan of mine, mostly because she favored European artists, especially Italians. Carol hired so many Italian singers, conductors, directors, and designers that people in the business began referring to the Chicago Lyric Opera as "La Scala West." That did not prevent me from singing in Chicago, though. During the summer, I used to perform at the Ravinia Festival in Highland Park, a Chicago suburb along Lake Michigan. Ravinia was then run by conductor James Levine. I first met Jimmy when I was living in Cleveland, just after George Szell had hired him as assistant conductor of the Cleveland Orchestra, the youngest in the orchestra's history. He's now the Met's artistic director.

Jimmy allowed me to pick the operas I wanted to sing. Consequently, although I never sang at the Lyric Opera, Chicago audiences heard my *Lucia, Norma, Abduction from the Seraglio, Traviata,* and God knows what else. The Festival's theater and grounds hold nearly 20,000 people, and I always attracted large turnouts.

Carol Fox and I didn't become friendly until late in my career. We met at a concert I sang for one hundred Chicago-area couples who had contributed something like $10,000 each to the March of Dimes. Carol had just come back from a trip to Europe, where she'd been mugged, leaving her with a broken arm. She walked up to me and said, "Okay, it's time we were friends." Right after that, Carol invited me to sing *Manon* with the Chicago Lyric Opera, but unfortunately, these were the last years of my career and I was solidly booked up.

Carol, Tito, and I agreed to present *Attila* in our respective opera houses, using different casts. Sam Ramey had a triumph in the production. That season I also produced the New York premiere of *Mary, Queen of Scots* by British composer Thea Musgrave—the piece had just had its American premiere at the Virginia Opera, and I brought it to New York to play alongside *Maria Stuarda*. Soprano Ashley Putnam sang both Marys and did extremely well.

The highlight of my first season was the company's premiere production of Leoš Janáček's *The Cunning Little Vixen,* a honey of an opera about a vixen that's adopted by a forester. The little fox eventually runs back to the forest, where she mates and has cubs and is then shot by a hunter. At the end, the forester adopts another little vixen.

The Janáček work is challenging to stage. The opera contains a lot of scenes and scenery, and scene changes must be made very quickly, because the music continues between scenes. Each scene starts at a specific moment in the score, so if you don't finish every scene change on time, you've got a real problem. You definitely don't want the audience to see a stagehand running out to push a sofa into the wings. We avoided trouble by flying most of the scenery down and up again from above the proscenium arch. In other words, we had to make things complicated in order to make them simple.

The look of our production was going to be absolutely crucial to its success. Frank Corsaro had once called me to rave about the sets artist Maurice Sendak had designed for a *Magic Flute* that Corsaro was then directing in Houston. I flew to Texas to see it, and Sendak's sets were indeed magical. Corsaro was then after me to do *Cunning Little Vixen,* and he wanted Sendak to design the opera's sets and costumes.

I'd long admired Sendak's work. When my daughter, Muffy, was about five years old, I bought her a series of fairy-tale books Sendak had illustrated. She still has them. One of Sendak's characters wore a derby and a checkered suit. I remember that every time Muffy saw that little fellow she'd get the giggles. I later bought her a poster Sendak had designed for a charity event, and she liked it so much we had it framed and hung in her bedroom.

As it happened, I was very interested in doing *The Cunning Little Vixen.* I invited Frank to bring Maurice around to meet me. The three of us sat down to talk about *Cunning Little Vixen,* and over tea and cookies I fell in love with Sendak, who's one of the sweetest men I know. Maurice looks a bit like the character in the derby he draws. He's shortish, powerfully built, with a moustache and a little beard and a somewhat impish air. It's almost impossible *not* to love Maurice. He's very soft-spoken and sensitive, and is an absolute perfectionist about his work.

When I told Muffy I'd hired him to do the sets and costumes for *Cunning Little Vixen,* she asked if I'd introduce her to Maurice. One day he came to my office with a bunch of posters for her, and on one of them he drew the little man with the derby and signed it "To Muffy." My daughter was *extremely* impressed. A few days later she wrote him a letter telling Sendak how she felt about his work and what fun he'd always given her. And they have continued to correspond. Both of them are crazy about dogs.

Set design was a new art form for Maurice; his paintings for children's books had naturally been done in a very flat context as opposed to the three-dimensional look of an opera set. It took him a long, long time to finish his renderings. Maurice worked so hard and agonized so much over every detail that I developed sympathy pains. When Maurice is in agony, so am I; I can't bear to see him unhappy. When his work was completed, however, Maurice had given us a wonderfully fanciful forest filled with dancing animals and insects, and a forester's house straight out of a fairy tale. Maurice's work was so brilliant he now spends almost as much time designing operas as he does working on his children's books. Soprano Gianna Rolandi sang the title role, and she was as foxy as they come. *Big,* big hit.

We played to 85 percent of our seating capacity that spring, and I felt I was off to a very good start. The one awful development that season was that John Samuels suffered severe financial reversals and resigned as our board chairman. That was really sad, because he was very good at the job. John's financial troubles also hurt the company. The large contributions we'd been getting from him would no longer be forthcoming.

In May, after the season ended, Peter, Muffy, and I traveled to China. The Chinese government had invited me to conduct four master classes in four cities, and I'd accepted. It seems that videocassettes of my televised operas had been brought into China by tourists and official visitors and had been duplicated *en masse*. The same thing had happened with recordings by the late Swedish tenor Jussi Bjoerling. The tapes were a staple of every music conservatory I visited. As a result, Bjoerling and I were China's favorite Western opera singers. I hasten to point out that he and I were practically the *only* Western singers most Chinese opera fans had ever heard. That's all changed now. In recent years, La Scala and Munich's Bavarian State Opera have sent touring companies to China, and in June 1986, Luciano Pavarotti brought over a TV crew and sang *La Bohème* in Beijing.

The Chinese gentleman who approached me about making the trip was affiliated with Columbia University, and initially had contacted Schuyler Chapin, who'd left the Met to become dean of the faculty of Arts at Columbia University. Schuyler was asked to coordinate the trip, so he and his wife, Betty, flew to China with Peter, Muffy, and me.

Let me tell you a cute story. When we arrived at the airport in Beijing, we were met by a large group of people who greeted us with candy and flowers. We couldn't help noticing that most of the crowd was gravitating toward Betty Chapin, and none of us could figure out why. We later learned that her passport read "Elizabeth Steinway Chapin"—she's part of the Steinway piano family. They greeted her so warmly because during the Cultural Revolution, China's government had pretty much banned music, and as a result the country's pianos had fallen into great disrepair. Chinese piano players needed felts and ivories and pedals. When they found out a Steinway was coming, they figured they might as well go ask her for help. And I think that after she got back to New York, Betty really *did* help them.

I had a good time in China. We spent our first week in Beijing.

The city was then undergoing an incredible heat wave, and the hotel was filled with rather pungent aromas. In Shanghai we stayed in the suite Richard Nixon had occupied at the Jin Jiang Hotel. All the rooms were done up in run-down art deco—the place was a shambles, and it was also headquarters for an army of cockroaches and all manner of insects. All the hotels we visited were in bad shape. I understand the situation has improved considerably since 1981, but at that point the Chinese felt that hotel work was menial. China really was unprepared for the hundreds of thousands of tourists that began visiting there each year.

In Xian, we stayed in a hotel built by the Russians, who aren't much better at that sort of thing. Maybe worse: The Russians had built a bathtub backward. The tub's drain was slanted higher than the opposite side, which meant water never could drain completely. It also meant that the other end of the tub was always filled with a lovely puddle of brown water. That bathtub somehow made me feel much safer about the Russians.

What surprised me most about Beijing were the hundreds of thousands of people out in the streets every day. The first morning we were there, I thought a national holiday was being celebrated, but nothing special was happening. The crowds were there every day. They were made up of unemployed people who had nothing else to do. The government apparently can't create jobs for all the millions of Chinese who live in Beijing, so at any given time the streets are teeming with people.

Like the majority of Western visitors to Beijing, we did a lot of our touring on foot. Peter noticed that most Americans we met in Beijing were elderly, and he wondered how well they endured all the walking and exposure to strange viruses. An official at the American consulate told us that was the source of a growing problem.

"They're dropping like flies," he said. "And the Chinese are cashing in on it. Whenever an American dies here, they ship the body back to the States—for twelve thousand dollars."

I expected Beijing's standard of living to be slightly higher than it was. The city's plumbing was fairly primitive—I saw outhouses all over the city. One section of Beijing reminded me of the barrios I'd seen in South America. There was a lot of bicycle traffic—only VIPs have cars—and I noticed very few dogs or cats on the streets. The department stores were also a bit of a jolt—they had *very* little merchandise to sell.

China's minister of culture and our translator, a wonderful woman named Kitty, were always along, so we didn't roam around by ourselves a lot. We were cautioned not to expect people to be friendly toward us, but the Chinese really were quite affectionate. They adored my daughter. Muffy was then twenty years old, had platinum-blond hair, and a size four figure. People would come up and stare at her, but in a very pleasant, good-natured way.

During our first day in Beijing, my daughter slipped on a step and sprained her ankle so badly—it blew up like a balloon—that I thought we might have to go home. But then a woman from the Ministry of Culture came by with a mustard-colored powder that she mixed into a paste with some foul-smelling alcohol. She rubbed it all over Muffy's leg and told her: "You're not going to have any more pain. Tomorrow your foot's going to turn bright purple, and two days later it will be bright yellow. The day after that, your ankle will be healed."

It happened just the way she said it would. I wanted to take some of that stuff home with me, but the woman wouldn't give me any, nor would she tell me what it was called. She did, however, laugh at my amazement and my desire to take some of those magic crystals back to the States.

The food served in the country's hotels was nothing to write home about, but we attended several banquets where the dishes tasted unlike any Chinese food I'd ever eaten. Even the *rice* was sensational. At a restaurant called the Sick Duck—it was next to a hospital!—we ate the best Peking duck a human being could ask for. We also had shark's-fin soup and a lot of other special soups, most of which looked highly unusual. I tried them all, but only after I made the waiters promise not to tell me what was in them. Between courses, everybody was very busy drinking what I called mai tais. I never found out the name of the drink, but it smelled like gasoline. I was told that once you get past the smell the taste ain't bad, but, my God, you could die from that smell.

I turned fifty-two while we were in Shanghai. The government people who were along with us baked me a birthday cake, and we had an early-evening birthday party. And then they sent the five of us—the Chapins, Peter, Muffy, and me—to a European-style restaurant and left us alone for the first time. The next night, they gave me a Chinese banquet with another birthday cake—and candles—they'd made.

On one level, my trip to China reminded me of my visit to Israel: The government scheduled a lot more work for me than we'd agreed upon. Instead of spending a week conducting four master classes, I wound up doing four master classes a day for three weeks. The classes were held in the Beijing Conservatory, the Shanghai Conservatory, and some small theaters out in the provinces. When I arrived, the auditoriums would be full, and you couldn't see to the end of the waiting lines. Instead of an agreed-upon forty students in each class, I had one hundred.

Those classes were attended by singers in their late teens or early twenties, along with their teachers. I can't account for it, but the men generally had much more extraordinary voices than the women. In one province we visited, people spoke their dialect very loudly, and those tenors had large, strong voices. Most Western tenors would give everything they own to hit high C's as powerfully and effortlessly as those young Chinese men did. But they had no music, and they had no technique—it was a tragedy.

I later found out the real reason I was invited over: If you'll pardon the expression, the Chinese wanted me to help them make a great leap forward in opera. Specifically, they wanted me to explain how the New York City Opera functions, which I did in front of about three dozen male officials who were seated in big brown velvet armchairs. Seems I'd been using the expression *People's Opera* in our advertising at home. Word of that had gotten back to Chinese officials, who were very curious to know how a "People's Opera" could get started in a capitalist society. So I told them. Through my interpreter, I also explained my plans for a development department, our need to raise money, and our marketing plans. They didn't seem to understand any of that.

When I began describing our dealings with unions that represent musicians, singers, stagehands, and so on, those men all started laughing. The idea of unionized opera companies really tickled them. In China, musicians and singers come in at eight in the morning and rehearse until they get it right or until they drop, whichever comes first. And there are no tea breaks.

As much as I helped them, they helped me. One night we all went to the Beijing Opera, where I saw operatic subtitles used for the first time. Vertical projection screens had been placed on either side of the stage, and as the opera went along, subtitles flashed on and off those screens. Since the opera was in Chinese, I asked our interpreter why it was being translated. Kitty told me that even if one spoke the dialect used by the singers, it was hard to understand them because their diction wasn't very good. A universal problem. More important, a wide variety of dialects are still spoken in China. The characters of the Chinese alphabet are the same in all dialects, however, so it was rather easy—and necessary—to translate the opera into other dialects besides the one used in the opera.

I told Kitty: "If *our* language went from north to south instead of west to east, I would project a translation of every opera."

Those subtitles intrigued me, but I must confess that I wasn't clever enough to visualize English translations being projected on a *horizontal* screen.

Before I left China, I knew I'd had more fun talking about the trip than I'd had living it. Even though I'm a whiz with chopsticks, I was always so tired that I couldn't seem to get food from my plate to my mouth without dropping some along the way. All my dresses wound up with huge stains all over the front. Only in America can you find excellent Chinese laundries; the stains on my dresses were made permanent by various hotel valet services. My husband gallantly named those stains "Beverlys." To this day, all Peter needs to say is "You've got a Beverly on your right bosom," and I'll know that I've just dropped some food on myself, and where.

After the success of our spring '81 season, I was confident we'd really knock everybody out come autumn. We again led off our fall season with *The Student Prince,* which continued to play to sold-out houses. I followed that up with another operetta: a new production of *Song of Norway.* Critics liked it, and all fourteen of our performances were winners at the box office, but I wasn't happy with the production. My dissatisfaction centered around the ballet scene at the end of the operetta, which is danced to the Edvard Grieg piano concerto. Robert Wright and George Forrest, who'd adapted *Song of Norway* from Grieg's music, were very devoted to the original Broadway version produced by Edwin Lester in 1944. They resisted every change I wanted to make. When it came to the ballet scene, they wanted the piano up on the stage, and I wanted it to remain in the pit. The scene ends with snow falling, and I felt that having a piano onstage at that moment would appear a bit strange.

The piano remained onstage, and I thought it ruined the look of that scene. I *know* it did. But I still hadn't learned to say, "Look, it's my way or no way at all. I'm paying for this. Case closed." When you try to reason with artists, especially those with a lot of experience, it's very difficult to find a middle ground. Sometimes you run into a brick wall, an attitude of "My mind's made up. Don't confuse me with the facts." I don't like ultimatums—either getting or giving them; that's seldom my style. But I knew that showdowns probably would become a way of life. When people assessed the City Opera, they invariably turned it into an assessment of yours truly. Fair enough. If I was going to receive a large part of the credit or blame for our work, I couldn't continue to back off when I had a strong opinion about any facet of a production. I could trust my taste.

Almost as soon as I reached that conclusion, I had cause to question it. My most ambitious undertaking that fall was a German opera by Carl Maria von Weber called *Der Freischütz*, which literally means "The Free Shooter," or hunter. We did an English version of *Der Freischütz*, and during our rehearsal period, the entire company thought we had a huge hit on our hands. The entire company was wrong. I still don't know why that opera didn't work. I've since seen three different productions of *Der Freischütz* in Germany, all of which are considered classics over there and none of which was as good as ours. Perhaps *Der Freischütz* doesn't travel well.

Our other City Opera premiere that fall was a shared production—courtesy of Bill Fisher again—of Verdi's *Nabucco*. I brought in Grace Bumbry to sing *Nabucco,* and she wasn't merely doing a turn as a guest star. Grace had agreed to come back and sing Cherubini's *Medea* the following spring, and we were discussing a number of possible roles for her.

Bill Fisher wanted *Nabucco* built so that it could accommodate five different opera companies. The heads of five opera companies all met, our technical people got together, and the set was built in Miami.

Nabucco was going to be one of eight productions we had hanging from pipes above the stage and crammed into wing space. When the set arrived, we had room for maybe half of it—the other half had to be left in the trucks. We had no choice but to improvise as best we could.

I invited John Bröcheler, a Dutch baritone, to sing the title role of *Nabucco*. I'd performed with John in *La Loca*—he played the three men in Juana's life and sang beautifully. I didn't know it when I hired Bröcheler, but after *La Loca,* John had developed stomach problems, and a lot of things unnerved him. *Nabucco* proved to be just a little bit too much for him. Grace did well, and even though *Nabucco* got mixed reviews, our six performances sold out. Like *Attila, Nabucco* is so rarely performed that when you *do* put it on, you invariably attract big crowds.

The season was a qualified success, but the City Opera continued to slide deeper and deeper into debt. Between 1980 and 1981 our operating expenses jumped from $10.8 million to $13 million. There wasn't a thing I could do about it. To begin with, labor costs had increased about 21 percent since 1979. The price of building materials had skyrocketed. A three-foot square of balsa wood that once cost us $5 was now up to $40; almost everything we built was made of balsa wood. Men's high leather boots that we once bought for $30 a pair could not be found for less than $300.

I had no other choice but to start nickel-and-diming. In *Carmen,* our soldiers wore rubber boots. Instead of silk gowns, our women wore synthetics. We even faked the embroidery on gowns by hand-painting the material. When I sang my first *Manon* at the City Opera in 1968, my costume was made with silk, embroidered ruffles, and pearl-encrusted lace. Sets and costumes for *Manon* originally cost $125,000. If the production were duplicated today—and we've done a rundown on it, not changing a button and using all the real stuff—it would cost $650,000.

We were so short of operating capital that I took a gamble and hiked the price of orchestra tickets from $20 to $25. Our audience could not sustain that kind of price increase. Attendance dropped from 85 percent of capacity in the fall of 1980 to 75 percent in the fall of 1981. The economy had gone into a recession, and opera houses all over America suffered similar setbacks at the box office.

It was no picnic, but I could deal with all that. What I couldn't deal with at first—what really *shocked* me—was the public's response to our subscription mailings for the spring 1982 season. Let me put it this way: There *was* no response. We mailed 'em out, and nobody returned them. I may be overstating the situation, but not by much. I had to do something to get our patrons back. The New York City Opera had been founded in 1943 with the mandate of presenting quality opera at prices the public could afford to pay. By raising the cost of tickets, I was driving away our audience. The problem was that simple; the solution was not. If we were going to continue referring to ourselves as the People's Opera, then we had to put our money where our mouth was. And so I came up with a plan that was strongly endorsed by our new board chairman, a smart, tough Wall Street investor named Robert W. Wilson. I then paid a visit to John McGillicuddy, chairman of Manufacturers Hanover Trust, and asked him to underwrite a two-page ad for us in *The New York Times*. Manny Hanny has always staunchly supported the City Opera. I wanted a two-page ad in the *Times*? Fine.

The ad appeared on Sunday, November 15, 1981. In addition to a ticket order form, a schedule, and a description of the operas we'd be presenting in the spring, the ad contained an open letter from me to our subscribers. I told them I was disturbed by the letters so many of them had written to me, all of them saying the same thing: They no longer could afford to subscribe to the City Opera. I told them that by raising prices in the spring, we'd brought in an additional $600,000 at the box office. But we'd lost people. Our audiences had been down by nearly 8 percent during the fall, and we wanted all of our opera lovers to come back.

To lure them back, I announced an immediate price cut of 20 percent on all City Opera subscriptions.

That ad—and my decision to lower ticket prices—generated a lot of comment, most of it positive, some of it negative. A few people predicted the public would view my action as an admission that our operas weren't worth very much. Others felt I was economically naïve, and said the 20 percent revenue loss on subscriptions already sold would put us deeper in the hole.

Anyway, here's what happened: Subscription sales went from 34 percent to 42 percent. Of our 9,500 subscribers, 4,500 contributed the discount back to the company or used it to buy more tickets. We were still alive, but I wasn't exactly feeling perky. The company's fiscal year runs from July 1 to June 30. As of July 1, 1981, we were $2.8 million in debt.

Up to that point, my fund-raising efforts primarily had been directed at private and corporate sponsors. Since Ed Koch had shown me we could get money from the local government, I decided to see what kind of help we could get from federal sources. I had few illusions about receiving such aid, but I soon found myself in a good position to ask for it. At the start of 1981, President Ronald Reagan appointed me to the President's Task Force for the Arts. Charlton Heston was chairman, and among the other members were Nancy Mehta, John Swearingen of Standard Oil, and David Packard of Hewlett-Packard.

The Task Force for the Arts came to the conclusion that since the government was about to cut back on what little money it contributed to the arts, organizations like the New York City Opera had to depend on private and corporate sponsors. A real waste of time.

The only benefit of joining the Task Force was the chance I got to meet President and Mrs. Reagan. Even though they both know my political leanings, I've had much closer and more frequent contact with the Reagans than with any other First Family. Pete and I were once invited to a small dinner for eight at the White House. In the course of the evening, President Reagan said he was sympathetic to the arts. "Don't forget that Nancy and I were both in the entertainment world," he pointed out.

"Yes, but you were in the profit-making sector of the arts," I told him. "Our opera company is a nonprofit organization—by law, we're not allowed to make money. If we do, we'll lose our nonprofit status, and then we won't get any money at *all*."

I happen to like Reagan a lot. He's a charming, clever politician who enjoys his work enormously. On a one-to-one basis, Nancy Reagan is a genuinely concerned and very sweet woman. It really tickles me—especially in today's funny world—to see a woman who's head-over-heels in love with her husband. The Reagans are extremely affectionate toward each other; if they're not holding hands, they're not in the same room.

The Reagans were the only presidential couple ever to invite Peter and me to dinner in their private apartments. They also invited us to the great historic state dinner at which they honored Zhao Ziyang, the Prime Minister of China. During the cocktail hour I bumped into Isaac Stern and other great American artists, and nothing struck me as unusual until we sat down to eat: Not only was I seated at the President's table, but I was seated on the Prime Minister's right.

Secretary of State George Shultz was in attendance, as was Defense Secretary Caspar Weinberger. It struck me as a little bit odd to seat China's Prime Minister next to a Jewish opera singer from Brooklyn.

When I whispered that to Nancy, she said, "The Prime Minister *asked* that he be seated next to you. You're the most famous opera star in China."

Nancy's remark simultaneously struck both of us as terribly funny. How many opera stars did China have? We started laughing and couldn't stop. Nancy Reagan is funny, and she's a participator. She doesn't just sit there and say: "Hello, I'm the First Lady of the land." She and her husband are both kind, warm people.

Looking back on all the First Families I visited at the White House, I must say I can't ever remember an unpleasant occurrence. I don't think any of the Presidents I sang for ever tried to use me for his own political ends—if any of them did, I was unaware of it. I never felt: *What's this all about? Why me, Charlie?* In a sense, no matter who the President is, when you perform at the White House, you're really paying homage to the country itself. And when you visit the White House, you suddenly realize that, my God, we may be a young country, but we've got remarkable traditions and a marvelous history. We've come a very long way in a very short time.

I hope that in the near future, the powers that be will finally understand that the arts deserve to be supported by the government. Some years back—and I doubt if the situation has changed significantly since then—I discovered that the Vienna Staatsoper received 77 percent of its operating budget from the government and needed to get only 23 percent from the box office. At the time, the New York City Opera was getting 17 percent of its budget from the government and had to raise 83 percent from the box office and outside sources. I know, I know: Who ever heard of the Austrian Air Force? Today, the federal government contributes less than 1.6 percent of our City Opera budget.

More and more, we seem to have the attitude that if the arts can't support themselves, then they don't deserve to survive. If that were the case, I don't know how many museums would remain open. I do know that an opera company *can't* make a profit. In order to do so, we'd have to charge $300 a ticket, and then no one would show up. People who know me have heard my views on this subject, but let me say it once more with feeling: Art is the signature of a civilization. It is through the arts—beginning with paintings left on the walls of caves—that we have always known who we were and who we are. The National Endowment for the Arts has been cut back to less than $150 million a year; the army has spent $1.2 billion on a new version of the jeep.

I *do* question our national priorities.

TWENTY-THREE

I wouldn't wish the kind of year I had in 1982 on my worst enemy. Well, maybe *only* on my worst enemy, but even then I'd have to think twice.

When I took over as general director of the City Opera, my husband suggested I conduct an administrative bloodbath and fire everyone connected with the previous regime. Not because they weren't good in their jobs, but because in order to start out fresh you have to hire people who have the same aims and goals you do. People you hire will see things your way and will come in ready to do exactly what you want them to do. If you allow a previous administration's employees to stay on, you run up against a set of preconceived ideas, aims, and ways of doing things drummed into them by your predecessor. Peter advised me to get my own people in there within two weeks. If I did it a little at a time, he said, I'd eventually wind up with the same bloodbath, but we'd be bleeding for years instead of two weeks.

Peter really gets on my nerves sometimes. He was very rational and caring as he gave me all this executive-suite kind of advice, but he probably knew damned well I was going to disregard it. A bloodbath? *Me?*

He was right, of course. I should have conducted a clean sweep. Instead, for two and a half years I put up with a lot of grumbling and a lot of conversations that began with "Well, we're not used to doing things that way."

In 1982, I finally got my own team. Peter's advice had also extended to our board of directors. I had been just as leery of removing a board member as I was of firing a secretary. But at a board meeting held just after I'd taken about six red-eye flights in a row to raise some money, a woman had the gall to say: "Well, maybe two opera companies in Lincoln Center is one too many."

I said, "Lady, you're on the wrong board. You should join the Met's board of directors—and the sooner the better, as far as I'm concerned."

The woman later referred to that as my "fishwife speech."

It made her mad enough to resign from the board.

When I wasn't flying around the country asking my friends, or Peter's friends, or friends of friends, for big donations, I was working fifteen hours a day in an underground office that sometimes felt like a dungeon. I was tired. I was *very* tired of board members who never attended meetings or who expected the kind of elaborate stroking they got from other companies in return for minor donations.

My most painful run-in with a board member was with Hedy Baum, whose late husband, Morton Baum, had been a co-founder of the City Opera and the whole City Center. Hedy didn't approve of a single thing I did, and she was very vocal about it. She was even critical of our Green Room, where VIPs and big potential donors are entertained. Hedy complained that other organizations' Green Rooms served hors d'oeuvres and fancy pastries, and we only put out peanuts. She resigned in January of 1982 and then told *Opera News:* "It hurts me to see an administration that brings the company to this low level."

She didn't know the half of it. I had to keep up a confident front or else we wouldn't have gotten a dime in donations, but the truth was, we barely had enough money to open our spring '82 season. We didn't even have enough money to pay our employees. Our season started in late February, and beginning in January, I'd leave New York on Tuesdays, visit four cities, and come back on Fridays with our weekly payroll of $250,000. That was grueling, but the worst part was that I'd arrive in time to see a dress rehearsal of an opera that would be premiering on Sunday. I'd spot some obvious flaws, and I'd think: *I can't let them go on like that,* but there was no time to fix things.

My biggest flops occurred in the spring of 1982. I'd seen a production of Montemezzi's *The Love of Three Kings* in Washington, D.C., directed by Frank Corsaro and with sets by Beni Montresor, both of whom worked regularly for the City Opera. I made a deal to bring it to New York, using as many of the same people as possible. To ensure its success, I got Samuel Ramey and soprano Carol Neblett to appear in our production. In Washington, *The Love of Three Kings* was hailed as a major triumph; in New York, with different singers, it got roasted. I still don't know why. I thought it was the most tasteful staging Corsaro had ever done—and he was *booed.* That shook me up a little, because I thought I had my finger on the pulse of what people liked. I'd sung *The Love of Three Kings* many years before, and I would have given my right arm for a production like the one I put on. It just was not well received.

We put on a new production of *Medea* for Grace Bumbry and created it the way I thought a Greek tragedy should be done. A huge head hung above the stage, and I found that very impressive. Nobody else did. I can't say *Medea* was a failure, but at best, its reception was no more than respectable.

The two operas we really got crucified for were *The Grand Duchess of Gerolstein* and Verdi's *I Lombardi. Gerolstein* is an Offenbach oper-etta, and to direct it, I again brought in Jack Hofsiss, who'd staged that marvelous *Student Prince* for us. Jack decided that our cast would pretend to be a traveling company of actors, so while the audience was still filing in, singers were onstage getting dressed, vocalizing, and putting on makeup. Fifteen minutes before the opera started, a girl walked across the stage and yelled, "Fifteen minutes!" to the cast. To open the performance, I had Walter Cronkite on tape saying, "Good evening, ladies and gentlemen. Tonight, the New York City Opera presents Madame Hortensius and her company in their triumphant production of *The Grand Duchess of Gerolstein.*"

I thought it was a terrific idea. Audiences didn't. The Grand Duchess is usually played by the sexiest singer you can find—the Duchess is a French nymphomaniac. I gave the role to Muriel Costa-Greenspon, one of the most gifted character actresses in American opera. Muriel is a little chubby, with a round apple face that glows onstage. Instead of having a sexpot play the role, I thought it would be fun to present the Duchess as a little fluffy puppy dog of a woman who just adores men. Muriel played the part exactly the way I hoped she would, but the opera also has an empty-headed ingenue who competes with the Duchess for the same man. By taking away the Duchess's sophistication and dangerous sensuality, we left very few contrasts between her and the bubblehead. My mistake.

For sheer catastrophe, however, you couldn't top our production of Verdi's *I Lombardi*. Sometimes you just have to bite the bullet. The fact is, I needed an opera, but I didn't have $200,000 to spend on one. So I began looking around for something the public hadn't seen before. I felt certain we could fill the house for six performances of a piece we'd never done and would never do here again. My only other requirements were that the opera could hold together vocally and that we could rent it for small change.

I Lombardi qualified on all counts. The City Opera had never performed it, we had a soprano who could sing it, and we were able to rent the set from a regional company for a mere $6,000. Judging by the renderings we received in the mail, we knew the set was hardly lavish. It consisted of a large revolving platform, rather like a huge turntable. Each time the platform made a complete revolution, a different backdrop and one of six different banners was supposed to drop down—that was it for both the scenery and the scene changes.

I was traveling around the country trying to drum up money during the entire rehearsal period for *I Lombardi*. But every night, I'd call Gilbert Hemsley, Jr., then our head of production, to check on whether the *Lombardi* set had arrived and how it seemed to be working. Gilbert got the revolving platform and the banners, but after a few weeks of waiting for them, he gave me the bad news about the backdrops: There weren't any. There never *had* been any. The company we rented *Lombardi* from had simply never built the backdrops.

"What do you think we can do?" I asked.

Gilbert said, "Well, I'm hanging the banners on a big black velvet curtain across the back, and every time the platform turns, a different banner will come down."

Gilbert told me that he and director Cynthia Auerbach were trying to devise a way of putting different platforms on the big platform, so that it would have a new look each time it came around.

I got back to New York in time to see the dress rehearsal. Every time the turntable revolved, a different six-foot by three-foot banner dropped down. That was it. Nothing else happened. To make things just a little worse, that turntable made a tremendous racket.

Our final piece of bad luck was that on opening night, soprano Ashley Putnam came down with a severe case of laryngitis. My one hope of overcoming the problems caused by our set—to have *I Lombardi* sung beautifully by a gorgeous woman—was now out the window. Ashley didn't cancel, although I wouldn't have blamed her if she had. Her singing was very labored, but I really admired her gutsiness.

Our opening night audience reacted to our production the only way they could: After the platform revolved a few times, people started laughing. The critics slaughtered us, but in spite of that, *I Lombardi* played to packed houses. My hunch was right; people who wanted to hear a *Lombardi* knew this was the only chance they'd ever get to see it in New York.

The season wasn't a complete artistic bust. Sam Ramey was sensational in a revival of Carlisle Floyd's *Susannah;* *The Pearl Fishers* was a hit, and so was Sarah Caldwell's production of *Ariadne auf Naxos* by Richard Strauss. But none of those operas had the kind of fine tuning they might have had if I'd been in New York instead of out of town rattling my tin cup. Nor did they wipe away the egg left on my face by *Three Kings, Gerolstein,* and *Lombardi.*

By the end of the season, I was being attacked for having no taste and for allowing the company's artistic product to go down the drain. Sir Rudolf Bing told *The Washington Post* that "Miss Sills has so far not shown any success in her job. If you begin to lose your audience and you have no subsidy, you'd better give up." Bing kept me out of the Met for twenty years, so I would hardly call him a success at his job, either. It's true, we didn't have a subsidy like the Met's, but I wasn't about to give up. Our attendance that spring actually had increased to more than 77 percent of capacity. That was no great shakes, but it was better than we'd done in either the spring or fall of 1981.

The press, however, behaved as if the company hadn't had a single flop in the thirty-five years before I came along. That simply wasn't the case. The New York City Opera has had a long history of flops, because we've often attempted untried pieces. We'll continue that tradition. We also have a long history of triumphs, and we'll continue *that* tradition. Every major opera company—and the Met is no exception—has had its share of turkeys. If ours sometimes seem more spectacular, it's because we take bigger risks. We take chances on new works, and we take fresh looks at standard operas. That's what this company is all about.

We couldn't have made it through that season without the help of Lloyd Rigler. During one seven-week stretch, Lloyd sent me $250,000 every Friday to cover our payroll. But we continued to sink like a stone. John White had retired on December 31, 1981, and without him keeping an eye on the cash register—and with me running around the country with my bottomless tin cup—our operating expenses increased from $13 million in fiscal year 1981 to $14.6 million in 1982. At that point I personally began minding the store. Every check, every contract, and every voucher now had to have my signature on it.

Before taking over the City Opera, I never realized how many people knew how to run an opera company. My fervent prayer is that every single person who feels that way should have the opportunity to do it for a week. That's also the way I feel about bullfight fans who whistle at matadors who displease them—I think they, too, should be given a chance to show everyone how it's done. The criticism I was taking hurt me a lot, and I had no way of defending myself, because I knew my only defense would finish the company: If I let people know how awful our financial picture was, contributions would dry up overnight. I had to keep quiet, because it's almost impossible to raise money for a bankrupt company, which is what we'd become. So I tried to keep a grin on my face in spite of all the criticism.

When we started up again that fall, I was still spending too much time raising money for the company, and liking it less and less. I don't recall precisely what triggered the thought, but at some point, I knew I just couldn't keep going the way I had been. The past spring, I'd decided that, temporarily, it was better for me to be a full-time fund-raiser and keep the company afloat rather than concentrate on our artistic problems. To me, it was a question of saving the patient's life and later taking care of his other ailments, versus letting the patient die. Setting aside all my rationalizations, however, I knew that we were putting out an artistically shoddy product.

That had to change, and I had to change it.

We were then entering the third year of our contract with the various unions that represented our employees. Our labor costs were due to go up another 8 percent, meaning that instead of $250,000 a week, I'd have to raise $270,000. I didn't think I could handle it. So I called a meeting of the whole company—orchestra, singers, chorus, and stagehands—and said that although I knew they were supposed to receive certain built-in salary increases, I was asking them to take a freeze on wages for a year. I told the company that I could not pay the increases. We were making payrolls by the skin of our teeth, and if they forced me to pay the increases, we'd have to consider bankruptcy.

"That's not a scare, and it's not a threat," I said. "You're dealing with someone who was a colleague of yours, and you can believe me or not believe me. I can't do more than I'm doing. The product is going to hell and I've got to get money so that we can pay you on time. But I can't do that exclusively—I've got to spend *some* time here supervising our productions. If you don't take the freeze, I won't be able to continue."

I was worn to a frazzle and everybody knew it. They took the wage freeze.

Our finances remained grim, but we shaped up artistically that fall. The New York State Theater's acoustical refurbishing had been completed, so we also sounded better than ever. I spent much more time working on our productions, and it showed. We presented two operettas, *The Merry Widow* and Hal Prince's razzle-dazzle version of Leonard Bernstein's *Candide,* and both were big hits. We did bread-and-butter pieces like *Carmen, Madama Butterfly, La Bohème,* and *La Traviata,* and *they* were hits. We did less-popular pieces like Thomas's *Hamlet,* with Sherrill Milnes returning to us in the title role, and Gluck's *Alceste,* and they, too, were well received. Attendance picked up from 75 percent of capacity in the fall of 1981 to better than 83 percent that fall. A real comeback, right?

Wrong. In December, when I sat down to begin putting our spring season in motion, no amount of paper-shuffling or playing with figures could disguise the fact that we'd finally hit rock bottom. Peter's prophecy had come true: We needed $1.2 million in start-up money for the next season, and we didn't have it. And there was no way for me to come up with that kind of cash between November 15, when our fall season ended, and February 1, when we would go into rehearsal for our spring season. To be more accurate about it, we were broke. Bankrupt. The game was over. It was time to fold my tent and steal away quietly into the night.

But dammit, I didn't *want* to steal away quietly into the night. Instead, I canceled the spring '83 season and made the happy announcement that I'd come up with a brilliant plan: Rather than having separate spring and fall seasons, we were going to compress both into one season that started in July and ended in November. I made the whole idea appear very positive, and said I was doing it to cut costs, which was true as far as it went. Each time we closed up a season, we had to move all our sets out of the theater to make way for the New York City Ballet. In 1982, nine of our productions were presented in both the spring and fall, but between seasons, they all had to be trucked out to our warehouse in Bayonne, New Jersey, and then trucked back in again. By pushing the two seasons together, and by having one rehearsal period instead of two, I automatically saved hundreds of thousands of dollars in load-in, load-out costs. Going to a one-season format also meant a sharp drop in the costs of printing up and mailing out separate brochures.

In reality, I bought myself five months of freedom to do nothing but raise money to get the company on its feet. I used the time to chase down every possible big contribution I could get. I had absolutely no shame. In some cases I said, "If you really love me, you'll help me keep our company going." In other cases, I said, "Look, four years ago I came down here and sang two concerts for your charity and gave you back my fee—you *owe* me."

I called in every chip. I pestered all of Peter's friends. My husband's view of the City Opera's financial condition hadn't changed. He again advised me to put the company in Chapter 11, but I wouldn't do it. I just didn't want people saying that Beverly Sills had killed the City Opera. Around then I got the reputation of being the most expensive breakfast in New York.

But people responded. A neighbor of mine in Martha's Vineyard arranged a party in New York at which I met Milton Petrie, who owns more than 1,300 stores that sell moderately priced clothes for women. Milton is one of the richest men in the world and a great philanthropist. I asked my friend to seat me next to Petrie at dinner, and after Milton and I talked for a while, I made my pitch.

Milton said, "You want money? Okay, I'll give you ten thousand dollars."

I decided to gamble. I said, "Mr. Petrie, I can get ten thousand dollars at breakfast tomorrow morning from my husband. You're not getting off that easy."

He looked at me and said, "I can see this is going to take another dinner. Why don't we meet at the Carlyle next Sunday? You bring your husband and I'll bring my wife, and they can talk to each other."

That's just what we did. When the four of us sat down at the table, Milton said, "Listen, Beverly, I'm going to order us a very good dinner, so let's talk before it's served, or else we might spoil it. What kind of bucks are you talking about?"

"A half a million to begin with," I said.

"All right, you have a half million." Milton whipped out his checkbook and wrote me a personal check for $500,000. I invited Carol, his wife, to join our board, and the four of us became quite friendly. Petrie subsequently made a couple of other donations that totaled $200,000. The following Christmas the Petries invited Peter, Muffy, and me to lunch at their home on Lyford Cay in the Bahamas. By then, Milton and Muffy had gotten acquainted, and they liked each other a great deal. Carol Petrie gave my daughter a pair of extraordinary little crystal earrings as a Christmas present, and gave Peter a handsome pair of cuff links. Their presents were on their plates, but mine was empty. I was seated next to Milton, and I said, "You know, you really are chintzy. You think because you gave me $700,000 this year you don't have to remember me at Christmas?"

Without looking at me, Milton said, "Pick up the damn plate, Bubbles."

I picked it up and underneath was a check for $100,000. He's really an exceptional man. Over the years, Milton probably has contributed tens of millions of dollars to charities, and he's also quietly given money to people who need a helping hand. In 1986, for instance, Marla Hanson, a twenty-four-year-old model, had her face slashed with razor blades by two thugs hired by her landlord, who was angry that she had refused to go out with him. The cuts required more than a hundred stitches, and her modeling career seemed over. Milton read about the case and sent her a check for $20,000, along with a letter saying Miss Hanson would receive the same amount from his estate each year for the rest of her life. Policemen's widows and children are among the many who also know his generosity.

Our new board chairman, Robert W. Wilson, was and is another sensationally generous benefactor. His personal donations to the company have run into seven figures.

In any case, my fund-raising went well, and the idea of a combined summer/fall season really captured the public's imagination. During the spring, we sold more than a million dollars' worth of subscriptions.

Early in 1983, director Lotfi Mansouri of the Canadian Opera called and asked me to come up to Toronto to see his production of Massenet's *Cendrillon*. The government had given him money to conduct an experiment: Lotfi was presenting the French opera with English surtitles, as he was calling them, projected on a screen above the stage. Remembering how much I'd admired the Chinese subtitled operas, I told him that of course I'd show up. I planned to fly to Toronto with Tony Bliss of the Met, but at the last minute I came down with the flu and had to cancel. I was extremely disappointed, because I was terribly interested in having the City Opera become America's first opera organization to pioneer the use of subtitles. When I called Lotfi to tell him how upset I was about not being able to make it to Toronto, he told me not to worry—a subtitled *Elektra* would be performed that June at Artpark in Lewiston, New York. So I went to the performance and saw how well it worked, and I was hooked. I borrowed the Canadian Opera's subtitles and scheduled a production of *Cendrillon* for our first combined spring/summer season.

And then, almost unbelievably, just before our season was to start on July 7, our orchestra went out on strike.

We'd been negotiating a new three-year contract, and I know that labor's leverage is always stronger the closer a company is to deadline—in our case, opening night—but I was still terribly depressed by the fact that our musicians walked out. To me, it was evident that the disagreement had to do mainly with lost weeks of employment. By moving over to a summer/fall season, I'd caused a lot of musicians to lose summer work, and after our sixteenth annual visit to Los Angeles in December 1982, our arrangement with the Los Angeles Civic Music Center Association had come to an end. I promised the orchestra I would find other touring work for us, and I subsequently did. We now play two weeks at California's new Orange County Center for the Performing Arts, one week at Wolf Trap, and one week at the Saratoga Performing Arts Center. We're also going to perform in Taiwan this year and in Tampa, Florida, in 1988.

But when the union went on strike, they didn't care about promises, no matter how well-intentioned. They wanted guarantees. Thus, our big fight was over guaranteed weeks plus a reduction of services. They wanted to work five performances a week; we wanted them to work six. Ultimately, both sides agreed to an average of five and a half.

The strike lasted for fifty-four days, and at one point, John Glasel, the union's newly appointed president, told *The New York Times* that I had my hand in the till. I can't tell you how much that offended me. Everyone there knew that I'd been donating all my time and a lot of money to the City Opera, and that without the fund-raising I'd been doing for four years, the company would long since have been out of business. I was in a rage. The next time we met, I found myself telling the union that our negotiations would not continue until I got an apology. And if I didn't get an apology I intended to sue Glasel for libel. I meant it too.

I got my apology, and Glasel disappeared from the bargaining sessions.

I spent the whole summer in New York trying to help settle that strike, and it was a very frustrating time for me. Peter and Muffy were up at our Martha's Vineyard home, and I was so completely involved in the negotiations that I couldn't spend any time with my family. Just to get to my office every morning I had to cross a picket line.

I used to arrive at the bargaining sessions with fruit and pastries for everybody. Early one hot, muggy Sunday morning, before a nine o'clock meeting with union officials, I was walking down Lexington Avenue looking for a place that sold Danish. The only thing open was a run-down coffee shop with a busted air conditioner. I sat in there thinking: *My God, look what's happening to me. Here I am, sitting on a stool drinking horrible coffee at eight-forty on a Sunday morning, the temperature is already up to ninety-five degrees, and I'm buying Danish for a dozen people. For what? It's just not worth it.*

I felt I was missing out on a lot in life. I was also home alone in that big apartment, and I was eating myself sick, growing fatter and fatter and feeling worse and worse.

That Sunday morning was my absolute low point. We finally settled the strike on August 29. Even though my first summer/fall season was shot to hell, I was elated when the wrangling stopped and the music began again.

I'd originally planned to open our season with Puccini's *La Rondine,* but because of the strike we had to postpone that production until 1984. On September 21, we instead opened our truncated fall season with *Cendrillon,* Massenet's version of "Cinderella." We rented the Canadian Opera's set of English supertitles and projected them on a dark six- by forty-seven-foot screen that hung unobtrusively just below our theater's proscenium arch. Those supertitles took both the public and the opera world by storm. Audiences loved them because they could finally understand what was going on without having to read librettos when they'd rather be looking at the stage. Supertitles aren't literal translations; we don't repeat every phrase, and we try to avoid antiquated usage.

Performers love to work with supertitles. I wish we'd had them when I was singing. In some comic operas, such as *The Barber of Seville,* I'd worked with truly funny people, yet we never got laughs from any of the wisecracks in that piece. How could we? Nobody understood what we were saying. So we usually played *The Barber of Seville* like the Marx Brothers, which is to say we exaggerated everything in order to get laughs. Singers don't have to do that anymore. With supertitles, people laugh in all the right places. Audience reactions to tragic operas have also changed. In America, body language is no longer an opera singer's only way of communicating with an audience. People can now follow every twist and turn of an operatic plot.

After we introduced supertitles to America, they were used in Boston, Chicago, Cincinnati, Houston, Pittsburgh, Portland, San Francisco, Seattle, Tulsa, and Washington, D.C. Our titles are photographed onto 35 mm slides, and there are usually five hundred to six hundred slides per opera. We rent them out, along with cues and timing to fit the score, for $3,000 a package.

When we first tried them in 1983, a number of opera critics and impresarios objected to supertitles. I was accused of turning opera into a lowbrow art form that anybody could enjoy. Well, better that than a highbrow art form that nobody could enjoy. Most of the traditionalists changed their minds as soon as they saw their first supertitled opera. Titles don't distract from an opera; they add meaning to it. People who were turned off by the thought of sitting through three hours of a performance sung in a language they don't understand have since flocked to opera houses. I think supertitles have played a large part in making opera more popular in America than it has ever been.

Cendrillon was so successful that I decided that, starting the following season, every one of our foreign-language operas would have English supertitles. And yes, there *was* going to be another season for us. In 1983, our attendance reached 86 percent of capacity, and we were also smiled upon by the critics. The City Opera was no longer an endangered species. We were alive and kicking. We weren't out of debt by any means, but we were healthy and whole. The bad times were finally, finally behind us.

TWENTY-FOUR

Believe it: Nothing succeeds like success. After our 1983 mini-season, it became a lot easier to persuade potential donors to support us. In 1982, I'd raised $6 million for the City Opera; in 1983 that figure increased to an all-time high of $9.7 million. Les Samuels had offered us a matching three-to-one challenge grant of $3 million, so when we topped $9 million in pledges—*hard* pledges—we were able to get the $3 million from the Fan Fox and Leslie R. Samuels Foundation. I'd known Les since I was seven years old and had sat in his lap to sing "Happy Birthday" to his wife. Les, a very special friend, died the following July.

In 1983 we also cleared our books of a major debt. In the two previous years, Lloyd Rigler had lent us a total of $3.1 million, most of which went for payroll expenses. Lloyd had known me for a long time and was terribly worried about my health and all the weight I'd gained. "I can't stand to see you like this," he told me. "What can I do to help you?"

My problem was fund-raising; I couldn't continue to do it alone. We needed more planning and a broader base of donors. In short, we needed a development department. Lloyd got me one. More specifically, he hired the C.W. Shaver Company to put together our company's development department. Nancy McDermott, a Shaver consultant, is an attractive, no-nonsense woman who knows her stuff. With her pointing us in the right direction, we got the development department we needed within a year. Since then we've been able to plan and carry out the level of fund-raising necessary to keep the City Opera functioning smoothly.

We owe that to Lloyd. We no longer owe Lloyd any money. In 1983, he forgave the City Opera the $3.1 million he had loaned us. Lloyd sometimes voices his differences with me about finances and marketing, and occasionally he puts me through a wringer, but I know it's all done out of love. Whenever I've needed his help, Lloyd's been there for me.

We were still almost $3 million in debt, but I was no longer walking around in a state of total anxiety. With the long strike settled, I felt as if I'd lived through an enormous crisis and had emerged in one piece. I was imperturbable. The only other time I've known that feeling was when I got my life in order after a long period of anguish about my babies' disabilities. In both cases, I felt as if I'd lived through an experience that set me apart—not above, just apart—from other people. That strike took a lot out of me, but it also strengthened me. Perhaps the most significant change it produced was to eradicate my longstanding fear of failure. I'd taken the New York City Opera from the brink of bankruptcy to the brink of success. I decided that the state of limbo I'd been living in had to end. In 1984 the City Opera would present its first combined spring and fall season, and for me, it was a make-or-break year. If it didn't work, I was prepared to say, "I've had enough."

If the 1984 season was a bust, no one would have to look twice to see who was responsible. I'd stand up and say, "Sorry, folks, I made a mistake," and then I'd step down. If the season *did* work, however, people were going to know I had made it work.

I was very ambitious in 1984, and I just hoped my reach wouldn't exceed my grasp. It was the City Opera's fortieth anniversary season, and we mounted eight new productions in twenty weeks. I don't think any opera company in modern history has done that. I lived in my office that summer. I came in at seven forty-five every morning and never left before eleven-thirty at night. Every day was a nonstop round of phone calls from every corner of the opera world and meetings with directors, set and costume designers, lighting technicians, and our business people. Rehearsals, auditions, performances, meals with contributors—if I wasn't there, I wasn't doing my job. I often brought along a change of clothing and stayed until two A.M. to watch our production crew unload the trucks that brought in our sets. I'd come home, fall into bed, and then get myself together again after four hours of sleep.

None of it bothered me. I really *did* feel imperturbable. That message, however, was having a tough time getting from my brain to my body. I think it's fair to say that I was literally killing myself. I was working like a horse, my blood pressure was way up, and I was eating six meals a day. And becoming obese. One night after a board meeting, I had double vision and realized I couldn't remember a single thing that had been discussed. I called my brother the doctor and told him: "I think something terrible is happening to me."

After I described what had just gone on, Sidney said, "You're eating yourself into a fast grave. Hang up. I'll call you back."

He did, and over the next few days I underwent a battery of tests and learned that I had a very high blood sugar count. It was suggested that I consult an endocrinologist. Donald Trump recommended one that Sidney had heard of, and off I went.

I came into my job as general director weighing 150 pounds; on June 16, 1984, when I visited the endocrinologist, I weighed 220 pounds. There was no great mystery as to the cause of my weight gain. I'd become a compulsive eater; any time I got tired or irritated, I stuffed myself. I don't know the moment one crosses the line that separates social drinkers from alcoholics, but I'd crossed it with food.

The doctor put me on a strict sugar-free diet. It was an abnormal diet only in the sense that I couldn't even eat fruits and vegetables that contain natural sugar—all citrus fruits and items like carrots, onions, beans, and tomatoes were out. On a typical day, I'd eat a limited amount of bran, broiled fish, and sugar-free vegetables like spinach and lettuce. I walked around feeling very heady, because I couldn't eat enough to total up much of a calorie count. I mean, a whole head of lettuce hardly adds up to twenty calories. The doctor supplemented my diet with calcium, iron, and potassium, and that was it. Within two weeks I dropped seventeen pounds. By December 16, exactly six months after going on that diet, I'd lost sixty pounds. In the spring, I lost twenty more.

*   *   *

Because of the splash we'd made the year before, a lot of people eagerly awaited the start of our 1984 season. We opened with a new production of *The Barber of Seville* that disappointed everyone who saw it, including me. I'd hired Toby Robertson, a director with the Old Vic, to stage the opera, and for some unfathomable reason he took a realistic comic opera and made it terribly abstract. He had two men singing while standing on ladders; he had other men shifting scenery, others juggling balls, and a couple more standing aimlessly on top of a suspended plank. It was yet another play-within-a-play, but this one was off the mark.

When you run an opera company, you can ask a director to make corrections, but you don't just tell him to direct it differently—his concept is what you're paying him for. The opening night audience was extremely cool to our *Barber of Seville*. The next day I telephoned every member of the cast and asked them to meet with me. Would they object if I restaged the opera? They had no objections whatsoever. Toby Robertson had already flown back to London. I called him there and told him the opera had gotten bad reviews and that I wanted to restage it.

"I don't believe in kowtowing to critics," he said.

"I'm not kowtowing to critics," I said. "The audience doesn't like it, and neither do I."

And so I restaged *The Barber of Seville*. I eliminated the play-within-a-play, made the opera more traditional and funnier, and brightened the look of it. When word got out about what I'd done, Donal Henahan of *The New York Times* came back and reviewed it again. He still found it flawed, but also thought it was much improved and vastly more entertaining than the first time around.

The Barber of Seville was our only real loser that season. We also performed *The Rake's Progress,* an opera inspired by Hogarth's pictures, with music by Stravinsky and libretto by W.H. Auden and Chester Kallman. The production was rented from the San Francisco Opera. Artist David Hockney's poster-colored sets were beautiful, and my only regret was that Donald Gramm wasn't alive to sing the role of Nick Shadow. In 1983, I had signed Donald to a five-year contract. He desperately wanted to play both Nick Shadow in *The Rake's Progress* and Sancho Panza in Massenet's *Don Quichotte,* which is why I went forward on both operas. In April 1983, Donald went to see a doctor for a routine checkup. He sat down in the doctor's waiting room and started reading a newspaper, and when the nurse told him the doctor was ready to see him, Donald didn't move—he was dead. Just like that. I have no words to tell you what Donald's death meant to me. I'd always referred to Gramm as "my Donald"—my funny, brilliantly talented pal and colleague. In his memory I created the Donald Gramm Fund for Young American Artists.

The Rake's Progress went on with Erie Mills, Jerry Hadley, and Frederick Burchinal—who played Nick Shadow—in the leads. They were excellent. But the surprise hit of our 1984 season was Puccini's *La Rondine,* a long-ignored masterpiece. *La Rondine,* which featured soprano Elizabeth Knighton and tenor Barry McCauley, got marvelous reviews and did standing-room-only business. I've never felt that operas are museum pieces. That summer, director Frank Corsaro set *Carmen* in the Spanish Civil War, and audiences loved it. Operatic stagings of Sondheim's *Sweeney Todd* and Bernstein's *Candide,* standards like *The Mikado, Rigoletto, La Traviata,* and *Turandot,* a *Mefistofele* for Sam Ramey, a rare *Lakmé,* Philip Glass's avant-garde *Akhnaten*—we presented an eclectic and, I think, exciting lineup of works. The public thought so too. We did eighteen productions that season, and 70 of our 136 performances were sell-outs. We conducted an audience survey, and 96 percent of our customers felt "positive" or "very positive" about our use of supertitles for all foreign-language operas. Except for the most hidebound operatic purists, supertitles were no longer a controversial issue.

Lawrence A. Wien, a New York lawyer, realtor, and philanthropist, and his wife, Mae, were among those who fell in love with the concept of titled operas. Larry and Mae had been patrons of the City Opera for several years when they were invited to attend a dinner in our Green Room before a performance of *La Bohème.* We give such dinners, for up to thirty people, throughout the season as a way of thanking longtime supporters. I made a short speech and invited everyone to come back to the Green Room for dessert after the first act.

When the Wiens returned, they were elated. They'd never seen supertitles before.

"I want you to title all your operas," Larry told me.

"As soon as I get the money, I will," I replied. "Meanwhile, we have to go one at a time."

Larry shook his head no. "*All* of them, Beverly—do all of them, and I'll pay for it," he said. "We can handle it on a yearly basis. Just let me know how many operas you're going to title each season and how much it'll cost, and I'll give you what you need."

A few days later, Larry and I met to work out the details. Over lunch he commented on how sad it was that generations of Americans would never see or hear our nation's great musical comedies, and he rattled off the titles of at least a dozen timeless Broadway hits. Larry then put forward an intriguing proposal.

"I'd like to give you seed money for a musical comedy season with the idea that three or four years down the road, you'll have a repertoire of classic musicals," he said.

I thought it was a terrific idea, and told Larry we could handle it. In November 1984, Wien made the first of five annual million-dollar donations, the purpose of which was to establish a spring musical comedy season.

We had a perfect spot to slot in musical comedies. The New York State Theater was dark during March and April, and we'd always rented it to outside companies during that period. March and April thus became the company's musical comedy season. We inaugurated our program of classic musicals with a five-week run of Lerner and Loewe's *Brigadoon* in 1986. This year, we'll be presenting musicals like Rodgers and Hammerstein's *South Pacific* for eight weeks. *Brigadoon* was a smash hit, and after our opening-night performance, Larry and Mae Wien threw the best party I've ever attended. Mae, a lovely lady, died that June.

I've been questioned about the propriety of an opera company performing musical comedies, and I can understand the concern. We have to be careful about what we present. I don't think we should produce musicals like *A Chorus Line* or *Dreamgirls* or any show that features a lot of choreography, because the point is to present singers, not dancers. To me, opera is musical theater, and I see no reason why we shouldn't showcase American musicals by the likes of Rodgers and Hammerstein, Lerner and Loewe, and Jerome Kern. By 1990, we'll be doing four musicals.

We also present operettas, the art form that was the precursor of the Broadway musical, our own so-called folk opera. Operettas traditionally have featured great singers, because they require operatic voices—you can't be a Mary Martin or Ethel Merman and sing operetta. Our company performs operettas beautifully, because the singers have the necessary vocal skills, they look the parts, are good actors, and have lovely music to sing. Each year we run a new production of an operetta for two weeks, and audiences love them.

The Wiens' initial gift topped off our 1984 season. After Labor Day, we played to 88.6 percent of capacity, our highest fall attendance since 1976. Our net gain for the season was $1.6 million. Bad news seemed to be a thing of the past. With the help of our development department, the City Opera raised a record $9.7 million in 1984. I was still serving peanuts in the Green Room, but our financial picture was all champagne and caviar.

Our 1985 season picked up where '84 left off, with critical and popular success. Gilbert and Sullivan's *The Mikado,* with David Eisler as Nanki-Poo, left very little to be desired. We did a number of *bel canto* pieces including *La Cenerentola,* which was Rossini's version of "Cinderella," *Lucia di Lammermoor,* and *I Puritani,* all of which garnered wonderful, wonderful reviews. Although the critics loved it, which delighted me, I was privately disappointed that director Renato Capecchi opted for a very mannered, far less comic *Daughter of the Regiment* than I'd hoped for.

In situations like those, I have to separate the diva from the impresario and realize that there are at least two ways to skin a cat. I find it awkward to criticize a soprano singing in a production originally created for me. Some of our singers—Gianna Rolandi, for example—will pick my brain on their way to emerging with their own concept of a role that I've sung. Others feel I want them to do it my way. I don't. Ideally, I want our sopranos to use me as a guide who can point out the trouble spots in a role and the opportunities to do something special of their own. I know our sopranos all trust me when I make suggestions about their makeup, wigs, and costumes, but it's a different story if I make suggestions about characterization or interpretation. I'm wary of criticizing sopranos singing in productions originally created for me. Nevertheless, I must and I do.

When the 1985 season ended, we compared it to 1984 and were able to discern a couple of trends. We learned that in the summer— exactly opposite to what transpires in the fall—our biggest nights are Tuesdays through Thursdays. In the fall, our biggest nights are Fridays through Sundays. During the summer, New Yorkers leave town on the weekends, so in order to attract big crowds on weekends in July and August, we have to put on lighter pieces—operettas like *The Student Prince* and musicals like *Kismet,* with Wright and Forrest's memorable score adapted from Borodin. We also discovered that during the summer, it's not advisable to present performances on Sunday nights. That's when a lot of visitors to New York go home, so in the summer of 1986 we eliminated all Sunday night performances.

Summer's a difficult time of year for me. My husband spends most of the season at our house on Martha's Vineyard, and I don't like being alone. Neither does he. Because of all our Friday and Saturday night performances, I really can't make it up to Martha's Vineyard. I'm not a very happy lady in July and August.

In the summer of 1985, when it became evident that the City Opera had reached a certain level of stability, I began having thoughts of retirement. The company's survival was no longer in question. I knew we'd be okay artistically. We had fine singers, designers, directors, and conductors, so our productions would not fall off if I stepped away. On an administrative basis, we'd come a long way from the days when I'd have to pore over balance sheets to discover whether we had the money to pay this vendor or that. We had a good, viable organization that, after several shaky starts, was running smoothly. The financial picture was brighter than it had been for at least a decade. In trying to be objective about our finances, however, I knew it would be tough for the company to find anyone as effective at fund-raising as I am. If I retired, perhaps I could stay on the board and continue to help raise money for the company.

There was still a lot that I wanted to accomplish financially. My number one priority was to establish an endowment fund for the City Opera. That's the easiest, most obvious way to make our company financially secure. The Metropolitan Opera, to point out a good example, set an endowment fund goal of $100 million in its centennial drive. The interest from such an amount, if achieved, would provide the Met with approximately $5 million each year. I wanted to get the same thing going for our company, so my departure wasn't imminent. But I was thinking about it.

I *know* I was thinking about it when I arrived at Martha's Vineyard to spend Labor Day weekend with my husband. Peter hasn't pushed me nearly as hard as he can in persuading me to retire, but our board members are well aware of how he feels. At an opera party a couple of years ago, Peter did his own version of Henny Youngman's most famous line. My husband turned to everyone in the room and said, "Fire my wife—*please!*"

All that was running through my mind on Labor Day of 1985. It was a beautiful, sunny afternoon, and I was so happy to be up there on the Vineyard. And then I got a telephone call from Susan Woelzl, our press and public relations director. Susan said, "Beverly, Joe Citarella has something to tell you."

Joe is our resident costumer. When he got on the phone, he said, "I have some very sad news."

"What happened?"

"You know that warehouse in Passaic, New Jersey, where we have all our costumes? It burned down today."

"What do you mean?" I asked.

Joe told me exactly what he meant. The warehouse where all our costumes were stored had burned to the ground. The costumes and stock—shirts, petticoats, jewelry, swords, uniforms, cummerbunds, boots, and the like—for seventy-four of our productions were now literally in ashes. As Joe talked, I realized that a whole bunch of kids were standing around him, and that he'd been elected to give me the bad news. I knew they were all waiting for my reaction, and that my reaction would influence theirs.

"Is *everything* gone?" I asked.

"Yes," he said. "We've lost at least twelve thousand costumes. The only ones left are for the eight operas that are in the theater."

"My costumes too?"

"Everything, Beverly."

"Okay. I'll fly back to New York today," I said. "We'll just have to build our inventory back up again."

After I said goodbye, I went into the bathroom and threw up.

I hope this won't be hard to understand, but my costumes for Donizetti's three queens had been such an integral part of my life that when we revived *Anna Bolena* and *Maria Stuarda*, I always felt that other women were wearing my clothes. Losing Queen Elizabeth's costume in *Roberto Devereux* was an especially low blow. Gigi and I had worked on that gown pearl by pearl. Elizabeth's costume alone would cost $9,000 to replace; it sported 2,000 hand-sewn pearls that now cost $3 each. My costumes for *Lucia*, *Puritani*, and *Manon* were still in the theater, so at least a few of them hadn't been destroyed. Cleopatra was gone, and I was able to avoid dwelling on how much that particular costume had meant to me. But when I thought about the magnificent and really irreplaceable gowns I'd worn in the three queens . . . let's just say I got a little weepy.

It turned out that two boys had been playing with matches in a compound of small businesses that included our warehouse. The site also contained a chemical plant, which went up first and spread the fire throughout the surrounding neighborhood. I couldn't feel too sorry for us. That fire killed one person and destroyed twenty-six homes and a number of small factories. It left 2,200 people out of work. We could replace our losses; they couldn't.

Any thoughts I had about retiring vanished. When I sat down with Joe Citarella, we estimated the loss at $10 million. Our insurance company gave us a check for $1.5 million.

On September 9, 1985, a week after the warehouse burned down, we established a $10 million Fire Emergency Fund, with $5 million to be raised by January 1 in order to guarantee a season in 1986. Joe and I worked hard and figured that a total of $6.5 million would solve the problem for 1986.

The first two contributors to our Fire Emergency Fund were Lloyd Rigler and PepsiCo. Roger Enrico, president and CEO of the Pepsi-Cola Company, was a member of our board and volunteered to chair the FEF committee. Lloyd and PepsiCo each presented the company with checks for $500,000. By the start of 1986, we reached our goal of $5 million. My only worry now is that our sets will look five thousand years old, while our costumes will look five *minutes* old.

Any lingering doubts about the City Opera's financial viability were finally dispelled in February 1986. We were still part of the City Center of Music and Drama, Inc., and in 1986, a builder named Bruce Eichner began construction of a skyscraper adjacent to the City Center's old theater on West 55th Street. New York has some peculiar zoning laws. Because the 55th Street Theater is not very tall, and because the skyscraper Mr. Eichner is building will be very tall indeed, he couldn't begin construction before purchasing "air rights" from the theater. The New York City Opera's cut of those air rights came to $3 million. We received a check in that amount in February 1986. We are now out of debt. Our budget is balanced. Suffice it to say that the City Opera is in the best financial shape of its life. But I still have to raise $9 million a year in order to meet an annual budget of $20 million.

It's very possible that our production budgets may soon go a bit higher than $200,000. It's certainly definite that we can continue to offer opera lovers a fascinating mixture of standard, overlooked, contemporary, and experimental musical theater. In 1986, our four new productions were Massenet's *Don Quichotte* and *Werther,* the Sigmund Romberg operetta *New Moon,* and *X (The Life and Times of Malcolm X),* by Anthony Davis. *X* was regarded as highly controversial, and a number of our contributors criticized me for producing it on the grounds that there were periods in his life when Malcolm X had been an immoral man as well as anti-Semitic. As I told *The New York Times,* if I wanted to suppress immorality, I would stop presenting *Rigoletto,* which is about a pimp and a rapist, and *La Traviata,* which is about a whore—no matter how well paid, that's what she was. Malcolm X had an enormous impact on America, and in *X,* he's neither deified nor crucified. I didn't produce *X* as a political state-ment I put it on because I thought it was a good opera. Audiences agreed with me. Our four performances of *X* sold out.

At the end of our 1986 season, I sat down to take a long look at what had transpired during my six years as head of the New York City Opera. I'm not criticizing Julius Rudel here, because for many years Julius was the only reason the company survived. Neverthe-less, the City Opera had been monetarily and artistically bankrupt when I took over. That was no longer true. For at least the foreseea-ble future, we were financially secure. I also knew we'd achieved a very high level of artistic excellence, and I wasn't being subjective about that. For the first time in our history, we had to struggle to hold on to our singers. La Scala grabbed Sam Ramey; the Vienna Staatsoper snapped up Jerry Hadley; Faith Esham was signed to make her Met debut. Carol Vaness now sings at the Metropolitan Opera, as do many of our singers. We've become a feeder company that sup-plies talent to every major opera house in the world. A number of singers still feel, however, that returning to the City Opera from guest appearances abroad is like coming home.

We've also stopped being looked upon as the Met's poor cousin. In the last couple of years, the Met's been criticized for not being nearly as innovative as we are. Although that lets me know how far we've come, I'm uncomfortable with such talk, because I want to keep the wonderful relationship that now exists between our two companies. After that disastrous warehouse fire, the very first person to telephone me in New York was Bruce Crawford, the Met's general manager. Bruce gave me carte blanche to go to his warehouse and pick out whatever we needed to finish our season. Our two companies now share a spirit of cooperation that never existed before. I remember a time when the Met and the City Opera played *Traviata* on the same night. Now we sit down and compare plans for upcoming seasons to ensure against an overlap in repertoire.

From my point of view we are two different companies that defy comparison. There is nothing to compare. Opera may have originated in Europe, but from a singer's point of view, the Met is *the* most prestigious opera house in the world, and the fact that it's in the United States is something we all can take pride in. The Met has often been sniped at for not presenting more contemporary and more American works. Bruce Crawford and James Levine don't feel at all uncomfortable about saying that presenting new American works is *our* function, not theirs. And, unlike their predecessors, they don't say that as a put-down. The Met's been wise enough to place its artistic direction in the hands of Jimmy Levine. Levine is one of the few performing artists who is artistic director of a major company, and he puts a personal stamp on every work he conducts. Jimmy is doing grand opera, and he should. He knows that parts of his audience will come to the City Opera to see contemporary works, and that parts of our audience will go next door to see productions like *Aida* and *Die Walküre,* which the City Opera could never properly produce. For the first time in their existences, the two companies are now perfectly willing to acknowledge each other's presence and each other's differences.

Forty years have flown by since my operatic debut in Philadelphia, and during that time opera has ceased being an alien entertainment and has taken its rightful place in the mainstream of American arts. I honestly don't have a clue as to how history will judge me as a singer. Frankly, I really don't have the time or inclination to be concerned about that. I did that already. I know that my career wasn't a fluke. I was a very good singer and musician, and when I was at the top of the heap, I produced. Nobody sang for me. But I can't finally analyze what I did or why people liked what I did. All that fits into the category of unnameable magic. And no matter who we are or what we do, we all have admirers and detractors. I think my admirers will far outnumber my detractors, and that's important to me. Beyond that, I have no concept of the niche I'll occupy in opera history, but I do know I'll have one.

I'm much clearer about the contribution I've made to popularizing opera in America. I knocked down a lot of barriers people had put between themselves and opera. Before I came on the scene, the public regarded opera stars as exotic hothouse plants. I think I changed that. I was a home-grown product the public could identify with. I looked and talked the way they did.

I also know what I accomplished as head of the New York City Opera. I kept prices low. I translated foreign noises into our language, so people no longer had to pretend they understood what was going on before them. I think I also upgraded the consistency of our product. We are now a company almost entirely made up of gifted young American artists. When you see a New York City Opera production, you see performers who can sing, act, and who look the parts they play. I've also tried to challenge the intellect of our audiences by deliberately varying our repertoire. I give them operetta, traditional works, classic Broadway musicals, contemporary pieces, and obscure operas they would never have a chance to see except at our house. Not long ago I made a list of all the operas we've produced that either hadn't been heard in New York for at least fifty years or hadn't been professionally staged there. During my six years as a general director, we've presented ten such works.

I don't know how many more years I'll stay in my job. I think our next general director should be someone who can make at least a ten-or fifteen-year commitment to the City Opera. My idea of the perfect general manager is an unmarried forty-five-year-old orphan.

One of these days, I'd like to spend a little time with my husband. I'm a very liberated woman and I think I'm good at my job, but I'm slowly coming to the realization that I won't have to fuss and worry when it's time for me to vacate that basement office for good. I knew when to stop singing. I think I'll be just as smart when I retire from my job as general director. I won't completely sever my ties with the New York City Opera, though. Nor will I retire from the workplace. As dotty as it might seem, the idea of unemployment still scares the daylights out of me. So what's in my future? I don't know, except that I'm going to have another career. I want to move on to another area where my experience can be put to use and my brain can be presented with fresh challenges. Someday you might well find me ensconced in the corporate world. You can't *imagine* how much I look forward to the day I'll never have to ask people for money again. I'm sure some of our donors are also looking forward to that day.

Recently, I mentioned the idea of a third career to a good friend of mine. The response I got was: "Have you ever figured out what makes Beverly run?"

The answer to that is no, I haven't. I only know that I've always tried to go a step past wherever people expected me to end up. I'm not about to change now.

INDEX